4th Edition

SPECIAL EDUCATION LAW

To the memory of my father,

Eric J. Friesen

LR

To Sara, Morgan, & Macy

SFJ

4th Edition

SPECIAL EDUCATION LAW

Laura Rothstein
University of Louisville
Louis D. Brandeis School of Law

Scott F. Johnson
Concord Law School

Los Angeles | London | New Delhi
Singapore | Washington DC

For information:

SAGE Publications, Inc.
2455 Teller Road
Thousand Oaks, California 91320
E-mail: order@sagepub.com

SAGE Publications Ltd.
1 Oliver's Yard
55 City Road
London EC1Y 1SP
United Kingdom

SAGE Publications India Pvt. Ltd.
B 1/I 1 Mohan Cooperative Industrial Area
Mathura Road, New Delhi 110 044
India

SAGE Publications Asia-Pacific Pte. Ltd.
33 Pekin Street #02-01
Far East Square
Singapore 048763

Printed in the United States of America

Library of Congress Cataloging-in-Publication Data

Rothstein, Laura
Special education law/Laura Rothstein, Scott F. Johnson. —4th ed.
p. cm.
Includes bibliographical references and index.
ISBN 978-1-4129-6771-6 (pbk.)
1. Special education—Law and legislation—United States. I. Johnson, Scott F. II. Title.

KF4210.R68 2009
344.73′0791—dc22 2008043218

This book is printed on acid-free paper.

09 10 11 12 13 10 9 8 7 6 5 4 3 2 1

Acquisitions Editor: Diane McDaniel
Editorial Assistant: Ashley Conlon
Production Editor: Astrid Virding
Copy Editor: Taryn Bigelow
Typesetter: C&M Digitals (P) Ltd.
Proofreader: Scott Oney
Indexer: Molly Hall
Cover Designer: Arup Giri
Marketing Manager: Christy Guilbault

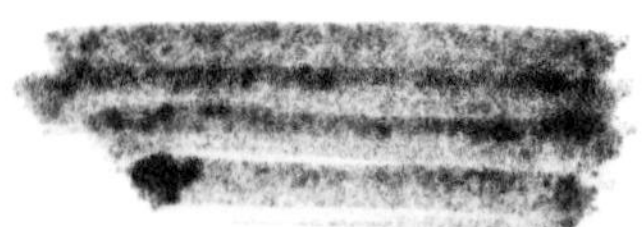

Brief Contents

Detailed Contents

Cases in Order of Appearance

Chapter 3
Smith v. Robinson, 468 U.S. 992 (1984)

Chapter 5
City of Cleburne v. Cleburne Living Center, 473 U.S. 432 (1985)
Plyler v. Doe, 457 U.S. 202 (1982)
Roe v. Commonwealth, 638 F. Supp. 929 (E.D. Pa. 1986)
Evans v. Independent School District 25, 936 F.2d 472 (10th Cir. 1991)
Timothy W. v. Rochester School District, 875 F.2d 954 (1st Cir. 1989)

Chapter 6
Quackenbush v. Johnson City School District, 716 F.2d 141 (2d Cir. 1983)
Larry P. v. Riles, 1992 LEXIS 13677 (N.D. Cal. 1992)
Parents in Action on Special Education (PASE) v. Hannon, 506 F. Supp. 831 (N.D. Ill. 1980)
Seals v. Loftis, 614 F. Supp. 302 (E.D. Tenn. 1985)

Chapter 7
Alvin Independent School District v. A.D., 503 F.3d 378 (5th Cir. 2007)

Chapter 8
Cerra v. Pawling School District, 427 F.3d 186 (5th Cir. 2005)

Chapter 9
Board of Education v. Rowley, 458 U.S. 176 (1982)
Alamo Heights Independent School District v. State Board of Education, 790 F.2d 1153 (5th Cir. 1986)

Chapter 10
Hurry v. Jones, 734 F.2d 879 (1st Cir. 1984)
Max M. v. Illinois State Board of Education, 629 F. Supp. 1504 (N.D. Ill. 1986)
Irving Independent School District v. Tatro, 468 U.S. 883 (1984)
Cedar Rapids Community School District v. Garret F., 526 U.S. 66 (1999)

Chapter 11

Roncker v. Walter, 700 F.2d 1058 (6th Cir. 1983)
Daniel R.R. v. State Board of Education, 874 F.2d 1036 (5th Cir. 1989)
Espino v. Besteiro, 520 F. Supp. 905 (S.D. Tex. 1981)
Hendricks v. Gilhool, 709 F. Supp. 1362 (E.D. Pa. 1989)
Lachman v. Illinois State Board of Education, 852 F.2d 290 (7th Cir. 1988)
A.W. v. Northwest R-1 School District, 813 F.2d 158 (8th Cir. 1987)

Chapter 12

Zobrest v. Catalina Foothills School District, 509 U.S. 1 (1993)
Kruelle v. New Castle County School District, 642 F.2d 687 (3d Cir. 1981)
David D. v. Dartmouth School Committee, 775 F.2d 411 (1st Cir. 1985)

Chapter 13

Brookhart v. Illinois State Board of Education, 697 F.2d 179 (7th Cir. 1983)

Chapter 14

Doe v. Maher, 793 F.2d 1470 (9th Cir. 1986)
Catlin v. Ambach, 644 F. Supp. 161 (N.D.N.Y. 1986)
In re Todd P., 509 A.2d 140 (N.H. 1986)

Chapter 15

Garcia v. Board of Education of Albuquerque Public Schools, 520 F.3d 1116 (10th Cir. 2008)

Chapter 16

Honig v. Doe, 484 U.S. 305 (1988)

Chapter 17

Schaffer v. Weast, 546 U.S. 49 (2005)
Winkelman v. Parma City School District, 127 S. Ct. 1994 (2007)

Chapter 18

Doe v. Belleville Public School District, 672 F. Supp. 342 (S.D. Ill. 1987)
School Board of Nassau County v. Arline, 480 U.S. 273 (1987)

Chapter 20

Board of Education v. Human Rights Commission, 385 S.E.2d 637 (W.Va. 1989)
Greider v. Shawnee Mission Unified School District, 710 F. Supp. 296 (D. Kan. 1989)

Chapter 21

Burlington School Committee v. Department of Education, 471 U.S. 359 (1985)
Board of Education v. Tom F., 2005 U.S. Dist. LEXIS 49 (S.D.N.Y. 2005)
Jefferson County Board of Education v. Breen, 853 F.2d 853 (11th Cir. 1988)

Cases Alphabetized

Alamo Heights Independent School District v. State Board of Education, 790 F.2d 1153 (5th Cir. 1986)	Chapter 9
Alvin Independent School District v. A.D., 503 F.3d 378 (5th Cir. 2007)	Chapter 7
A.W. v. Northwest R-1 School District, 813 F.2d 158 (8th Cir. 1987)	Chapter 11
Board of Education v. Human Rights Commission, 385 S.E.2d 637 (W.Va. 1989)	Chapter 20
Board of Education v. Rowley, 458 U.S. 176 (1982)	Chapter 9
Board of Education v. Tom F., 2005 U.S. Dist. LEXIS 49 (S.D.N.Y. 2005)	Chapter 21
Brookhart v. Illinois State Board of Education, 697 F.2d 179 (7th Cir. 1983)	Chapter 13
Burlington School Committee v. Department of Education, 471 U.S. 359 (1985)	Chapter 21
Catlin v. Ambach, 644 F. Supp. 161 (N.D.N.Y. 1986)	Chapter 14
Cedar Rapids Community School District v. Garret F., 526 U.S. 66 (1999)	Chapter 10
Cerra v. Pawling School District, 427 U.S. 186 (5th Cir. 2005)	Chapter 8
City of Cleburne v. Cleburne Living Center, 473 U.S. 432 (1985)	Chapter 5
Daniel R.R. v. State Board of Education, 874 F.2d 1036 (5th Cir. 1989)	Chapter 11
David D. v. Dartmouth School Committee, 775 F.2d 411 (1st Cir. 1985)	Chapter 12
Doe v. Belleville Public School District, 672 F. Supp. 342 (S.D. Ill. 1987)	Chapter 18
Doe v. Maher, 793 F.2d 1470 (9th Cir. 1986)	Chapter 14
Espino v. Besteiro, 520 F. Supp. 905 (S.D. Tex. 1981)	Chapter 11
Evans v. Independent School District 25, 936 F.2d 472 (10th Cir. 1991)	Chapter 5
Garcia v. Board of Education of Albuquerque Public Schools, 520 F.3d 1116 (10th Cir. 2008)	Chapter 15
Greider v. Shawnee Mission Unified School District, 710 F. Supp. 296 (D. Kan. 1989)	Chapter 20
Hendricks v. Gilhool, 709 F. Supp. 1362 (E.D. Pa. 1989)	Chapter 11

Special education is an area in which elaborate sets of regulations exist at both the federal and state levels. At the federal level, the IDEA regulations spell out in considerable detail the procedures and programming that must be provided to children with disabilities in order for states to receive federal funding.[7] States must submit their state plans to the federal Department of Education to qualify for IDEA funds. States may go beyond what is required in the IDEA regulations as long as their regulations are not inconsistent with the federal requirements. For example, some states have broadened the definition of which children are entitled to special education by including gifted children in their special education programming. States also often regulate areas such as bus transportation, pupil/teacher ratios, and other issues that are more appropriate for state regulation.

Case Law

Case law is the law developed in the courts. Historically, it was a means of establishing law before there was a great deal of written statutory law. Judges would render opinions that incorporated custom. This early law was known as common law. Most judicially rendered law today is opinion not about custom but rather interpreting a constitutional provision or statute as it applies to a particular set of facts. Courts are limited to rendering opinions about the specific facts in the cases before them. Pronouncements of a broader nature are not prohibited, but they do not have the force of law. Broader pronouncements are known as *dicta*, and they provide guidance to potential litigants about their chances of success should they decide to seek a remedy in the courts.

In the United States, there is a fairly universal acceptance of the concept of *stare decisis*, which means that courts are bound to render decisions consistent with previous decisions in the same jurisdiction and with decisions of higher courts over that jurisdiction. If a court reaches a result different from a previous decision, it must usually justify the decision by explaining why the set of facts before it is different, or why circumstances have changed, or why the previous decision was wrong. So that judicial law can be known to the public, most judicial opinions at the federal level, and a significant portion of opinions within state judicial systems, are published. These published opinions are available in law libraries, and part of a legal education includes training in how to find relevant court opinions as well as how to research statutes and regulations.

Administrative Decisions and Opinions

Administrative decisions and opinions are issued at the federal, state, and local levels. The federal Department of Education often issues interpretive statements and letters of opinion. Some state educational agencies do this as well. At both the federal and state levels, there are also findings in specific cases that are resolved by administrative agencies. While these are important as guides to how an agency is likely to interpret or decide a particular matter, such decisions and opinions do not carry the same weight or have the same precedential value as statutes, regulations, and judicial decisions. Because of their lesser value, such opinions and decisions are not a substantial basis for the material included in this text. In addition, these statements are not consistently reported publicly in the same way as statutes, regulations, and judicial decisions; therefore, keeping up with them on a comprehensive basis is difficult.

It is very useful for individuals involved with special education issues to obtain access to the administrative decisions and opinions in their particular state. The difficulty or ease of obtaining these statements varies dramatically from state to state. For that reason, individuals should initially contact their state education agencies to determine the best means of accessing such materials. The Internet has made these decisions somewhat more accessible.

Federal regulations must be published in the *Federal Register* with an opportunity for public comment before they are finalized. Federal agency opinion letters, however, do not go through the notice and public comment process. For that reason, they do not have precedential value, although they certainly should be accorded some deference. Unless one has access to a loose-leaf service or similar distribution of such materials, or can access them through the Internet, obtaining these letters and decisions may be difficult.

The Judicial System

To understand which court opinions on the relevant subject matter apply to a specific case, it is necessary to understand the court system in the United States. The system includes both federal and state courts and various appellate levels within those systems.[8]

> In the United States there are really 51 court systems: the federal court system, and a court system in each of the 50 states. Each system has the power to decide both criminal cases and civil cases, but the jurisdiction of the federal courts is limited by the Constitution. Article III, which defines the judicial power of the federal courts, says that this power extends only to cases "arising under this Constitution [and] the Laws of the United States."[9] This limitation on the types of cases that can be decided by courts of the United States is the most important limitation for those who deal with legal issues in education. Often referred to as "federal question jurisdiction" it means that cases concerning the fourteenth amendment's equal protection provision or cases involving sex discrimination in education (which is prohibited by federal law) can be decided by federal courts. On the other hand, a case involving alleged defamation cannot be decided by a federal court, but would generally have to be tried in a state court because it is based on state law only. State courts, in addition to dealing with a variety of criminal and civil matters, also have the power to decide cases concerning issues of federal statutory and constitutional law. Because many legal problems in education involve federal questions (either constitutional or statutory), litigants in such cases have a choice as to which court system (federal or state) they will initially choose. A case filed in a state court can reach the U.S. Supreme Court if a controversy still exists after it has been heard and decided by the highest state court. Figure 1.1 shows the alternative paths of a judicial controversy.
>
> The federal judicial system and most state judicial systems are three-tiered. They have a relatively large number of trial courts, where the facts are determined and where the law is applied to the particular facts; a smaller number of intermediate appellate courts, which review the way the law has been applied to the facts; and one final court of appeals, which is the highest court of the particular jurisdiction. The names of these courts vary from state to state; they are often called superior court, court of appeals, and supreme court,

respectively; but this is not always true, so care should be taken in determining whether one is reading a case from a trial court or from the highest court of a state. In New York State, for example, the lowest trial court of general jurisdiction is the Supreme Court, whereas the state's highest court is the Court of Appeals. In the federal system, the nearly 100 trial courts are called United States District Courts, the 13 courts of appeals are called the United States Courts of Appeals, and the highest court is officially called the United States Supreme Court.

Figure 1.1 Alternative paths of a judicial controversy

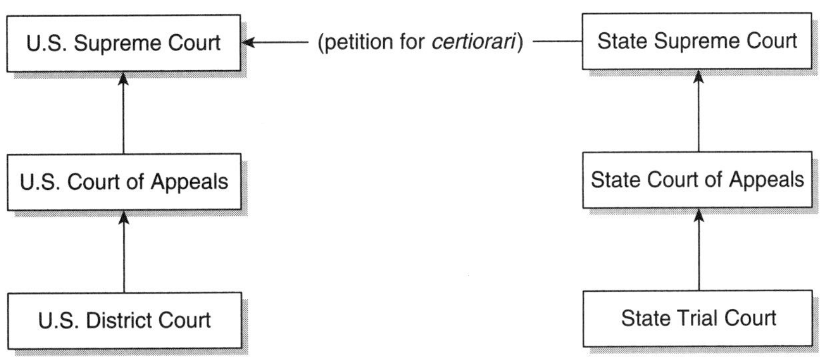

Judicial controversies generally move from the trial court level to the intermediate appellate court level and, finally, to the highest court of the jurisdiction. Additionally, a case can move from the highest court of a state to the U.S. Supreme Court, if the losing party submits a request to the Supreme Court to consider the case. This request usually comes in the form of a "petition for certiorari," which the U.S. Supreme Court can either accept or reject. After careful consideration, a vote is taken by the nine justices; if four vote in favor of considering the case, the justices will issue a "writ of certiorari" asking that the case be sent to the Court. This often occurs when the various federal courts of appeals are in conflict over a particular issue.

When reading one of the many cases decided by the various state and federal courts, an important point to consider is whether or not the particular decision of the court (often called the court's "holding") is binding in your state or region. Decisions of the Supreme Court are binding everywhere, but the decisions of the lower federal courts are binding only in their respective territories. All federal courts of appeals (except for the one in Washington, D.C., and one dealing with special patent and copyright issues) cover more than one state, and there is more than one federal district court in most states. A map of the jurisdictions covered by the federal courts of appeals is contained in Appendix A. The opinions of state courts are binding only in the state where they are decided. However, decisions from courts other than the one deciding the case may be used as precedent; although not binding, these decisions are often considered persuasive in other jurisdictions.

Regulatory Decision Making

Congress sometimes delegates to an administrative body the function of deciding disputes or determining whether a statute has been violated. The reason is often one of efficiency and quality of decision making. It is costly and time-consuming to litigate disputes in court. A resolution before an administrative hearing officer is often quicker and less expensive, although it is not always so. In addition, in some cases an administrative decision maker may have a particular area of expertise that could lead to better decisions than might be made by a judge in court.

Special education is one of the areas in which Congress has delegated dispute resolution and other decision making to administrative process. Where parents or the administrative agency dispute the appropriateness of the proposed special education program, the IDEA sets up a detailed framework providing an opportunity for an impartial hearing, with a right of review by the state educational agency and a subsequent right of review in state or federal court. In addition, anyone believing that the school has violated Section 504 of the Rehabilitation Act or the Americans with Disabilities Act may complain to the federal Department of Education, which may then investigate and possibly hold a hearing to determine whether a violation has occurred. In this forum, the complaining party is not a party in the hearing. In other words, it is not really a hearing to provide a remedy to the individual complainant but to determine whether a violation has occurred and whether corrective action, such as withholding future federal financial assistance, is an appropriate remedy. Because this administrative decision making does not really resolve the problem for the individual complainant, many individuals choose to go directly to court to seek relief. As later chapters indicate, whether doing so is permissible is not entirely clear. Chapter 18 clarifies that even if one can claim a violation of Section 504 or the ADA in court, most claims involving special education must be decided under the IDEA, and the parents must first seek relief through the impartial hearing process mentioned above.

Relationship of Constitutional Law, Statutory Law, Regulatory Law, and Case Law in the Development of Special Education Laws

Laws are not developed by the various governmental entities (Congress, administrators, judges) in a vacuum. Often, laws are made by one entity as a response to developments in other arenas. State and federal laws are frequently interactive in this process. The development of special education law is an excellent example of this metamorphosis.

While many states had laws providing for some education for children with at least some types of disabilities before the 1970s (such as blindness and deafness), the real watershed year for special education law was 1971. In that year, and a year later, two judicial opinions interpreted the fourteenth amendment to the United States Constitution as follows: Because the District of Columbia and the Commonwealth of Pennsylvania provided education to children within their jurisdictions, they were denying due process and equal protection to children with disabilities by excluding these children from the educational system.[10]

As a result of these federal judicial opinions and the number of similar lawsuits awaiting final decision throughout the United States, Congress responded. To bring consistency to and to assist states in what appeared to be constitutionally mandated education of students with disabilities, Congress created a federal program of subsidization.[11]

The program that resulted was set out in the Education for All Handicapped Children Act (EAHCA), passed in 1975. This act made federal funds available to states that developed plans to ensure education for all children with disabilities who were of school age. This education was to be individualized, provided at no cost to the parents, made available in the least restrictive appropriate setting, and provided under required procedural safeguards. In 1990, the name of the act was changed to the Individuals with Disabilities Education Act (IDEA). Two other major amendments to the IDEA (in 1997 and 2004) further developed the requirements of the law but did not substantially change the primary principles and procedures under the original 1975 statute.

The statute itself set the general framework, but a great deal of detail was needed to clarify what was meant by the various provisions relating to procedural safeguards. The Department of Health, Education, and Welfare (now separated into the Department of Education and the Department of Health and Human Services) developed an elaborate set of regulations to spell out these details. These regulations became effective in 1977 after extensive public comment. As of now, all states have elected to seek funding support under the IDEA, and, as a result, they have all developed state statutes and regulations incorporating the requirements of the IDEA and usually providing for additional requirements relating to special education.

Even with detailed statutory and regulatory requirements, a number of issues became the subject of debate. These issues included matters such as whether states were required only to provide the same number of school days to students with disabilities that they provided to students without disabilities, whether residential placements must be paid for entirely by the state and under what circumstances, and whether services such as catheterization must be provided at no charge. Several issues reached the level of the Supreme Court, which then issued its interpretation of the law. When Congress disagrees with the Court's interpretation, Congress can rewrite or pass new legislation. One Supreme Court case that prompted Congress to amend the IDEA to clarify its intent was the 1984 case of *Smith v. Robinson*.[12] In that case, the Supreme Court held, among other things, that under the IDEA as it was then written, parents could not recover attorneys' fees. Congress subsequently passed the Handicapped Children's Protection Act (HCPA) in 1986 to allow for attorneys' fees in certain circumstances under the IDEA. Already there has been a substantial amount of litigation concerning situations in which those attorneys' fees can be awarded.[13] Interaction among the various agents in the development of law has continued as the interpretation of the IDEA continues to evolve.

Summary

The basic legal framework applicable to education of children with disabilities is currently found primarily in a federal statute, the IDEA, and in its regulations and the state statutes passed in conjunction with the federal law. These requirements developed as a result of the dynamic workings of our legal system. The United States Constitution (through the fourteenth amendment equal protection and due process requirements) was interpreted by federal courts (in *Pennsylvania Association of Retarded Children [PARC] v. Pennsylvania* and *Mills v. Board of Education*), which set out a general framework for what the Constitution required of states in providing special education. The general framework of the decisions was then the basis for the passage of a federal statute (the IDEA) and the detailed regulations developed pursuant to it.

Although the IDEA and its regulations now are the primary source of law for special education, numerous judicial interpretations of the IDEA are essential additional reference points. The Supreme Court has issued several opinions clarifying certain issues but leaving others unresolved. An enormous body of case law at lower court levels continues to provide additional and sometimes conflicting interpretations of the IDEA. Statutory amendments have been passed in response to judicial decisions and recognized gaps or needs for clarification in the statute.

With this expanding body of statutory, regulatory, and judicial law, it might seem that answers to most questions about what is required of schools in providing special education would by now be found within existing laws. As the following chapters illustrate, however, many questions remain unanswered, and it is likely that the development of law on these issues will continue for some time.

Appendix A provides a more detailed explanation of the American legal system, the way it works, and information on how to stay abreast of legal developments.

Questions for Reflection

1. Why doesn't Congress develop all the details of the IDEA and other statutes rather than leaving that to administrative agencies?

2. Is it good policy to enact a statute that may be intentionally somewhat vague on certain points?

3. Which is the fastest and most efficient way to develop law—through the court system or the legislative process? What are the advantages and disadvantages of each?

NOTES

1. See *U.S. Const.* art. I, § 8, cl. 1.
2. 20 U.S.C. §§ 1400 *et seq.*
3. 29 U.S.C. § 794.
4. See *U.S. Const.* amend. XIV.
5. See *U.S. Const.* art. X.
6. See *U.S. Const.* art. I, § 8, cl. 18.
7. See 34 C.F.R. §§ 300.1–300.818.
8. The following four paragraphs and the chart are from Louis Fischer & Gail Paulus Sorenson, *School Law for Counselors, Psychologists, and Social Workers,* published by Allyn & Bacon, Boston, MA. Copyright © 1985 by Pearson Education. Reprinted with permission of the publisher. See also Appendix A, *Education and the American Legal System.*
9. *U.S. Const.* art. III, § 2, cl. 1.
10. This is a somewhat simplified statement of the holdings in *Pennsylvania Association for Retarded Children (PARC) v. Pennsylvania,* 334 F. Supp. 1257 (E.D. Pa. 1971), 343 F. Supp. 279 (F.D. Pa. 1972), and *Mills v. Board of Education,* 345 F. Supp. 886 (D.D.C. 1972).
11. The history of these developments is discussed more fully in Chapter 2.
12. 468 U.S. 992 (1984).
13. See Laura Rothstein & Julia Rothstein, *Disabilities and the Law* § 2.51 (Thomson West 2006).

History of Special Education Law

Special Education Before the 1970s

The development of educational philosophy toward students with disabilities in schools occurred in several phases.[1] The first phase, in the late 1800s, reflected an intention of relieving stress on the teacher and other students by removing students with disabilities to separate, special classes. This segregationist attitude continued in later years, but the underlying basis was to avoid stress on the individual with a disability. Eventually, some educational programming was provided, first in the form of diluted academic training and later as training for manual jobs. The students were still segregated for the most part, and there was a continued concern to avoid disruption in the classroom. Many students with disabilities were never sent to school.

By the mid-1900s an important shift had begun—the recognition of the self-worth and dignity of the person that led to the goal of teaching self-reliance. Also about this time, vocal leaders in education recognized that separation, or segregation, in the educational process was usually inherently negative. The education of students with hearing and visual disabilities had a somewhat different history in terms of the types of training they received. There was a similarity historically, however, in that education was usually provided in a segregated setting. The statements from congressional hearings included later in this chapter provide a firsthand perspective on the state of affairs at that time. These attitudes are a far cry from the attitudes that exist today. Advocates for independent living, however, would argue that the status today is still far from where it should be.

A Constitutional and Political Framework for Change

It was *Brown v. Board of Education*[2] that most forcefully stated the philosophy of integration. That decision was based on the federal constitutional principle of the fourteenth amendment, which provides that the states may not deprive anyone of "life, liberty, or property, without due process of law" nor deny anyone "equal protection of the laws."[3] While the Supreme Court has held consistently that there is no federally protected right to education, nonetheless if the state undertakes to provide education (which all states do), a property interest is thereby created by the state. The *Brown* decision recognized that if black children were educated separately, even in facilities "equal" to those of white children, their treatment was inherently unequal because of the stigma attached to being educated separately and the deprivation of interaction with children of other backgrounds.

The concept of educating the child with a disability in the regular classroom as much as possible (known as "mainstreaming" or "inclusion") paralleled the movement away from racial segregation and helped lead to the determination that separating children was detrimental to them. Congress made preliminary efforts to provide for special education by enacting grant programs in 1966 and 1970,[4] but these were primarily incentive programs with little in the way of specific guidelines and enforcement. Although mainly for personnel development, these programs attempted to address the issue of educating children with disabilities in the regular school system.

By 1975, about three million children with disabilities were not receiving appropriate programming in public schools. In addition, about another one million were excluded totally from public education. So, of the more than eight million children with disabilities in the United States, more than half were receiving either inappropriate or no educational services.[5]

Financing was one reason that special education was inadequate; special education is costly and supporting it is burdensome for local school districts. By 1975, state education agencies had taken on a substantial role in special education, both by mandating it and by allocating funds to help subsidize it in local school districts.

By the 1970s, special education could usually be described by a number of common practices. Identification and placement of children with disabilities was haphazard, inconsistent, and generally inappropriate. African American, Hispanic, and some other ethnic groups were often stereotyped and disproportionately placed in special education programs. Parental involvement was generally discouraged. Special education placements were often made with the goal of avoiding disruption in the regular classroom. Special educators and regular educators were competitors for resources, and the two groups did not work in a spirit of cooperation.

The application of the principles set forth in the *Brown* decision to the education of children with disabilities became a legal theory in more than 30 separately filed cases throughout the country. Two of these cases culminated in landmark decisions in 1971 and 1972. In *Pennsylvania Association for Retarded Children (PARC) v. Pennsylvania*[6] and *Mills v. Board of Education*,[7] district courts approved consent decrees that enjoined states from denying education to students who were mentally retarded and students with other disabilities without due process. The *Mills* consent decree went so far as to set out an elaborate framework for what that due process would entail. Both of these cases were based on constitutional theories of equal protection and due process under the fourteenth amendment and were the impetus for similar cases in several other states.

As previously noted, there is no federal constitutional right to education. It is only when the state undertakes to provide education that the fourteenth amendment comes into play. When states provide education, they must do so on equal terms, and they must not deny this state-granted right without due process.

In its evaluation of what is meant by equal terms, the Supreme Court has traditionally applied different degrees of scrutiny to the practices of governmental entities. If the individual affected by the practice is a member of a "suspect class" such as a racial minority, or if the right at issue is a "fundamental right" such as privacy, the practice will be strictly scrutinized (evaluated very carefully). Where the classification is not a specially protected class, or if the right is not an important one, the practice will usually be upheld if there is any rational basis for it. Individuals with disabilities have not been held to be members of a suspect class,[8] but education has been recognized as deserving of "special constitutional treatment," and an intermediate test of heightened scrutiny has been applied.[9] It is important to note that in assessing whether children with disabilities are receiving equal protection in their educational programming, one should not use equal expenditures of money as the measure, although it is often difficult to determine exactly what constitutes equality.[10]

The due process clause of the fourteenth amendment requires procedures to be appropriate to the protected interest at stake. Obviously in a criminal proceeding, states must be extremely careful that the individual has received appropriate due process because incarceration is a serious deprivation of liberty. Education is recognized as an important property interest by states because without it, a person may not succeed in life. Education is important for helping individuals with disabilities to live independently or semi-independently. For that reason, the court in the *Mills* decision mandated that due process include procedures relating to the labeling, placement, and exclusionary stages of decision making. The procedures should include a right to a hearing (with representation, a record, and an impartial hearing officer), a right to appeal, a right to have access to records, and written notice at all stages of the process.[11] The basic framework set out in *Mills* was incorporated into the Education for All Handicapped Children Act (EAHCA) (now known as the Individuals with Disabilities Education Act or IDEA).

Because of potential confusion that might result from varying decisions in other jurisdictions and pressure from administrators at the state level concerned about the cost of providing special education, Congress intervened. It passed federal grant legislation to encourage states to adopt appropriate procedures for providing education to children with disabilities, procedures that would be consistent with judicial decisions. The civil rights movement and related activities provided a favorable political atmosphere for the enactment of strong legislation.

Statutory Responses

The Individuals with Disabilities Education Act

While the constitutional principles theoretically would mandate equal protection and due process for children with disabilities in the public school setting without any statutory requirement at the federal level, Congress recognized that states might have difficulty implementing the constitutional requirement to provide education to these children. And although most states already had statutes in place requiring the education of children with disabilities, there was a great deal of inconsistency in what states required, and many states did not have very strong programs of special education when *PARC* and *Mills* were decided.

During the 1973–1974 congressional hearings on educational services for children with disabilities, a number of problems with the status of special education were revealed through testimony and statements. These statements indicated that, to a large extent, states that were acting in good faith and attempting to provide special education had serious problems of administration and financing. In other instances, parents had been successful in getting the school administration to implement a local program benefiting one or a few individuals, but at a cost of substantial effort and energy on the part of the parents. And, perhaps most troubling, in some areas significant numbers of students were still being excluded.

The following statements from those hearings[12] illustrate more graphically some of these problems. The first statement indicates the most severe crisis—the child who is simply institutionalized and not given an education.

Statement of Dr. Oliver L. Hurley, Associate Professor of Special Education, University of Georgia, Athens (p. 657)

Some years ago, during the course of a visit to the State Institution for the mentally retarded, I encountered a little girl who was lying in a crib. Wondering why she was so confined while the other children were not, I began to play with her. I found that even though I could make eye contact with her, she was unable to follow me with her eyes for more than about 12 inches. I began to try to teach her. In about 15 minutes she could follow me about a quarter of the way around the bed. I was convinced then, and still am, that with a little work the child could have been taught some useful behavior and could have been gotten out of the crib. It seems safe to say that no one with any authority was concerned about the education of that little girl.

For me, this child, who showed some ability to learn, typified our reactions to these difficult cases—hide them away, exclude them, forget them. Such a prejudicial attitude toward those who are different must be changed. The "Education for All Handicapped Children Act" will help in this regard. Someone must assume responsibility for the education of such children. To me, the State education agencies are a logical choice. It seems antithetical to American philosophy, as I see it, that whether or not a handicapped child gets proper care and proper educational treatment depends on the fatness of that child's father's wallet.

The problem of different levels of services from state to state was raised by a parent of a child with a hearing impairment.

Statement of Mrs. Gordon Wuddleston, Orangeburg, S. C., Parent of a Severely Hard-of-Hearing Child (pp. 796–799)

My husband and I are particularly interested in this bill because we have experienced education in four States for our hearing-impaired son, and in these four States we have found a vast difference in what is provided for him. Perhaps by telling my story, I can best illustrate to you some of these differences that we have experienced.

In 1950, our son David was born with a severe hearing impairment. We discovered this when David was 2 years of age. We were living in Parkersburg, W. Va., at the time, and because of limited medical facilities we were referred to Dr. Helmer Michelbust, at the Institute of Language Disorders at Northwestern University, in Evanston, Ill. Dr. Michelbust and his staff told us that David had a severe hearing impairment and was delayed in language, but with proper early education he could develop speech and lip reading ability, to function in society, and the emphasis was on early education. We were told that early ideology and language training was a must.

West Virginia did not have any facilities, but we were fortunate that we lived in an area where we could get to the speech and language clinic at Ohio University. So for 2 years David and I drove 100 miles a day for speech therapy. When David was 4, the educators at Ohio University told us that he was ready for academic training and should be placed in a school for hearing-impaired children, that because of the potential that he had shown during his period of work there they recommended that we definitely seek an oral deaf school placement for our son. There was such a school as part of the public school program in Columbus, Ohio, so at that time our family moved to Columbus, and at age 4 David entered the Alexander Graham Bell Oral School for Hearing-Impaired Children, as part of the public school program in Columbus.

He worked in a classroom with a trained teacher of the deaf, in a public school setting, with a maximum of eight students per class. After $2\frac{3}{4}$ years in this setting, we were told that David could integrate into the regular classroom in his own district: with supportive help, resource teachers, he could probably function very well. His teacher made use of audiovisual aids, and resource teachers were available to him. He was promoted to the second grade with a B-plus average.

At this time we were transferred to Wilmington, Del., with the Du Pont Co., and moved David there. There were facilities; there were resource teachers; there was also an oral school for hearing-impaired children at Newark, Del. David received from these resource teachers, in a regular classroom setting in Wilmington, one-to-one help in math, reading, and language. At the end of second grade, David was evaluated by the school psychologist and by a staff from

(Continued)

(Continued)

the Margaret Struck School for Hearing-Impaired Children, in Newark, Del. It was determined at that time that David was functioning very well in a normal classroom and it would be in his best interest to continue in a regular classroom setting. This is where he could reach his potential, with supportive help. He completed third grade, had a B average, and we were told that he was on his way, and with supportive help he should be able to continue in a normal classroom setting with normal children.

Meanwhile, we were faced with two transfers from the company and felt compelled to turn them down. My husband was then transferred into the international department with Du Pont and was going to be faced with a lot of travel. This concerned us, this being away from home and the possibility of more transfers, and a job opportunity came along in South Carolina that would be a permanent job for us, so we felt that we must think in terms of finding a permanent location for our family. But before we would go for the job interview we came to South Carolina first and had an interview with the superintendent of schools in Orangeburg district, with the school psychologist, and with the director of curriculum there. We told them of David's problems and his needs thus far in his education. Yes, they explained, they did have reading teachers, they did have a speech therapist, and they did have a school psychologist for the district.

Services Not Available in South Carolina

We moved, and we started the school year, and David entered Sheridan Elementary School in Orangeburg, in the fourth grade. We were dismayed to find that he was not able to have a reading teacher help him. He was placed for one-half hour a week in a group session speech therapy with children who did not have a similar defect to his. There were no resource teachers. We sought counseling from the school psychologist: he was very sympathetic. But they explained to us that because of their caseload they just were not able to take him into therapy; consequently, we would have to go it on our own.

Being concerned, I volunteered as a parent to work at school 4 days a week in David's science and math classes to help him come through the year. He did come through. He was in an individual math program. We came through the year, and at the end of the year we tested out 4.9. He had made progress in this area. However, his language and reading teacher was not able to give him the benefit from extra help, and David started downhill. He became frustrated. He started falling behind. His behavior became disruptive. And I might add that he had two teachers, and when he was working in the area of math and areas where he could still compete, his behavior was fine. When he entered the reading and the language area, his behavior became a problem.

The Child Should Adapt

Rather than find help for him, he was given such tasks, as punishment, to write 500—not 50 or 100—500 times a night, "I will sit in my seat and I will behave."

We again sought help from the school psychologist, but again were told that they would really like to help but the caseloads were just so heavy that it was just impossible to give him the help that he needed. . . .

Our son has been evaluated at the Institute for Language Disorders at Northwestern University; Ohio State University; Mid-American Hearing Association, headed by Dr. George Shambaugh, in Chicago; and Margaret Sturk School for Hearing-Impaired Children. All have felt that David had potential and emphasized that he would be able to take his place in a hearing society, and with proper resource teachers in education would not be a burden to society, in that someday, if he were allowed to reach his potential, he could take his place and function in society and would not have to have residential placement or wind up in a correctional institution. He could be a self-supporting member of this society.

I am here today because we have experienced vast differences in education in the different States that we have been in. Quite honestly, we have seriously considered leaving the State of South Carolina, but my husband likes his work, and we very, very much like this State. We would like to remain here. In addition to that, we have met other parents facing the same problems in Orangeburg. If we leave, that's not going to help them a bit. But hopefully this bill will help others, and all across the country, not just in certain States.

Other parents noted that even when appropriate programming was provided, parents often were required to provide transportation in order to obtain the programming for the child.

Statement of Mrs. Mary Ellen Ward, Avon Park, Fla., Member of the Ridge Area Association for Retarded Children and the Florida and National Associations for Retarded Children (pp. 812–813)

I'd like to describe a particular case, and this is of a multihandicapped girl now 10 years old, severely crippled by cerebral palsy, mentally retarded, and with very limited speech. She was enrolled in our Association-sponsored Division of Retardation funded developmental training

(Continued)

(Continued)

program at the age of 4, when she was beginning to roll and crawl on the floor. Before she moved to another county last July she had learned to walk with crutches and braces, to feed herself; she'd been toilet trained and was learning to swim and to perform some self-care chores. She, with her family, moved to another Florida county in order to maintain the father's employment status. Beginning 10 days after the move, the mother started investigating, as carefully as her abilities would permit, the educational opportunities for Jerri.

The parents completed a number of applications, submitted to tests and examination, met appointments for interviews, and paid for medical and psychological exams. Eight months after first making application, 10-year-old Jerri, who had been in a training program for 5½ years in our county, was accepted in a program for 2 hours daily, provided the mother transport Jerri a distance of 7 miles and remain as her babysitter while Jerri attends this particular school. At the end of the first week the mother reported Jerri's instructions were coming from her, and at last hearing there is still no program for Jerri.

This happened in 1973 in one of the highest-ranked States in terms of percentages of handicapped persons served. I think it demonstrates the need for further statewide help in designing, funding, evaluating, and accounting for local services for the handicapped. It emphasizes the need to provide services for the low functioning handicapped, who may never qualify for a job but who certainly need to know skills of self-help and self-care.

The problems of funding in states with limited resources, the need for funding to support construction of physical facilities, and a program to support training of qualified personnel were also noted.

Statement of Dan Delon, Executive Director, South Dakota Association for Retarded Children (p. 1296)

We have been fortunate in South Dakota to have successfully passed mandatory special education legislation, which requires the provision of appropriate educational opportunities to all exceptional children from birth to 21 years. Since the passage of that bill in 1972, rapid progress has been made in the development of public school programs for handicapped children, but still it has not been enough. DHEW [Department of Health, Education, and Welfare] estimates indicate that only 24.8% of our handicapped children are receiving appropriate educational services. We feel that the estimate may be too high and that the actual figure is closer to 20%.

Leading special education experts in our state estimate that more than 5,000 handicapped children will exit from our school systems during the next four years almost totally lacking in skills which will allow them to move into competitive employment areas or successful adjustment to community living.

As an advocate group, we are in the business of making ideals become realities. We recognize that it is ideal that all handicapped children receive a free public education, and in our efforts to make that a reality, we have had to face some very harsh realities about education in a rural state with large impoverished areas.

Statement of Edward Kirsch, Parent of a Retarded Child (p. 1550)

[T]he ratio as I understand it in speech therapy is approximately three full-time or two full-time speech therapists and one part-time speech therapist for the needs of 737 children, and this is rather a ridiculous ratio. These people are really only involved with trainable children so it's hardly likely the children will get much speech therapy. Then again there are the facilities the speech therapists have to share. In one instance there is a speech therapy room sharing space with a piano tuner and a music class. It's hard to imagine anybody can accomplish anything in a situation like that.

One of our biggest concerns is the lack of funds to provide facilities for these children because presently a plan the school board has in mind is to move these children, all 562 of them, to an 88-year-old building on the north side of Pittsburgh in the Manchester area. It's certainly not adequate for the needs of these children in view of the fact that some of them are multiply handicapped and blind and have many other physical handicaps. To put these children in a four-story building seems ridiculous, but there doesn't seem to be any place else for them to go because there are no funds available for new construction.

Many of the parents complain that the children that are teenagers and don't have many more years to spend in the system, and that they are very much concerned because their children have received very minimal vocational and occupational training and shortly they will be out of the system. Where will they go to from there? Many of them were 15 years old when the consent agreement came down so they maybe only have three more years left and agewise they will have to be removed from the system and put into supportive programs outside of the right to education program.

Statement of Carl Wass, Pennsylvania Mental Health, Inc. (p. 1556)

There are many school districts we find throughout the State who leave it to the intermediate unit to provide services for the handicapped child. And the intermediate units sometimes are not providing these services and when they do we find that the classes that provide

(Continued)

(Continued)

services for the handicapped are either overcrowded, as was suggested in the case of Pittsburgh, or that the personnel, the teaching personnel, is not equipped to handle the particular problem. The end result is that many of these children who have an identifiable handicap are not getting the kind of education that is contemplated by the Department of Education or by the consent order. I think on the grass roots level competent personnel are needed.

Perhaps of unique interest were statements from a variety of individuals from Pennsylvania, a state under a consent decree to implement the *PARC* decision. *PARC* was the judicial settlement that mandated serving children who are mentally retarded in the public schools. Many of the comments illustrate the frustration of wanting to carry out the intent and spirit of the order but needing supportive funding to do so. The following is one of many comments from Pennsylvania that indicate the gaps left by the consent agreement.

Statement of William W. Wolfinger, Director Special Education Services, Hamburg State School, Pennsylvania (pp. 1538–1539)

We are now at a point of having had over a year and a half of time go by with certainly many accomplishments, but also much remaining to be done.

First, this act, in my opinion, will be a stimulus for our state legislature to look at the total problem of education for all handicapped children since the consent agreement was limited to only the mentally retarded.

Second, it soon became apparent in our implementation of programs for the mentally retarded that much more money was needed for staff, equipment, and physical facilities.

Third, perhaps from such a review by our legislature will emerge the potential for providing a better balance of programs for the handicapped, one that will provide these children with the same program advantages afforded the so-called "normal" child.

Fourth, perhaps a year-round, twelve-month school can also emerge since this is so important for handicapped children; 220 days of school instead of the customary 180. . . .

Much remains to be done and without adequate financing most of our needs at each of the state schools will remain unanswered.

> Most pressing is the need for adequate physical facilities in which to conduct the educational programs and the related services that are so critical in order to reach the total needs of the child. Buildings are desperately needed that are equipped for the handling of the physically handicapped, since most of the severely and profoundly retarded children found in institutions are also inflicted with severe multiple handicaps. Handicapped children should not be compelled to attend classes or individual sessions in crowded or substandard facilities.

In response to these concerns, as an initial stopgap measure, Congress passed an interim funding bill in 1974 that required states, as a condition of receiving federal funds, to adopt "goal/s/ of providing full educational opportunities to all handicapped children."[13] The interim bill was adopted to give Congress a year to study the issue more carefully, and the following year Congress passed the Education for All Handicapped Children Act (EAHCA) of 1975,[14] which became effective in 1977. There was significant congressional concern about the cost of the legislation. The result of that concern is that the EAHCA is not intended to fund the costs of special education fully but is meant to subsidize state and local educational agencies.

The EAHCA is technically an amendment to the 1970 Education of the Handicapped Act (EHA),[15] which had provided for grants to states to provide special education. The EAHCA amends Part B of the EHA and is significant because it provides the important elements of procedural safeguards, integration, and nondiscriminatory testing and evaluation materials and procedures.

The EAHCA is basically a grant statute that creates individual rights. A state can receive federal funding to support payment for children with disabilities ages 3 through 21 based on a formula of average per-pupil expenditures (which has been adjusted under subsequent amendments), if the state develops a plan to provide for *all* children with disabilities in the state a "free, appropriate public education which emphasizes special education and related services designed to meet their unique needs."[16]

The act specifies the general parameters of the procedural safeguards required of the recipients, and the details of these requirements were eventually developed in the regulations finalized in 1977.[17] The basic underlying principles of the EAHCA (now IDEA) should be noted here, however.

- *All* children with disabilities must be given an education.[18]
- It must be provided in the *least restrictive appropriate* placement.[19]
- Education is to be *individualized* and *appropriate* to the child's unique needs.[20]
- It is to be provided *free*.[21]
- *Procedural protections* are required to ensure that the substantive requirements are met.[22]

In 1990, the EAHCA was amended and the title was changed to the Individuals with Disabilities Education Act (IDEA). The language of the act changed also, with *handicap* replaced by *disability* throughout. Controversy over what the IDEA mandates mean has resulted in a multitude of cases, and there are now hundreds of reported judicial decisions relating to these issues. Before 1990, the IDEA was often referred to by its Public Law number, 94-142, or as the EHA or the EAHCA. Although any of these designations is acceptable, in this book EAHCA is used in older judicial decision excerpts and the IDEA is most often used in the textual material.

In 1997, the IDEA went through another major amendment. Although the major underlying substantive and procedural principles of the statute remained, they were extended in a number of ways. Prior versions of the law were concerned with ensuring that students were not excluded from school, or excluded from free and appropriate services at school. In 1997, Congress went beyond that purpose and started addressing the quality of services provided to students with disabilities by including provisions regarding the expectations and outcomes for students with disabilities.

Congress noted that the implementation of the IDEA had been impeded by low expectations and an insufficient focus on applying replicable research on proven methods of teaching and learning for children with disabilities.[23] To address this, Congress enacted provisions to the IDEA in 1997 that required high expectations for students with disabilities along with access to the "general curriculum." Congress required schools to provide services that would allow students with disabilities "to progress" in the general curriculum.[24] The general curriculum is the curriculum available to all students.

The rationale behind the requirement was that the general curriculum would contain high educational standards and expectations for students because of a variety of other state and federal laws about education standards that governed the development of the general curriculum by local school districts. These state and federal laws include Title I of the Elementary and Secondary Education Act of 1965, which would become part of No Child Left Behind a few years later.

There were other changes to the law as well, including changes in the areas of discipline, attorneys' fees, provision of special education services to students in private schools, statewide assessment (testing) requirements, individualized education plan (IEP) requirements, transition requirements, and the funding formula. The statute also received its first renumbering since its initial passage in 1975. This renumbering makes it difficult to cross-reference current provisions with pre-1997 provisions, although the case excerpts throughout this book attempt to provide appropriate cross-referencing by bracketing the current citation to the statute.

Congress amended the statute again in 2004 and continued down the path of high expectations and outcomes for students with disabilities, stating that "the education of children with disabilities can be made more effective by having high expectations for such children and ensuring their access to the general education curriculum in the regular classroom, to the maximum extent possible, in order to—(i) meet developmental goals and, to the maximum extent possible, the challenging expectations that have been established for all children; and (ii) be prepared to lead productive and independent adult lives, to the maximum extent possible."[25]

Along these lines, Congress made a change to the name of the law. It is now called the Individuals with Disabilities Education Improvement Act (IDEIA). However, Congress also stated that it could still be referred to under its old name, the Individuals with

Disabilities Education Act (IDEA), so the old name is often used in publications (including this book). It also expressly addressed the overall goal of the law in terms of outcomes for students with disabilities by noting that a purpose of the law was to prepare students with disabilities "for further education, employment, and independent living."[26]

The 2004 changes contain a number of express connections between the IDEA and the 2002 requirements in No Child Left Behind (NCLB).[27] These connections include the quality of services provided to students with disabilities, more express provisions regarding students with disabilities taking statewide assessment tests, and the qualifications for school personnel and others who provide services to students with disabilities.[28]

One example of a connection between the IDEA and NCLB is the integration of the term "scientifically based research," which comes from NCLB.[29] Under the 2004 changes to the IDEA, scientifically based research plays an important role in a number of areas, including (1) professional development and training for school personnel; (2) the procedures used to determine if students have learning disabilities; and (3) the supports and interventions provided to students, including positive behavioral interventions and supports provided to students with behavioral issues. Similarly, the IDEA now requires that the special education and related services and the supplementary aids and services provided to students with disabilities be based on "peer-reviewed research to the extent practicable."[30]

The findings and purpose of the IDEA in 2004 also focus on prevention and technology. Congress emphasized the importance of providing "scientifically based early reading programs, positive behavioral interventions and supports, and early intervening services to reduce the need to label children as disabled in order to address the learning and behavioral needs of such children."[31] Early intervening services are for students who are not currently identified as needing special education services, but need additional academic and behavioral support to succeed in a general education environment.[32] Congress also noted that the education of children with disabilities can be made more effective with the use of assistive technology.[33]

One example of following a preventive approach is in the area of identifying students with learning disabilities as eligible for services under the law. The IDEA 2004 allows and encourages states to use "response to intervention" or similar approaches that are premised on concepts of early intervention and student achievement and progress in grade-level content.[34]

Other changes made in 2004 include changes to IEP requirements, IEP development, and IEP team meeting requirements, reevaluation requirements, parental rights, discipline, dispute resolution, attorneys' fees, and paperwork requirements. These changes are discussed in detail in the appropriate sections of this book.

State Statutes

Initially, every state except New Mexico elected to receive federal grant support under the EAHCA (hereinafter referenced as IDEA). The *PARC* and *Mills* decisions and similar actions in other states had arguably made it necessary for the states to implement much of what was being required under the IDEA, even states not electing to apply for the federal support. In addition, statutory authority in Section 504 of the

Rehabilitation Act of 1973 required states to provide education in a nondiscriminatory manner to children with disabilities. Perhaps because of all these pressures, New Mexico eventually also elected to apply for IDEA funding.

The IDEA and its regulations set out minimum requirements that states had to meet to be eligible for funding. Those states with statutes and regulations already in place before enactment of the IDEA sometimes had difficulty adjusting to the new law, and those with no policy in place had the task of developing one. Occasionally, conflicts still arise between state and federal mandates over what constitutes appropriate education for students with disabilities.

Section 504 of the Rehabilitation Act

Even before passage of the IDEA, Congress passed the Rehabilitation Act of 1973, which includes Section 504. That section requires that

> [n]o otherwise qualified individual with a disability . . . shall solely by reason of her or his disability, be excluded from the participation in, be denied the benefits of, or be subjected to discrimination under any program or activity receiving Federal financial assistance.[35]

In addition to federal financial assistance provided under the IDEA to states specifically for "the purpose of providing special education," states receive a great deal of funding from the federal government to support other educational programs. Although Section 504 did not grant funds to the states to provide education for students with disabilities, the law made it illegal for any programs receiving federal funding to discriminate against an individual on the basis of disability.

The IDEA might appear to be unnecessary because Section 504 already provides protection. It is important, however, to recognize several factors that make the IDEA essential to the provision of special education. First, Section 504 refers only to nondiscrimination, and the IDEA contemplates that a substantial amount of subsidization will take place to ensure that children with disabilities not only receive educational services but also benefit from this education. While Section 504 case law has indicated that some reasonable accommodation must be provided to meet the nondiscrimination standard, the level of accommodation being provided in public education under the IDEA goes beyond what is required in other contexts. Second, while Section 504 was passed in 1973, before the 1975 IDEA, the regulations under Section 504 were not finalized until 1978, and there was no detailed framework for the schools to follow. Finally, because the Section 504 regulations were finalized after the IDEA regulations, they are much less detailed, and in fact incorporate by reference the IDEA regulations. Should the IDEA be repealed or deregulated (as was attempted in the early 1980s), Section 504 would provide much less protection in terms of both substantive requirements and procedural safeguards. The fact that Section 504 is not a funding statute provides an additional problem with it as a source of ensuring educational services.[36]

The Americans with Disabilities Act

In 1990, Congress passed the Americans with Disabilities Act (ADA)[37] prohibiting discrimination on the basis of disability. The reason for its passage was to expand the protection found in the Rehabilitation Act to the private sector. While education was not its primary focus, the ADA does apply to both public and private schools. Most of the ADA requirements for schools already exist through Section 504 of the Rehabilitation Act, and it is likely the IDEA will preempt the ADA to the same extent it preempts Section 504. There will remain, however, at least some situations where the ADA will apply.[38]

Sequential Listing of Major Special Education Law Developments

Brown v. Board of Education, 347 U.S. 483 (1954)

Established that "separate but equal" was not equal in education.

PARC v. Pennsylvania, 334 F. Supp. 1257 (E.D. Pa. 1971), and *Mills v. Board of Education,* 348 F. Supp. 866 (D.D.C. 1972)

Established the constitutional basis for providing education to children with disabilities by finding that denial of education to these children and denial of due process in so doing violates the fourteenth amendment to the Constitution.

Rehabilitation Act of 1973 (Section 504), 29 U.S.C. § 794

Recipients of federal financial assistance may not discriminate on the basis of disability.

Education for All Handicapped Children Act of 1975 (EAHCA), 20 U.S.C. §§ 1400–1461

A grant statute to provide for the support of special education to states that implement a plan to provide a free appropriate public education to all children with disabilities so that special education and related services will be available on an individualized basis; due process protection must be in place to ensure compliance.

Final Regulations for EAHCA, passed August 15, 1977

Now found at 34 C.F.R. Part 300

Battle v. Commonwealth, 629 F.2d 269 (3d Cir. 1980)

Established that educational policies (such as one limiting the school year to 180 days) would violate the EAHCA if such policies denied students with disabilities a free appropriate public education. (This was eventually incorporated into the IDEA principles.)

Board of Education v. Rowley, 458 U.S. 176 (1982)

An "appropriate" education under the EAHCA is found when a program of special education and related services is provided such that the child benefits from education and where the due process procedures have been followed in developing the program.

Irving Independent School District v. Tatro, 468 U.S. 883 (1984)

Catheterization and similar health-type services are "related services" because they need not be provided by a physician and are relatively simple procedures to provide. If these services had been determined to be medical services, they would not be required under the EAHCA.

Smith v. Robinson, 468 U.S. 992 (1984)

Where the EAHCA provides the basis for protection in special education, it is the exclusive avenue of relief, and Section 504 and Section 1983 are not available.

Perkins Act of 1984, 20 U.S.C. §§ 2301, 2332–2334

Ten percent of all federal funding for vocational education must go toward the education of students with disabilities. Vocational education is to be provided in the least restrictive environment. This was an important step toward recognizing the importance of special education in the secondary schools and as part of the transition to adulthood.

City of Cleburne v. Cleburne Living Center, 473 U.S. 432 (1985)

Mentally retarded individuals are not a suspect or even a quasi-suspect class for determining the appropriate level of constitutional scrutiny. The *Plyler v. Doe*, 457 U.S. 202 (1982), decision, which provides that while education is not a fundamental right it deserves heightened scrutiny, will mean that although individuals with disabilities will not be given any special deference by the courts, education will.

Burlington School Committee v. Department of Education, 471 U.S. 359 (1985)

Where the parents unilaterally place a child in an appropriate placement and the school did not provide an appropriate placement, the parents may receive reimbursement for the expenses incurred.

Handicapped Children's Protection Act of 1986 (HCPA)

An amendment to the EAHCA providing for attorneys' fees and costs to be awarded to parents who are prevailing parties.

Education of the Handicapped Act Amendments of 1986, 20 U.S.C. §§ 1471 *et seq.* and 1419 *et seq.*

Provides for a phase-in of early intervention services for 3- to 5-year-olds, to be mandatory by 1990; also contains an incentive program for younger children.

School Board of Nassau County v. Arline, 480 U.S. 273 (1987)

Contagious diseases are a handicap under Section 504 of the Rehabilitation Act, and individuals with these diseases are protected from discrimination in federal financially assisted programs, although the individuals must also be otherwise qualified. Risk to the health and safety of others, if actual, may deem the individual unqualified.

Civil Rights Restoration Act of 1987, 29 U.S.C. § 706(7)(8)(c)

Amended Section 504 of the Rehabilitation Act to clarify that *all* portions of an educational agency are considered to be part of the program; adopted the *Arline* characterization of contagious diseases as handicaps within the Rehabilitation Act.

Honig v. Doe, 484 U.S. 305 (1988)

Expulsion of a child for more than 10 days constitutes a change in placement for which all EAHCA due process protections must take place. Temporary removals are permissible for emergency situations.

Dellmuth v. Muth, 491 U.S. 223 (1989)

States and state agencies are immune from suits under the EAHCA, which was later amended to provide that states and state agencies are not immune.

Individuals with Disabilities Education Act of 1990 (IDEA)

Amended the EAHCA by changing the title of the act, providing for transitional programming and assistive technology as related services, and a number of other provisions. Did not significantly change the existing act.

Americans with Disabilities Act of 1990 (ADA)

Major civil rights statute prohibiting discrimination on the basis of disability by most employers, public agencies, and public accommodations. Similar coverage to Section 504, but does not require one to receive federal financial assistance to be subject to the ADA. Title II applies to public schools; Title III applies to private schools.

Zobrest v. Catalina Foothills School District, 509 U.S.1 (1993)

Public educational agencies may provide sign language interpreter services to special education students in parochial schools without violating the first amendment prohibition against establishing religion.

Florence County School District Four v. Carter, 510 U.S. 7 (1993)

Public schools may be required to fund private education in unapproved programs where the public school fails to provide special education.

Board of Education v. Grumet, 512 U.S. 687 (1994)

Creating a school district to correspond to a Hasidic Jewish religious neighborhood in order to provide special education programming to children in that neighborhood violates the establishment clause of the Constitution.

Individuals with Disabilities Education Act (IDEA) (1997), 20 U.S.C. §§ 1400 *et seq.*

Expanded on prior requirements in the law by including requirements for high expectations and outcomes for students with disabilities.

Cedar Rapids Community School District v. Garret F., 526 U.S. 66 (1999)

Intensive nursing services required for student are related services within the IDEA.

No Child Left Behind (NCLB) (2002)

Federal legislation requiring state education standards to have high expectations for all students (including those with disabilities), statewide assessment testing, and personnel requirements.

Individuals with Disabilities Education Act (IDEA) (2004) 20 U.S.C. §§ 1400 *et seq.*

Continued to expand on high expectation and outcome requirements for students with disabilities and incorporated some requirements from No Child Left Behind (NCLB). Made a number of changes to the details of the law. Implementing regulations to the law were developed and released by the United States Department of Education in 2006.

Schaffer v. Weast, 546 U.S. 49 (2005)

Burden of proof falls on the party seeking relief in IDEA cases.

Arlington Central School District Board of Education v. Murphy, 548 U.S. 291 (2006)

Expert fees are not available as a remedy.

Winkelman v. Parma City School District, 127 S. Ct. 1994 (2007)

Parents can represent themselves in challenging their children's rights under the IDEA.

Board of Educ. of City School Dist. of City of New York v. Tom F., 128 S. Ct. 1 (2007)

Equally divided Supreme Court decision affirms without decision a Second Circuit Court of Appeals decision regarding payment for private school tuition reimbursement. Circuit court held that student need not first receive special education services from the public school in order for the parents to be eligible for reimbursement.

Americans with Disabilities Act Amendments of 2008, Pub. L. No. 110-325

Amends the definition of disability for both the ADA and the Rehabilitation Act in a way that might provide greater protection for students with certain types of learning disabilities and certain types of health conditions.

Summary

The right to education for students with disabilities did not become a comprehensive program until 1975 with passage of the Education for All Handicapped Children Act (EAHCA). Before 1975, some states provided some educational programming to some children with certain disabilities. Federal law before 1975 provided incentive funding to those states that provided special education.

The 1975 amendment to the federal incentive programs was the real guarantee of a comprehensive and consistent program for providing education to children with disabilities. The 1975 EAHCA included the important requirements that appropriate education must be provided to all children with disabilities in the least restrictive appropriate setting at no cost to parents and that procedural safeguards for parents must be in place to enforce these rights.

Although the EAHCA (now IDEA) does not mandate that states comply with its requirements unless they seek funding under the IDEA, states need the additional federal funding. They also recognize that public educational agencies are subject to the 1973 Rehabilitation Act and the 1990 Americans with Disabilities Act prohibiting discrimination on the basis of disability as well as constitutional equal protection and due process requirements. For these reasons, all states have elected to accept funding under the IDEA.

The requirements of the IDEA have developed and evolved over the years, but the concepts of providing students with disabilities with a free and appropriate public education and including parents in the process remain central components of the law. Newer provisions of the law include requirements aimed at increasing and improving the expectations and outcomes for students with disabilities.

Courts have issued many decisions interpreting federal statutes. These include a number of Supreme Court opinions. In some situations, Congress has responded to a Supreme Court decision by amending the statute. This continuing dynamic relationship among Congress, the courts, and regulatory agencies is likely to continue.

Questions for Reflection

1. Why has the IDEA evolved over the years to include requirements regarding high expectations for students with disabilities? What effect have these provisions had on the services provided to students with disabilities? Do these requirements have any effect on students without disabilities? Why or why not?

2. One of the requirements in the IDEA since 1997 is that students with disabilities progress in the general curriculum. This requirement, along with the least restrictive environment requirement mentioned in this chapter (see Chapter 11 for more information about this topic), encourages schools to educate students with disabilities in the regular classroom along with students without disabilities to the maximum extent appropriate. At the same time, the law requires schools to provide students with disabilities with individualized instruction that meets each student's unique needs. Is

there a conflict between these provisions? Are there ways that schools can differentiate instruction for students within the same class to meet everyone's needs?

3. Consider the following scenario:

> Jeff is a second grade student with a learning disability in reading. His individualized education plan (IEP) includes direct individualized instruction in basic reading concepts and phonics for 30 minutes per day. The instruction is different from the instruction his fellow students receive in class and needs to be provided by a special education teacher, as opposed to the regular classroom teacher.

How should the services be provided? Would it be stigmatizing to remove Jeff from the regular classroom for 30 minutes per day and place him in a group of other students with similar needs for reading services? If so, should that stigmatization factor into the decision on where or how he receives services?

NOTES

1. These phases are described in more detail in Max L. Hutt & Robert G. Gibby, *The Mentally Retarded Child*, pp. 386–391 (1958).
2. 347 U.S. 483 (1954).
3. *U.S. Const.* amend. XIV.
4. Pub. L. No. 89-750, § 161, 80 Stat. 1204; Pub. L. No. 91-230, 84 Stat. 175, Part B.
5. Pub. L. No. 94-142.
6. 334 F. Supp. 1257 (E.D. Pa. 1971); 343 F. Supp. 279 (E.D. Pa. 1972).
7. 348 F. Supp. 866 (D.D.C. 1972).
8. *City of Cleburne v. Cleburne Living Center*, 473 U.S. 432 (1985).
9. *Plyler v. Doe*, 457 U.S. 202 (1982).
10. For a more in-depth discussion of these issues, see Laura Rothstein & Julia Rothstein, *Disabilities and the Law* §§ 2:34–2:43 (Thomson West 2006). See also Katharine T. Bartlett, "The Role of Cost in Educational Decisionmaking for the Handicapped Child," 48 *Law & Contemporary Problems* 7 (1985).
11. 348 F. Supp. at 878–883. See also *Disabilities and the Law* §§ 2:34–2:48.
12. To Provide Financial Assistance to the States for Improved Educational Services for Handicapped Children: Hearings on S. 6 Before the Subcomm. on the Handicapped of the Senate Comm. on Labor and Public Welfare, 93rd Cong., 1st Sess. (May 14, 1973, Oct. 19, 1973, and March 18, 1974) (hereinafter referred to by witness and page number).
13. Pub. L. No. 93-380, 88 Stat. 579, 583 (1974). The first major effort to provide special education at the federal level had occurred in 1966 when Title VI of the Elementary and Secondary Education Act, Pub. L. No 98-750 (1966), was passed. Title VI provided a single administrative body to coordinate efforts, namely the Bureau of Education for the Handicapped (BEH). Title VI was replaced in 1970 by a separate act, the Education of the Handicapped Act (EHA), Pub. L. No. 91-230 (1970). Part B of the EHA authorized grants to states to assist in providing special education.
14. Pub. L. No. 94-142, enacted November 29, 1975, 20 U.S.C. §§ 1400 *et seq.*

15. Pub. L. No. 91-230 (1970).
16. 20 U.S.C. § 1400(c) (1975); section numbers have been changed.
17. See Chapter 5.
18. See Chapter 5.
19. See Chapter 11.
20. 20 U.S.C. § 1414(d)(1)(A)(i)(IV).
21. See Chapter 14.
22. See Chapter 15.
23. 20 U.S.C. § 1401(b)(4)(1).
24. 20 U.S.C. § 1414(b)(5).
25. 20 U.S.C. § 1400(c)(5).
26. 20 U.S.C. § 1400(d)(1)(A).
27. NCLB is explained in more detail in Chapter 3.
28. For provisions on assessments, see 20 U.S.C. § 1414(d)(1)(A); 34 C.F.R. § 300.320(a); and Chapter 8 of this book. For school personnel qualifications see 20 U.S.C. § 1402(10)(B); 20 U.S.C. § 1412 (a)(14)(C); 34 C.F.R. § 300.18; and Chapter 4.
29. The term is defined in the regulations at 34 C.F.R. § 300.35.
30. 20 U.S.C. § 1414(d)(1)(A)(i)(IV).
31. 20 U.S.C. § 1400(c)(5)(F).
32. 34 C.F.R. § 300.226(a).
33. 20 U.S.C. § 1400(c)(5)(H).
34. See Chapters 6 and 7 for more information about response to intervention.
35. 29 U.S.C. § 794.
36. See Chapter 18.
37. 42 U.S.C. §§ 12101 *et seq.*
38. See Chapter 18.

Statutory Provisions

A General Overview

The material in this book focuses primarily on the requirements of the Individuals with Disabilities Education Act (IDEA).[1] Before detailed requirements of the IDEA are examined, it is important to have an overall picture not only of the IDEA but also of the other statutory provisions that relate to the education of students with disabilities. These provisions include the Americans with Disabilities Act,[2] Section 504 of the Rehabilitation Act[3] (basically nondiscrimination statutes), state laws (which usually fill in some of the gaps and supplement the federal IDEA), and a variety of other laws that relate to student records, confidentiality issues, and even tortious conduct. A broad overview of all of these laws is important for placing the IDEA in context.

Section 504 of the Rehabilitation Act

Before 1990, the most comprehensive disability rights statute other than the IDEA was the Rehabilitation Act, specifically Section 504.[4] The 1973 Rehabilitation Act was actually an amendment to a much older law providing for vocational rehabilitation—the focus of the older law being solely on employment.[5] Section 504 provides, among other things, that recipients of federal financial assistance, such as schools, should not discriminate on the basis of disability. It provides that

> [n]o otherwise qualified individual with a disability . . . shall solely by reason of her or his disability, be excluded from the participation in, be denied the benefits of, or be subjected to discrimination under any program or activity receiving Federal financial assistance.[6]

This requirement is significant because it reaches not only employment, where the recipient has federal grants or other assistance, but also institutions such as welfare providers, hospitals, federally supported transportation providers, and, of course, schools.

Most early litigation under the Rehabilitation Act focused on procedural and jurisdictional issues, such as whether the recipient actually received federal financial assistance, whether there was a private right of action, and whether one must exhaust administrative remedies before going to court.[7] More recent judicial opinion has addressed substantive issues such as whether the particular person is within the protected class, whether discrimination has actually occurred, and whether reasonable accommodations are required.

Who Is Protected Under Section 504?

To be entitled to protection under Section 504, an individual must meet the definition of a person with a disability. That definition is as follows:

> any person who (i) has a physical or mental impairment which substantially limits one or more of such person's major life activities, (ii) has a record of such an impairment, or (iii) is regarded as having such an impairment.[8]

Major life activities include

> caring for oneself, performing manual tasks, seeing, hearing, eating, sleeping, walking, standing, lifting, bending, speaking, breathing, learning, reading, concentrating, thinking, communicating, and working.[9]

Simply having a disability does not lead to success in a discrimination claim. The individual must also be "otherwise qualified." That has been interpreted to mean that the individual must be someone "who is able to meet all of a program's requirements in spite of his handicap."[10] For example, in the employment setting, an employee with a hearing impairment must be able to carry out the essential requirements of the job. Although the recipient need not make substantial modifications or fundamental alterations to the program, the recipient must still make reasonable accommodations.

What Programs Are Covered?

Recipients under Section 504 are those who receive funds, personnel services, and interests in property, whether received directly or through another recipient.[11] In *Grove City College v. Bell*,[12] the Supreme Court addressed the question of whether Title IX[13] (a sex discrimination statute similar to Section 504) applies to an entire college when the college receives only indirect federal financial assistance by having students with federally subsidized loans attend the college.

The Court held that only the program that receives the federal financial assistance is subject to Title IX. A similar analysis was subsequently applied to Section 504. After several years of effort, Congress passed the Civil Rights Restoration Act in 1987, which amended Section 504 of the Rehabilitation Act by providing that a program or activity means *all* the operations of a local or state educational agency.[14] Thus, it is rare when Section 504 would not apply to public schools. Many private schools receive federal financial assistance through school lunch programs and other subsidies, and thus are frequently also subject to Section 504.

Enforcement

Anyone with a grievance against a recipient of federal financial assistance can file a complaint with the Department of Education within 180 days of the adverse action.[15] After investigation by the Department of Education, if informal resolution does not address the complaint satisfactorily, the department may hold a hearing.[16] The agency may also refer the matter to the Department of Justice. The individual who complained to the funding agency is not a party to the hearing and does not receive an individual remedy, although that person will be given notice of the hearing.[17]

If a violation of Section 504 is found, the agency issues an appropriate order, which would normally be termination of federal funds. Following the *Grove City* holding, the termination would apply only to the program subject to the discrimination claim. The recipient may also be barred from receiving federal financial assistance in the discriminating program in the future.[18] As a practical matter, this is unlikely to happen. The burden of having records reviewed by federal government staff members can be a deterrent even though the likelihood of losing federal funding is small. Decisions by administrative agencies are subject to judicial review.[19]

For the student claiming discrimination, it will be of little comfort to know that the school's federal funding has been terminated. What the student may want is reimbursement for counseling or some other monetary remedy. This is usually not available through administrative procedures. The question then is whether the individual may bring an action directly in court to obtain an individual remedy. While the clear majority of federal circuit courts have decided that there is a private right of action under Section 504,[20] the Supreme Court has not yet directly ruled on this question, although it has addressed several Section 504 claims.[21] Most commentators and judges who have applied this test to Section 504 have found that the standard has been met. Thus, in most cases an individual would be allowed to bring suit to seek an individual remedy.

A related question is whether a party must exhaust administrative remedies before bringing an action in court. The weight of authority on this matter is not quite as strong as on the matter of whether there is a private right of action at all. Most authorities, however, indicate that because administrative remedies do not provide relief to the individual and because of the general ineffectiveness of administrative procedures, exhaustion of administrative remedies is not required in Section 504 cases.

Assuming that the individual does have a private right of action, the more difficult questions are what the burden of proof is in these cases and what remedies are available to the individual who is successful in proving a Section 504 discrimination claim. Where the individual can prove that he or she is an otherwise qualified individual with a disability within Section 504, and that benefits were denied to him or her, the general rule seems to be that the burden then shifts to the recipient to demonstrate either that the individual is not qualified or that the denial was for some reason other than the disability.[22]

Remedies

The usual remedy when an administrative agency finds a violation of Section 504 is the termination of federal assistance. The individual who has been discriminated against is usually more interested in a remedy that will redress the specific injury. One remedy that may benefit the individual is an injunction. Courts have generally found that injunctive relief is available under Section 504.[23]

There is less consistency relating to monetary relief in the form of damages as a remedy under Section 504. This would provide compensation for out-of-pocket expenses, prospective expenses, or recovery such as lost potential earnings. There is no question that damages are available if the action is brought under Section 1983 of the Civil Rights Act[24] for a violation of Section 504. Section 1983 permits individuals deprived of the rights, privileges, or immunities of the Constitution or federal laws to bring action in courts and also to recover damages. It is not yet well settled whether Section 1983 may be used to remedy Section 504 violations, although there is some precedent allowing it.

The remedy where there is the most clarity is that of attorneys' fees. The Rehabilitation Act has a specific provision allowing attorneys' fees for individuals who are successful in Section 504 actions. Individuals who are successful in Section 1983 actions are also entitled to attorneys' fees.[25]

In the first years after the passage of the IDEA and Section 504 of the Rehabilitation Act, it was unclear whether an individual could seek redress under both statutes or use Section 1983 of the Civil Rights Act as the basis for bringing an equal protection claim. The following decision initially resolved this issue to a significant extent.

SMITH V. ROBINSON

468 U.S. 992 (1984)

Justice Blackmun delivered the opinion of the Court.

This case presents questions regarding the award of attorney's fees in a proceeding to secure a "free appropriate public education" for a handicapped child. . . .

We turn to petitioners' claim that they were entitled to fees under sec. 505 of the Rehabilitation Act, because they asserted a substantial claim for relief under sec. 504 of that Act.

Much of our analysis of petitioners' equal protection claim is applicable here. The [Education of the Handicapped Act (EHA)] is a comprehensive scheme designed by Congress as the most effective way to protect the right of a handicapped child to a free appropriate public education. We concluded above that in enacting the EHA, Congress was aware of, and intended to accommodate, the claims of handicapped children that the Equal Protection Clause require that they be ensured access to public education. We also concluded that Congress did not intend to have the EHA scheme circumvented by resort to the more general provisions of sec. 1983.

Section 504 and the EHA are different substantive statutes. While the EHA guarantees a right to a free appropriate public education, sec. 504 simply prevents discrimination on the basis of handicap. But while the EHA is limited to handicapped children seeking access to public education, sec. 504 protects handicapped persons of all ages from discrimination in a variety of programs and activities receiving federal financial assistance.

Because both statutes are built around fundamental notions of equal access to state programs and facilities, their substantive requirements, as applied to the right of a handicapped child to a public education, have been interpreted to be strikingly similar. In regulations promulgated pursuant to sec. 504, the Secretary of Education has interpreted sec. 504 as requiring a recipient of federal funds that operates a public elementary or secondary education program to provide a free appropriate public education to each qualified handicapped person in the recipient's jurisdiction. The Secretary declined to require the exact EHA procedures, because those procedures might be inappropriate for some recipients not subject to the EHA, but indicated that compliance with EHA procedures would satisfy sec. 104.36.

On the other hand, although both statutes begin with an equal protection premise that handicapped children must be given access to public education, it does not follow that the affirmative requirements imposed by the two statutes are the same. The significant difference between the two, as applied to special education claims, is that the substantive and procedural rights assumed to be guaranteed by both statutes are specifically required only by the EHA. . . .

In *Southeastern Community College v. Davis,* the Court emphasized that sec. 504 does not require affirmative action on behalf of handicapped persons, but only the absence of discrimination against those persons. In light of *Davis,* courts construing sec. 504 as applied to the educational needs of handicapped children have expressed confusion about the extent to which sec. 504 requires special services necessary to make public education accessible to handicapped children.

In the EHA, on the other hand, Congress specified the affirmative obligations imposed on States to ensure that equal access to a public education is not an empty guarantee, but offers some benefit to a handicapped child. Thus, the statute specifically requires "such . . . supportive services . . . as may be required to assist a handicapped child to benefit from special education," including, if the public facilities are inadequate for the needs of the child, "instruction in hospitals and institutions."

There is no suggestion that sec. 504 adds anything to petitioners' substantive right to a free appropriate public education. The only elements added by sec. 504 are the possibility of circumventing EHA administrative procedures and going straight to court with a sec. 504 claim, the possibility of a damages award in cases where no such award is available under the EHA, and attorney's fees. As discussed above, Congress' intent to place on local and state educational agencies the responsibility for determining the most appropriate education plan for a handicapped child is clear. To the extent sec. 504 otherwise would allow a plaintiff to circumvent that state procedure, we are satisfied that the remedy conflicts with Congress' intent in the EHA. The Act appears to represent Congress' judgment that the best way to ensure a free appropriate public education for handicapped children is to clarify and make enforceable the rights of those children while at the same time endeavoring to relieve the financial burden imposed on the agencies responsible to guarantee those rights. Where sec. 504 adds nothing to the substantive rights of a handicapped child, we cannot believe that Congress intended to have the careful balance struck in the EHA upset by reliance on sec. 504 for otherwise unavailable damages or for an award of attorney's fees.

We emphasize the narrowness of our holding. We hold only that where, as here, whatever remedy might be provided under sec. 504 is provided with more clarity and precision under the EHA, a plaintiff may not circumvent or enlarge on the remedies available under the EHA by resort to sec. 504.

The Supreme Court decision in this case applied similar reasoning to the use of Section 1983 of the Civil Rights Act of 1871[26] to cases involving education and children with disabilities. Following the *Smith v. Robinson* decision, Congress amended the IDEA to allow attorneys' fees and costs under the IDEA. The amendment did not change the Supreme Court's decision that the IDEA is the exclusive avenue where it provides redress for the matter at hand.

While there will still be some situations involving children with disabilities in the public schools, most questions must be resolved by using the IDEA procedures and remedies.

Defenses

There are a number of defenses to a Section 504 action. As was pointed out by the *Smith v. Robinson* decision, there will be few situations in the future where Section 504 will be applicable to a special education case. For that reason, these defenses will not be discussed in detail. They should, however, be mentioned.

One defense that is no longer relevant for cases arising since 1986 is the defense of immunity. The eleventh amendment to the Constitution prohibits actions that are not based on constitutional violations, against states or state agencies. There are two exceptions to this rule: (1) where Congress has specifically abrogated immunity and (2) where the state has expressly waived immunity. The Supreme Court in 1985, in *Atascadero State Hospital v. Scanlon,*[27] held that states and state agencies were immune from suits under Section 504 of the Rehabilitation Act because neither exception applied. As a result of that decision, Congress amended the Rehabilitation Act to specify that states are not immune from Section 504.[28]

Other defenses under Section 504 include cost, and safety or health risks. The defense of cost could arise if the defendant claimed that it would be unduly burdensome to provide reasonable accommodation to allow participation to persons with disabilities in a program. This is an issue that has not frequently been raised in Section 504 cases involving special education, so there is little case law to provide guidance. The health issue has begun to be addressed, as it relates to children with infectious diseases, and it will be discussed more fully in Chapter 5. The safety issue arises most frequently in cases involving the participation of students with physical impairments in contact sports and students with psychological conditions.

Under Section 504, schools can raise the defense that the requested accommodation would fundamentally alter the program. This defense has not been litigated to any great extent in the special education context, but in other cases it means that the program need not lower standards nor substantially modify the program in order to comply.

The Americans with Disabilities Act

In 1990, Congress enacted the Americans with Disabilities Act (ADA).[29] The ADA is similar to the Rehabilitation Act in terms of who is protected, but it is much more far-reaching because it does not require entities to be recipients of federal financial assistance.[30] The two major provisions applicable to the special education context are Title II (applicable to public agencies, i.e., public schools) and Title III (applicable to private providers of programs of public accommodation, which includes private schools). Under the ADA, both public and private schools are prohibited from discriminating on the basis of disability and are required to provide reasonable accommodations that do not cause an undue hardship.

The ADA is more far-reaching than Section 504 in some significant ways in addition to covering the private sector much more comprehensively. It clearly establishes that individuals with contagious diseases are protected from discrimination so long as they do not directly threaten the health or safety of others. The original definition under Section 504 was not so clear, although it has been amended to provide similar protection to individuals with contagious diseases.

The ADA also extends protection to individuals who are associated with someone with a disability. For example, a child could not be excluded from enrolling in school because that child's mother is HIV positive.

The ADA, like Section 504, requires schools not to discriminate and to provide reasonable accommodations in all programming aspects. For example, the school auditorium may be required under the ADA to be accessible because of its use for public events while the IDEA might not mandate that same level of access. The ADA also benefits students with disabilities in a very important way that goes beyond their on-site educational programming. First, it requires that places of public accommodation (such as museums) be accessible, thus making it easier for schools to ensure that field trips and special events can be in accessible locations. Second, because the ADA prohibits most employment and public accommodation discrimination, students with disabilities will be more likely to achieve full participation even after they have left the comprehensive protection of the IDEA in public schools. Thus, the student with a disability will more likely be able to enter postsecondary education and the world of employment successfully.

It is important to recognize that the ADA and Section 504 are primarily nondiscrimination statutes requiring reasonable accommodation. For that reason and because of the *Smith v. Robinson* decision, most issues involving students with disabilities in the schools will be resolved by the IDEA rather than the ADA or Section 504. There will, however, most certainly be instances in which Section 504 and the ADA will apply.

The ADA may be applicable to situations involving architectural barriers. Title II (relating to public schools) requires that the program as a whole is to be accessible. Public school programs were also required to conduct a self-evaluation (to the extent one was not already done under Section 504) by January of 1993. Title III (relating to private schools) requires that by January of 1992 barriers were to have been removed to the extent it was readily achievable to do so. No self-evaluation is required under Title III.

Enforcement of the ADA under Title II is through the procedures of Section 504 and includes the same remedies and rights. Title III enforcement involves both private enforcement through the remedies and procedures of the Civil Rights Act of 1964 and Attorney General enforcement. Remedies available under Title III include injunctive relief and attorneys' fees and costs. Damages are only available under Title III if the Attorney General intervenes. The issue of immunity under the ADA in an educational setting has not yet been addressed by the Supreme Court.[31]

The Individuals with Disabilities Education Act

As was pointed out in Chapter 2, the IDEA was founded on constitutional principles of equal protection and due process. While there is no direct federal constitutional right to education or special education, states that provide education to their citizens must do so on an equal basis. Any denial of this state-created right requires due process.

States could choose to comply with these equal protection and due process requirements by setting up a program of special education without following the federal requirements of the IDEA, as long as the special education program meets the constitutional standards of equal protection and due process.

Congress recognized, however, that the additional costs of special education are burdensome, and that as a policy matter it made sense to encourage some degree of consistency among the various states. To that end, Congress passed the IDEA (effective in 1975), formerly referred to as Public Law 94-142. The original title of the act was the Education for All Handicapped Children Act. In 1990, Congress passed some amendments to the act and changed the title to reflect the new preference for using *disability* instead of *handicap* throughout the statute.

As noted in Chapter 2, Congress amended the law again in 1997 and 2004. The current goals of the IDEA include the following:

1. To ensure that all children with disabilities have available to them a free appropriate public education that emphasizes special education and related services designed to meet their unique needs and prepare them for further education, employment, and independent living;

2. To ensure that the rights of children with disabilities and parents of such children are protected; and

3. To assist States, localities, educational service agencies, and Federal agencies to provide for the education of all children with disabilities.[32]

The IDEA is a funding statute that creates substantive rights. Under the IDEA, the federal government will provide supportive funding to those states that provide special education within the framework of federally developed guidelines. An exploration of many of these guidelines is the major substance of this book, but an overview of the guidelines is useful before the requirements are examined in depth.

The Funding Mechanism

The IDEA is not intended to cover the entire cost of special education. The assumption after the *PARC* and *Mills* decisions and numerous other similar actions throughout the country is that states are obligated to provide special education anyway. Appropriations under the IDEA assist states in providing what they must provide even without the IDEA.

To qualify for federal funds, the state educational agency is required to submit an annual program plan setting out how it intends to provide education to children with disabilities within the state. A detailed framework of information must be provided in this annual program plan.[33] Details of the plans include what services will be provided (including a comprehensive system of personnel development) and what procedural safeguards will be in place to ensure that programming is being provided. The services must include not only the education itself but also a system for identifying, evaluating, and locating children in need of special education. States must also set up a system for allocating the funding to schools and ensuring that schools and school districts comply with the law's requirements.

The funding formula itself is fairly complicated. A basic explanation is that the formula sets up a maximum amount of funding that each state could receive from IDEA grants. That maximum amount is based on a count of the age eligible children who are receiving special education and related services within the state. The number is multiplied by 40 percent of the average per-pupil expenditure in public elementary and secondary schools in the United States and then adjusted by certain factors noted in the law. The 2004 changes to the law also included different maximum amounts for fiscal years 2005 and 2006, and then for 2007 and beyond.[34] The formula funding has created a number of issues. One issue, of course, is simply the complexities of counting the children with disabilities. Another major issue is the fact that Congress has never appropriated or allocated the maximum amount of funding to states. The appropriated amount has never gone beyond 19 percent, which leaves state and local funding to make up the difference.[35]

The funding amount is also based on a national average cost of educating a pupil with a disability (based on national figures), which can result in figures being much lower than the actual costs in certain areas. Additionally, the cost of educating children who have severe disabilities can be much higher than the average costs. For example, the cost of two or three residential placements within a small local school district could easily surpass the total amount of federal funding the school receives.

The Substance of Special Education

One of the major principles of the IDEA is that special education and related services be provided to *all* children who meet the age and other eligibility requirements in the law.[36] This principle is based on the idea that all children are capable of benefiting from education.[37] The IDEA's requirements for services also include students who have been suspended or expelled from school.[38]

The special education and related services to be provided include more than just the academics. Services under the IDEA can include basic self-help skills such as feeding, toilet training, and vocational training.

Those children who meet the general age eligibility requirements are those aged 6 through 17. In addition, states that provide education to children between ages 3 and 5 and ages 18 and 21 must also provide special education to eligible students in these age ranges on an equal basis.

A 1986 amendment to the IDEA provided for additional coverage for infants, toddlers, and preschoolers under the age of 3. These requirements remain today as part of the IDEA.[39] The specific requirements in these sections are different in some areas as compared with the requirements for older students, but include many of the same basic concepts. The other eligibility requirements in the law are discussed in more detail in Chapter 7, but generally require that the child fit into one of the categories of disability covered by the law and need special education and related services.[40]

A second major principle of the IDEA was initially referred to as the "mainstreaming" mandate. Current terminology is more likely to refer to this concept as "inclusion." Regardless of what term is used, the principle arises from the IDEA requirement that special education and related services are to be provided in the *least restrictive environment,* which generally means that students with disabilities should be educated with students without disabilities to the maximum extent appropriate.[41]

One of the early fears of educators was that the IDEA inclusion mandate meant that all children with disabilities, regardless of the severity of disability, were to be "dumped" into the regular classroom without support. While there are certainly instances of inappropriate placements of children with severe disabilities into the regular classroom, the IDEA requires that the child be placed in the least restrictive *appropriate* setting, which means that the student must be able to receive the services he or she requires in the placement. If the services that a student requires cannot be provided in the regular classroom, then it is not an appropriate placement for that particular student.

The IDEA requires states to develop a continuum of alternative learning environments to help ensure that least restrictive environment requirements are considered by the school along with the parents when making decisions about where the student will receive services.[42]

While the goal of the law is to move the child to less restrictive settings, for some children full time in the regular classroom may never be an appropriate placement. The theory underlying the mainstreaming goal includes the "separate is not equal" principle of *Brown v. Board of Education.*[43] Segregated placements are inherently stigmatizing. In addition, for many children, interaction with peers who do not have disabilities is an essential component of role-modeling and appropriate social development. It is important to emphasize that the IDEA does *not* require placement in the *best* placement, only the least restrictive appropriate placement. While states may choose to make the *best* placement a part of special education, it is not required under federal law.

A third major principle of the IDEA is that education is to be *individualized* and *appropriate* to the child's needs.[44] The IDEA requires that once a child is identified as a "child with a disability" as that term is used in the law, a team of people that are defined in the law must develop an individualized education program (IEP) for that student. The team includes teachers, service providers, and the parent(s).[45] The IEP must meet the unique needs of that specific child based on evaluations and other information about that student's needs and abilities.[46]

It is important to note that the goals set forth in these plans are not contracts between the parents and the educational agency, and that schools are not always held liable simply because certain goals have not been met. Rather, the law requires the team to address the reasons why the goals were not met by meeting and revising the services provided to the student, or perhaps the goals themselves as appropriate for that particular student.

The final substantive principle of the IDEA is that education is to be provided free.[47] This basically means that the special education and related services provided to the student must be provided at no cost to the parents, regardless of their ability to pay. Schools may charge parents for incidental fees that are charged to students without disabilities.[48] Disputes have arisen about whether certain kinds of expenses were really medical rather than educational, and whether expensive residential placements must be paid for by the educational agency.[49]

In some situations, state or local social service agencies may be involved with the services provided to a student, or otherwise responsible for paying for the cost of services. Insurance providers such as Medicaid may also provide payment for some services, and changes to the IDEA in 2004 allow school districts to ask parents to consent to having the parents' private health insurance pay for services that may be covered under the health insurance plan.[50] Parents may choose to consent to the request or not.

These substantive principles and other issues are discussed in greater detail in subsequent chapters.

Procedural Safeguards Under the IDEA

Congress recognized that for the substantive requirements to be carried out, procedural protections would need to be in place. These are discussed in greater detail in Chapters 8 and 15, but the following is a general overview. These protections are in place at all stages of the special education process, including identification, evaluation, IEP development, placement decision making, and implementation. The protections fall into four general categories: (1) the right to *notice* about meetings and proposed actions by the school at all stages of the special education process, (2) the right to *participate* in decisions as an equal team member at all stages in the special education process, (3) the right to *consent* or to not consent to proposed actions during the special education process, and (4) the right to *have disagreements* about decisions and proposals during the special education process *resolved* through various dispute resolution mechanisms. Parents have the right to challenge a decision as well as withdraw consent at any stage of the process.

The specific procedural protections also include a right to notice of all of the procedural and substantive protections available. Parents also have a right to access the student's educational records.

One of the ways the parties can resolve a dispute that arises during the special education process is through a due process hearing. The hearing process itself includes a number of procedural protections for the parties. The hearing must include an impartial hearing officer, the parties are entitled to be represented at the hearing, the parties may call and cross-examine witnesses, and there is a right both to a record of the hearing and to written findings of fact and decisions. There is also a right of review with the state educational agency and an ultimate right to seek review in the courts.

There has been litigation over circumstances that might permit the parents to seek redress directly in court, and this issue is discussed more fully in subsequent chapters. An initially unresolved issue was whether one can use Section 504 of the Rehabilitation Act or Section 1983 to seek relief, or whether one is limited to using the procedures of the IDEA. The Supreme Court in *Smith v. Robinson*[51] held that where the IDEA provides relief, that statute, and not Section 504, must be the basis for seeking redress.

What remains under dispute, however, are questions about situations in which Section 504 (and now the ADA) might still be available.

There are some who criticize the IDEA procedures as really providing protection only to aggressive middle-class parents. Others argue that the procedures are cumbersome and an inefficient use of educational resources. Congress enacted provisions in the 1997 and the 2004 amendments to the IDEA to address these issues and lessen the paperwork burdens on school personnel. The existence of these procedures has been an important and essential component of ensuring compliance with the goals of the IDEA.

No Child Left Behind

No Child Left Behind (NCLB), enacted in 2002, is a federal statute that evolved from Title I of the Elementary and Secondary Education Act, which was originally enacted as a part of the "War on Poverty" in the 1960s to help children from low-income homes.[52] NCLB has numerous requirements. The three categories of requirements that are most relevant to special education are (1) developing state education standards with high expectations for all students, (2) statewide assessment testing, and (3) personnel requirements.

NCLB requires states to develop or adopt content and proficiency standards and assessment mechanisms to determine what all students should know and be able to do at various grade levels. The law requires that these standards be challenging, contain high expectations, and apply to all students.[53]

These requirements are relevant to special education in a number of ways. First, the state-developed or -adopted content and proficiency standards are used by states and local schools to develop the curriculum used by local schools to teach all students. When Congress amended the IDEA in 1997 and in 2004, it modified the focus of the law in some ways by including a requirement that students with disabilities have access to and progress in the general curriculum, which is the curriculum that schools use for all students. As a result, the services that are provided to students with disabilities are now designed to allow them to access and progress in the same curriculum as students without disabilities. The curriculum is based on the challenging, high expectations in the content and proficiency standards.[54]

Second, NCLB requires states to adopt a statewide assessment program to measure student proficiency in meeting the state content and proficiency standards. The law divides students into various subgroups and requires each of those subgroups to make adequate yearly progress (AYP).[55] Schools and school districts that do not make AYP are subject to various sanctions. Students with disabilities are one of the subgroups under the law, which has led to an increased focus on providing students with disabilities with services to assist them in the areas covered in the statewide assessment test.

The 1997 and 2004 amendments to the IDEA also include a number of requirements for students with disabilities aimed at ensuring that students with disabilities participate in statewide assessment programs and receive required accommodations during the process. The other major connection between NCLB and the IDEA comes in the highly qualified teacher (HQT) requirements. NCLB requires teachers that teach "core academic subjects" to meet certain standards delineated under the law. The general HQT requirements include a bachelor's degree, licensure or certification by the state in which they teach, and demonstrating competency in the subject matter in which they teach.[56] From there, the requirements vary depending on various factors including whether the teacher is experienced or new and the grade level taught by the teacher.

The law also requires paraprofessionals at Title I schools to have a high school diploma and be supervised by a highly qualified teacher, and the law places limitations on the duties and tasks that a paraprofessional can perform.[57] The 2004 amendments to the IDEA incorporated the HQT requirements from NCLB for special education teachers and included requirements for paraprofessionals as well. These requirements are discussed in detail in Chapter 4.

The application of NCLB principles to students with disabilities has been the source of much discussion. Policymakers and educators recognize the benefits of including students with disabilities in ensuring high expectations, the presence of highly qualified teachers, and accountability. There are concerns, however, about the impact.[58]

State Education Statutes

Although education is primarily state controlled, special education, in practice, has become federally controlled by the IDEA. Although states are not required to follow the IDEA requirements, they must do so if they wish to receive federal funding for special education. The federal budgetary support for special education is of extreme importance to states. In addition, states may well be required to comply with many of the substantive and procedural requirements of the IDEA in any case, as a result of the *PARC* and *Mills* decisions incorporating constitutional principles. All states have elected to develop annual program plans to be eligible for federal funding under the IDEA.

For those states providing special education even before the IDEA, it was necessary for them to adapt their existing state educational programs to fit the requirements of the IDEA. States that did not have special education programs in place were required to develop them.

Virtually all states have adopted the federal regulations as a basic framework. Many have expanded on these regulations and have provided more detailed or additional requirements for special education programming. To the extent that these do not conflict with federal requirements and do meet the federal minimums, they are permissible.

There are a number of areas in which some states expand on the federal special education requirements. For example, states may elect to provide special education to children outside the age mandates of the IDEA. States may include other categories of children entitled to special education, such as gifted students. As long as the procedures are consistent with the IDEA, states may allow for additional procedural safeguards, such as having a panel of hearing officers rather than just one. In addition, states set out their own specific requirements relating to matters such as teacher certification, age span requirements in the classroom, teacher-pupil ratios, and maximum time for transportation.

One area in which there has been some difficulty involving state policies relates to the deinstitutionalization movement. In a significant number of states, litigation under state constitutions, mental health and mental retardation laws, and other statutes resulted in moving institutionalized individuals (both children and adults) into the local community. For those children who are eligible for public education, there are often disputes over which agency has responsibility for funding the child's placement. State health and human service agencies have sometimes tried to shift fiscal responsibility for these placements and certain services to state educational agencies. While there have been some recent efforts to establish interagency cooperation in a number of states, this is an area in need of greater policy clarity. In challenging economic times, these issues can become even more critical because less local, state, and federal funding support is available to finance these programs. Even where funding is available, there can be challenges in finding sufficient trained staff.

It should be noted that states are given a substantial degree of deference in the choice of educational programming to be provided within the framework. The role of the federal government is not intended to be one that mandates how states are to educate a deaf child, for example. This point was emphasized in the first Supreme Court case to decide an IDEA issue, *Board of Education v. Rowley.*[59]

Other Relevant Laws

When a parent or school is concerned about the requirements for educating a child with a disability, the primary laws will be the IDEA, state education laws, and to a lesser extent Section 504 of the Rehabilitation Act and the Americans with Disabilities Act. There are, however, a number of other federal and state laws relevant to the education of students with disabilities.

Student Education Records Laws

The Family Educational Rights and Privacy Act (FERPA)[60] is more commonly known as the Buckley Amendment. It is intended to provide protections in two major areas—access to and accuracy of school records. It requires that schools subject to FERPA, which includes public schools, must permit parents and students over 18 to have access to their records in most cases, and it provides for protections against unauthorized disclosure of school records. By having access to the records, the student can ascertain whether the information in the records is accurate and complete. FERPA provides mechanisms for making appropriate changes and corrections.

In addition to FERPA, most states have a variety of state record laws. These may have additional protections and may provide for additional rights and remedies where violations have occurred. State confidentiality requirements and related laws are particularly important in cases involving children with HIV or other communicable diseases. It can be critical to know when certain information must be reported to public health officials, and to whom it is permissible to disclose information about the condition of a child. Many states have revised their state confidentiality and communicable disease laws because of these concerns.[61]

Student Health Record Laws

State laws relating to communicable diseases can be of importance in the special education context. Where a child has a communicable disease that may be viewed as one posing a risk to others, but where that same child is potentially considered to be "disabled" within the IDEA, the ADA, or Section 504, there is the potential for tension between the various laws. This is an area where the need for policy revision has become apparent, but until a clear-cut national policy is developed, or until a statewide policy is established in the state where the child is attending school, it is important at least to recognize that there may be conflicting policies.

In addition to communicable disease laws, there are state mental health/mental retardation statutes. These laws usually involve the provision of services to individuals who are mentally ill or mentally retarded. A child with a severe emotional disturbance or autism, who might have simply been institutionalized before 1975, will now be entitled to at least the educational component of a placement under state special education laws. There is considerable tension between agencies in many states, and the laws themselves do not always clearly delineate the agency having the primary administrative or fiscal responsibility for the services needed by the child.

Finally, the Health Insurance Portability and Accountability Act of 1996 (HIPAA),[62] which is discussed in Chapter 19, provides for privacy for medical records. Records covered by FERPA, however, are not covered by HIPAA even if they have health-related information in them.

Tort and Contract Law

In addition to the major laws noted previously, there are numerous instances where issues of tort and/or contract law may become relevant. While this is not a major area of concern, it is one where a brief general overview is appropriate.

Tort law includes a variety of potential actions that could arise relating to special education. These could include defamation, libel, slander, or invasion of privacy, where information about a child is improperly or inaccurately conveyed by school officials to others who are not authorized to receive the information.

The tort issue most likely to arise, however, is negligence—or special education malpractice. As will be discussed in more depth in Chapter 20, there is currently little judicial acceptance of the malpractice theory in special education cases, although there are some exceptions in egregious cases. Related to the negligence issue is a breach of contract issue. The question that is raised in some circumstances is whether the failure to accomplish the goals of an individualized education plan constitutes a breach of contract. As a general rule, such a theory will not be accepted by the courts, but it is important to be aware that it may be raised.

Summary

Section 504 of the Rehabilitation Act prohibits recipients of federal financial assistance (such as educational agencies) from discriminating on the basis of disability. This provides some protection for the student who has a disability. The Americans with Disabilities Act, which applies to virtually all schools, prohibits discrimination on the basis of disability and has application to Section 504. Neither Section 504 nor the ADA contains a basis for the additional support services and major accommodations necessary in many cases for appropriate provision of special education, nor do they have elaborate procedures focused on the education setting.

The IDEA provides these missing elements. It goes beyond a mere nondiscrimination mandate and requires special education and related services to be provided to all students with disabilities in the least restrictive appropriate setting at no cost. Perhaps the most important feature of the IDEA is its elaborate set of procedural protections including notice, participation, and an opportunity to have a disagreement resolved by an impartial decision maker.

Because of the detailed requirements of the IDEA, the Supreme Court has held that Congress intended the IDEA to be the exclusive avenue through which special education claims were to be addressed—at least where the substantive rights of the child are protected through the IDEA. The *Smith v. Robinson* decision left open the question of what circumstances remain to justify reliance on other avenues of redress.

What remedies are available remains somewhat unresolved under both the IDEA and Section 504. The Supreme Court has yet to clarify this issue, and lower courts have reached a variety of conclusions about the question of damages and other remedies in special education cases.

While Section 504, the ADA, and the IDEA provide the federal statutory framework, state special education statutes and regulations incorporate the IDEA mandates and frequently expand on various issues. The No Child Left Behind statute, which is not directly a federal law for students with disabilities, includes key elements that are coordinated with the IDEA.

In addition, student academic record and student health record statutes, tort and contract laws, and federal and state law relating to privacy for students must also be reference points in evaluating legal requirements affecting students with disabilities. While it is important to recognize state law requirements, the wide variance from state to state makes an in-depth examination of these laws impossible in this text.

Questions for Reflection

1. With the Rehabilitation Act and the ADA providing protection against discrimination on the basis of disability, why is the IDEA necessary?

2. What are some ways that Congress could address some issues noted in this chapter with the IDEA funding formula?

3. Why are the procedural protections of the law important? Do you think the goals of the law that were noted in this chapter could be met without these protections? Why or why not?

4. What do state education statutes relating to special education add to the IDEA? Why doesn't the IDEA cover these issues?

NOTES

1. 20 U.S.C. §§ 1400 *et seq.*
2. 42 U.S.C. §§ 12101 *et seq.*

3. 29 U.S.C. § 794.

4. A more detailed discussion of how Section 504 works in specific disputes is found in Chapter 18.

5. See 1973 U.S. Code Cong. & Ad. News 2076.

6. 29 U.S.C. § 794. Other provisions of the Rehabilitation Act prohibit discrimination by federal employers and federal contractors. Early versions of these provisions used the term "handicap" instead of disability. In 1990, the Act was amended to change the language to "disability."

7. See generally Laura Rothstein & Julia Rothstein, *Disabilities and the Law* §§ 2:40–2:46 (Thomson West 2006).

8. 29 U.S.C. § 706(8)(B).

9. 34 C.F.R. § 104.3(j)(2)(ii).

10. *Southeastern Community College v. Davis,* 442 U.S. 397 (1979).

11. 34 C.F.R. § 104.3(f)&(h).

12. 465 U.S. 555 (1984).

13. 20 U.S.C. § 1681(a).

14. Pub. L. No. 100-259.

15. The United States Department of Education's Web site provides information about how to file a complaint. See http://www.ed.gov/about/offices/list/ocr/docs/howto.html (last accessed August 5, 2008). The address is U.S. Department of Education, Office for Civil Rights, 400 Maryland Avenue, S.W., Washington, DC 20202. The procedures are those used for implementation of Title VI of the Civil Rights Act. See 34 C.F.R. §§ 100.6–100.10.

16. 34 C.F.R. § 100.9.

17. *Id.* at 100.9(a).

18. 34 C.F.R. § 100.10(f).

19. 34 C.F.R. § 100.11.

20. See *Disabilities and the Law* § 2:02.

21. *Southeastern Community College v. Davis,* 442 U.S. 397 (1979); *Camenisch v. University of Texas,* 451 U.S. 390 (1981); *Bowen v. American Hospital Association,* 476 U.S. 610 (1986); *United States Department of Transportation v. Paralyzed Veterans of America,* 477 U.S. 597 (1986); *County of Los Angeles v. Kling,* 474 U.S. 936 (1985); *Consolidated Rail Corporation v. Darrone,* 464 U.S. 624 (1984); *Atascadero State Hospital v. Scanlon,* 473 U.S. 234 (1985); and *School Board of Nassau County v. Arline,* 480 U.S. 273 (1987).

22. See *Disabilities and the Law* §§ 2:02, 2:54–2:55.

23. *Id.* at § 2:55.

24. 42 U.S.C. § 1988. See *Disabilities and the Law* § 2:56.

25. 42 U.S.C. § 1988 (the Civil Rights Attorney's Fees Awards Act of 1976).

26. See *Disabilities and the Law* § 1:15.

27. 473 U.S. 234 (1985).

28. Pub. L. No. 99-506, 100 Stat. 1807 (1986); 29 U.S.C. § 701.

29. 42 U.S.C. §§ 12101 *et seq.* See also *Disabilities and the Law* § 2:06.

30. A more detailed discussion of the application of the ADA to cases involving students with disabilities is found in Chapter 18.

31. See *Disabilities and the Law* § 1:08.

32. 20 U.S.C. § 1400(d)(1).

33. 42 U.S.C. § 1412.

34. 20 U.S.C. § 1411.

35. See Congressional Research Service Report to Congress, *Individuals with Disabilities Education Act, Current Funding Trends,* Richard N. Apling, February 11, 2005.

36. See Chapter 5.

37. *Timothy W. v. Rochester School District,* 875 F.2d 954 (1st Cir. 1989).

38. 20 U.S.C. § 1412(a)(1).

39. 20 U.S.C. §§ 1419 & 1431.

40. 34 C.F.R. § 300.8; 34 C.F.R. § 300.306.

41. 20 U.S.C. § 1412(a)(5). See Chapter 11.

42. 34 C.F.R. § 300.115.

43. 347 U.S. 483 (1954).

44. See Chapter 9.

45. 20 U.S.C. § 1414(d)(1)(B).

46. 20 U.S.C. § 1414(d)(1)(A).

47. See Chapter 14.

48. 34 C.F.R. § 300.39(b).

49. See *Cedar Rapids Community School District v. Garret F.,* 526 U.S. 66 (1999) and *Abrahamson v. Hershman,* 701 F.2d 223, 227–228 (1st Cir. 1983).

50. See 34 C.F.R. § 300.154.

51. 468 U.S. 992 (1984).

52. See Laurence Parker, *The Elementary and Secondary Education Act at 40: Reviews of Research, Policy Implementation, Critical Perspectives, and Reflections* (Sage 2007).

53. 20 U.S.C. § 6311.

54. 20 U.S.C. § 1400(c)(5).

55. 20 U.S.C. § 6311(b)(2)(B).

56. 20 U.S.C. § 6319; 20 U.S.C. § 7801(23).

57. 20 U.S.C. § 6319.

58. See Cassandra Cole, "Closing the Achievement Gap Series: Part III, What Is the Impact of NCLB on the Inclusion of Students With Disabilities?" 4 *Education Policy Brief, Center for Evaluation & Education Policy, Indiana Institute on Disability and Community* 11 (Fall 2006) (publications can be found at the center's Web site: http://www.ceep.indiana.edu); Judy A. Schrag, "No Child Left Behind and Its Implications for Students With Disabilities," 16 *The Special Edge* 2 (Spring 2003) (download at http://www.calstat.org, link to "Publications").

59. 458 U.S. 176 (1982).

60. 20 U.S.C. § 1232.

61. A more detailed discussion of this issue is found in Chapter 19.

62. 42 U.S.C. §§ 300gg–300gg-2; 29 U.S.C. §§ 1181–1191c.

The People

Before examining in detail the substantive and procedural requirements and the remedies available under the laws relating to special education, it is useful to have a sense of the various individuals who are involved in these issues. These include the students themselves, their parents, educators, administrators, related service providers, advocates, and decision makers. The following sections describe the major characteristics of these people.

Students

Categorization

Not all students with disabilities are covered by the Individuals with Disabilities Education Act (IDEA). To be eligible for the protections under the IDEA, a student must fit into the definition of a "child with a disability" under the law. The definition includes 13 categories of disabilities. The definition states,

> Child with a disability means a child evaluated in accordance with §§ 300.304 through 300.311 as having mental retardation, a hearing impairment (including deafness), a speech or language impairment, a visual impairment (including blindness), a serious emotional disturbance (referred to in this part as "emotional disturbance"), an orthopedic impairment, autism, traumatic brain injury, an other health impairment, a specific learning disability, deaf-blindness, or multiple disabilities, and who, by reason thereof, needs special education and related services.

Each of these categories of disability has its own specific requirements that must be met in order for a student to be eligible to receive services under the law. These requirements are discussed in more detail in Chapter 7. States may also have a category for children ages 3 through 9 experiencing developmental delays with physical development, cognitive development, communication development, social or emotional development, or adaptive development.[1]

It should be emphasized that the child must not only fit into one or more of the listed categories, but must also require special education and related services because of the disability in order to be eligible for services. Some have raised concerns about the categorization system used for providing special education services under the IDEA. One concern is that the categorical labels do not always accurately reflect the characteristics of the children. Additionally, labeling may stigmatize the child, and once a child is labeled, it may be difficult to change the label. Some believe that attaching a label to a child may well produce a self-fulfilling prophecy.[2]

Some contend that the labels or categories do not help teachers in finding the appropriate means of providing instruction and training. As a result, some professionals have recommended that the classification of children be noncategorical. These recommendations have been implemented in some states. For example, Texas, Colorado, and California train and certify special educators noncategorically. The move away from categories has been achieved positively in a variety of programs throughout the country. The 2004 amendments to the IDEA provide states with some additional discretion in this area by stating that the IDEA does not require states to classify students by disability as long as each child who has a disability as defined by the law and needs special education and related services is regarded as a "child with a disability." In other words, a state does not have to categorize students as learning disabled, speech-language impaired, other health impaired, and so on. It could instead just develop a system that provides that students who meet any of the categories of disability under the law are simply "children with disabilities."[3]

While some of the legal issues relating to labeling will be discussed more fully in Chapter 6, a few general points should be noted here. Within the categories set out by the IDEA definition of a child with a disability, a wide degree of difference exists among children. The educational needs of children within these categories is correspondingly widely disparate. And even children with the same functional level may have differing educational needs because of a variety of factors. It should, therefore, be apparent that attaching a label to a child provides only the most general information about that child. It is one of the reasons that individualized educational programming that goes beyond the student's label is required for children with disabilities under the IDEA. Placement and services cannot be based just on the child's label.

Gaps in Coverage

One category not covered by the IDEA is the gifted and talented. Although the IDEA does not provide coverage for this group of children, many states provide special educational programming for gifted children. Several other categories of children are not comprehensively covered by the IDEA. The first is the chronically ill child, the child with an illness such as cancer or diabetes who may be frequently absent from school for treatment or because of illness. Children could be covered under the law in the "other health impaired" category, but only if they require special education and related services by reason of the disability. A child who is frequently absent and needs a program of homebound instruction because of illness may fit the definition.

Similarly, a child with HIV or another infectious disease may meet the definition of a "child with a disability" for purposes of the IDEA, but only if the child requires special education and related services as a result of the disability. If the child does not require special education services, the child could still be protected under Section 504 of the Rehabilitation Act and the Americans with Disabilities Act (ADA).

This distinction in coverage can be important if the child is seeking to take advantage of the procedural safeguards noted in Chapter 3 that are available under the IDEA that are not available under Section 504 or the ADA. More information about the differences between the IDEA and Section 504 and the ADA is provided in Chapter 18. More information about the procedural safeguards in the IDEA is provided in Chapter 15.

An additional category of children are those with attention deficit disorder (ADD) or attention deficit hyperactivity disorder (ADHD). These conditions may affect the concentration abilities and other behaviors of some children. At one time, there was a debate about whether this condition should be treated as a separate disability under the IDEA or whether it would fall under the definition of learning disability or other health impaired. Because of this debate, the 1990 amendments to the IDEA required that the United States Department of Education solicit public comments on the issue.

As a result of the comments, the United States Department of Education listed ADHD as one of the chronic or acute health problems that can fit in the other health impaired category.[4] As with other students with chronic illness, having ADHD alone is not sufficient to be eligible for services under the IDEA. The student must meet the other requirements of the other health impaired category and must require special education services.

The medically fragile child in most cases is protected under the IDEA, but such children are a group for whom education agencies may have difficulty providing services. Medically fragile children include those who might require suctioning[5] or some other similar attention to ensure that medical conditions do not cause injury to the child. Until 1999, there was an unsettled legal debate involving some of these children: Must intense nursing or similar care be provided to them in transit and at the school site, or is it permissible for the child to be provided homebound education?

The mainstreaming principle discourages homebound instruction, so the issue for school districts became how far they had to go in providing related services that some may consider medical in nature (like suctioning, catheterization, operating a portable ventilator for the child, etc.). A related issue is who has to provide the services. Does a school nurse provide the services, or can an aide or classroom teacher provide services?

Understandably, teachers are often concerned about liability related to the safety and health of medically fragile children. If teachers are to provide services, school districts must ensure that teachers are appropriately and adequately trained to provide them, that a backup plan is available when there are emergencies, and that a clear procedure has been developed for providing such services.[6]

A case that helped to resolve this issue is the Supreme Court decision in *Cedar Rapids Community School District v. Garret F.*[7] In that case, a high school student who had been paralyzed at age four required a variety of services for his physical needs while in school. These services included bladder catheterization, suctioning of a tracheotomy tube, feeding, positioning, and ventilator services. The services required some degree of training, but did not require that a physician perform them. The Supreme Court held that, although they are intensive and costly, if a doctor is not required to perform the services, and the student requires the services to be able to attend school, then the educational agency has the obligation to provide or fund these services during school hours under the IDEA.

Another category of children who may fall through the cracks between special and regular education is the "slow learner." Unless a child is defined as learning disabled, mentally retarded, or one of the other categories of disability under the IDEA, he or she is not entitled to the individualization and special attention accorded to the child with a disability under the IDEA.

Historically, regular education was often geared toward the average student, which meant that the slow learner's needs might not be met in a traditional educational program. Today, there are ongoing efforts in many places to provide "differentiated instruction" within the classroom for all students to address the different learning styles and abilities of students. These efforts are outside of the IDEA's requirements.

Additionally, over the years, there has been some disagreement among professionals about the definition of learning disabled. Some contend that the definition used in the IDEA has led to the misclassification of some students, with some children who are really slow learners being classified as learning disabled under the law and others who are actually learning disabled not being classified as learning disabled under the law. Congress and the United States Department of Education attempted to address some of the issues with the learning disability classification when the IDEA was amended in 2004, and new implementing regulations were issued in 2006. These changes are discussed in more detail in Chapter 7.

Children who are socially maladjusted constitute another category that is not specifically covered under the IDEA. There has been a substantial controversy over the years about whether to identify or even separate socially maladjusted children from those who meet the definition of emotionally disturbed and whether it is possible to do so. The definition of emotional disturbance in the IDEA's regulations states that it does not include children who are socially maladjusted unless they have an emotional disturbance.[8] Thus, the issue becomes whether the social maladjustment can be separated diagnostically from other ailments the student may have that could be covered under the emotionally disturbed category.[9]

Children who are addicted to drugs or alcohol present unique difficulties. Alcohol and drug addiction itself is not considered a disability under the IDEA. These children would be protected under the IDEA only if they required special education and related services under one of the recognized categories of disability. Even when such students are not entitled to special education under the IDEA, there may be instances in which they would be given some protection against adverse treatment because of Section 504 of the Rehabilitation Act or the ADA. Clearly, this is an area where there is an increasing need for services, but at this point the primary responsibility for these services does not fall on the school system within special education mandates.

In sum, most children entitled to special education are more different from each other than they are alike. They are more like other children in the school system than they are different. But for most of them, their differences require specialized instruction and some accommodation if they are to benefit from the educational system.

It is also important to note that historically, most attention to special students has occurred on the elementary school level. This is reflected in programming and teacher training. There has, however, been an increasing recognition in the education field of the importance of early education and the transition at the secondary level to the workplace or postsecondary opportunities. This recognition is reflected in changes to the IDEA promoting prevention and early intervention including early childhood and infant programs, and an increasing emphasis on vocational training and transition services for special education students.

Parents

Who Are Parents?

When determining the special education placement of an individual entitled to services under the IDEA, the individual who will usually be asked to consent to the evaluation, placement, or other decision is the parent. Children under the age of majority as defined in state law (usually 18 years of age) are generally presumed legally incompetent under the IDEA to consent to decisions made on their behalf. The preferences of the child may be a consideration, particularly with matters such as transition services, and the child may participate in the special education process, but the parents make the decisions. As a result, the procedural protections under the IDEA mentioned in Chapters 3 and 15 belong to the parents and not the student while the student is under the age of majority. Once the student reaches the age of majority, the procedural and other rights under the IDEA transfer to the student unless the student has been determined to be incompetent under state law.[10] The parents maintain a right to notice along with the student under the IDEA even when the student reaches the age of majority.[11]

For purposes of the IDEA, whenever reference is made to decision making or involvement by the parent, the term is intended to include not only the actual parent but also possibly a grandparent, a stepparent, a surrogate parent appointed by the court or a social service agency, or a court-appointed guardian.[12] The intent is that the person who is legally responsible for the child shall be the person responsible for making special education decisions. In instances where the child is a ward of the state, a surrogate parent would have to be appointed or some other arrangement would have to be made because the term does not include the state itself in the role of parent.

Given the divorce rate in the United States, it is not unusual for a child to have parents who do not live in the same household. When one parent has legal custody, ordinarily that parent will have the authority to make decisions about special education placement and will be the party to whom notice of special education decisions is to be sent. In fact, both parents continue to have rights under the IDEA unless the divorce decree specifies otherwise. Problems can arise, however, where divorced parents have joint legal custody of a child. Must the school send both parents copies of all general school notices, or only notices about special education matters? While there is not a great deal of litigation in this area, it is an issue that arises from time to time. One of the few cases to address this issue indicates that while it is unreasonably burdensome to send copies of routine announcements about school activities to both parents with legal custody, they are probably both entitled to access to school records.[13] It is probably also advisable to send both parents notices about testing, placement, and other special education matters that relate to the individual child.

The Role of Parents

Parents are an essential component to the effectiveness of the IDEA. Only by requiring that parents be apprised of their rights and informed of the procedures available is the attainment of the IDEA goals possible. Parental participation requirements include mandatory notification of parents at various stages of the process and mandates ensuring that the opportunity for parental participation is available.[14]

Although there is probably a general consensus about the significance of the parental role in carrying out the requirements of the IDEA, there are those who believe that not all children with disabilities are benefiting from the IDEA because they do not all have strong parental advocates. The thought is that aggressive middle-income parents who are not intimidated by the educational or legal system will take advantage of the procedural and substantive protections available, and the child whose parents may be less well-informed is less likely to benefit.

Middle-income parents are more likely to be aware of both the availability and the benefits of special education. The same may be true of wealthy parents, but they are more likely to pay for a private placement in order to have the "best" educational programming rather than seek special education through the public education system. It is difficult to know whether children with disabilities from lower-income families are being less well served, but this may be the case. If so, additional policy changes may be needed. In any case, it seems undeniable that the parents play a significant role in carrying out the requirements of the IDEA.

A number of situations arise in which the interest of the parent conflicts with that of the child. Some parents seek very restrictive placements out of fear that their children may become lost in the mainstream or because they feel overwhelmed by the responsibility of caring for the child. Often, the attorney who has been consulted by the parent has difficulty deciding whether the rightful client is the parent or the child. It may be important for the attorney to discuss this dilemma at the outset. It is also important to recognize that the school district's obligation is to ensure appropriate education *regardless* of parental wishes. Schools sometimes give in to parents even when doing so means the child's best interest is not served.

Having a child with a severe impairment that is demanding in terms of time and family resources can cause substantial stress on a family. The high emotional and financial costs can lead to tensions. There is a higher incidence of divorce in families with children with disabilities.[15] Those demands should be recognized and taken into account by the educational agency when it is responding to what may seem like unreasonable and difficult demands and expectations from parents.

Educators

Teachers

The primary contact person for the child with a disability is, of course, the teacher. Often there is a regular classroom teacher and a special education teacher. Sometimes there are teachers of special subjects such as art, physical education, vocational education, and music.

For many regular classroom teachers, the implementation of the IDEA brought a great deal of stress. They feared that masses of children with disabilities would be "dumped" into the regular classroom. Regular education teachers (as well as teachers in general) had already been faced with increasing professional demands at the same time that financial and professional rewards were diminishing. This new pressure was not welcomed. Most of these teachers had received their degrees and teaching certificates before special education was mandatory and had little exposure to the requirements of being a teacher in a "mainstream" classroom. The added requirements of recordkeeping were often viewed as an unnecessary burden.

Another concern was the lack of role clarification. Regular teachers who had been teaching for some time questioned why they should consult with a young, newly trained special education teacher. There was additional anxiety because a number of requirements were initially unclear, and it was difficult to learn all of the requirements even when they were clear. For example, if a regular education teacher wanted to place the child in a speech therapy or other remedial program, the teacher could no longer simply do this. Notice to parents of the plan and an opportunity for them to be involved in the decision was now required.

In spite of the initial negative reaction to the IDEA, teachers have come to accept and embrace the inclusion requirement as a fact of life in public education, and there is improvement in the amount of support provided to the regular classroom in the form of consultation with special educators, teaching assistants, volunteers, and others. In addition, the teacher education programs for new teachers are likely to include experience with special education issues and educational methodology for children with disabilities. Some states now require experience with special education for all teachers. Teachers are also more likely to have access to in-service training relating to special education issues to compensate for knowledge they did not get while acquiring their teaching degrees.

Although the attitude and preparation of the regular education teacher has improved since 1975, there are still some serious obstacles for this teacher. The initial funding promises and plans of the IDEA have not been entirely fulfilled by the federal government, and there remain significant problems of understaffing in the regular classroom. For example, placement for a child who is mildly mentally retarded may be appropriate in the regular classroom, but the child may need additional support for certain aspects of the educational program and there may not be funding to provide a teacher's assistant.

In addition, coordination and cooperation between regular classroom teachers and special education teachers are needed. These two groups should communicate needs, problems, and solutions to each other. Another concern is that the regular education teacher may need more in the way of training relating to identification of disabilities, behavior management, and direct instruction methods for students who do not learn from the traditional teaching strategies. Teacher education programs, state certification requirements, and local hiring practices should require regular education teachers to demonstrate these skills. A number of positive improvements have occurred in these areas, but the need to improve regular education teacher preparation for providing special education programming in the regular classroom is ongoing and in serious need of attention. In addition to providing training and support services, increasing the financial compensation of educators will be an essential component if future efforts are to be successful.

The 2004 amendments to the IDEA recognize the need to have high quality teachers and high quality professional development training so that teachers who provide services to students with disabilities have the skills and knowledge necessary to use scientifically based instructional practices to improve the academic achievement and functional performance of children with disabilities.[16] Under No Child Left Behind (NCLB) and the 2004 amendments to the IDEA, both regular teachers and special education teachers must contend with the highly qualified teacher (HQT) requirements in NCLB. To be highly qualified under the IDEA, a special education teacher now must (1) obtain full state certification as a special education teacher, or pass the state special education teacher licensing examination and hold a license to teach in the state as a special education teacher; and (2) hold at least a bachelor's degree.[17] There are slightly different requirements for teachers who teach students to meet "alternative achievement standards."[18]

Special education teachers that teach "core academic subjects" to students with disabilities must meet the requirements for a highly qualified special education teacher noted above and they must also meet the NCLB requirements for each core area taught. This means the teacher must have a bachelor's degree, obtain state certification, and demonstrate competency in the core academic area taught.[19] Core academic subjects are defined as English, reading or language arts, mathematics, science, foreign language, civics and government, economics, arts, history, and geography.[20] Special education teachers who teach two or more core subjects exclusively to students with disabilities are subject to different requirements. These teachers must (1) meet the requirements of NCLB for any elementary, middle, or secondary school teacher who is new or not new to the profession; or (2) if the teacher is not new to the profession, demonstrate competence in the core academic subjects taught in the same way that NCLB requires for an elementary, middle, or secondary school teacher who is not new to the profession; or (3) in the case of a new special education teacher who teaches multiple subjects and who is highly qualified in mathematics, language arts, or science, demonstrate competence in the other core academic subjects in which the teacher teaches in the same manner as required by NCLB within two years of hire.[21]

To ensure that special education teachers are highly qualified, the IDEA requires states that receive funds to establish and maintain qualifications to ensure that personnel that provide services to students with disabilities are appropriately and adequately prepared and trained. They must have the content knowledge and skills to serve children with disabilities.[22]

One of the skills of the special education professional is being able to work with the regular educators in developing an appropriate program to maintain the child in the least restrictive setting. Historically, many special education teacher training programs were developed to match definitional categories, and this practice continues in some programs today. For example, training programs for teachers of children with learning disabilities existed separately from teacher training programs for teachers of children with behavior disorders. But the interrelationship of the various special education teacher preparation programs was minimal. While there have been improvements in this area, it is important that this trend continue.[23]

In recent years, regular and special education teachers have begun working in collaboration. Such positive interaction is most likely to occur where there is supportive school leadership. With the increase in another education trend—site-based management—it will be critical that school principals have a mechanism by which to stay current on special education requirements and the best practices to implement them.

A major concern for both the regular classroom and the special education program is teacher shortages. There continues to be a shortage of teachers adequately trained to provide education to special students. While the IDEA requires program personnel development for states receiving funding, the low pay and high demands of teaching in general (and special education teaching in particular) continue to keep special education understaffed. This situation is even more problematic in rural and inner city areas.[24] Some schools have responded to teacher shortages by using temporary certification as a vehicle to meet certification requirements. There is much concern about whether teachers with temporary certificates are adequately prepared.

Previously, one of the ironies of the IDEA was that often teachers of specialized subjects—such as art or woodworking—were the least likely to have teacher preparation to address the needs of the special student, but were the most likely to have the child with a disability placed in the class. It was not unlikely for a child with certain disabilities to be placed in a segregated special education class for most of the academic-type subjects, but to be placed with his or her age-appropriate peers for music or art. Over the years, this practice has dissipated due to the least restrictive environment requirements in the IDEA and increasing focus on inclusion and mainstreaming, but it is still important that teacher certification and teacher training programs recognize that teachers of special subjects need training in behavior management, in communicating with the regular and special education teacher, and in teaching methodology.

Another important area is vocational education teacher training. There is an increasing awareness today that high school students, who are chronologically at the end of the public education service system, need to be provided with skills that will enable them to be productive members of society. One of the primary goals of the IDEA is to provide students with the knowledge and skills they need to lead productive and independent adult lives, including preparing them for further education and employment.[25] With recognition of the importance of this transition has come the knowledge that our public school systems are not adequately staffed with appropriately trained vocational teachers.

Administrators

One of the most important administrators in providing special education is the local director of special education. That person has the responsibility for ensuring that local schools are adequately staffed with appropriately trained personnel and for overseeing the development and implementation of the individualized education programs for each child in the local school district. The special education director must also develop the data necessary for obtaining funding from the state educational agency. The special education director must plan systematic steps to help students move between regular and special education. It is essential that special education directors be able to communicate with the local principal and local board of education to ensure that appropriate policies are made and carried out.

The attitude and knowledge of the local superintendent and the school principal are also critical to the effective implementation of special education policy. The tone and philosophy comes from the top. These are individuals who signal by their prioritization and personal attitudes the importance of various educational issues.[26]

At the state level, administrators responsible for special education must develop the program plans for federal and state funding, ensure appropriate funding to the local school districts, and have teacher certification requirements that ensure comprehensive teacher preparation. It is important that state administrators be able to coordinate and cooperate with other social service providers as certain types of placements fall under the responsibility of several agencies. It is necessary not only to coordinate the appropriate services to be provided but also to establish which agency's budget will fund those programs.

In many states, particularly states with large populations, an intermediate level of regional administration has been developed. Regional activities often include development of in-service programs and cooperative plans for providing certain services among local education agencies within the regions.

Other Personnel

Providing special education involves a variety of other individuals within the educational system who may not be directly involved with providing educational programming or related services. These include teachers' aides, custodial staff, and clerical staff. While these individuals may not be directly involved in programming for these children, it is important nonetheless that they be able to communicate with those responsible for developing education plans for special students. It is also important that they be alerted to special situations that may require their attention. For example, they may need to alert the principal's secretary about a child with severe emotional problems who may exhibit violent behavior if sent to the principal's office. Lunchroom monitors may need to be prepared to respond to a child who has frequent epileptic seizures.

The failure to train such individuals adequately could result in harm to the child or others. Not only would such a result be detrimental to the child, it could result in legal liability to the school district for failure to provide adequate training. This issue is discussed more fully in Chapter 20. The challenges for regular and special educators in supervising these individuals were noted previously.

Related Service Providers

Because of the need to provide related services, such as transportation, individuals that might as a group be referred to as related service providers are often involved in providing educational programming and supportive services to children with disabilities. The following would be included in this group: speech and language therapists, physical therapists, occupational therapists, school social workers, counselors (to provide counseling to the child or the parents), nurses (for nonmedical health services), physicians (for diagnostic purposes only), and individuals providing transportation services.

Some of these individuals provide services for both children with disabilities and those who do not have disabilities. For example, a school nurse may provide catheterization service to a child with spina bifida and also provide cough medicine to a child who is not disabled but who has a cold. Others, such as speech and language therapists, may provide services only to children with disabilities. Regardless of the degree to which these individuals are involved with services for children with disabilities, it is essential that they be adequately trained and prepared to work with children with special needs. The IDEA now includes qualifications for related services personnel.[27]

The requirement that states ensure that personnel are appropriately and adequately prepared and trained, and have the content knowledge and skills to serve children with disabilities, includes qualifications for related services personnel and paraprofessionals. The IDEA requires states to develop or include qualifications that

- Are consistent with any state-approved or state-recognized certification, licensing, registration, or other comparable requirements that apply to the professional discipline in which those personnel are providing special education or related services;
- Ensure that related services personnel who deliver services in their discipline or profession meet these requirements and have not had certification or licensure requirements waived on an emergency, temporary, or provisional basis; and
- Allow paraprofessionals and assistants who are appropriately trained and supervised, in accordance with state law, to be used to assist in the provision of special education and related services to children with disabilities.[28]

No Child Left Behind also imposes some training and qualification requirements for paraprofessionals that work in Title I schools or that receive payment from Title I funds. Training for both regular and special educators related to supervising paraprofessionals can be particularly challenging where paraprofessionals have lengthy experience in the schools and may resent supervision from younger, less experienced teachers.

Advocates

Passage of the IDEA was in large part due to the concerted efforts of advocacy groups in bringing litigation and lobbying for legislation that has affected children with disabilities. The role of advocates continues to be a vital part of the implementation of special education law. Advocates are not only necessary to press for implementation, but in many cases can be valuable resources for information.

There are currently many advocacy, consumer, and voluntary health organizations at the national, state, and local level. Many of these organizations focus on advocacy on behalf of one particular group, such as children with deafness, autism, learning disabilities, and other disabilities. The value of these organizations in advocacy is demonstrated by the fact that the Pennsylvania Association for Retarded Citizens was the plaintiff in the landmark *PARC* case, which, along with *Mills,* set the stage for passage of the IDEA. A 1975 federal law provides grant money to any agency that will implement a protection and advocacy program for developmentally disabled persons. The current Protection and Advocacy system is funded through grant programs within the United States Department of Health and Human Services and the United States Department of Education.[29]

In 1975, one of the challenges to effective attorney advocacy in special education cases was the lack of knowledge and experience. That is no longer the case. Many law schools teach courses in disability discrimination, special education law, or education law (which includes attention to special education issues). There are numerous reference books including treatises, manuals, and loose-leaf services. So, at least the lack of information for lawyers is no longer a barrier, but it can still be difficult for parents to find an attorney to represent them in special education matters.[30] In many areas of the country, lay advocate organizations at the local level are helpful in advising parents on how to obtain appropriate special education for their children. These groups can suggest strategies for working with school systems and can even help to prepare parents for due process hearings. In some cases, they may actually represent the parents in these proceedings.

The passage of the Handicapped Children's Protection Act (HCPA) in 1986, an amendment to the IDEA, was an important step in ensuring effective advocacy. Before that point, it was unclear whether parents could be reimbursed for attorneys' fees and certain costs incurred in disputes involving special education placements and other decisions. The HCPA clarified that these fees are available to prevailing parties in appropriate circumstances.[31] While there are still some areas of confusion about what the HCPA requires in certain instances, it would seem that the availability of attorneys' fees has made this an area of law that is somewhat more attractive to the practicing attorney, and as a result it should follow that an increase in advocacy will occur. Parents may have difficulty, however, in finding an attorney willing to wait for payment until resolution of the dispute. Expert fees, however, are not available, and this can be a cost barrier to parents in deciding whether to seek legal help in advocacy efforts.

An important point for advocates to keep in mind is that resolution of special education disputes involves parties who must maintain an ongoing close relationship. After the dispute is resolved, the child may often be placed in a setting where the educator has had an adversarial and perhaps defensive attitude toward the parent(s). It is important that both the anger and the frustration resulting from resolving disagreements do not adversely affect the child's education. In recognition of this, negotiation and other alternative dispute resolution should be used when appropriate.

In addition to representation in particular disputes, advocacy is important for general policy changes or development. Advisory councils are mandatory at the state level[32] and are also used at the local level. These offer important opportunities for advocacy. These councils include parents and other advocates who play an important role in recommending practices and policies to state and local school boards.

Decision Makers

Another group of people involved in the special education process are the decision makers, or those who help resolve disputes that may arise between the school and parents in the special education process. Whenever there is a dispute between the parents and the educational agency that cannot be resolved regarding the appropriate program, related services, or another special education matter covered by the IDEA, there are a number of parties who may become decision makers or intermediaries to resolve those disputes. These include mediators within state or local school district dispute resolution procedures, hearing officers who conduct impartial hearings, and judges.

Mediators do not themselves make decisions about the dispute, but they help the parties try to reach an agreement that resolves the dispute. Hearing officers oversee due process hearings and issue binding decisions about disputes between the parties based on evidence presented at the hearing. Either party can appeal the hearing officer's decision to state or federal court. If they do, a state or federal court judge can issue a decision about the dispute.

These decision-making or decision-facilitating individuals may have different levels of knowledge, awareness, and understanding about students with disabilities and the laws that protect them. While some states have special training programs specifically for special education administrative hearings, others have more training for administrative hearings generally. Many federal and state court judges have considered special education cases, but many have not. It will be important for the parties to the dispute to be aware of the level of knowledge in various settings, and to take it into account in educating the decision maker about disabilities, education, and the laws protecting students with disabilities in preparing a case for these different decision makers.

Another group of decision makers are the administrators at the local level discussed above as they generally have the authority to allocate school resources and can make such allocations to try and help resolve a dispute between the parties. More information about dispute resolution procedures and mediators, hearing officers, and judges is provided in Chapter 17.

Summary

Participants in special education include the students, the parents, the educators (teachers, related service providers, administrators, and others), and advocates. These participants play varying roles in ensuring appropriate special education.

The students are a varied group that includes individuals with mobility, sensory, mental, emotional, and health impairments. The wide diversity of types and degrees of impairments under the IDEA makes individualization in providing special education an essential component of the Act.

There are numerous unsettled controversies about whether labeling should be done at all and whether certain categorical labels (such as learning disability) are appropriately defined or applied. Gifted and talented students and those with certain health impairments are not really protected by the IDEA, although Section 504 and the ADA may provide some relief to the latter group and some states protect students in the former. Students with drug or alcohol problems do not have comprehensive coverage, nor does a student who is just a slow learner.

The parents in special education situations have important rights and an essential role. They have a right to a hearing and an opportunity to challenge the school's proposal decisions. With that right comes an important role—that of being a participant at all stages of the development of an appropriate program and deciding on an appropriate placement for the child. These rights and roles are fairly unique to special education. In no other aspect of public education do parents have such specific rights.

Educators have numerous obligations as a result of special education legal requirements. These demands may at times overburden understaffed, underpaid, and undertrained educational personnel. Educators must nonetheless comply with the legal requirements while advocating increased resources. The issues to be resolved at a policy level include how to fund educational agencies at an appropriate level to meet these demands. Within the legal framework of the IDEA, the issue is related more to accountability—for personnel development and for conduct toward and programming for the student.

Advocates had a strong role in the initial passage of the IDEA. Initially, lay advocates were probably the primary force in the enforcement of special education mandates, but the 1986 attorneys' fees amendment to the IDEA has led to an increased advocacy role for practicing attorneys.

Decision makers are also involved in the special education process. When disagreements arise during the special education process, decision makers help the parties resolve their differences either by agreement of the parties or by decision of a hearing officer or court order.

Questions for Reflection

1. Should training and certification for special education teachers be categorical? In other words, should a teacher be trained and certified in a specific category of disability like specific learning disabilities. If not, what is a more desirable way to train teachers and how can it be accomplished?

2. Should gifted and talented students be included among the children protected under the IDEA? Why or why not? What about slow learners? Socially maladjusted students?

3. As a policy matter, should any changes be made to the IDEA to include students with chronic illness or infectious diseases who currently would not receive protection under the IDEA, but would under Section 504 or the ADA? (Remember from the discussion above that students with chronic illness or infectious disease may be covered under the IDEA, but only if they meet the requirements of the "other health impaired" category and require special education services.)

4. As a policy matter, how can the IDEA be designed to ensure that not only middle-income, well-educated parents take advantage of the requirements relating to special education?

5. As a policy matter, should schools be required to give notice under the IDEA to both parents if they are divorced? Should it matter whether the parents have joint legal

custody? What administrative burdens might result if both parents must be given notice? What are the alternatives?

6. How can educational systems ensure that their teachers are adequately trained? Should regular education teachers be required to take courses in special education? What requirements can be imposed on teachers who already have been certified and who have a teacher contract in existence?

7. Who should be liable if teachers are not adequately trained and a physical or education injury occurs as a result?

8. Is the availability of attorneys' fees and the resultant increase in attorneys involved in the special education process positive or negative in carrying out the goals of the IDEA?

NOTES

1. 34 C.F.R. § 300.8(b).
2. See, e.g., Robert T. Tauber, *Self-Fulfilling Prophecy: A Practical Guide to Its Use in Education* (Greenwood Publishing 1997).
3. 20 U.S.C. § 1412(a)(3)(B).
4. 34 C.F.R. § 300.8.
5. In basic terms, suctioning refers to using a device to suction food, saliva, or other things out of the child's mouth, or feeding tubes, so the child does not choke.
6. See, e.g., David C. Ogg & Thomas E. Elfers, "Medically Fragile Children: How Far Are Schools Responsible?" *School Business Affairs* (May 1988).
7. 526 U.S. 66 (1999).
8. 34 C.F.R. § 300.8(c)(4).
9. Virginia Costenbader & Roberta Buntaine, "Diagnostic Discrimination Between Social Maladjustment and Emotional Disturbance: An Empirical Study," 7 *Journal of Emotional and Behavioral Disorders* 2–10 (1999).
10. 34 C.F.R. § 300.520.
11. *Id.*
12. 42 U.S.C. § 1401(23).
13. *Taylor v. Vermont Department of Education,* 313 F.3d 768 (2d Cir. 2002). See also Laura Rothstein & Julia Rothstein, *Disabilities and the Law* § 2:30 (Thomson West 2006) (regarding school records).
14. See Chapters 6–8 and 15.
15. C. Amber Havens, "Becoming a Resilient Family: Child Disability and the Family System," *Access Today,* Special Volume, Issue 17 (Spring 2005), http://www.indiana.edu/~nca/monographs/17family.shtml for a discussion of this issue and citations for research on it.
16. 20 U.S.C. § 1400(c)(5).
17. 20 U.S.C. § 1402(10)(B); 34 C.F.R. § 300.18.
18. *Id.*
19. 34 C.F.R. § 300.18(a).
20. *Id.*; 34 C.F.R. § 300.10.

21. See 20 U.S.C. § 1401(10)(D); 34 C.F.R. § 300.18(d).

22. 20 U.S.C. § 1412(a)(14)(A); 34 C.F.R. § 300.156.

23. For a discussion of this issue, see J. Matt Jameson & Dixie S. Huefner, "'Highly Qualified' Special Educators and the Provision of a Free Appropriate Public Education to Students With Disabilities," 35 *Journal of Law & Education* 29 (January 2006).

24. Glori Chaika, "Scrambling for Staff: The Teacher Shortage in Rural Schools," *Education World*, http://www.educationworld.com/a_admin/admin/admin142.shtml (last accessed August 6, 2008).

25. 20 U.S.C. § 1401(d).

26. Michael F. DiPaola & Chriss Walther-Thomas, "Principals and Special Education: The Critical Role of School Leaders," *COPPSE Document No. IB-7*, Center on Personnel Studies in Special Education (February 2003).

27. 34 C.F.R. § 300.156(b).

28. 20 U.S.C. § 1412(a)(14)(B); 34 C.F.R. § 300.156(a)–(b).

29. An overview of these programs and links to their provisions are found at http://www.drcnh.org/federalauthority.htm (last accessed August 12, 2008). See also *Disabilities and the Law* § 9:10.

30. See *Maroni v. Pemi-Baker Sch. Dist.*, 346 F.3d 247, 258 n.9 (1st Cir. 2003) (noting the difficulty that parents have in obtaining representation in special education matters).

31. 20 U.S.C. § 1415(i)(3).

32. 20 U.S.C. § 1412(a)(21).

Who Is Protected

Who is protected depends on what avenue is being used for redress. The courts have defined protection under constitutional theories differently from the statutory definitions in some cases. The statutes themselves differ from each other.

Constitutionally Based Cases

Under the fourteenth amendment to the United States Constitution, states may not deprive their citizens of "equal protection of the laws." In determining whether a state has complied with the equal protection clause of the fourteenth amendment, the courts have traditionally applied different levels of scrutiny depending on the type of case involved. Two major factors are at issue in deciding what level of scrutiny to apply. One is whether the person claiming a denial of equal protection is a member of a class of individuals who are or should be entitled to special consideration. The other is the importance of the right at issue.

Classification of Individuals With Disabilities

The following opinion excerpt demonstrates the level of scrutiny that is to be applied to individuals who are mentally retarded. The decision did not involve the educational setting, but it is instructive in evaluating potential constitutional claims involving individuals with disabilities. The case involved a city council's denial of a special use permit to operate a group home in a residential neighborhood. The applicant for the permit wanted to operate a group home for 13 men and women who were mentally retarded. They would have had constant staff supervision. The reason for the city's denial included negative attitudes and fears of nearby property owners, concern that residents would be harassed by junior high students from a nearby school, the location of the home on a flood plain, and concern that a group home would result in crowded conditions. In deciding what level of scrutiny to apply in evaluating whether the denial was constitutional, the Supreme Court examined the classification of the group affected.

CITY OF CLEBURNE V. CLEBURNE LIVING CENTER

473 U.S. 432 (1985)

Justice White delivered the opinion of the Court.

The Equal Protection Clause of the Fourteenth Amendment commands that no State shall "deny to any person within its jurisdiction the equal protection of the laws," which is essentially a direction that all persons similarly situated should be treated alike. Section 5 of the Amendment empowers Congress to enforce this mandate, but absent controlling congressional direction, the courts have themselves devised standards for determining the validity of state legislation or other official action that is challenged as denying equal protection. The general rule is that legislation is presumed to be valid and will be sustained if the classification drawn by the statute is rationally related to a legitimate state interest. . . .

When social or economic legislation is at issue, the Equal Protection Clause allows the states wide latitude, and the Constitution presumes that even improvident decisions will eventually be rectified by the democratic processes.

The general rule gives way, however, when a statute classifies by race, alienage or national origin. These factors are so seldom relevant to the achievement of any legitimate state interest that laws grounded in such considerations are deemed to reflect prejudice and antipathy—a view that those in the burdened class are not as worthy or deserving as others. For these reasons and because such discrimination is unlikely to be soon rectified by legislative means, these laws are subjected to strict scrutiny and will be sustained only if they are suitably tailored to serve a compelling state interest. Similar oversight by the courts is due when state laws impinge on personal rights protected by the Constitution. Legislative classification based on gender also calls for a heightened standard of review. . . .

A gender classification fails unless it is substantially related to a sufficiently important governmental interest. Because illegitimacy is beyond the individual's control and bears "no relation to the individual's ability to participate in and contribute to society," official discriminations resting on that characteristic are also subject to somewhat heightened review. Restrictions "will survive equal protection scrutiny to the extent they are substantially related to a legitimate state interest."

We have declined, however, to extend heightened review to differential treatment based on age. The lesson is that where individuals in the group affected by a law have distinguishing characteristics relevant to interest the state has the authority to implement, the courts have been very reluctant to closely scrutinize legislative choices as to whether, how and to what extent those interests should be pursued. In such cases, the Equal Protection Clause requires only a rational means to serve a legitimate end.

Against this background, we conclude for several reasons that the Court of Appeals erred in holding mental retardation a quasi-suspect classification calling for a more exacting standard of judicial review than is normally accorded economic and social legislation. First, it is undeniable, and it is not argued otherwise here, that those who are mentally retarded have a reduced ability to cope with and function in the everyday world. Nor are they all cut from the same patterns:

as the testimony in this record indicates, they range from those whose disability is not immediately evident to those who must be constantly cared for. They are thus different, immutably so, in relevant respect, and the states' interest in dealing with and providing for them is plainly a legitimate one. How this large and diversified group is to be treated under the law is a difficult and often a technical matter, very much a task for legislators guided by qualified professionals and not by the perhaps ill informed opinions of the judiciary. Heightened scrutiny inevitably involves substantive judgments about legislative decisions, and we doubt that the predicate for such judicial oversight is present where the classification deals with mental retardation.

Second, the distinctive legislative response, both national and state, to the plight of those who are mentally retarded demonstrates not only that they have unique problems, but also that the lawmakers have been addressing their difficulties in a manner that belies a continuing antipathy or prejudice and a corresponding need for more intrusive oversight by the judiciary. . . .

Such legislation thus singling out the retarded for special treatment reflects the real and undeniable differences between the retarded and others. That a civilized and decent society expects and approves such legislation indicates that governmental consideration of those differences in the vast majority of situations is not only legitimate but desirable. . . . Especially given the wide variation in the abilities and needs of the retarded themselves, governmental bodies must have a certain amount of flexibility and freedom from judicial oversight in shaping and limiting their remedial efforts.

Third, the legislative response, which could hardly have occurred and survived without public support, negates any claim that the mentally retarded are politically powerless in the sense that they have no ability to attract the attention of lawmakers. Any minority can be said to be powerless to assert direct control over the legislature, but if that were a criterion for higher level scrutiny by the courts, much economic and social legislation would now be suspect.

Fourth, if the large and amorphous class of the mentally retarded were deemed quasi-suspect for the reasons given by the Court of Appeals, it would be difficult to find a principled way to distinguish a variety of other groups who have perhaps immutable disabilities setting them off from others, who cannot themselves mandate the desired legislative responses, and who can claim some degree of prejudice from at least part of the public at large. One need mention in this respect only the aging, the disabled, the mentally ill, and the infirm. We are reluctant to set out on that course, and we decline to do so.

Doubtless, there have been and there will continue to be instances of discrimination against the retarded that are in fact invidious, and that are properly subject to judicial correction under constitutional norms. But the appropriate method of reaching such instances is not to create a new quasi-suspect classification and subject all governmental action based on that classification to more searching evaluation. Rather, we should look to the likelihood that governmental action premised on a particular classification is valid as a general matter, not merely to the specifics of the case before us. Because mental retardation is a characteristic that the government may legitimately take into account in a wide range of decisions, and because both state and federal

(Continued)

(Continued)

governments have recently committed themselves to assisting the retarded, we will not presume that any given legislative action, even one that disadvantages retarded individuals, is rooted in considerations that the Constitution will not tolerate.

Our refusal to recognize the retarded as a quasi-suspect class does not leave them entirely unprotected from invidious discrimination. To withstand equal protection review, legislation that distinguishes between the mentally retarded and others must be rationally related to a legitimate governmental purpose. This standard, we believe, affords government the latitude necessary both to pursue policies designed to assist the retarded in realizing their full potential, and to freely and efficiently engage in activities that burden the retarded in what is essentially an incidental manner. The State may not rely on a classification whose relationship to an asserted goal is so attenuated as to render the distinction arbitrary or irrational. Furthermore, some objectives—such as "the bare . . . desire to harm a politically unpopular group"—are not legitimate state interest. Beyond that, the mentally retarded, like others, have and retain their substantive constitutional rights in addition to the right to be treated equally by the law.

We turn to the issue of the validity of the zoning ordinance insofar as it requires special use permits for homes for the mentally retarded. . . . Requiring the permit in this case appears to us to rest on an irrational prejudice against the mentally retarded, including those who would occupy the Featherston facility and who would live under the closely supervised and highly regulated conditions expressly provided for by state and federal law. [The denial of the permit was invalid.]

The *Cleburne* case demonstrates that individuals who are mentally retarded specifically, and individuals with disabilities generally, will not be given any heightened level of scrutiny, because they are neither a suspect nor a quasi-suspect class. It is important to note, however, that the Supreme Court emphasized that irrational prejudice could not be the basis for unequal treatment. This standard will be important in assessing the exclusion of children with HIV, because it is well documented that the fear of being infected with HIV through the types of casual contacts that occur in the education setting is irrational.

It is also noteworthy that when Congress enacted the Americans with Disabilities Act (ADA), the preamble findings stated that "historically, society has tended to isolate and segregate individuals with disabilities; . . . [and] individuals who have experienced discrimination on the basis of disability have often had no legal recourse to redress such discrimination; . . . [and] individuals with disabilities are a discrete and insular minority . . . subjected to a history of purposeful unequal treatment, and relegated to a position of political powerlessness in our society, based on characteristics that are beyond the control of such individuals. . . ."[1] It would appear that Congress was setting the stage for possible future cases that might address disability under a constitutional challenge that would overrule the determination in *Cleburne.* Since 1990, however, the Supreme Court has not addressed a case where this issue was raised. Thus, it is not clear whether the Court would change its analysis. Given the comprehensive statutory coverage, however, it is less necessary to bring a case under the Constitution's equal protection and due process clauses.

Heightened Scrutiny for Education

The *Cleburne* case examined the classification of individuals with disabilities and concluded that their status does not give them any special protection. As the following case excerpt demonstrates, however, special education cases will be examined with special scrutiny, not because children with disabilities are involved, but because education is considered to be a right entitled to "special constitutional sensitivity." The case involved whether undocumented alien children residing in the United States were entitled to public education.

PLYLER V. DOE

457 U.S. 202 (1982)

Public education is not a "right" granted to individuals by the Constitution. But neither is it merely some governmental "benefit" indistinguishable from other forms of social welfare legislation. Both the importance of education in maintaining our basic institutions, and the lasting impact of its deprivation on the life of the child, mark the distinction. . . .

We have recognized "the public schools as a most vital civic institution for the preservation of the democratic system of government," and as the primary vehicle for transmitting "the values on which our society rests." . . .

[H]istoric "perceptions of the public schools as inculcating fundamental values necessary to the maintenance of a democratic political system have been confirmed by the observations of social scientists." In addition, education provides the basic tools by which individuals might lead economically productive lives to the benefit of us all. In sum, education has a fundamental role in maintaining the fabric of our society. We cannot ignore the significant social costs borne by our Nation when select groups are denied the means to absorb the values and skills upon which our social order rests. In addition to the pivotal role of education in sustaining our political and cultural heritage, denial of education to some isolated group of children poses an affront to one of the goals of the Equal Protection Clause: the abolition of governmental barriers presenting unreasonable obstacles to advancement on the basis of individual merit. Paradoxically, by depriving the children of any disfavored group of an education, we foreclose the means by which that group might raise the level of esteem in which it is held by the majority. But more directly, "education prepares individuals to be self-reliant and self-sufficient participants in society." Illiteracy is an enduring disability. The inability to read and write will handicap the individual deprived of a basic education each and every day of his life. The inestimable toll of that deprivation on the social, economic, intellectual, and psychological well-being of the

(Continued)

(Continued)

individual achievement make it most difficult to reconcile the cost or the principle of a status based denial of basic education with the framework of equality embodied in the Equal Protection Clause. . . .

In these days, it is doubtful that any child may reasonably be expected to succeed in life if he is denied the opportunity of an education. Such an opportunity, where the state has undertaken to provide it, is a right which must be made available to all on equal terms. . . .

If the State is to deny a discrete group of innocent children the free public education that it offers to other children residing within its borders, that denial must be justified by a showing that it furthers some substantial state interest. No such showing was made here.

As the preceding two opinions demonstrate, it would seem that constitutionally based cases involving unequal treatment in the education system are going to incorporate a "heightened equal protection" test, which will probably result in a very close examination of the state's treatment of children with disabilities. The judicial opinion in the *PARC* case, issued before either *Plyler* or *Cleburne*, similarly indicated that exclusion of retarded children is unlikely to be rationally based.[2]

Inasmuch as a constitutionally based challenge to unequal treatment or denial of education without due process is likely to succeed for children with disabilities, why then are all special education cases not brought alleging constitutional violations? In answering this question, it should be noted first that some are brought alleging constitutional violation. The two major reasons, however, that more are not constitutionally based are that constitutional cases are cumbersome and complex to litigate, and that the *Smith v. Robinson*[3] decision established that most special education claims must be brought under the Individuals with Disabilities Education Act (IDEA). Chapter 3 included an excerpt of the opinion in that case. While that excerpt focuses solely on the preemption of special education by the IDEA as related to Section 504 of the Rehabilitation Act, the Supreme Court also concluded in that case, "Where the [IDEA] is available to a handicapped child . . . [it] is the exclusive avenue through which the child and his parents or guardian can pursue their [equal protection claim]."[4] In most cases, the IDEA will provide an adequate basis for redress.

Cases Under the IDEA

What Is a Disability?

As noted in Chapter 4, the IDEA defines children with disabilities as those

> having mental retardation, a hearing impairment (including deafness), a speech or language impairment, a visual impairment (including blindness), a serious emotional disturbance (referred to in this part as "emotional disturbance"), an orthopedic impairment, autism, traumatic brain injury, an other health impairment, a specific learning disability,

> deaf-blindness, or multiple disabilities, and who, by reason thereof, needs special education and related services.[5]

Chapter 4 mentioned briefly some of the problems of labeling. This section will focus on some of the issues that arise under the definition of "child with a disability" under the IDEA. More detailed information about eligibility under the IDEA is provided in Chapter 7.

One of the key provisions in the "child with a disability" definition is that the child must require special education services as a result of the disability. A child who needs only related services that are not special education services is not covered under the IDEA.

For example, a child who is able to participate fully in the regular classroom, but who has a mobility impairment and needs assistance in moving from class to class, may not be protected by the IDEA. Similarly, a child with spina bifida who is mentally and physically able to participate in the regular academic program, but who requires intermittent catheterization, is likely not disabled within the Act. Failure to provide needed services to these children, however, is probably a violation of Section 504 and the Americans with Disabilities Act requirements to provide reasonable accommodation.

One of the more unusual early cases involving a disability and related services was *Espino v. Besteiro.*[6] In that case, the boy had a condition that made it impossible for him to regulate his body temperature. Although his condition was unusual, the student was covered under the IDEA, and, as a result, the court held that the school was required to air-condition the entire classroom in order to meet the least restrictive environment requirements under the IDEA. The court reasoned that providing air-conditioning would give the child maximum classroom interaction with his classmates.

Another interesting decision involved a 13-year-old intellectually gifted girl who had anorexia nervosa. The court concluded that this physical condition resulted from underlying emotional disturbance, and that she was classified as emotionally disturbed and disabled within the IDEA.[7] An expanded discussion of the application of Section 504 and the ADA to students with disabilities is found in Chapter 18.

Age Eligibility

To be eligible for federal funding under the IDEA, states are to provide special education to all children with disabilities as defined under the law aged 3 through 21, including those who have been suspended or expelled from school.[8] But for those aged 3, 4, 5, 18, 19, 20, and 21, education need only be provided to the extent consistent with state law. Additional limitations are placed on incarcerated individuals. The state has an obligation to identify, locate, and evaluate all children entitled to special education.[9] This "child find" mandate is an important element for identifying students with disabilities and preparing schools to provide education for these children once they are age eligible. In some situations, as when the child is attending private school by the choice of the parent, the IDEA does not always mandate that the schools actually provide services, but they do have to offer them to the student. More information about this topic is provided in Chapters 6 and 12.

In recognition of the value of early intervention to the individual and societal cost benefits in the long run of such intervention, in 1986 Congress amended the IDEA to provide additional incentives to states to provide programming earlier than school age. The 2004 amendments again recognized the value of early intervention.[10]

Schools that wish to receive federal grants under the IDEA for special education and related services for children ages 3 to 5 must now provide special education to *all* children with disabilities in that age-group.[11] Previous to the effective date of the amendment, incentive grants did not mandate coverage for *all* age eligible children. Children entitled to services under this section must meet the definition of disabled child, but are also entitled to coverage at the state's discretion if they have developmental delays in physical, cognitive, communication, social, emotional, or adaptive development. State education agencies that elect to apply for grants for this age-group must have in place procedural safeguards and state plans that already apply to children ages 6 to 18.

For infants and toddlers up to 2 years of age, grants can be awarded to an agency other than the state education agency. The goal is early intervention as a means of reducing educational costs over the long run, maximizing the potential for independent living, and enhancing the capacity of families to meet the needs of this population. The services are to be provided to "individuals under 3 years of age who would be at risk of experiencing a substantial developmental delay if early intervention services were not provided to the individual."[12]

The policy of the infant and toddler provisions does not mandate that the grantee agency actually *provide* all the needed services, but that it be the agency responsible for coordinating the development, implementation, and payment of such services. Education agencies, while recognizing the value of these programs, are challenged with the financial and practical difficulties in implementing them.

At the other end of the age spectrum, the IDEA provides that services end at age 21 or when the student receives a regular high school diploma.[13] Students who have reached the age of 18, but who have not graduated, or who have been given a diploma even though they do not actually meet the competency requirements for graduation, can raise issues for educational agencies. State policies differ substantially in their treatment of these individuals. In some states, once the individual has been given a diploma, the individual is no longer eligible for public education. Some states even prohibit educational agencies from providing public education once the student has graduated, basing this on state constitutional or state statutory provisions. In these states, it may violate state policy to provide compensatory education even in cases where it is determined that the state had not provided appropriate education to the student before he or she graduated. Other states are more permissive about providing education beyond the receipt of a diploma. There is a developing body of state administrative decisions and judicial decisions on this issue, and thus far the federal special education policymakers have not chosen to override state policies that conclude state responsibility at graduation.[14]

Cases Under Section 504 and the Americans with Disabilities Act—Broader Coverage

Section 504 of the Rehabilitation Act of 1973 provides that "no otherwise qualified individual with a disability . . . shall solely by reason of her or his disability, be excluded from the participation in, be denied the benefits of, or be subjected to discrimination under any program or activity receiving Federal financial assistance."[15] The Americans with Disabilities Act, which defines a protected individual in similar terms, prohibits such discrimination by both public and private schools.

A person with a disability is an individual with a physical or mental impairment that constitutes a substantial impairment to one or more major life activities, an individual who has a record of such an impairment, or an individual who is regarded as having such an impairment.[16] This definition contrasts with the IDEA definition, which is a categorical listing.

While *Smith v. Robinson*[17] makes it unlikely that most cases involving children with disabilities will be brought alleging a violation of Section 504, there will be cases in which Section 504 or the ADA is relevant. As noted earlier in the chapter, the application of Section 504 and the ADA to situations that may not be covered by the IDEA is discussed in greater detail in Chapter 18.

Special Situations

Gifted Students

The following case illustrates the current status of education for gifted children under the IDEA.

ROE V. COMMONWEALTH

638 F. Supp. 929 (E.D. Pa. 1986)

Plaintiff, a student in the Bensalem Township School District, raises various statutory and constitutional challenges to her exclusion from gifted education. . . .

The extent to which Pennsylvania chooses to apply the same [as the IDEA] procedural protections to its determinations regarding the placement of students in gifted and handicapped educational programs is within constitutional limitation. Plaintiff alleges that gifted education is the preferred educational placement, and therefore that defendants violated her rights by placing her in regular education classes without prior notice and an opportunity to be heard. Second, she alleges that when she initiated due process proceedings to determine her eligibility for gifted education, the procedures employed by defendants were constitutionally defective.

A threshold issue in any due process inquiry is whether the plaintiff was deprived of a constitutionally protected interest. Plaintiff argues that because gifted education is the preferred educational assignment, she has both a property and a liberty interest in being placed in gifted education. I disagree.

(Continued)

(Continued)

Property interests are not created by the Constitution, but by independent sources, such as state law. As to placement in gifted education, Pennsylvania law provides as follows:

> Persons shall be assigned to a program for the gifted when they have an IQ of 130 or higher. A limited number of persons with IQ scores lower than 130 may be admitted to gifted programs when other educational criteria in the profile of the person strongly indicate gifted ability. . . .

Assuming, without deciding, that this regulation creates a property interest in gifted education for students with IQs of 130 or higher, it does not confer such an interest upon plaintiff, as she does not allege that her IQ falls within the specified range. To have a property interest in a benefit, a person must have "more than an abstract need or desire for it. . . . He must . . . have a legitimate claim of entitlement to it." Neither the provision in the regulation that select students with IQs under 130 may be admitted to gifted programs, nor, if such is the case, the fact that gifted education is the preferred educational assignment, creates in plaintiff a legitimate claim of entitlement to it. Therefore, I conclude that plaintiff does not have a property interest in being placed in gifted education. [The court also denied that liberty interest had been denied.] . . .

Count III of plaintiff's complaint alleges four equal protection and substantive due process violations. Summarized briefly, plaintiff challenges the use of IQ scores to define mental giftedness, the fact that students with IQs of 130 or higher are placed in educational programs purportedly designed to maximize their potential, while students with IQs under 130 are not entitled to be placed in such programs, and the fact that only exceptional students, i.e. those deemed gifted or handicapped, are legally entitled to be placed in the least restrictive educational environment. . . .

Plaintiff's claims must be evaluated under the rational relation standard. Under this standard, the proper inquiry is whether the regulations challenged by plaintiff are "so unrelated to the achievement of any combination of legitimate purposes" that one can only conclude that defendants, in promulgating the challenged regulation, acted irrationally. . . .

Plaintiff's argument that the creation by defendants of the gifted student classification is irrational in light of the enabling legislation is not convincing as either a logical or a factual matter. The enabling legislation requires the Board of Education to prescribe standards for the education of all exceptional children, and defines exceptional children as those who "deviate from the average . . . to such an extent that they require special educational facilities or services." I fail to see how it could be irrational for the Board of Education to conclude that children with high IQs "deviate from the average" and thus come within the purview of the enabling legislation. Moreover, since the creation of the gifted student classification by the Board of Education, the legislature has placed its imprimatur upon the provision of special education to gifted children.

Most, if not all other courts addressing this issue have reached similar conclusions. Although there may be philosophical support in favor of ensuring gifted education, scarce resources are probably the reason why gifted education is not mandatory in most states.

Children in Private Schools

Education services for children in out-of-district placements and in private schools is one of the areas where the 1997 IDEA amendments provide clarification. Additional clarification comes from the 2004 amendments. There had been some dispute about children who had been placed in private schools by their parents and whether they were entitled to the same level of special education services as those children who had been placed in or referred to private schools by the public agency. This issue is discussed in greater detail in Chapter 12. The following, however, is a brief overview of the issue.

Under current policy, the programmatic and financial responsibility of the public educational agency depends primarily on the role the public agency had in making the placement decision. In general, for children placed by their parents in private schools within the local school district, there is a proportionate payment of educational costs and an obligation to find and identify these students. However, the child is not entitled to a free and appropriate public education and does not have the same rights under the IDEA as a student who is enrolled in public school.[18] Where the public agency makes the placement at a private school, the public agency is still responsible for ensuring that the child receives a free and appropriate public education and the child has the same rights under the IDEA as a child who is enrolled in public school.[19] Where the public agency had been previously involved with the special education placement, but the parents place the child in a private placement without that agency's consent or referral, reimbursement of the costs may still be required if a free appropriate public education had not been made available to the child in a timely manner.[20] There are obviously a number of potential issues for dispute.

Incarcerated Juveniles

Another issue that arises relating to eligibility is how special education is to be provided to incarcerated juveniles. In some instances, these individuals are in trouble because of problems relating to their disabilities. How to prevent that from occurring is perhaps one of the underlying goals of the IDEA. But once the individual is in a juvenile detention facility or otherwise incarcerated, the individual is technically still entitled to special education if he or she is eligible otherwise. The logistics of providing special education in detention facilities are quite difficult in many instances, and this is a topic that is receiving increasing attention. In addition, many children with learning disabilities and psychological problems have never been identified and are therefore not receiving services. The transient nature of this population is a further obstacle to satisfactory implementation of the IDEA. Some of these challenges are discussed in Chapter 13.

Students With Learning Disabilities and Related Disabilities

Students with learning disabilities present unique challenges under the IDEA. One challenge arises from disagreements at the policy level about which individuals should be included in a definition of learning disability. Another challenge is what kinds of services should be provided. This area of law underwent significant changes in the 2004 amendments to the IDEA. The changes are discussed in detail in Chapter 7.

The definition for learning disability under the IDEA refers to a "disorder in one or more of the basic psychological processes involved in understanding or in using language, spoken or written, which disorder may manifest itself in an imperfect ability to listen, think, speak, read, write, spell, or to do mathematical calculation." The term does not include children who have learning problems that are primarily the result of visual, hearing, or motor disabilities, of mental retardation, of emotional disturbance, or of environmental, cultural, or economic disadvantage. It does include disorders such as "perceptual disabilities, brain injury, minimal brain dysfunction, dyslexia, and developmental aphasia."[21]

The number of children identified as learning disabled increases every year. The reasons for what may be overidentification of children as learning disabled include overburdened regular education teachers, improperly trained personnel, and, to a lesser extent, federal reimbursement for identifying a child as learning disabled. More positive reasons for the increase include greater public awareness, improved assessment methods, reevaluation of minority placement where children had been identified as mentally retarded, and the less stigmatizing label of learning disability versus mental retardation.[22] Whatever the reasons, the number of students with learning disabilities continues to increase, and this is an area where there is likely to be dispute about whether a child really meets the definition.

The condition of attention deficit disorder (ADD), or attention deficit hyperactivity disorder (ADHD), has been the subject of much debate. In recognition of this, the 1990 amendments to the IDEA mandated that the United States Department of Education solicit public comments regarding ADD and ADHD. The Education Department was to resolve whether children with ADD or ADHD, should be categorized as eligible for services under learning disability, other health impaired, or some other separate category. As a result of its evaluation, the Education Department decided that there should not be a separate category for ADD, but listed ADD and ADHD as specific conditions recognized as chronic or acute health problems under the other health impaired category.[23] In some instances, school districts are required to provide special services to students with ADD or ADHD under Section 504 or the ADA.

Students Who Are Emotionally Disturbed or Socially Maladjusted

Students with behavior problems present special difficulties for educational agencies and their obligations under the IDEA. While it is clear that students who are seriously emotionally disturbed or socially maladjusted need services, it is not clear that the school must provide them under special education mandates. In the following case, a 14-year-old girl who was suicidal and had engaged in behavior indicating serious social maladjustment was held not to be protected by the IDEA. This issue is discussed more fully in Chapter 10 on the related service of psychological counseling.

EVANS V. INDEPENDENT SCHOOL DISTRICT 25

936 F.2d 472 (10th Cir. 1991)

The material facts in the case are not in dispute. A.E. is a minor child, who was born on September 25, 1973. She is a student in the Stilwell, Oklahoma, Public Schools. It is agreed that A.E. is learning disabled in math. She has also experienced problems with peer interaction, impulse control, and excessive anxiety while in school. In November 1987, she was suspended from school for theft, fighting, tardiness, smoking, disruptions of class, and use of improper language. The school determined that these behavioral problems were not related to her learning disability. In reaction to news of the suspension, A.E. made a suicidal gesture by cutting herself on the arm with a broken bottle.

A.E. was admitted to the Children's Medical Center psychiatric unit on December 17, 1987. She was diagnosed as having a conduct disorder related to emotional problems and a borderline personality disorder. Her psychologist recommended that she remain in a homebased program until the fall, when she could be placed in a class for seriously emotionally disturbed students and then slowly returned to regular classes. A.E. was discharged from the Children's Medical Center on April 25, 1988.

In the fall of that year, the parents of A.E. requested that the school district develop an Individualized Education Plan (IEP) for A.E., and classify her as seriously emotionally disturbed rather than merely learning disabled. The IEP team determined that A.E. was categorically not covered by the Act. The team concluded that A.E.'s behavioral problems were not related to her learning disability. Further, the team refused to classify her as seriously emotionally disturbed. Although the team determined that A.E. was not handicapped within the scope of the Act, an IEP was prepared to assist A.E.'s progress in a mainstream classroom.

After receiving notification of this determination, the Evanses requested a due process hearing. The hearing was held on September 15, 1988. The Hearing Officer concluded that A.E. was not emotionally disturbed, but was properly categorized as learning disabled with a deficiency in mathematics. The Hearing Decision was appealed on November 25, 1988. The Appeal Officer agreed that A.E. was not seriously emotionally disturbed. The United States District Court for the Eastern District of Oklahoma affirmed. At issue is whether seriously emotionally disturbed children who are diagnosed as having a conduct disorder are properly excluded from the coverage of Public Law 94-142 by the language in 34 C.F.R. § 300.5(b)(8).

Seriously emotionally disturbed children are clearly included within the Education for All Handicapped Children Act [EAHCA]. 20 U.S.C. § 1401(a)(1) [Now § 1401(a)(3)]. The Supreme Court has noted:

> Among the most poorly served of disabled students were emotionally disturbed children: Congressional statistics revealed that for the school year immediately preceding passage of the Act, the educational needs of 82 percent of all children with emotional disabilities went unmet. *Honig*, 484 U.S. at 309.

(Continued)

(Continued)

The legislative history confirms this proposition.

In drafting Public Law 94-142, Congress was concerned with the emotional trauma and educational difficulties inherent in misclassification of children as handicapped or not handicapped. For that reason, Congress attempted to develop concise definitional regulations and a due process procedure that would allow review of any classification decision. The school district does not dispute that A.E. is properly classified as learning disabled in math; however, the district declined to reclassify A.E. based on the definition of seriously emotionally disturbed found in 34 C.F.R. § 300.5(b)(8). The language of 34 C.F.R. § 300.5(b)(8) excludes children who are socially maladjusted from coverage under the Act, unless they are also seriously emotionally disturbed. That a child is socially maladjusted is not by itself conclusive evidence that he or she is seriously emotionally disturbed. The evidence before us clearly supports the trial court's decision that A.E. was not seriously emotionally disturbed within the purview of the Act. In reviewing the district court decision, we find no error of law or unsupportable findings of fact. The testimony supports the finding that A.E. suffered from a conduct disorder, but was not seriously emotionally disturbed within the federal definition. There is no evidence of bad faith on the part of the Stilwell Public Schools. Although A.E.'s IEP team refused to reclassify her as seriously emotionally disturbed, the team did prepare an IEP designed to combat her learning disability and behavioral problems. The school district has made every effort to assure that A.E. can be educated in the least restrictive environment possible.

Dr. Graybill was called as a witness for the plaintiff. Dr. Graybill has been employed by numerous school districts to evaluate students for serious emotional disturbance and evaluated A.E. on behalf of the school district. He diagnosed A.E. as having a conduct disorder with related emotional disturbance. The challenged testimony arose due to confusion over the psychological, lay, and legal definitions of the terms used in the federal regulation. While Dr. Graybill admitted that A.E. had emotional problems, he did not feel that her problems were of such a magnitude as to meet the federal definition of seriously emotionally disturbed. On redirect, he was directly asked whether A.E. fit within the definitions of the Act. Plaintiff-Appellant now seeks to challenge the testimony. Any error was invited by the questioning and is harmless.

Accordingly, the Judgment of the district court in favor of Defendant Appellee Stilwell Public Schools is AFFIRMED.

One of the issues more likely to arise in light of recent tragedies on college campuses is whether an institution of higher education should be informed of behavior and conduct issues or any diagnosis of an emotional disturbance. Policies resulting from recent attention to this concern have not yet resolved these challenging issues.[24]

Infants and Toddlers and Preschool Children

The value to the learning process of early intervention is generally recognized by experts in child development. This is particularly true for children with disabilities. The earlier they are provided with developmental programming, the better able to benefit from public education they will be. It is also generally recognized that while it is costly to provide early educational programs, in the long run there is a significant cost savings to the public. The child who is provided early programming will be less likely to require substantial public support after public educational programming has been completed.

In recognition of this, Congress in 1986 amended the IDEA to provide for special education benefits for children up to the age of five. This mandate was updated with amendments that provide that states should make available programming to infants and toddlers (from birth to age 2) who are disabled.[25] A similar grant program is provided for children with disabilities ages 3 to 5.[26] The financial incentives are particularly strong for the program for preschoolers, in terms of additional federal support to be made available to states electing to take advantage of the program.

To receive grants under either of these programs, the state must demonstrate that it has a policy of making the programming available to all eligible children meeting the definition within the state. The Infants and Toddlers grant program contemplates a statewide, comprehensive, coordinated, multidisciplinary, interagency system to provide early intervention services.

"Uneducable" Children

One of the IDEA principles is the concept of "zero reject." This is found in the requirement that states are to provide education to *all* children with disabilities.[27] In spite of this seemingly clear mandate, a few courts have adopted a position that at least some children are uneducable.[28] While the Supreme Court has not yet addressed this issue, one federal appellate court has done so with detailed discussion of the congressional history, the statute and regulations, and case law interpretation, and overruled a lower court decision that had held that a child was ineligible for special education services because he was incapable of benefiting from such services. The case involved Timothy W., born in 1975, two months premature to a 15-year-old mother. He weighed only 4 pounds at birth and had numerous severe developmental disabilities, including severe spasticity, cerebral palsy, brain damage, joint contractures, cortical blindness, quadriplegia, severe respiratory problems, and hearing defects. Although he received some services from a child development center, he did not receive any services from the school district when he reached school age. As part of the school's initial evaluation of his eligibility for special education services in 1980, it was determined that "Timothy was not educationally handicapped . . . since he was not 'capable of benefitting' from an education." For the next three and a half years he received no educational programming from the school district. At this point, in response to attorney intervention, the school reevaluated Timothy, and the placement team recommended a program of special education at the Child Development Center. The school board rejected this recommendation based on their finding that he was ineligible for services. A complaint was filed in federal district court in November of 1984. After four years of legal debate including hearings and rulings by both the court and administrative agencies, the district court rendered a final decision that "under EAHCA, an initial determination as to a child's ability to benefit from special education must be made in order for a handicapped child to qualify for education under the Act." The court held that this was an implicit part of the act and applied only in cases where there were extreme disabilities.

The following is an excerpt from the appellate court's reversal of that decision.

TIMOTHY W. V. ROCHESTER SCHOOL DISTRICT

875 F.2d 954 (1st Cir. 1989)

II. The Language of the Act

The language of the Act could not be more unequivocal. The statute is permeated with the words "*all* handicapped children" whenever it refers to the target population. It never speaks of any exceptions for severely handicapped children. Indeed . . . the Act gives priority to the most severely handicapped. Nor is there any language whatsoever which requires as a prerequisite to being covered by the Act, that a handicapped child must demonstrate that he or she will "benefit" from the educational program.

III. Legislative History

Not only did Congress intend that all handicapped children be educated, it expressly indicated its intent that the most severely handicapped be given priority. This resolve was reiterated over and over again in the floor debates and congressional reports, as well as in the final legislation. The principal author . . . stated that the bill "assures that handicapped children in the greatest need will be given *priority* by requiring that services be provided first to those children not receiving an education; and second, *to those children with the most severe handicaps* receiving an inadequate education."

This priority reflected congressional acceptance of the thesis that early educational intervention was very important for severely handicapped children. . . . [Timothy] would be in the *highest priority*—as a child who was not receiving any education at all.

In mandating a public education for all handicapped children, Congress explicitly faced the issue of the possibility of the non-educability of the most severely handicapped.

Thus, the district court's major holding, that proof of an educational benefit is a prerequisite before a handicapped child is entitled to a public education, is specifically belied, not only by the statutory language, but by the legislative history as well. We have not found in the Act's voluminous legislative history, nor has the school district directed our attention to, a single affirmative averment to support a benefit/eligibility requirement. But there is explicit evidence of a contrary congressional intent, that no guarantee of any particular educational outcome is required for a child to be eligible for public education.

IV. Case Law

The courts have also made it clear that education for the severely handicapped under the Act is to be broadly defined, to include not only traditional academic skills, but also basic functional life skills, and that educational methodologies in these areas are not static, but are constantly evolving and improving. It is the school district's responsibility to avail itself of these new approaches in providing an education program geared to each child's individual needs.

Since the *Timothy W.* decision, the "zero-reject" concept has been generally accepted and no court has disagreed with the decision. The decision in this case may resolve the issue for Timothy while he is within the age eligibility for public education. Unresolved as a policy matter, however, is who bears these costs when he is no longer eligible for public educational services.

Summary

Students with disabilities who seek to challenge practices and policies of public educational agencies will find their rights affected by the theory under which they bring action. A constitutionally based case offers students with disabilities protection from school policies and practices by applying a standard of heightened scrutiny—that is, the school must show that its action furthers some substantial state interest. This standard is applied, not because individuals with disabilities fall into a specially protected class, but because education is deemed to be such an important interest.

Federal statutes offer more specific and special treatment for students with disabilities. The IDEA is categorical in its definitional coverage and requires not only that the individual have one or more of the listed disabilities, but also that the individual require special education and related services because of the disability. The student must also be within the specified age range. While it might seem that the law is fairly specific in defining who is covered, a number of questions remain subject to varied judicial interpretations. These questions include who is actually learning disabled, whether chronically ill children or those with contagious diseases (such as HIV) fit within the definition, and whether students who are still age eligible, but who have received a high school diploma, are covered.

The Rehabilitation Act and ADA's definition is much broader—covering not only those with substantial impairments, but also those who have a record of or are perceived to have an impairment that substantially hinders a major life activity. This different coverage necessitates an understanding of the procedures and remedies available under those statutes and how they overlap and differ from the IDEA.

Special situations relating to who is protected include the issue of gifted students. The IDEA does not provide protection for this group, but many state laws do. The issue then is whether the criteria for selection of these students and the application of these criteria are valid. As a general rule, courts give a great deal of deference to educational agencies in their implementation of such programs.

Students with disabilities who are in private schools are eligible for some special education through the public education agency. The same is true for incarcerated juveniles. With both groups, however, there are logistical problems of identifying the children and providing the education to students who are geographically separate from the public school program.

Recognition of the value of early intervention and education services for young children led to the development of additional incentive grant programs for children to the age of five. While states are not required to provide these programs to be eligible for general IDEA funding, there is a clear recognition of the value of these programs and the importance of having federal subsidization of state efforts to provide preschool programming. Although these programs have been in existence for many years, courts have not yet addressed many issues related to the mandates for this age-group. Recent amendments to the IDEA have clarified some requirements.

One other group of individuals has received special attention by courts and administrators, namely those who are deemed by some to be "uneducable." While the zero-reject principle of the IDEA would seem to prevent the exclusion of any child with a disability from public education, the zero-reject policy raises an important general question, namely, whether educational agencies should be the parties responsible for providing certain expensive quasi-custodial, quasi-medical services to children with severe disabilities. Those who would argue that they should would probably agree, however, that additional funding or better interagency funding responsibility is required if educational agencies are to carry this burden.

Questions for Reflection

1. Keeping in mind the age eligibility criteria of the IDEA, should a 19-year-old individual with a neurological impairment who has not yet graduated from high school be permitted to be on the basketball team, when ordinarily the age criterion limits participation to students age 18 or under?

2. Brittany is an 18-year-old individual with a hearing impairment whose parents have been disputing during the past three years whether the school has been providing an appropriate education. Brittany is bright, and has earned a C average in spite of not receiving appropriate programming. She has done well enough to pass the graduation competency tests. The school now concedes that it did not provide entirely appropriate programming over the past three or four years, but the programming was not grossly inadequate. Now that Brittany has qualified for graduation, the school claims that if she accepts the diploma, she is no longer eligible for public education. Should Brittany be entitled to services beyond graduation? If so, what kind of services should she receive since she will no longer be in the high school?

3. Suppose Brittany (question number 2) was 16 instead of 18, and in the 11th grade, and wanted to drop out. In most states there is no mandatory public school attendance after age 16. If Brittany is receiving a special education program and wants to drop out, and her parents are agreeable to allowing her to do so, is there any obligation on the school system to keep Brittany in school?

4. In 1980, Josh was found to be emotionally disturbed and was placed in a public school junior high program. He was to be provided psychological counseling, parent consultation, and academic monitoring. In 1984, Josh was found by the local court to be a juvenile delinquent. The court placed him in a juvenile delinquent center, and subsequently a special school for juvenile delinquents. Who is required to pay for the placement, the school district or the town?

5. Is a state-established experimental program for gifted children, for which eligibility is based on having a certain IQ and subsequent selection based on lottery, likely to be upheld? This would mean that only some children identified as gifted would receive special programming.

6. If a state has a program for gifted children based only on IQ score, doesn't this eliminate children who are musically or otherwise talented? Could this have disparate impact on some groups?

7. Under the 2004 amendments to the IDEA, the school where the child attends, rather than the school where the child resides, is responsible for special education services, although the responsibilities are limited. Is this a good policy shift? Why or why not? What are the logistical challenges to such a policy?

8. As a policy matter, how should the dispute about the definition of learning disability be resolved? At the federal level, state level, or local level? Through what process—hearings by educational administrative agencies, litigation, or amendment to statutes?

9. Because preschool is not mandatory in most states, how can the mainstreaming goals of the IDEA be accomplished for children under 5?

NOTES

1. 42 U.S.C. § 12101(a).
2. *Pennsylvania Association for Retarded Children v. Commonwealth of Pennsylvania*, 343 F. Supp. 279 (E.D. Pa. 1972).
3. 468 U.S. 992 (1984).
4. 468 U.S. at 1013.
5. 20 U.S.C. § 1401(3); 34 C.F.R. § 300.8.
6. 520 F. Supp. 905 (S.D. Tex. 1981).
7. *Antkowiak v. Ambach*, 638 F. Supp. 1564, 1577, 1579 (W.D.N.Y. 1986). Pending a final decision in the case, the court also ordered that Lara Antkowiak be placed in the Deveraux Treatment Center, an extremely expensive private treatment center, at no cost to the parents.
8. 20 U.S.C. § 1412(a)(1)(A)&(B).
9. 20 U.S.C. § 1412(a)(3).
10. 20 U.S.C. § 1400(c)(5)(F).
11. 20 U.S.C. § 1419(b).
12. 20 U.S.C. § 1432(1). See Laura Rothstein & Julia Rothstein, *Disabilities and the Law* § 2:15 (Thomson West 2006).
13. 34 C.F.R. § 300.102.
14. See Chapter 21 for a discussion of compensatory education as a remedy.
15. 29 U.S.C. § 794.
16. 29 U.S.C. § 706.
17. 468 U.S. 992 (1984). See Chapter 3 for excerpts from the opinion.
18. 34 C.F.R. § 300.137(a).
19. 20 U.S.C. § 1412(a)(10)(B); 34 C.F.R. § 300.146.

20. 20 U.S.C. § 1412(a)(10)(C).

21. 20 U.S.C. § 1401(30).

22. See G. R. Lyon et al., "Rethinking Learning Disabilities," Thomas B. Fordham Foundation and Progressive Policy Institute, 2001, http://www.ppionline.org/documents/SpecialEd_ch12.pdf (last accessed September 1, 2008).

23. 34 C.F.R. § 300.8.

24. The report following the April 16, 2007, Virginia Tech shootings recognized that there are a number of gaps in policy with respect to these issues and made recommendations about areas to be addressed by policymakers. See *Mass Shootings at Virginia Tech, April 16, 2007, Report of the Review Panel Presented to Governor Kaine, Commonwealth of Virginia* (August 2007).

25. 20 U.S.C. §§ 1431–1444.

26. 20 U.S.C. § 1419.

27. 20 U.S.C. § 1412(a)(1)(A).

28. See *Disabilities and the Law* § 2:15; Laura Rothstein, "Educational Rights of Severely and Profoundly Handicapped Children," 61 *Neb. L. Rev.* 586 (1982).

Identification and Evaluation

Before a child can receive special education or related services under the Individuals with Disabilities Education Act (IDEA), the child must be identified as being a "child with a disability" under the IDEA. This chapter focuses on identification and evaluation of students in terms of when an evaluation can and should be done, when parental consent must be obtained, what happens if consent is refused, and what occurs if there is disagreement about the evaluation or other identification procedures. The chapter also notes limitations of assessment instruments.

Identification—The Beginning of the Special Education Process

The special education process under the IDEA generally has five steps: (1) identification and referral, (2) evaluation, (3) eligibility, (4) developing an IEP (individualized education program), and (5) placement. The identification and referral process is part of the school district's "child find" obligations.[1] The process requires schools to identify, locate, and evaluate any student who is suspected of being a child having a disability.[2] Local school districts must have procedures in place to ensure that all children educated in the school district (including children who attend private schools in the district and children in other settings) who are suspected or known to have a disability are referred to the school for further evaluation.[3]

A referral is simply someone asking the school district to determine if the student is a "child with a disability" under the IDEA. A parent or a teacher or another appropriate individual within the public agency (the school) can make a referral. Circumstances when a child may be referred to the special education process are wide ranging and not specified in the IDEA itself, but may be defined under state special education statutes or regulations. The 2006 federal regulations to the IDEA make clear that child find and referral obligations include students who have passing grades and are being promoted from grade to grade.[4] In other words, these students may still be a "child with a disability" under the law and entitled to a free and appropriate public education even though they have passing grades and are advancing from grade to grade.[5]

For children with some disabilities, such as orthopedic impairment or blindness, identification will have occurred long before the child enters public school. The parent or family physician will have identified the problem and referred the child to the special education process. In some cases, the child may already be receiving early educational programming. For others, however, it will not be until the child enters the educational system that a problem will be noticed. A child with a hearing deficit or a learning disability or with certain behavior problems may have functioned fairly well until the demands of reading, arithmetic, or simply remaining in a seat were placed upon the child by the school system.

Group Screenings and Assessments

The school may also have "sweep screenings" of all children or group assessments that may identify a need to refer a child to the special education process, or the regular classroom teacher may notice something of concern. One of the most common types of sweep screening of all children is for hearing and vision problems. Ordinarily, these are very quick and routine screening programs, where any deviation from normal performance results in a referral or recommendation that the child be further assessed either by a school evaluator or by the family's personal physician. Other types of sweep screenings that commonly occur in many schools include testing of basic fine motor skills (the ability to manipulate small objects, for example), gross motor skills (such as the ability to throw a ball or jump on one foot), and basic perceptual motor skills (such as drawing a triangle). Often kindergarten-age children are screened for basic cognitive development by testing the ability to recognize common objects and common words. If a problem is identified in one of these areas at this level, the student may be referred to the special education process for further evaluation.

Statewide achievement tests could also be considered examples of sweep screening to assess academic performance levels. Under No Child Left Behind, states have developed statewide assessments in reading, math, and science for various grade levels beginning in Grade 3. Very low scores on these may be the basis for a referral to the special education process for further special education eligibility testing. Schools also may conduct other types of group assessments such as norm-referenced academic achievement tests that compare individuals to a group norm or average.

Group testing also occurs every day at the classroom level. Whenever a class is given a chapter review math test or spelling test, the student's competency is being measured at the same time as that of the entire group. To at least some extent, the performance of other members of the class will be a determining factor in the student's competency. For example, if a teacher gives a test on geography to the fifth grade class, asking class members to name the capitals of all the states, the average performance of the entire class will probably be a factor in the teacher's assessment of what is a competent level of performance.

Schools are *permitted* to do these types of sweep screenings and group assessments of students. Such screenings are helpful in meeting the IDEA's obligations to proactively develop policies and procedures for the identification, location, and evaluation of all children with disabilities in the state or local school district.[6]

Team Meeting

Whenever a sweep screening, group assessment, personal observation, or other factor signals the need to refer the child to the special education process, the IDEA requires the school to do so and to convene a team meeting to make a decision about whether the student has a disability that is covered by the IDEA and whether the student requires special education services as a result of that disability. The members of the team are defined by law and include the parents.[7]

The team reviews existing data about the student that can include evaluations provided by the parents, classroom-based assessments and observations by teachers or related service providers, and statewide assessments.[8] The team then determines what additional information is needed, if any, to answer the following questions:

1. Does the child have a disability that fits into one of the categories of disability protected under the IDEA?
2. Does the child need special education and related services?
3. What are the child's educational needs?
4. What are the child's present levels of academic achievement and related developmental needs?[9]

If the team determines that evaluations are necessary to answer these questions, it must determine what evaluations are necessary to conduct a "full and individual evaluation" of the student.[10] The school must also provide the parent with notice of the evaluations the school will conduct and obtain the parent's written consent to conduct the evaluations.[11]

Obtaining Consent to an Evaluation

Under the IDEA, consent means that the parent has been fully informed of all the information relevant to what the school is proposing and the parent understands and agrees in writing.[12] The school must provide written notice about the proposed action, the evaluation procedure to be used, and the procedural safeguards available under the IDEA.[13] The notice must be understandable to the parent, and therefore must be in the parent's native language or other mode of communication used by the parent. To ensure that the request is understood by the parent, written evidence, usually a signature, must be obtained by the educational agency. The importance of these requirements is noted in the following excerpt from a judicial decision.

QUACKENBUSH V. JOHNSON CITY SCHOOL DISTRICT

716 F.2d 141 (2d Cir. 1983)

Jason was placed in a regular kindergarten class in the defendant district in September 1978, although the district then knew or should have known that he was a handicapped child in need of special educational services. Plaintiff Quackenbush, Jason's mother, took no action at that time because district employees told her to wait until the following year. However, during the following year Jason repeated kindergarten, again in a regular classroom setting.

Concerned about her son's lack of progress in the second year, Quackenbush had Jason evaluated by a psychologist who recommended that he be classified as learning disabled. A copy of the psychologist's evaluation was sent to the district's COH [Committee on the Handicapped] in April 1980. In June 1980 Quackenbush requested that Jason be reviewed by the COH. Immediately thereafter, defendant Rowlind [a school district employee] came to Quackenbush's home with a "parental permission form" which Quackenbush filled in. On instructions of defendant Rowlind, Quackenbush left blank the area to be checked with respect to giving permission to conduct an evaluation of Jason. Rowlind took the form.

Although the complaint does not allege what action the school district took on plaintiff's request for special services, we infer that the district took no action whatsoever from that time forward. We also infer from the allegations that the district took no action on the request because Rowlind, without plaintiff's authority, put a check mark on the form in the box indicating that she denied the district permission to conduct an evaluation of Jason. Plaintiff alleges that Rowlind altered the form "for the sole purpose of denying [Jason] the special education he is entitled to." She further alleges that he acted pursuant to a policy of the defendant school district to refuse special education to handicapped children for financial reasons. As a result Jason was denied the special education to which he was entitled, suffered damages to his intellect, emotional capacity, and personality, and was impeded in acquiring necessary training. In addition, plaintiff alleges that she moved to a different school district to get the services Jason needed and that she herself suffered emotional distress. . . .

It is unthinkable that Congress would have intended that a plaintiff such as Quackenbush, who as the case presented itself sought for two years to have the school district provide services, made a direct request for evaluation, and was deprived of that request by school district forgery, should be left without any remedy. Particularly in a statutory scheme such as the EHA [Education of the Handicapped Act] where great emphasis is placed upon procedural safeguards, we must assume that Congress intended some kind of relief when, through school district policy or misconduct of school officials or both, a handicapped child is deprived of the procedural safeguards guaranteed by sec. 1415. Assuming, then, that Congress intended a remedy here, the question remains whether that remedy, which all parties to this appeal assume to exist, is to be implied in sec. 1415(e)(2), or whether it is to be found in sec. 1983, which guarantees a citizen relief from state deprivations of federally granted rights.

> Section 1983 is a general remedial statute aimed at preventing lawlessness by state and local governments. Defendants' deliberate interference with procedural safeguards guaranteed by Congress for the purpose of depriving Jason of special educational services necessary to provide him with free appropriate public education would constitute the deprivation of a right guaranteed under federal law within the meaning of sec. 1983. . . .
>
> We express no opinion on what damages, if any, plaintiff might be entitled to recover should she prove her allegations. We find it fitting, however, that defendants should be required to respond in damages for those injuries caused by their conduct which deprived plaintiffs of access to the administration system and procedural safeguards guaranteed to them by Congress.

If the parents agree to the evaluations, the process moves to the evaluation phase of the special education process. If the parent does not agree to evaluate the child, the school must make reasonable efforts to obtain consent and may try to override the parent's refusal to consent by going through the dispute resolution process, but the school is not required to do so under the law.[14] Public schools may not try to override a refusal to consent if the student is homeschooled or placed in a private school by the parents.[15]

Disagreements may also arise after an evaluation has been made. If the parents do not accept the results of the school's evaluation, they may request an independent evaluation as part of the eligibility decision. The independent evaluation requirements are discussed in a subsequent part of this chapter.

Evaluation Procedures and Limitations

The IDEA's evaluation provisions require the team to use a variety of assessment tools and strategies to gather relevant information about the child in order to answer the four questions noted previously, and to help provide information to use in developing the content of the child's IEP.[16] Changes to the IDEA in 2004 make clear that the schools must meet the student's academic, developmental, and functional needs.[17] This means that the evaluations must address more than just academics. The student's functional performance and development[18] must also be considered and evaluated by a team of qualified professionals and the parents.[19]

The IDEA includes a number of specific requirements regarding evaluation procedures. These requirements include the following:

- Assessing the student in all areas related to the suspected disability including, as appropriate, health, vision and hearing, social and emotional status, general intelligence, academic performance, communicative status, and motor disabilities.

- Using sufficiently comprehensive evaluations in order to identify all the child's special education and related services needs.

- Evaluating specific needs, not just general IQ, and selecting and administering tests to reflect aptitude or achievement accurately.

- Not relying on any single measure or assessment as the sole criterion for making decisions about the student's eligibility or services.

- Using technically sound instruments that are valid and reliable and tailored to assess specific areas of educational need.

- Using evaluations or assessments that are not racially or culturally biased, and that are in the child's native language or other mode of communication.

- Taking into account any impairments the child has with sensory, manual, or speaking skills so that the assessments accurately reflect the student's aptitude or achievement.

- Having trained and knowledgeable personnel administer the evaluations or assessments.[20]

An example of why some of these requirements are necessary can be illustrated by considering a child with cerebral palsy who is given the WISC-R, a commonly used IQ test. The test includes several different types of verbal and performance (i.e., nonverbal) tests. Several of the items on the test are timed. The child with limited motor skills and slow speech would have difficulty with many of the performance (nonverbal) tests requiring manipulation of objects and would have difficulty in many cases with items that require speed to perform. The child with cerebral palsy may very well have high intelligence, but the use of this particular testing instrument could inaccurately indicate that the child is mentally retarded.

Testing and evaluation are necessary to identify children who have special needs and to identify what type of programming is appropriate. Once special needs are identified and services are provided, evaluations continue to be necessary to test and evaluate in order to assess whether programming being provided is effectively meeting the child's needs (see the section on reevaluation later on in this chapter).

Protection Against Discrimination

As noted previously, the IDEA requires testing to be individualized and that no single procedure be used as the sole criterion for determining an appropriate educational program for a student.[21] In addition, it is essential that the testing procedures are not discriminatory, are valid and reliable, and are administered by trained and knowledgeable personnel.[22] While there has been much criticism of certain types of testing procedures in general, there has been specific criticism about the disproportionate placement of some children in special education classes. In particular, some court cases have addressed questions about whether certain groups of children (behaviorally disordered/emotionally disturbed, learning disabled, and mildly mentally retarded) are being appropriately identified.[23]

LARRY P. V. RILES

1992 LEXIS 13677 (N.D. Cal. 1992)

This dispute concerns the 1979 Larry P. decision in which this court enjoined the use of standardized intelligence tests ("IQ tests") for the identification and placement of African-American school children into classes for the "educable mentally retarded" ("EMR"), or their substantial equivalent. See *Larry P. by Lucille P. v. Riles,* 495 F. Supp. 926 (N.D. Cal. 1979), aff'd in part, rev'd in part, 793 F.2d 969 (9th Cir. 1984). In 1986, as a result of a stipulation submitted by the Larry P. parties, this court expanded the 1979 injunction to prohibit the use of IQ tests in the assignment and placement of African American school children in special education classes and programs. Plaintiffs claim that this modification violated their due process and equal protection rights guaranteed by the United States Constitution.

Background

This action is consolidated with the *Larry P.* action previously before this court. Over twenty years ago, the *Larry P.* plaintiffs brought a class action challenging the use of certain IQ tests for the placement of African-American students in EMR classes for the "educable mentally retarded."

These classes were deemed to be dead-end classes for students with no hope of returning to regular classrooms. The purpose of the classes was not to provide remedial training for students who would return to the mainstream, but rather to provide training to make them "economically useful and socially adjusted." The primary instructional goals of the EMR program were limited to "physical health and development, personal hygiene and grooming, language and communications skills, social and emotional adjustment, basic home and community living skills, occupational and vocational information and skills, and citizenship." Reading, writing and arithmetic were excluded as primary goals for students enrolled in the EMR programs.

Children were most often placed in these classes at the ages of eight to ten. Because the programs deliberately deemphasized academic skills in favor of "adjustment," the students typically fell further and further behind students in the regular classes. Evidence presented at trial indicated that fewer than twenty percent of the students placed in EMR classes ever returned to the regular classroom.

Because the EMR program was such a dead-end "track" for children who were considered incapable of progressing beyond a minimal education, the court considered the decision to place students in such a program to be "crucial." After the presentation of extensive data and testimony by experts in the field this court found that the use of IQ tests to determine placement in EMR classes was resulting in the disproportionate placement of African American school children in such classes. While African-American students comprised roughly ten percent of the state student population, they comprised nearly twenty-five percent of the total EMR population.

(Continued)

(Continued)

As a result of this finding, the court enjoined the *Larry P.* defendants from "utilizing, permitting the use of, or approving the use of any standardized intelligence tests . . . for the identification of black EMR children or their placement into EMR classes, without securing the prior approval of this court." The court also ordered the defendants to direct each school district to reevaluate every African-American child currently identified as an EMR pupil without using standardized intelligence tests. Further, the defendants were ordered to monitor and eliminate disproportionate placement of African-American children in California's EMR classes. In anticipation of the elimination of the EMR program from California's special educational system, the court directed that the injunction would apply to any educational category that is the substantial equivalent of EMR and to any special class serving "substantially the same functions."

By 1986, the category of EMR had been completely eliminated from the California special educational system. On September 18, 1986, this court approved a proposed modification of the injunction, which was presented to the court through a stipulation between the parties. The stipulated modification expanded the original injunction to prohibit the use of intelligence tests in the assessment of African-American pupils who have been referred for any special education classes. In the current educational system, special educational classes include any service or curriculum developed for a child requiring special attention, whether that child is mentally, emotionally, or physically handicapped. On November 19, 1986, the September, 1986 stipulated modification was amended to emphasize that IQ tests may not be used to determine whether an African-American child is learning disabled because it is possible that the resulting score could identify the pupil as mentally retarded. Pursuant to the modification order, the State Department of Education issued a directive to school districts prohibiting their use of IQ testing for African-American children in the context of special educational services.

The instant action was filed by plaintiffs [from earlier litigation] who are African-American school children with learning disabilities. These plaintiffs are challenging the state defendants' refusal, pursuant to the 1986 stipulated modification, to allow certain African-American school children to take IQ tests for special education assessment purposes. The[se] plaintiffs claim that they have been unfairly and unlawfully deprived of the opportunity to take intelligence tests, solely on the basis of their race. Plaintiffs also include the parents of these school children, who claim that they have been deprived of the full range of educational testing opportunities enjoyed by parents of children who are not African-American.

In May, 1988, plaintiffs filed their complaint alleging that the ban on using the IQ test issued by this court's *Larry P.* order had been unfairly and unlawfully expanded to encompass the plaintiffs [from earlier litigation] through the 1986 stipulated modification of the *Larry P.* injunction. Plaintiffs charged that they had been deprived "of their right to equal protection of the laws . . . by [the state's] establishing a racially discriminatory regulation precluding parents of black children, and black children, from voluntarily using intelligence tests for special education purposes and services."

The vacation of the 1986 stipulation leaves the original *Larry P.* ruling standing. The original ruling enjoined the use of IQ testing for placement of African-American school children in EMR or its substantial equivalent. Because the EMR program is no longer operative, however, further action is required to give meaning to the 1979 ruling in the current educational system. In order to avoid the difficulties encountered with the 1986 modification, this court will require a hearing to determine the contemporary meaning of the "substantial equivalent" language of the original injunction.

At the hearing, the court will consider evidence and determine the substantial equivalent of EMR for the present California educational system. Despite defendants' attempts to characterize the court's 1979 order as a referendum on the discriminatory nature of IQ testing, this court's review of the decision reveals that the decision was largely concerned with the harm to African-American children resulting from improper placement in dead-end educational programs. Thus, the inquiry into the contemporary equivalent of EMR will require the search for such dead-end programs.

Alternatively, the court would entertain suggestions for a more extensive proceeding to examine evidence of the racial bias of IQ tests and their disparate effect upon the placement of African-American children, or members of other racial or ethnic minorities, referred for special educational services to determine whether a broad injunction similar to that achieved through stipulation in 1986 can be reinstated with the adequate factual support and sufficient participation by affected individuals to pass constitutional muster.

The decision to vacate the 1986 modification as a void judgment entered in violation of due process prevents this court from reaching the equal protection challenge raised by plaintiffs. This court is mindful, however, of the equal protection implications of any injunction based upon racial classifications. Consequently, in determining the scope of the 1979 injunction in the present day educational system, this court will ensure that the injunction is narrowly tailored and supported by sufficient evidence.

The parties to the *Larry P.* action are directed to contact the court within fourteen days of the date hereof to schedule a hearing to discuss the feasibility of these suggested alternatives.

The following is a much-condensed opinion from the *Parents in Action on Special Education (PASE)* case. The case covered 52 pages in the official reporter, and includes a detailed discussion of the various versions of IQ tests. These portions are omitted, but review of the full opinion on these points is useful for those interested in greater detail.

PARENTS IN ACTION ON SPECIAL EDUCATION (PASE) V. HANNON

506 F. Supp. 831 (N.D. Ill. 1980)

This case presents the question whether standard intelligence tests administered by the Chicago Board of Education are culturally biased against black children. The action is brought on behalf of all black children who have been or will be placed in special classes for the educable mentally handicapped ("EMH") in the Chicago school system. The defendants are the Chicago Board of Education and its officers responsible for administration of the relevant programs. The named plaintiffs are two black children who were placed in EMH classes after achieving low scores on standard intelligence tests. . . .

(Continued)

(Continued)

Three and $\frac{7}{10}$ percent of all black students enrolled in the system are in EMH, whereas only 1.3 percent of the white students are in EMH. . . .

[Lengthy discussion of intelligence tests and their validity and bias according to various experts is omitted.]

The Assessment Process

Defendants' system for the identification and placement of mentally handicapped children, which is spelled out in manuals and printed regulations, involves several levels of investigation. It is important to understand that an IQ test is not the first level, nor is an IQ score the catalyst for the assessment process. The first level of investigation is the classroom. Unless the child is having difficulty with his studies in the classroom, the question of EMH placement will never arise and there is no occasion for an IQ test. Individually administered IQ tests of the kind involved in this case have never been given routinely in the Chicago school system, and the former practice of giving group-administered general intelligence tests to all students was discontinued some years ago.

If the classroom teacher has reason to believe the child has an educational handicap, the matter is taken up with the school principal. The teacher prepares a written report concerning the child, using the prescribed form. The principal then convenes a screening conference. The participants are the principal, the classroom teacher, a parent of the child and any other appropriate persons.

The screening committee makes a recommendation to the principal as to whether a case study should be requested for the child. If the principal determines on the basis of this recommendation that a case study is warranted, the matter is referred to the Special Education Bureau for the development of an appropriate case study program.

Various professional personnel then determine what areas of evaluation are appropriate for the child. On the basis of this determination, the child is examined by persons in the appropriate disciplines. This may involve a medical examination, a psychiatric examination, a psychological assessment or reference to a social worker or a speech therapist.

When the case study evaluation has been completed, the principal convenes a multidisciplinary staff conference. The members of this staff include a representative of the special education program, all of the professionals who evaluated the child, the school principal, and parents of the child. The purpose of this multidisciplinary staff meeting is to determine whether the child should be placed in a special education program, and if so, what program it should be. The report of the staff conference is in writing. Each participant must sign it and indicate whether he or she concurs in the recommendation.

No child can be placed in an EMH class unless the placement is recommended by a psychologist who has evaluated the child. While the conference can decline an EMH placement recommended by the psychologist, it cannot make such a placement without the psychologist's recommendation.

If either the child or his parents on the one hand or the school officials on the other are dissatisfied with the decision, they may request further hearings on the matter. Placement of the child is stayed pending the hearing, which is conducted by an impartial hearing officer assigned from another school district by the State Department of Education. Ultimately, the matter is subject to administrative review in the courts of Illinois.

The evaluation and placement process is not carried out hastily. There are more children in need of placement than there are available seats in the EMH classrooms. Sometimes the decision is against placement even though the parent desires it. A motive for unnecessary placement is nonexistent, since the cost to the local system of administering the program far exceeds the state and federal aid received for it. The total cost of the Chicago special education program exceeds by 50 million dollars per year the state and federal funds received to support it. . . .

In the circumstances of this case, where defendants have shown that IQ scores are only one factor which enters the EMH assessment and that a low IQ score frequently does not result in such placement, I believe the burden of showing an absence of racial bias in the tests does not rest on the defendants. . . .

It is unfortunately true that, despite what I believe are sincere efforts on the part of the defendants to avoid erroneous placements, some children are placed in EMH classes who should not be there. Small but significant numbers of EMH students are constantly being moved out of EMH classes back into the regular curriculum. Some of these transfers are due to the fact that the child has progressed in the EMH class and is ready for a greater challenge. In other instances, however, the child is transferred because it is belatedly discovered that he should not have been there in the first place.

These erroneous placements have not been shown to be due to racial bias in the IQ tests. The situations of the two named plaintiffs illustrate this failure of proof. These two black children, Barbara B. and Angela J., were each evaluated as being mentally retarded and were transferred out of their regular classes to EMH classes. Each child was evaluated by a school psychologist and achieved a low score on one of the WISC tests or the Stanford-Binet. . . .

The Larry P. Case

This is not a case of first impression. The exact issue of racial bias in the WISC, WISC-R and Stanford-Binet tests has been decided by Judge Robert E. Peckham of the United States District Court for the Northern District of California in the case of [*Larry P. v. Riles* (1984)].

Plaintiffs rely upon that decision heavily, since Judge Peckham held that the tests are culturally biased against black children. Judge Peckham heard a number of the same witnesses who testified here. He found their testimony persuasive. Judge Peckham's lengthy and scholarly opinion is largely devoted to the question of what legal consequences flow from a finding of racial bias in the tests. There is relatively little analysis of the threshold question of whether tests bias in fact exists, and Judge Peckham even remarked that the cultural bias of the tests " . . . is hardly disputed in this litigation . . ." I find reference to specific test items on only one page of the opinion. . . .

(Continued)

(Continued)

As is by now obvious, the witnesses and the arguments which persuaded Judge Peckham had not persuaded me. Moreover, I believe the issue in the case cannot properly be analyzed without a detailed examination of the items on the tests. It is clear that this was not undertaken in the *Larry P.* case.

Conclusion

I have found one item on the Stanford-Binet and a total of eight items on the WISC and WISC-R to be culturally biased against black children, or at least sufficiently suspect that their use is in my view inappropriate. These few items do not render the tests unfair and would not significantly affect the score of an individual taking the tests. The evidence fails to show that any additional test items are racially or culturally unfair or suspect.

I believe and today hold that the WISC, WISC-R and Stanford-Binet tests, when used in conjunction with the statutorily mandated "other criteria for determining an appropriate educational program for a child" (20 U.S.C. § 1412(2)(D)(5) [Now § 1412(a)(6)(B)], do not discriminate against black children in the Chicago public schools. Defendants are complying with that statutory mandate.

Intelligent administration of the IQ tests by qualified psychologists, followed by the evaluation procedures defendants use, should rarely result in the misassessment of a child of normal intelligence as one who is mentally retarded. There is no evidence in this record that such misassessments as do occur are the result of racial bias in test items or in any other aspect of the assessment process currently in use in the Chicago public school system.

The *Larry P.* and *PASE* decisions have been the two lead cases involving the use of IQ tests and their implications for racial and cultural bias. In a case alleging that the use of achievement tests for special education placement had a disproportionate impact on black children, the court held that while relief was not available under the Rehabilitation Act, IDEA (then the Education for All Handicapped Children Act) procedures could be applied.[24]

In another decision, the court approved guidelines for placement to avoid disproportionate racial impact and included a requirement that the students be observed in the classroom to note any personality clashes between the regular classroom teacher and the student that may have resulted in the recommendation for removal.[25]

Payment for Evaluations

When the school conducts, requests, or arranges for the evaluation, it is paid for at public expense. Sometimes, the evaluations are done by people who are not employed by the school, such as doctors, psychologists, and speech-language pathologists. For example, students who are being evaluated for eligibility under the "other health impaired" (OHI) category of disability may need to have a physician render a medical diagnosis of the underlying chronic medical condition. School districts have an obligation to pay for a physician to evaluate the student in this situation.

Problems can sometimes arise when an evaluation is done by someone outside of the school when the scope or extent of the requested evaluation is not clear. The following case illustrates the issue.

SEALS V. LOFTIS

614 F. Supp. 302 (E.D. Tenn. 1985)

[Travis Seals has special education needs relating to a seizure disorder, visual difficulty, and learning disabilities. He began elementary school at one school, and was later transferred to another school to better meet his needs. It was noted at the time of his transfer that his behavior had changed and his school performance had deteriorated. The multidisciplinary team met and recommended to his parents that Travis be evaluated by a pediatrician because they did not want to do anything that would affect his education without a recent medical evaluation.]

Acting on the recommendation of the Department's M-Team, Travis' parents brought him to Dr. Richard E. Poehlein, a pediatrician of their own choice. Dr. Poehlein referred Travis to Dr. Lawrence T. Ch'ien for a neurological evaluation. Upon completion of this evaluation, Dr. Ch'ien, along with Dr. Poehlein, referred Travis to Dr. William M. Hillner, a psychologist, for a psychological evaluation. While the M-Team had not specifically requested the neurological and psychological evaluations, it is quite clear that Dr. Poehlein felt that both of those evaluations were necessary to help him ascertain the source of Travis' difficulties. It is also clear that the Department became aware of the evaluations by Drs. Ch'ien and Hillner, and made some use of a written report by Dr. Hillner in ascertaining Travis' special education needs. The neurological and psychological evaluations did not result in any changes in Travis' individualized education plan, but might have resulted in changes had the evaluations reached different conclusions.

When a dispute arose over whether the Department or Travis' parents were to pay for the evaluations done by Drs. Ch'ien and Hillner, a "due process" hearing was convened before a hearing officer. The hearing officer concluded that the Department "pay the amount which is in excess of the cost borne by the Seals' insurance for Travis' medical and neurological evaluations." [The total cost of evaluations was close to $450, some of which had been paid for by the Seals' insurance company. This had not affected their insurance premium payments, but had reduced their lifetime maximum benefit for psychological services.]

The Seals elected to bring this action pursuant to 20 U.S.C. sec. 1415(e)(2), seeking *inter alia* reimbursement of the insurance proceeds paid by the Seals' insurer to Drs. Ch'ien and Hillner. The Seals contend that the hearing officer erroneously required them to use their insurance coverage to pay for the evaluations done by Drs. Ch'ien and Hillner. The Department contends that the hearing officer decided the insurance question properly, but erred in requiring the Department to pay the rest of the cost of these evaluations. This Court has . . . received the records of the administrative proceedings and has heard additional evidence at the request of the parties.

(Continued)

(Continued)

The questions which must be decided here are:

1. Whether the evaluations by Drs. Ch'ien and Hillner are within the scope of aid which is to be provided the Seals pursuant to the EAHCA [Education for All Handicapped Children Act], and if so,

2. Whether the Seals can be required in this case to utilize the proceeds of their medical insurance to pay for the evaluations of Drs. Ch'ien and Hillner.

It is apparent that these services were requested and required by the Department to assist Travis, in the words of 20 U.S.C. sec. 1401(7) "to benefit from special education." As such, they must be furnished to Travis by the Department pursuant to the EAHCA. . . .

There is little specific guidance from the EAHCA on this insurance reimbursement issue. On the one hand, the EAHCA requires the furnishing of a free appropriate public education to handicapped children. On the other hand, the United States Department of Education has promulgated a rather cryptic regulation which is found at 34 C.F.R. sec. 300.301(b) which provides:

> Nothing in this part relieves an insurer or similar third party from an otherwise valid obligation to provide or to pay for services provided to a handicapped child.

The above regulation, being directed only at the obligations of insurers, does not deal directly with whether the Seals may be required to use their medical insurance for the services of Drs. Ch'ien and Hillner. Because of EAHCA's emphasis upon a free appropriate public education, this Court concludes that parents of a handicapped child cannot be required to utilize their private medical insurance benefits where the utilization of those benefits would cause them to incur a financial cost. Any other conclusion would be inconsistent with the concept of a free appropriate public education which underlies the EAHCA.

This Court further holds that the Seals in this case did incur a cost with respect to the insurance payment to Dr. Hillner in that the payment reduced the lifetime benefits available to them under their policy. Defendants must therefore reimburse the Seals in the amount of Ninety Nine and 70/100 Dollars ($99.70). [This is the amount by which the lifetime maximum benefit would be reduced.]

Since the Seals' insurance payment to Dr. Ch'ien did not result in a "cost" to the Seals, the decision of the hearing officer, the extent that it requires the Seals to use their insurance for this purpose, is affirmed. [This amount did not affect the Seals' insurance benefits or premiums in any way.]

The 2004 amendments to the IDEA provided some specific provisions regarding schools' ability to use parents' private insurance to pay for evaluations. Schools may now access parents' private health insurance to pay for services if the parents agree to allow them to do so.[26] The school must seek parental consent each time it proposes to access the parents' insurance to cover an expense or service. The parents are not required to agree and the school must inform the parents that if they do not consent, the school will still provide the required services at no charge to the parents.[27] The law now also specifies that schools can use public funds to pay for any co-pays or deductibles that may apply.[28]

Independent Evaluations

If the parents agree with the evaluations, then the process moves to the eligibility phase. At this point, the team meets to determine whether or not the information from the evaluations process demonstrates that the student is a child with a disability requiring special education services under the law.

As noted previously, if the parents do not agree with the evaluations, the parents have the right to request that an independent evaluation be done at public expense. If the parents request an independent evaluation at public expense, the school must, without unnecessary delay, either (1) initiate a due process hearing to show that its evaluation is appropriate under the law (meaning that it met all the evaluations requirements noted in this chapter), or (2) ensure that an independent education evaluation is provided at public expense.[29] If the school believes its evaluations are appropriate, it must request an administrative due process hearing to determine the appropriateness of the evaluations.[30] Chapter 17 provides more information about due process hearing procedures.

The school must also provide parents with information about where an independent education evaluation may be obtained and provide the parents with any criteria applicable for independent education evaluations (such as the qualifications or location of the evaluators).[31] These criteria must be the same as the criteria the school uses for its evaluations and must be consistent with the parents' right to an independent evaluation.[32] Changes to the law in 2004 specify that parents are only entitled to one independent evaluation at public expense each time the school conducts an evaluation.[33]

Parents may also obtain independent evaluations at their own expense at any time. If parents do so, the result of such an evaluation must be considered by the school in any decision regarding the provision of a free appropriate public education (FAPE) to the student, as long as the evaluation meets the school's criteria for evaluations.[34] The parental evaluation may also be presented as evidence at a due process hearing.

Reevaluation

Once the child has started to receive an individualized education program, it is important to ensure that the program remains appropriate for the child. To accomplish that goal, the IDEA requires that the child's program be reviewed at least annually,[35] and that the child be reevaluated at least every three years, or more frequently if warranted or requested by the parents or school.[36] The 2004 amendments to the IDEA specify that parents may only request reevaluation once per school year unless the parents and school agree otherwise.[37]

The necessity of the periodic reevaluation is illustrated in the case of *Hoffman v. Board of Education*, a case that predates the 1975 passage of the IDEA.[38] In that case a kindergarten-age boy was tested by a psychologist and was placed in a class for children who were mentally retarded. Although the psychologist recommended reevaluation within 2 years, the boy was not retested for intelligence until 12 years later. When he was retested, in 1969, it was determined that he was not mentally retarded and had been inappropriately placed for 12 years. In recognition of the significantly negative consequences of such a wrongful placement, the trial court awarded the parents $750,000 to compensate for the boy's lost potential earnings. Although that decision was eventually overruled at the appellate court level because of New York State judicial deference to educational decision making, it is arguable that this failure to retest could today be the basis for liability because the IDEA clearly establishes a requirement that such children be periodically reevaluated.[39]

During the reevaluation process, the evaluation team meets and gathers information just as they do for the original evaluation process. After reviewing the existing information, the team decides if further evaluations are required to determine the child's educational needs, if the child continues to be a "child with a disability" under the law, and if additions or modifications are needed to the special education and related services being provided.[40] The evaluations or assessments selected must meet the same standards for evaluations discussed previously in this chapter.

If the team decides that additional information is not required, then the parent must receive notice and the reasons for the decision. Parents have the right to request that additional evaluations be performed.[41]

Reevaluations also come up when the school believes that a student may no longer be eligible for special education services (meaning the child is no longer a child with a disability under the law). The school must go through the reevaluation process before it can determine that the student is no longer eligible for services and before it can stop providing services.[42] There are two exceptions to this requirement: (1) when the termination of services is due to the child graduating with a regular high school diploma, or (2) when the student reaches the maximum age eligibility for special education services.[43] More information about ending services is provided in Chapter 13.

Schools must obtain consent from parents before performing a reevaluation. Consent does not need to be obtained if the school can demonstrate that it made reasonable efforts to obtain consent and the child's parents failed to respond.[44] If the parents do not consent to reevaluation, the school may utilize the dispute resolution mechanisms to try to resolve the dispute, but is not required to do so.[45]

Summary

Before a child can receive special education or related services under the IDEA, the child must first be identified as having a disability under the law, and an assessment of the particular needs of that child based on the condition must be made. Because of the importance of parental participation, the IDEA requires that parental notice and consent occur before an individual evaluation can be made. The regulations are quite specific as to the form of the notice to ensure that informed consent is actually provided. The law is not settled on whether a parent can recover monetary damages if the school does not comply with these requirements.

When the educational agency provides appropriate notice and requests permission to evaluate, it is clear that parents may refuse. A disagreement about whether to evaluate may be resolved through an administrative hearing under the IDEA. Changes to the IDEA in 2004 no longer require schools to pursue this avenue when parents refuse to consent. Schools may now simply honor the parents' request and not go forward with the evaluations. Where permission to evaluate has been granted, but the parents disagree with the results of the evaluation, the parents may request an independent evaluation at public expense. Results of an independent evaluation must be considered in making programmatic and placement decisions.

The use of certain testing procedures, such as IQ tests, has been challenged in several major court cases in which it has been claimed that these procedures discriminate on the basis of race. While these cases have reached differing results in terms of upholding the validity of IQ tests, there is clarity on the requirement that such tests should never be the sole criterion for making a placement decision. The IDEA is specific in that regard, and judicial attention to this issue is consistent on that point. Inherent in the IDEA policy is a recognition that no assessment procedure is perfect and that evaluation by a number of different individuals using different types of evaluation instruments is essential for a reasonably accurate assessment of needs and abilities.

Flaws in testing instruments and the fact that a child's abilities and performance can change over time (and in fact should change with appropriate programming) is foundation for the IDEA's mandate that a child placed in a special education program should be reevaluated as needed, and at least every three years, and the child's program reviewed at least annually. Failure to comply with that requirement can have disastrous results if a child is permitted to remain in an inappropriate program over an extended period of time.

Questions for Reflection

1. The court left open the question of what damages, if any, would be recoverable in the *Quackenbush* case. What damages or other remedy would compensate Jason and his mother for the denial of procedural safeguards in this case? What action should be taken with respect to Rowlind, assuming that any monetary recovery is collected from the school system, rather than Rowlind as an individual? Keep these questions in mind in reading material in later chapters on procedural safeguards, special education malpractice, and remedies.

2. In *Seals v. Loftis,* how might the school have avoided this type of referral evaluation expense or at least controlled the referral to some extent?

3. Who has the burden of proving the validity or invalidity of assessments used in the evaluation process described in this chapter?

4. In the *PASE* decision, the court notes that because of the high cost of EMR placement, the "motive for unnecessary placement is nonexistent." While the local educational agency's motive for unnecessary placement may not exist, isn't it possible that the classroom teacher may have a motive to refer out children who are disruptive?

5. How might NCLB school performance standards affect these decisions?

NOTES

1. 34 C.F.R. § 300.111.
2. 20 U.S.C. § 1412(a)(3); 34 C.F.R. § 300.111.
3. 20 U.S.C. § 1412(3), (10)(A); 34 C.F.R. § 300.111.
4. 34 C.F.R. § 300.111(c).
5. 34 C.F.R. § 300.101(c).
6. 20 U.S.C. § 1412(a)(3).
7. 34 C.F.R. § 300.305.
8. 34 C.F.R. § 300.305(a).
9. 20 U.S.C. § 1214(c)(1); 34 C.F.R. § 300.305.
10. 20 U.S.C. § 1414(a)(1); 34 C.F.R. § 300.301.
11. 34 C.F.R. §§ 300.300 & 300.301.
12. 34 C.F.R. § 300.9.
13. 20 U.S.C. §§ 1414–1415.
14. 34 C.F.R. § 300.300(a).
15. 34 C.F.R. § 300.300(d)(4).
16. 20 U.S.C. § 1414(b)(2); 34 C.F.R. § 300.304(b)(1).
17. 20 U.S.C. § 1414(b)(3)(A)(ii); 34 C.F.R. § 300.304(b)(1).
18. See also *Comments* to federal regulations indicating that "functional" includes the student's nonacademic needs. 71 Fed. Reg. 46753 (Aug. 14, 2006).
19. 20 U.S.C. § 1414(b)(4)(A).
20. 34 C.F.R. § 300.304(b)–(c).
21. 20 U.S.C. § 1414(b)(2)(B).
22. 20 U.S.C. § 1414(b)(3)(B).
23. See, e.g., Martha J. Coutinho & Donald P. Oswald, "The Influence of Sociodemographics and Gender on the Disproportionate Identification of Minority Students as Having Learning Disabilities," 23 *Remedial and Special Education* 49–59 (2002).
24. *Georgia State Conference of Branches of NAACP v. Georgia,* 775 F.2d 1403 (11th Cir. 1985). In the case of *Crawford v. Honig,* 37 F.3d 485 (9th Cir. 1994), the court further modified the ruling in the *Larry P.* case. See also Shaver D. Jeffries, "The Structural Inadequacy of Public Schools for Stigmatized Minorities," 34 *Hastings Const. L. Q.* 1 (2006); Lisa Suzuki & Joshua Aronson, "The Cultural Malleability of Intelligence and Its Impact on the Racial/Ethnic Hierarchy," 11 *Psychology, Public Policy, and Law* 320–327 (2005); Daniel J. Losen, "Challenging Racial Disparities: The Promise and Pitfalls of the NCLB's Race Conscious Accountability," 47 *Harv. L. J.* 243 (2004).
25. *Lora v. Board of Education,* 587 F. Supp. 1572 (E.D.N.Y. 1984).
26. 34 C.F.R. § 300.154(e).
27. *Id.*
28. *Id.*
29. 34 C.F.R. § 300.502.
30. 20 U.S.C. § 1415(b)(3)&(6).
31. 34 C.F.R. § 300.502.
32. 34 C.F.R. § 300.502(e).
33. 34 C.F.R. § 300.502(b)(5).

34. 34 C.F.R. § 300.502(c).

35. 20 U.S.C. § 1414(d)(4)(A).

36. 20 U.S.C. § 1414(a)(2)(B).

37. 34 C.F.R. § 300.303.

38. 49 N.Y.2d 121, 400 N.E.2d 317, N.Y.S.2d 387 (1979).

39. Laura Rothstein, "Accountability for Professional Misconduct in Providing Education to Handicapped Children," 14 *Journal of Law & Education* 349 (1985).

40. 34 C.F.R. § 300.305(a)(2)(B).

41. 20 U.S.C. § 1414(c)(3); 34 C.F.R. § 300.305(d).

42. 20 U.S.C. § 1414(c)(5); 34 C.F.R. § 300.305(e).

43. *Id.*

44. 34 C.F.R. § 300.300(c).

45. *Id.*

7

Eligibility

General Requirements and Evolving Standards

After the school completes the evaluations agreed to by the team, the team meets to review the evaluations and other information to determine if the student is a "child with a disability" under the Individuals with Disabilities Education Act (IDEA).[1] In making this determination, the team must draw upon information from a variety of sources, including the evaluations it performed, parent input, teacher recommendations, and information about the child's physical condition, social or cultural background, and adaptive behavior. The team must ensure that information obtained from all of these sources is documented and carefully considered.[2]

There are three parts to the definition of a "child with a disability" under the IDEA. The first two parts are that

1. The student must meet the requirements of one or more of the thirteen categories of disability noted in the law; and

2. The student must require special education and related services as a result of the disability.[3]

The third part of the analysis is that the disability must "adversely affect" the student's educational performance. This requirement comes from the definitions of the categories of disability in the IDEA.[4] For example, speech-language impairment is one of the categories of disability, and the regulations state,

> Speech language impairment means a communication disorder, such as stuttering, impaired articulation, a language impairment, or a voice impairment, that adversely affects a child's educational performance.[5]

Similarly, another category of disability that has been mentioned earlier in this book is "other health impaired." The definition of other health impairment states,

> Other health impairment means having limited strength, vitality, or alertness, including a heightened alertness to environmental stimuli, that results in limited alertness with respect to the educational environment, that—
>
> (i) Is due to chronic or acute health problems such as asthma, attention deficit disorder or attention deficit hyperactivity disorder, diabetes, epilepsy, a heart condition, hemophilia, lead poisoning, leukemia, nephritis, rheumatic fever, sickle cell anemia, and Tourette syndrome; and
>
> (ii) Adversely affects a child's educational performance.

While the IDEA provides definitions for the 13 categories of disability recognized under the law, it does not elaborate on when a child requires special education services, nor does it define "adversely affects a child's educational performance." Congress and the United States Department of Education left these issues to the states and local schools. Some states have specific definitions or provisions in their state statutes or regulations; others do not provide any additional information.[6] As a result, courts have often had to determine what these terms mean in the context of specific situations.

Courts have rejected the idea that the "adversely affects education performance" requirement means a "significant negative impact on the child's educational performance." Rather, the requirement "demands that a disability cannot qualify a child for IDEA benefits unless it has a negative effect on educational performance; no effect, or a positive one, will not do. The regulation does not, however, put any quantitative limit, "significant" or otherwise, on the disability."[7]

Educational performance includes more than just academic performance. Social and emotional difficulties must also be considered.[8] Along these lines, the changes to the IDEA in 2004 specify that schools must meet the functional, developmental, and academic needs of students with disabilities, including students who have passing grades and are advancing from grade to grade.[9]

When deciding whether a child needs special education and related services, courts will often review how the student is doing in school without such services and whether the student is able to do required class work without specialized instruction.[10] Specialized instruction, or specially designed instruction under the IDEA, means "adapting as appropriate to the needs of an eligible child under this part, the content, methodology, or delivery of instruction" to address the unique needs of the child that result from the disability and to ensure access to and progress in the general curriculum.[11]

Disputes often arise about whether the child's disability adversely affects his or her education and whether the student requires special education services. While the concepts overlap in some respects and have some similarities, it is important to remember that they are different requirements under the law. The following case illustrates the point.

ALVIN INDEPENDENT SCHOOL DISTRICT V. A.D.

503 F.3d 378 (5th Cir. 2007)

A.D. is a student in AISD diagnosed with Attention Deficit Hyperactivity Disorder ("ADHD"). A.D. receives medical treatment for his ADHD, including prescriptions for ADHD medications. He has attended AISD schools since he was three years old, and he participated in the district's Early Childhood and Preschool Program for Children with Disabilities on the basis of a speech impediment. Because of both the speech impediment and the ADHD, A.D. qualified for special education services through third grade, at which point his mother and school personnel agreed that he no longer qualified for those services. After his dismissal from special education, A.D. performed well throughout elementary school.

Starting in seventh grade, however, A.D. began to exhibit behavioral problems. He received numerous discipline referrals, and teachers removed him several times from the classroom and sent him to in-school suspension. A.D. was placed in the "At Risk" program at Alvin Junior High, which involved a Student Success Team consisting of several school personnel meeting regularly to discuss his performance. A.D. continued to pass all of his classes and met the statewide standards required by the Texas Assessment of Knowledge and Skills ("TAKS").

A.D.'s behavioral problems continued throughout eighth grade. . . . A.D.'s behavioral issues culminated in theft of property and robbery of a school-sponsored concession stand. Due to the latter incident, A.D. was sent to in-school suspension for ten days, and AISD eventually recommended A.D.'s placement in an alternative education program. Even with these issues, however, A.D. passed the eighth grade with one A, three Bs, two Cs, and one D and passed the TAKS test, receiving an evaluation of "commended" on the reading portion. While the disciplinary decision for A.D.'s theft was pending, A.D.'s mother requested that A.D. receive special education services.

III

The IDEA places several conditions on the provision of federal aid to state special education programs, including that the state provide a "free appropriate public education" [for] children with disabilities. 20 U.S.C. § 1412(a)(1). A "free appropriate public education," which involves special education and related services, *see* 20 U.S.C. § 1401(9), must be "specifically designed to meet the child's unique needs, supported by services that will permit him 'to benefit' from the instruction."

Only certain students with disabilities, however, are eligible for IDEA's benefits. Specifically, to qualify for special education services a student must both: (1) have a qualifying disability and (2) "by reason thereof, need . . . special education and related services." 20 U.S.C. § 1401(3)(A). In making this determination, a state or local education agency (here, the ARD [Admission, Review and Dismissal] Committee) must conduct a "full and individual evaluation" following statutorily prescribed standards. 20 U.S.C. § 1414.

In this case, there is no dispute that A.D. satisfies the first prong because ADHD is considered an "other health impairment," a recognized qualifying disability. 20 U.S.C. § 1401(3)(A)(i). Thus,

(Continued)

(Continued)

the central dispute pertains to the second prong: *by reason of* his ADHD, does A.D. *need* special education and related services? AISD contends that A.D. does not need special education services because his educational performance is adequate without them, and, in the alternative, any need for special education services derives from sources other than his ADHD.

B

A.D. also argues that the district court applied the wrong legal standard when determining "need" under 20 U.S.C. § 1401(3)(A). Specifically, A.D. argues that the district court should have looked to whether or not his ADHD "adversely affects his educational performance" rather than whether his ADHD adversely impacts his ability to "benefit from regular education."

A.D.'s argument is flawed for two reasons. First, the "adversely affects a child's educational performance" standard is a subpart of the definition of "other health impairment." 34 C.F.R. § 300.8(c)(9). Thus, establishing an adverse effect on educational performance demonstrates that A.D. has an "other health impairment." As described above, however, determining that a child has an "other health impairment" only fulfills the first prong of the "child with a disability" analysis under 20 U.S.C. § 1401(3)(A). A.D. must still fulfill the second prong by demonstrating that, by reason of his ADHD, he needs special education services. Therefore, the fact that A.D.'s ADHD adversely affects his educational performance does not necessarily mean that he is eligible for special education services under the IDEA.

Second, contrary to A.D.'s assertion, the district court did not base its holding upon the "benefit from regular education" standard. Under this standard, the district court would have focused exclusively on A.D.'s passing grades and TAKS scores. Rather, the district court also considered "a variety of sources, including aptitude and achievement tests, parent input, and teacher recommendations, as well as information about the child's physical condition, social or cultural background, and adaptive behavior. . . ." 34 C.F.R. § 300.306(c)(1)(i) (outlining procedures for determining "eligibility and educational need"). Therefore, in determining whether A.D. needs special education services by reason of his ADHD, the district court properly considered the unique facts and circumstances of this case.

C

Finally, A.D. argues that the district court reached an incorrect conclusion in holding that he has no need for special education by reason of his disability. A.D. relies primarily on the reports and testimony of his doctors; his past behavioral issues; his failing grades on various exams and progress report cards; and AISD's attempts to assist A.D., such as the Academic and Behavior Contract and A.D.'s placement in the "At Risk" program. He argues that the district court placed undue weight on his academic performance, as determined by the TAKS test and final class grades.

AISD responds, and the district court agreed, that A.D. does not need special education services for several reasons. First, A.D.'s passing grades and success on the TAKS test demonstrate academic progress. *See Rowley*, 458 U.S. at 207 n. 28 "[T]he achievement of passing marks and advancement from grade to grade will be one important factor in determining educational benefit." Second, A.D.'s teachers testified that, despite his behavioral issues, he did not need special education and was achieving social success in school. AISD argues that the district court properly determined that the testimony of A.D.'s teachers, who observed his educational progress first-hand, is more reliable than much of the testimony from A.D.'s physicians, who based their opinions on faulty information culled from isolated visits, select documents provided by A.D.'s mother, and statements from A.D.'s mother about what she believed was happening in school. Finally, AISD argues that much of A.D.'s behavioral problems are derived from non-ADHD related occurrences, such as alcohol abuse and the tragic death of A.D.'s brother. Thus, AISD asserts, any educational need is not by reason of A.D.'s ADHD, as required by the statute. We agree with AISD's argument and find that the district court's factual findings were not clearly erroneous.

After reviewing the record, we hold that the district court properly considered evidence of A.D.'s academic, behavioral, and social progress in determining that A.D. does not need special education services by reason of his ADHD and, therefore, is not a "child with a disability" under the IDEA. Because we find that A.D. does not qualify for special education services, we need not reach his final argument regarding AISD's alleged procedural errors.

Note that the court in *Alvin* used the *Rowley* standard for determining if the student has received a free appropriate public education (FAPE), as part of the analysis of whether the student is eligible for special education services. *Rowley* and FAPE are discussed in more detail in Chapter 9, but it is worth noting here that not all courts agree that the *Rowley* standard should be used in the eligibility analysis. *Rowley* involved questions about whether a student who was already eligible for services received FAPE from the services the school provided. The eligibility requirements under the IDEA are different from the FAPE requirements.[12]

Other factors can also lead to a student not being eligible for special education services. For example, the IDEA states that a student cannot be eligible for special education services if the "determining factor" for eligibility is a lack of appropriate instruction in reading, including the essential components of reading instruction, math, or limited English proficiency.[13] The essential components of reading instruction are defined in the No Child Left Behind Act. They are phonemic awareness, phonics, vocabulary development, reading fluency, and reading comprehension strategies.[14]

Specific Learning Disabilities and Response to Intervention (RTI)

General Requirements for Identifying Learning Disabilities

The category of specific learning disability under the IDEA has been subject to much scrutiny and debate over the years. More students are identified under this category than any other category of disability under the IDEA.[15] As mentioned in prior chapters of this book, there are concerns about the requirements or criteria in the definition of specific learning disability in the IDEA and whether it overidentifies by including students who do not actually have learning disabilities, or underidentifies by not including students who do have learning disabilities.

One of the criticisms about the specific learning disability requirements in the IDEA in the past was that the federal regulatory requirements imposed a severe discrepancy model that focused on the student's ability and achievement. One of the primary criticisms of this approach is that it is a "wait to fail" model that requires that performance or achievement must be sufficiently bad in comparison to ability before the student is eligible to receive special education services.[16] Another criticism about the severe discrepancy approach is that it is too rigid. Some states and schools developed strict formulas under this approach that required the student's achievement to be a specific or exact amount below ability before the student could be eligible.[17]

The 2004 amendments to the IDEA and the resulting federal regulations to the law remove that severe discrepancy requirement and prohibit states from requiring local schools to use such a formula.[18] Schools are still allowed to use a severe discrepancy formula if they choose to do so, and although a state's regulations may allow for severe discrepancy models, the state can no longer require schools to use that model. States are also free to prohibit discrepancy models from being used at all, but are not required to do so.

The law also requires states to permit schools to use a process that determines if the child responds to scientific, research-based intervention (generally referred to as response to intervention or responsiveness to intervention or "RTI" for short).[19] States may also permit the use of other alternative research-based procedures for determining whether a child has a specific learning disability.[20]

As a result of these changes, the criteria in the federal regulations for determining if a student has a specific learning disability are now geared toward an RTI or research-based process. The federal regulations now focus on the student's achievement and progress based on grade-level content, appropriate for the child's age, or in relation to state-approved grade-level standards.

Under the new requirements, a child has a specific learning disability if

> (1) the child does not achieve adequately for the child's age or to meet State-approved grade-level standards in one or more of the following areas, when provided with learning experiences and instruction appropriate for the child's age or State-approved grade-level standards:
>
> (i) Oral expression.
> (ii) Listening comprehension.
> (iii) Written expression.
> (iv) Basic reading skill.
> (v) Reading fluency skills.
> (vi) Reading comprehension.
> (vii) Mathematics calculation.
> (viii) Mathematics problem solving.

(2) (i) The child does not make sufficient progress to meet age or State-approved grade-level standards in one or more of the areas identified in paragraph (a)(1) of this section when using a process based on the child's response to scientific, research-based intervention; or

(ii) The child exhibits a pattern of strengths and weaknesses in performance, achievement, or both, relative to age, State-approved grade-level standards, or intellectual development, that is determined by the group to be relevant to the identification of a specific learning disability, using appropriate assessments. . . .[21]

The lack of achievement and progress or the patterns of strengths and weaknesses cannot be primarily the result of a visual, hearing, or motor disability; mental retardation; emotional disturbance; cultural factors; environmental or economic disadvantage; or limited English proficiency.[22]

To ensure that underachievement in a child suspected of having a specific learning disability is not due to lack of appropriate instruction in reading or math, the group making the eligibility decision must consider, as part of the evaluation process,

(1) Data that demonstrate that prior to, or as a part of, the referral process, the child was provided appropriate instruction in regular education settings, delivered by qualified personnel; and

(2) Data-based documentation of repeated assessments of achievement at reasonable intervals, reflecting formal assessment of student progress during instruction, which was provided to the child's parents.[23]

The changes to the requirements for specific learning disability in the IDEA demonstrate the intent of Congress and of the United States Department of Education to move away from the severe discrepancy model that has been used to identify students with learning disabilities.[24] Congress and the United States Department of Education are emphasizing that states should utilize methods based on scientifically based research and instructional assessment that focus on prevention and intervention for students that may have learning disabilities. Congress and the Department of Education also intend students to receive high-quality classroom instruction that is based on state-approved grade-level standards that were developed to comply with No Child Left Behind.[25]

Response to Intervention (RTI)

A detailed description of the response to intervention process is beyond the scope of this book, but a basic description is provided.[26] One very important aspect of RTI is that it is a schoolwide approach. It is not something that is intended to be implemented for just a specific student, or for just special education students.

Under an RTI approach, students are screened and their skills are monitored to determine whether they show adequate growth (responsiveness) to high-quality instruction (having high-quality instruction in the classroom for all students is a prerequisite for being able to use RTI). The RTI process is intended in part to rule out ineffective instruction as the reason for inadequate academic performance.

Students who do not respond adequately to instruction delivered in the general education classroom are provided with increasingly intensive interventions. Students' progress in skill areas is monitored frequently and the data collected help determine if students are responding appropriately, or need more intensive instruction.

RTI has three tiers or phases. In the first tier, high-quality instructional and behavioral supports are provided for all students in the general education classroom. School personnel conduct universal screening of literacy skills, academics, and behavior for all students. Teachers implement a variety of research-supported teaching strategies and approaches and utilize ongoing, curriculum-based assessment along with continuous progress monitoring. All students receive differentiated instruction based on data from ongoing assessments.

Students whose performance and rate of progress lags behind move on to the second tier where they receive more specialized prevention or remediation still within the general education program. Curriculum-based measures are used to identify which students continue to need assistance with specific kinds of skills. Collaborative problem solving is used to design and implement instructional support for students that may consist of a standard protocol or more individualized strategies and interventions. Students receive more intensive scientific, research-based instruction targeted to their individual needs.

Student progress is again monitored to determine the effectiveness of the intervention and the need for modifications. Systematic assessment is conducted to determine the integrity with which instruction and interventions are implemented. Parents are informed and included in the planning and monitoring of their child's progress with these interventions. General education teachers receive support (e.g., training, consultation, direct services for students), as needed, from other qualified educators in implementing interventions and monitoring student progress.

Those students who still do not respond sufficiently move to tier three, where more intensive, systematic, specialized instruction is provided, additional data is collected, and the student is referred to the special education process for evaluation and eligibility determination. The process then follows the evaluation and eligibility process required under the IDEA as noted in this book.

The RTI information will be part of the information the team relies on in the evaluation and eligibility process, but it cannot be the only information used by the team.[27] Further information is necessary to determine the reasons for the lack of achievement or progress, to rule out other possible identifications, to determine the needs of the student, and to develop an individualized education plan or program (IEP).

Eligibility Determination

If the team, which includes the parents, determines that the student is eligible for special education, under specific learning disability or any of the other categories of disability, the process moves to the IEP phase. If the team finds that the student is not eligible and the parents disagree, the parents can pursue the dispute resolution mechanisms in the law to try to resolve the dispute. These mechanisms are discussed in detail in Chapter 17.

If a student is found not to be eligible for special education services under the IDEA, the student may still be eligible for services or protections under the Americans with Disabilities Act (ADA) or Section 504. As noted in Chapters 5 and 18, these statutes require that a student have a physical or mental impairment that substantially limits one or more major life activities, or have a record of such an impairment, or be regarded as having such an impairment.[28]

These requirements are different from the IDEA's requirements and may provide coverage when the IDEA does not. For example, a student with a disability such as ADHD that does not have an adverse effect on his or her educational performance, or does not require special education services, may still be eligible for protection under the ADA or Section 504.

Summary

The eligibility requirements under the IDEA have remained fairly consistent over the years. Not every child with a medical disability will be covered under the law. Rather, the child's disability must fit within one or more of the 13 categories of disability recognized by the law. Most of these categories have a requirement that the disability adversely affect the child's educational performance. The final requirement is that the student must require special education and related services to address the adverse effect on educational performance. If regular classroom techniques or accommodations are all that is required, the student is likely not eligible under the law.

Congress and the United States Department of Education have defined educational performance to include more than just academic performance. It also requires that functional and developmental needs must be met.

One area of eligibility that has changed is that of learning disabilities. Due to concerns over a variety of issues, the 2004 amendments to the IDEA and subsequent regulations changed the eligibility criteria for this disability and now focus on a more preventive approach with techniques such as response to intervention.

If students with disabilities are not eligible for services under the IDEA, they may still be eligible for some services or protections under Section 504 or the Americans with Disabilities Act.

Questions for Reflection

1. Assume Tony is a 10-year-old fourth grade student with ADHD. The special education evaluation process reveals that Tony has a slightly above average intelligence and ability and a slightly below average result in performance on academic subjects. He has a C+ average on his grades in academic subjects. What information or data would be necessary to establish that Tony's ADHD adversely affects his educational performance? What kind of information would be necessary to show that Tony needs special education and related services?

2. Referring back to question number 1, assume for purposes of discussion that Tony is found not eligible under the IDEA. What would need to be established for him to be eligible under the ADA or Section 504? What kinds of services or protections might he receive under these laws that differ from what he could receive under the IDEA?

3. How is the RTI model noted in this chapter different from the severe discrepancy model for specific learning disabilities?

4. Should courts use the *Rowley* standard for determining if a student received FAPE to also determine if a student is eligible for special education services?

NOTES

1. 20 U.S.C. § 1414(b)(4)&(5); 34 C.F.R. § 300.306.
2. 34 C.F.R. § 300.306.
3. 34 C.F.R. § 300.8, § 300.306.
4. The only categories that do not have this requirement are deaf-blindness, multiple disabilities, and traumatic brain injury, all of which have slightly different requirements. Additionally, the definition of specific learning disability does not include the "adversely affects the student's educational performance" language, but it has a number of more detailed requirements that are discussed in this chapter.
5. 34 C.F.R. § 300.8(c)(11).
6. For a discussion of this topic, see *Mr. I v. Maine Admin. Sch. Dist. No. 55,* 480 F.3d 1 (1st Cir. 2007).
7. *Mr. I v. Maine Admin. Sch. Dist. No. 55,* 480 F.3d 1 (1st Cir. 2007).
8. See, e.g., *Mr. I v. Maine Admin. Sch. Dist. No. 55,* 480 F.3d 1 (1st Cir. 2007); *Lenn v. Portland Sch. Comm.*, 998 F.2d 1083, 1089 (1st Cir. 1993).
9. 20 U.S.C. § 1400(c)(5); 34 C.F.R. § 300.101(c), § 304(b)–(c), § 305(a)(2), § 300.43.
10. See, e.g., *Hood v. Enctias,* 486 F.3d 1099 (9th Cir. 2007); *Yankton v. Schramm,* 93 F.3d 1369 (8th Cir. 1996).
11. 34 C.F.R. § 300.39(b)(3).
12. See Robert A. Garda, Jr., "Untangling Eligibility Requirements Under the Individuals with Disabilities Education Act," 69 *Missouri L. Rev.* 441 (2004).
13. 20 U.S.C. § 1414(b)(5).
14. 20 U.S.C. § 6368.
15. See *Twenty-fifth Annual Report to Congress on the Implementation of the Individuals with Disabilities Education Act,* available at http://www.ed.gov/about/reports/annual/osep/2003/execsumm.html (last accessed August 7, 2008).
16. National Research Center on Learning Disabilities, *And Miles to Go . . . : State SLD Requirements and Authoritative Recommendations,* available at http://www.nrcld.org/about/research/states/section3.html (last accessed August 7, 2008).
17. *Id.*
18. 20 U.S.C. § 1414(b)(6); 34 C.F.R. § 300.307.
19. 34 C.F.R. § 300.307(b).
20. 34 C.F.R. § 300.307(a)(3).

21. 34 C.F.R. § 300.309.

22. 34 C.F.R. § 300.309(a)(3).

23. 34 C.F.R. § 300.309(b).

24. The legislative history of the IDEA states that the discrepancy formula has not worked and that other methods should be used instead. House Committee on Education and the Workforce Report 108-077, to accompany H.R. 1350 at 107–108; Senate HELP Committee Report 108-185 to accompany S. 1248 at 28.

25. *Id.*

26. The information for this description of RTI came from a variety of sources, including IRIS Center, STAR Legacy Modules: *RTI (Part I): An Overview,* available at http://iris.peabody.vanderbilt.edu/browsebytopic04.html (last accessed August 7, 2008); Douglas Fuchs & Lynn S. Fuchs, "Responsiveness-to-Intervention: A Blueprint for Practitioners, Policymakers, and Parents," 38 *Teaching Exceptional Children* 57–61 (2005); National Joint Committee on Learning Disabilities June 2005 Report, *Responsiveness to Intervention and Learning Disabilities,* available at http://www.ldanatl.org/pdf/rti2005.pdf (last accessed August 7, 2008). These sources provide more information about RTI as well.

27. Assistance to States for the Education of Children With Disabilities and Preschool Grants for Children With Disabilities; Final Rule 71 Fed. Reg. 46646, 46647 (August 14, 2006).

28. 29 U.S.C. § 706(8)(b); 42 U.S.C. § 12102(2).

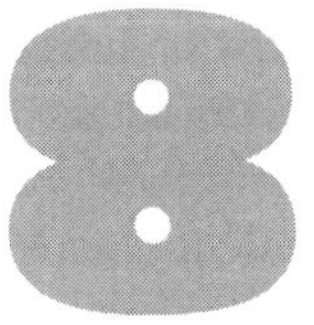

Individualized Education Program

The Individualized Education Program (IEP) Overview

Once a child has been identified as being in need of special education and related services, the team must use the information from the evaluation process noted in Chapter 6 to develop an individualized education program or IEP. An IEP is a written statement that provides information about the child's unique needs and the special education and related services that the child will receive.[1] It is a package that must "target all the child's special needs whether they be academic, physical, emotional, or social."[2] The IEP is in some ways the most important step in the special education process. IEPs have been called the cornerstone of the Individuals with Disabilities Education Act (IDEA) as they provide the information required for the school to provide the student with a free and appropriate public education (FAPE).[3]

The IEP is developed at team meetings[4] that include a representative or representatives with appropriate qualifications from the educational agency, the teacher (not less than one regular education teacher if the child is in a regular education environment), not less than one special education teacher, the parent(s) (or other person acting as a parent), an individual who can interpret the instructional implications of evaluations results (in appropriate circumstances), other individuals the parent or agency deems to have appropriate knowledge or special expertise, and the child (in appropriate circumstances).[5]

Development of the IEP is an extremely important opportunity for parental participation. The IDEA regulations recognize the importance of requiring parental attendance at this meeting by requiring that notice of the meeting must be provided in a timely fashion to ensure attendance and by requiring that meetings be scheduled at mutually agreeable times and locations. The notice given of the meeting is to include a specification of the time, place, and participants and the purpose of the meeting.

Even with the best of efforts by an educational agency, the unfortunate fact is that there will be instances when the parents cannot or will not attend an IEP meeting. The agency must, however, attempt to use other methods of participation, such as telephone communication. The agency must also document in detail its attempts to ensure parental participation. Such documentation would include records of telephone calls made or attempted, copies of correspondence, and records of attempts at actual contact with the parents.[6]

One of the issues around IEP development and team meetings has been the strain that it can place on educators in terms of the amount of time spent in numerous meetings discussing and developing an IEP.[7] The 2004 amendments to the IDEA changed some of the team meeting requirements for developing and modifying IEPs to try to address some of these issues. A team member now does not need to attend an IEP meeting, in whole or in part, if the team will not be discussing the team member's area of services or curriculum.[8]

For example, a science teacher does not need to attend an IEP meeting if the meeting is only going to cover goals for math that would be unrelated to anything the science teacher is doing. Similarly, an occupational therapist does not need to attend a meeting if the team is not going to discuss occupational therapy, or an area that is affected by the student's occupational therapy services. For this provision of the law to apply, the parent and the school must agree in writing that the team member's attendance is not necessary because the team member's area of services or curriculum will not be discussed or modified at the meeting.[9]

A team member may also be excused from a meeting even if his or her area of services or curriculum is going to be discussed if the parent and the school agree to the excusal and the team member submits input in writing to the team that can be used at the meeting.[10] The agreement and the parent's consent to excuse must be in writing.[11]

Similarly, the IDEA now states that regular education teachers are members of the team and shall, to the extent appropriate, participate in the development of the IEP, including helping to make decisions when necessary about the appropriate use of positive behavioral interventions and supports, the use of supplementary aids and services, program modifications, and support for school personnel.[12] Just like other providers, the regular education teacher may be excused from team meetings under the methods discussed above.

IEP Development and Content

When developing an IEP, the team must consider the strengths of the student, the results of evaluations, and the academic, developmental, and functional needs of the child. It must also consider the concerns of the parents for enhancing the education of the student.[13] The team must also consider some "special factors" including, among other things, whether the student's behavior impedes the student's learning or the learning of others. If it does, the IEP team must consider the use of positive behavioral interventions and supports and other strategies to address the behavior.

Another special factor that the team must consider is whether the student needs assistive technology devices and services.[14] If the student needs assistive technology services or devices as part of the special education, related services, or supplementary aids and services to receive FAPE, then it must be provided to the student at no charge.[15] Assistive technology devices and services are defined very broadly. Devices include items and equipment used to "increase, maintain, or improve the functional capabilities of a child with a disability," while assistive technology services simply means any service that directly assists a child with a disability in the selection, acquisition, or use of an assistive technology device.[16] This type of service could include a functional evaluation to determine how assistive technology could assist the child.

The goal of assistive technology is to assist the student in becoming an independent learner and to supplement instruction as opposed to the technology being used as a substitute for teaching the student. The IEP team determines the specific services to be required and the nature and extent of these services.

There are three other special factors for the team to consider as well. They involve students with limited English proficiency, students who are blind or otherwise visually impaired, and the communication needs of students, including students who are deaf or hard of hearing. If the team determines that any one of the special factors needs to be addressed in order to provide the student with FAPE, then the goals and services to address these needs must be included in the student's IEP.

The IEP itself describes the special education and related services and accommodations or modifications that will be provided to meet the student's academic, functional, and developmental needs and to enable the student to receive FAPE.[17] One very important component of IEPs and providing FAPE is enabling the student to be involved in and progress in the general education curriculum, meaning the curriculum used by the local school district for all students.[18]

Generally, the local school district curricula will be based on the state content and proficiency standards that set targets for what students should know and be able to do by certain grades and are part of No Child Left Behind (NCLB) requirements. Another connection to NCLB is that the IDEA also now requires that the special education and related services provided to the student be based on peer-reviewed research to the extent practicable.[19]

IEPs must also address developmental and functional needs that can include a variety of matters beyond academics such as emotional issues, socialization, independent living, and orientation and mobility.[20] Specifically, the IDEA and its implementing regulations require IEPs to contain the following information:

1. A statement of the student's present levels of academic achievement and functional performance, including how the student's disability affects the student's involvement and progress in the general education curriculum.

2. A statement of measurable annual goals, including academic and functional goals, designed to meet the student's needs that result from the student's disability so that the student will be involved in and progress in the general education curriculum and to meet the child's other educational needs that result from the child's disability.

3. A statement of the special education and related services, and supplementary aids and services, based on peer-reviewed research to the extent practicable, to be

provided to the student, and a statement of the program modifications or supports for school personnel that will be provided to enable the student to

a. advance appropriately toward meeting the annual goals in the IEP;
b. be able to be involved in and make progress in the general education curriculum and participate in extracurricular and nonacademic activities;
c. be educated and participate with other children with disabilities and children without disabilities in educational and extracurricular and nonacademic activities.

4. An explanation of the extent, if any, that the student will not participate with nondisabled children in the regular class or in nonacademic or extracurricular activities.

5. A statement of any individual-appropriate accommodations necessary to measure academic achievement and functional performance on state- or districtwide assessment tests.

6. The projected date for the beginning of services and modifications and the anticipated frequency, location, and duration of the services and modifications.

7. A statement of how the student's progress toward annual goals in the IEP will be measured and when the parents will be informed of the progress (such as the use of quarterly reports or periodic reports concurrent with the issuance of report cards).

8. Beginning not later than the first IEP to be in effect when the child turns 16 (or younger than 16 if the IEP team finds it appropriate), IEPs must contain information about the transition needs of the student. Chapter 13 of this book provides more information about transition services.[21]

The school must provide the parents with a copy of the child's IEP at no charge.[22] The child's IEP must also be accessible to each regular education teacher, special education teacher, and service provider (such as therapists, pathologists, school psychologists, etc.), and they must also be informed of their specific responsibilities in implementing the IEP and the specific accommodations, modifications, and supports that must be provided to the child under the IEP.[23]

Consent and Disputes

During the IEP development process, parents (as part of the IEP team) must be given an opportunity to suggest additions, deletions, or other changes to what the school proposes. If the school district and parents disagree over the IEP, either side may request another meeting to discuss the IEP, or the parties can attempt to resolve the dispute through the dispute resolution mechanisms in the IDEA, which are discussed in Chapter 17.

Once the document is finalized, the school must obtain parental consent before actually implementing the program, at least for the initial provision of services. In the past, if the parent did not consent to services, schools could attempt to override the refusal by going to a due process hearing and obtaining an order to provide services from a hearing officer. The order would be based on the child's need for FAPE. However, changes to the IDEA in 2004 prohibit schools from attempting to override a parent's refusal to consent. The changes also absolve the school from any liability for not providing FAPE to the student when the parent refuses services.[24]

Disputes over IEPs generally fall into two categories: procedural and substantive. Procedural claims can include, among other things, allegations that the parents were not provided proper notice of meetings, or not given a chance to participate in meetings, or that the team did not properly consider the parent's views in the team meeting process.

With procedural violations, courts have generally used something of a "no harm no foul rule," meaning that a student (or parent) is not entitled to certain remedies for a procedural violation unless the procedural violation impeded the right to receive FAPE, significantly impeded the parents' right to participate in the special education process, or caused a deprivation of educational benefit. The IDEA incorporated this approach when it was amended in 2004, but still allows a hearing officer or court to order the school to comply with procedural requirements prospectively.[25]

Common areas of dispute between parents and the school regarding IEP substance include whether the IEP addresses the student's unique needs, whether certain services or provisions have to be included in an IEP, whether the amount or type of services provided is sufficient, and whether the student is making sufficient progress under the IEP as written.

The legal standard governing these substantive questions is whether the IEP provides the student with FAPE. To provide FAPE, an IEP must be reasonably calculated to enable the student to receive educational benefit.[26] The following case illustrates some of these issues.

CERRA V. PAWLING SCHOOL DISTRICT

427 F.3d 186 (5th Cir. 2005)

Background

In January 2001, midway through the school year, the Cerras enrolled Kathryn in Pawling High School, where she completed the ninth grade in the regular education program. In June 2001, Kathryn received a psychological evaluation by Karen Arnhold, a school psychologist. Mrs. Arnhold's report indicated that Kathryn had average overall intelligence, but that she was a "remediated dyslexic" whose "[r]eading comprehension [was] seriously discrepant with grade expectations" and whose "verbal memory [was] mildly disordered." The report also indicated that she had an attention disorder. Consequently, on June 24, 2001, the District classified Kathryn as learning disabled and developed an Individualized Education Program ("IEP") for her for the summer of 2001, as required by IDEA. *See* 20 U.S.C. § 1414(d).

At the end of the summer, Kathryn was given an IEP for the 2001–02 school year. It placed her in the school's regular education program, supplemented by weekly consultant teacher services sessions. . . . These special sessions consisted of group instruction with a student to teacher ratio of up to 5 to 1. The IEP also required "preferential seating" in the classroom and gave Kathryn twice the amount of time to take tests.

(Continued)

(Continued)

On October 23, 2001, the District's Committee on Special Education ("CSE") held a meeting with Mrs. Cerra in attendance to discuss and revise Kathryn's 2001–02 IEP based on a report by Dr. Ronda Facchini, who had conducted a neuropsychological evaluation of Kathryn at her parents' request. Dr. Facchini's report concluded that "Kathryn [would] be most appropriately educated in a specialized school for children with learning issues" and noted that she "should be engaged in psychotherapy to aid her emotional development." The CSE determined that Kathryn could "successfully progress in the regular classroom with modifications and support in skill development," but amended the 2001–02 IEP to provide one-on-one tutorials two days a week after-school instead of consultant teacher services. The revised IEP also added after-school educational counseling sessions two days a week.

While Kathryn availed herself of these services in November and early December, she did not attend the tutoring or counseling sessions from December 15, 2001 through March 20, 2002. Consequently, members of the CSE met with the Cerras in March to develop a more workable program. Without formally amending Kathryn's IEP, it was decided that Kathryn would stop attending one-on-one tutoring and counseling sessions at the elementary school, and instead would resume consultant teacher services at the high school in a small group setting. Kathryn attended the small-group sessions through most of May, except during a short period when her mother told her not to go because of a dispute with her teacher.

On May 17, 2002, seventeen days before the school year ended, the District's Director of Special Education, Althea Schepperly, convened a meeting with Mrs. Cerra and some of Kathryn's teachers and counselors to make short-term plans to help Kathryn pass the Regents exams. The group discussed Kathryn's reading comprehension difficulties and arranged for her to be tutored daily during lunch and after-school.

On June 14, 2002, the CSE held its annual review of Kathryn's educational program, with Mrs. Cerra in attendance. The group first discussed Kathryn's fourth quarter grades, all of which were passing, but very low. Mrs. Cerra expressed that she believed the poor grades showed that Kathryn had regressed during the year and that the CSE needed "to come up with a better plan." The group then discussed Kathryn's 2002–03 IEP. The CSE proposed offering Kathryn one period of resource room instruction and one period of a special reading class each day, both of which would have 5 to 1 student-teacher ratios. . . . The CSE also recommended study guides, class notes, an additional set of textbooks, testing modifications, and preferential seating away from social peers. Mrs. Cerra requested that she and her husband be sent Kathryn's new IEP early in the summer so that they would have an opportunity to review it.

Near the end of the meeting, Kathryn's consultant teacher, Mrs. Schreiber, provided Mrs. Cerra with a draft copy of the goals and objectives for Kathryn's proposed 2002–03 IEP. Mrs. Schreiber explained that she was providing the draft so that "when you do get the IEP over the summer, you can check it against what I submitted here today in June." The draft was apparently coded in a confusing way, leading Mrs. Cerra to say, "[i]t's all Greek to me." Mrs. Schreiber explained that the final IEP would not be coded and also reiterated that the draft was only intended to provide an advance copy of the objectives that she could compare with the IEP when she received it.

Over the summer, the Cerras sent several letters to the School District requesting the IEP and also asking for class profiles for the proposed reading class and resource room sessions, which would identify the other students in the classes. Having not yet received the IEP, on August 19 and 20, 2002, Appellees sent letters to the District requesting an impartial hearing pursuant to IDEA, informing the District that they were enrolling Kathryn in the Landmark School, a private residential school in Massachusetts, and demanding reimbursement for tuition, legal fees, expenses, associated costs and transportation. *See* 20 U.S.C. § 1415(f).

Discussion

In reviewing the administrative proceedings, it is critical to recall that IDEA's statutory scheme requires substantial deference to state administrative bodies on matters of educational policy. Although the district court must engage in an independent review of the administrative record and make a determination based on a "preponderance of the evidence," the Supreme Court has cautioned that such review "is by no means an invitation to the courts to substitute their own notions of sound educational policy for those of the school authorities which they review." As our Court has explained, "[w]hile federal courts do not simply rubber stamp administrative decisions, they are expected to give 'due weight' to these proceedings, mindful that the judiciary generally 'lacks the specialized knowledge and experience necessary to resolve persistent and difficult questions of educational policy.'"

I. Compliance with IDEA's Procedural Requirements

In considering whether the District fulfilled IDEA's procedural obligations, we focus on whether the Cerras had an adequate opportunity to participate in the development of Kathryn's IEP. To ensure parental participation, the Act requires, *inter alia,*

> [a]n opportunity for the parents of a child with a disability to examine all records relating to such child and to participate in meetings with respect to the identification, evaluation, and educational placement of the child, and the provision of a free appropriate public education to such child, and to obtain an independent evaluation of the child.

20 U.S.C. § 1415(b)(1). The regulations governing parental participation provide that "[e]ach public agency shall take steps to ensure that one or both of the parents of a child with a disability are present at each IEP meeting or are afforded the opportunity to participate[.]" 34 C.F.R. § 300.345(a). The regulations go on to state that "[t]he public agency shall give the parent a copy of the child's IEP at no cost to the parent." 34 C.F.R. § 300.345(f). "[T]he importance Congress attached to these procedural safeguards cannot be gainsaid." The district court concluded that the proposed IEP for Kathryn's 2002–2003 school year was procedurally inadequate because the District "fail[ed] to provide Plaintiffs with the requested documents concerning her proposed classes, and [failed] to provide the IEP in a timely fashion which would have afforded Plaintiffs an opportunity to evaluate the proposed program." By contrast, the SRO [State Review Officer]

(Continued)

(Continued)

found that IDEA's procedural requirements were satisfied because the Cerras were "significantly involved" in developing Kathryn's special education plans, as evidenced by Mrs. Cerra's participation at the May 17, 2002 and June 14, 2002 meetings. The SRO noted that the transcripts of the two meetings reflected that Mrs. Cerra actively participated in discussing Kathryn's needs, the goals of her 2001–02 and 2002–03 IEPs, and her teachers' concerns.

We agree with the SRO that the District fulfilled the Act's procedural obligations. The Cerras had numerous opportunities to "participate in meetings with respect to the identification, evaluation, and educational placement of the child" throughout the 2001–02 school year, as well as in preparation for the 2002–03 school year. 20 U.S.C. § 1415(b)(1). In addition to attending meetings on October 23, 2001, March 20, 2002 and May 17, 2002, Mrs. Cerra participated actively in the June 14, 2002 CSE meeting, which was specifically focused on developing Kathryn's 2002–03 IEP. The transcript of that meeting shows that the group discussed Kathryn's educational progress, her health, and the goals and objectives she should be achieving, and that Mrs. Cerra was frequently consulted for input about the CSE's proposed plan. Moreover, as soon as the District found out that the Cerras intended to send Kathryn to a private residential school, it scheduled another meeting to discuss the IEP before the school year began.

Although the district court acknowledged Mrs. Cerra's participation in the June 14, 2002 meeting, it suggested that her participation in that meeting was not "meaningful" because she could not understand the "coded" document Mrs. Schreiber gave her toward the end of the meeting. The U.S. Department of Education has instructed that when a school district "bring[s] drafts of some or all of the IEP content to the IEP meeting, [the relevant inquiry is whether there was] a full discussion with the child's parents, before the child's IEP is finalized, regarding drafted content and the child's needs and the services to be provided to meet those needs." 34 C.F.R. § 300, App. A–Notice of Interpretation, Question 32. When Mrs. Schreiber gave Mrs. Cerra the draft document near the end of the meeting—after a lengthy discussion of Kathryn's past performance and future goals—the teacher explained that she was giving her the draft so that she could compare it against the final IEP later in the summer. The document was clearly given to Mrs. Cerra as a supplement to the discussion and the IEP, not in place of either one. Under these circumstances, we are satisfied that Mrs. Cerra's participation in the meeting was meaningful despite her initial confusion about the draft.

The district court also faulted the District for failing to provide the IEP in a timely fashion. However, the Cerras have not directed us to any statutory provision or regulation requiring that an IEP be produced at the time parents demand. Instead, school districts must only ensure that a child's IEP is in effect by the beginning of the school year and that the parents are provided a copy. *See* 34 C.F.R. § 300.342(a) ("At the beginning of each school year, each public agency shall have an IEP in effect for each child with a disability within its jurisdiction."); 34 C.F.R. § 300.345(f) ("The public agency shall give the parent a copy of the child's IEP at no cost to the parent."). Although the Cerras might have preferred to receive the IEP sooner, and we are sympathetic to the frustration they undoubtedly felt in not receiving it sooner despite repeated requests, the District fulfilled its legal obligations by providing the IEP before the first day of school.

The District also was not obligated to provide student profiles for Kathryn's special education classes, particularly when they did not yet exist. Unlike an IEP, the Act's statutory and regulatory provisions do not expressly require school districts to provide parents with class profiles. . . .

In sum, given Mrs. Cerra's extensive participation in the June 14, 2002 meeting and the District's compliance with the requirement of providing an IEP before the first day of the 2002–03 school year, we are satisfied that it fulfilled IDEA's procedural obligations. While the Cerras may have been dissatisfied by the District's slow pace, we cannot conclude that they were denied a meaningful opportunity to participate in the formulation of their daughter's IEP.

II. Substantive Adequacy of the IEP

Under *Rowley,* a school district complies with IDEA's substantive requirements if a student's IEP is "reasonably calculated to enable the child to receive educational benefit[s]." *Rowley,* 458 U.S. at 207. A school district is not, however, required to furnish "every special service necessary to maximize each handicapped child's potential." *Id.* at 199. Rather, a school district fulfills its substantive obligations under the IDEA if it provides an IEP that is "likely to produce progress, not regression," and if the IEP affords the student with an opportunity greater than mere "trivial advancement."

In order to avoid "'impermissibly meddling in state educational methodology,'" a district court "must examine the record for any 'objective evidence' indicating whether the child is likely to make progress or regress under the proposed plan." Because administrative agencies have special expertise in making judgments concerning student progress, deference is particularly important when assessing an IEP's substantive adequacy. *See, e.g., M.S.,* 231 F.3d at 105 ("An assessment of educational progress is a type of judgment for which the district court should defer to the SRO's educational experience, particularly where . . . the district court's decision was based solely on the record that was before the SRO."). We have not hesitated to vacate district court opinions where the district court "erred in substituting its judgment for that of the agency experts and the hearing officer." *Briggs v. Bd. of Educ.,* 882 F.2d 688, 693 (2d Cir. 1989); *see also Grim v. Rhinebeck Cent. Sch. Dist.,* 346 F.3d 377, 383 (2d Cir. 2003) ("[I]n violation of *Rowley,* the District Court impermissibly chose between the views of conflicting experts on a controversial issue of educational policy—effective methods of educating dyslexic students—in direct contradiction of the opinions of state administrative officers who had heard the same evidence."); *M.S.,* 231 F.3d at 105 ("We believe the district court thus inappropriately substituted its own subjective judgment about what are appropriate measures for educational progress.").

Here, the district court cited three reasons why it believed the proposed 2002–03 IEP "was *not* likely to produce progress nor confer any meaningful benefit upon Kathryn." First, the court noted that the IEP did not provide for one-on-one instruction, even though one of Kathryn's teachers had "indicated the importance of and the likelihood of success when tutoring Kathryn one on one as compared to group tutoring." Second, the court expressed doubt that Kathryn's passing grades were evidence that she had actually mastered the material she was taught because her grades were also based on class participation and homework completion. Third, the district court observed that the 2002–03 IEP failed to provide Kathryn with any counseling sessions, even though Mrs. Cerra had informed the District that Kathryn felt stressed and overwhelmed.

(Continued)

(Continued)

The District argues that the district court erred in substituting its judgment for that of the SRO, which specifically addressed the three issues cited by the district court. The SRO was satisfied that "small group instruction two periods per day"—which took the place of one-on-one sessions in the 2002–03 IEP—was "designed to support content area subjects, and would have provided skills training as well as support and instruction in compensatory strategies." The SRO also determined that there was evidence in the record that Kathryn had made progress in 2001–02, despite the fact that her 2001–02 IEP was not fully implemented since her attendance was sporadic. The SRO cited not just her passing grades, but also "[p]rogress reports," "teacher testimony," and "formal evaluation reports" that showed she had made progress. Finally, the SRO found that the proposed IEP adequately accounted for Kathryn's emotional and psychological needs even though it discontinued counseling because (1) "[t]he record indicate[d] that the student's reported anxiety and emotional distress were not observed in school," (2) "petitioners did not advise respondent that their daughter was receiving counseling for anxiety or depression," and (3) any counseling that had been provided in the 2001–02 IEP "was being provided to address her organizational and cognitive deficits rather than social and emotional concerns."

We agree with the District that the district court failed to give "due weight" to the SRO's lengthy, reasoned opinion. As a preliminary matter, "[d]eference is particularly appropriate when, as here, the state hearing officers' review has been thorough and careful." Furthermore, the district court's determination that Kathryn was unlikely to make progress under the proposed IEP is precisely the kind of educational policy decision a district court may not make absent objective evidence in the record suggesting that the SRO has reached an erroneous conclusion. Although the district court minimized the significance of Kathryn's passing grades, we have expressly held that when a learning-disabled child is in a mainstream class, "the attainment of passing grades and regular advancement from grade to grade" will generally constitute evidence of satisfactory progress. Furthermore, the SRO's finding that Kathryn could make progress under the proposed IEP was based on more than simply her low but passing grades. The SRO noted, for example, that Kathryn's inconsistent use of the services provided to her under the 2001–02 IEP might have affected her performance and that she could make more progress in the future with regular attendance. The district court, by contrast, failed to take into account the shared belief among Kathryn's teachers and other professionals that her poor performance was due largely to her inconsistency in accessing special education services.

The district court's other conclusions are also not supported by sufficient evidence to justify rejecting the SRO's reasoned findings. The district court emphasized the importance of one-on-one tutoring because it found that "[d]uring the May 17, 2002 meeting, Kathryn's teacher indicated the importance of and the likelihood of success when tutoring Kathryn one on one as compared to group tutoring." Even if it were appropriate for the district court to focus on a single comment in a voluminous record, Mrs. Schreiber's remarks, read in context, do not support the district court's conclusion. Rather than comparing the benefits of one-on-one work to group tutoring generally, Mrs. Schreiber was simply observing that Kathryn did well on her Math

Regents after receiving one-on-one tutoring over the summer. In fact, Mrs. Schreiber made clear that she thought "a reading program with no more than five students" was adequate.

The district court also concluded that the proposed IEP was deficient because it failed to provide counseling services even though Dr. Facchini had concluded that "Kathryn should be engaged in psychotherapy to aid her emotional development." However, the SRO was justified in finding that the record suggests otherwise. Kathryn's teachers uniformly testified at the hearing that she came across as a bubbly, social, and relaxed teenager, and Mrs. Arnhold, the school psychologist, testified that she knew of "nothing" to "support the fact that [Kathryn] had any type of a serious mental problem or disorder at that time." Moreover, school officials testified that the Cerras had not told the school that she was being treated for anxiety or depression. Accordingly, we see no reason for the district court to have substituted its judgment for that of the SRO.

Conclusion

For all of these reasons, we conclude that the District complied with IDEA's procedural and substantive requirements. Accordingly, we reverse the judgment below and remand to the district court with instructions to enter judgment in favor of the District.

Reviewing and Revising the IEP

After the IEP is developed, the IEP team must continue to review the IEP to see if the student's IEP goals are being achieved and revise the IEP when they are not. The team must review and revise the IEP at least annually and must do so more frequently if necessary to address a lack of expected progress toward IEP goals, or in the general education curriculum. Other factors that may lead the team to review and revise the IEP include new evaluations, input from the parents, and the student's anticipated needs.[27]

To make the IEP development process more efficient, the IDEA now allows the parents and the team to agree to make changes to an IEP after the annual meeting without having additional IEP meetings.[28] In other words, if the IEP team meets to review and revise the IEP and agrees to make some changes to the IEP, the parents and the team do not have to keep coming back for additional meetings to discuss the specific language or the particular changes. This can now be done outside of the team meeting, with a member of the team and the parents communicating about the changes outside of the team meeting setting. The parent must agree to proceed this way and must consent to the final changes and the revised IEP. The parent must also be given a copy of the revised IEP.[29]

Summary

The IEP is a critical component of the Individuals with Disabilities Education Act (IDEA) and the provision of FAPE to students with disabilities. It is a document that is developed by a team that includes that parents and details the special education and related services the student will receive. Amendments to the IDEA in 1997 and 2004 include requirements that the IEP provide special education and related services that will allow the student to have access to and progress in the general curriculum. The reason behind the requirement is to ensure that students with disabilities have access to the same high expectations and standards as students who do not have disabilities.

The IDEA and its implementing regulations have a very specific listing of IEP requirements that must be followed in terms of IEP development and content. If disputes arise in the IEP development or content, the parties can access the dispute resolution mechanisms to try to resolve the dispute.

Questions for Reflection

1. As noted in this chapter, the 2004 amendments to the IDEA included several changes to make the IEP process more efficient and to ease the time constraints of attending multiple team meetings. Are these changes sufficient? Where should the balance be in terms of reducing the amount of meetings and paperwork on the one hand and still ensuring that enough information is generated to measure progress, provide accountability, and ensure parental participation in the team process?

2. Why do you think Congress and the United States Department of Education included requirements in the IDEA that students with disabilities be involved in and progress in the general education curriculum? Are there any advantages to having a separate curriculum for students with disabilities?

3. In the *Cerra v. Pawling School District* case, the Fifth Circuit Court of Appeals found that the school district's IEP was reasonably calculated to provide the student with FAPE. Based on the information and the legal standards discussed in the opinion, why did the court come to that conclusion? What kind of information would the parents need to present in that case in order to show that the IEP was not reasonably calculated to provide FAPE?

4. In the *Cerra v. Pawling School District* case, the court noted that "when a learning-disabled child is in a mainstream class, 'the attainment of passing grades and regular advancement from grade to grade' will generally constitute evidence of satisfactory progress." Other courts have ruled that these factors are just issues to consider and not necessarily determinative of progress, particularly when the student's grades are modified. What weight should a court place on student grades and the fact that the student is passing from grade to grade? What kind of information may show that a student with passing grades is not making satisfactory progress under the IDEA?

5. The parents in the *Cerra v. Pawling School District* case sought tuition reimbursement for a private special education school as the remedy for the IEP allegedly not providing FAPE. This remedy and others are discussed in subsequent chapters of this book. What should the remedy be if a court or hearing officer determines that an IEP is not reasonably calculated to provide FAPE? How would that remedy be carried out?

6. Consider the following fact pattern:

> Sherry is a 13-year-old student with a specific learning disability and ADHD. She is halfway through the eighth grade and has been eligible for special education since second grade. She has IEP goals in reading, spelling, writing, and social skills. She also has a number of accommodations in her IEP regarding preferential seating in class, providing instruction to her in various modalities, and allowing her to take breaks from class when needed. During the first two quarters of school, her grades were average, she made modest progress on some goals and no progress on others, and she mastered some of her goals in reading. She also had a number of in-class behavioral incidents that led to disciplinary measures, which is something that has not occurred in the past.

Should the team meet to review and revise her IEP? What types of changes, if any, might the team want to make? Should the team take any other actions?

7. As noted in this chapter, the school is absolved from any liability for not providing FAPE when the parent refuses services. What if school personnel strongly believe that the parents' actions are grossly inappropriate and will cause significant harm to the child if the special education services are not provided? Should the school have an obligation in that case even if the IDEA does not require it?

NOTES

1. 34 C.F.R. § 300.320(a).
2. *Lenn v. Portland School Committee,* 998 F.2d 1083, 1086 (1st Cir. 1993).
3. *Honig v. Doe,* 484 U.S. 305, 310 (1998); *Roland M. v. Concord School Committee,* 910 F.2d 983, 987 (1st Cir. 1990).
4. 20 U.S.C. § 1414(d)(1)(B).
5. 34 C.F.R. § 300.321.
6. 34 C.F.R. § 300.322, § 300.328.
7. Megan Roberts, "The Individuals with Disabilities Education Act: Why Considering Individuals One at a Time Creates Untenable Situations for Students and Educators," 55 *UCLA L. Rev.* 1041 (2008).
8. 20 U.S.C. § 1414(d)(1)(C); 34 C.F.R. § 300.321(e).
9. 34 C.F.R. § 300.321(e).
10. 20 U.S.C. § 1414(d)(1)(C); 34 C.F.R. § 300.321(e)(2).
11. *Id.*
12. 20 U.S.C. § 1414(d)(3)(C); 34 C.F.R. § 300.324(a)(3).
13. 20 U.S.C. § 1414(d)(3)(A); 34 C.F.R. § 300.324.
14. 20 U.S.C. § 1414(d)(3)(B); 34 C.F.R. § 300.324.
15. 20 U.S.C. § 300.105.
16. 20 U.S.C. § 1401(2); 34 C.F.R. § 300.6.
17. 34 C.F.R. § 300.324(a)(1); 34 C.F.R. § 300.320.
18. 34 C.F.R. § 300.320; 34 C.F.R. § 300.347.
19. 34 C.F.R. § 300.320.

20. The United States Department of Education interprets the term *functional* to mean activities and skills that are not considered academic or related to a child's academic achievement as measured on statewide achievement tests. Assistance to States for the Education of Children With Disabilities and Preschool Grants for Children With Disabilities; Final Rule 71 Fed. Reg. 46579 (August 14, 2006).

21. 20 U.S.C. § 1414(d)(1)(A); 34 C.F.R. § 300.320(a).

22. 34 C.F.R. § 300.322(f).

23. 34 C.F.R. § 300.323(d).

24. 20 U.S.C. § 1414(a)(1)(D); 34 C.F.R. § 300.300(b).

25. 20 U.S.C. § 1415(f)(3)(E); 34 C.F.R. § 300.513(a)(2).

26. *Board of Education v. Rowley,* 458 U.S. 176, 207 (1982); *Roland M. v. Concord Sch. Comm.*, 910 F.2d 983, 991 (1st Cir. 1990).

27. 20 U.S.C. § 1414(d)(4)(A); 34 C.F.R. § 300.324(b).

28. 20 U.S.C. § 1414(d)(4)(A); 34 C.F.R. § 300.324(a)(4)–(6).

29. *Id.*

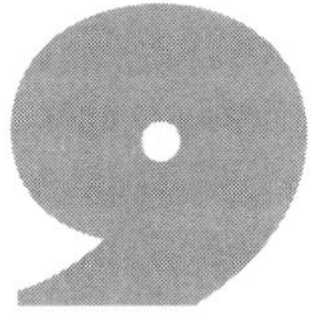

Free Appropriate Public Education

THE *ROWLEY* STANDARD

In order to qualify for federal support under the Individuals with Disabilities Education Act (IDEA), the state must have a policy that provides that a *free appropriate* public education (referred to as FAPE) is available to all children with disabilities in the state.[1] As noted in Chapter 8, the development of a program of appropriate special education and related services for a specific student occurs through the vehicle of the individualized education program (IEP).[2] The IEP must be reasonably calculated to provide the student with FAPE, and the special education and related services provided pursuant to the IEP should provide the student with FAPE.

FAPE has two major components: (1) the services provided must be free, meaning they must be provided at public expense and at no cost to the parents, and (2) the services provided must be appropriate for the child based on the child's individual, unique needs.[3] The definition of FAPE also requires that the special education and related services provided meet the standards of the state educational agency; include an appropriate preschool, elementary, or secondary school education in the state involved; and be provided in conformity with the student's individualized education program.

The term *appropriate* is not defined in the IDEA or its implementing regulations. The first Supreme Court case to address any issue of the IDEA was concerned with precisely what the term *appropriate* means.

BOARD OF EDUCATION V. ROWLEY

458 U.S. 176 (1982)

Justice Rehnquist delivered the opinion of the Court.

I

The Education of the Handicapped Act provides federal money to assist state and local agencies in educating handicapped children, and conditions such funding upon a State's compliance with extensive goals and procedures. . . .

In order to qualify for federal financial assistance under the Act, a State must demonstrate that it "has in effect a policy that assures all handicapped children the right to a free appropriate public education." That policy must be reflected in a state plan submitted to and approved by the Secretary of Education, which describes in detail the goals, programs, and timetables under which the State intends to educate handicapped children within its borders. States receiving money under the Act must provide education to the handicapped by priority, first "to handicapped children who are not receiving an education" and second "to handicapped children . . . with the most severe handicaps who are receiving an inadequate education," and "to the maximum extent appropriate" must educate handicapped children "with children who are not handicapped.". . .

The "free appropriate public education" required by the Act is tailored to the unique needs of the handicapped child by means of an "individualized educational program" (IEP). . . .

In addition to the state plan and the IEP already described, the Act imposes extensive procedural requirements upon States receiving federal funds under its provisions. . . .

Thus, although the Act leaves to the States the primary responsibility for developing and executing education programs for handicapped children, it imposes significant requirements to be followed in the discharge of that responsibility. . . .

II

This case arose in connection with the education of Amy Rowley, a deaf student at the Furnace Woods School in the Hendrick Hudson Central School District, Peekskill, N.Y. Amy has minimal residual hearing and is an excellent lip reader. During the year before she began attending Furnace Woods, a meeting between her parents and school administrators resulted in a decision to place her in a regular kindergarten class in order to determine what supplemental services would be necessary to her education. Several members of the school administration prepared for Amy's arrival by attending a course in sign-language interpretation, and a teletype machine was installed in the principal's office to facilitate communication with her parents who are also deaf. At the end of the trial period it was determined that Amy should remain in the kindergarten class, but that she should be provided with an FM hearing aid which would amplify words spoken into a wireless receiver by the teacher or fellow students during certain classroom activities. Amy successfully completed her kindergarten year.

As required by the Act, an IEP was prepared for Amy during the fall of her first-grade year. The IEP provided that Amy should be educated in a regular classroom at Furnace Woods, should continue to use the FM hearing aid, and should receive instruction from a tutor for the deaf for one hour each day and from a speech therapist for three hours each week. The Rowleys agreed with parts of the IEP, but insisted that Amy also be provided a qualified sign-language interpreter in all her academic classes in lieu of the assistance proposed in other parts of the IEP. Such an interpreter had been placed in Amy's kindergarten class for a 2-week experimental period, but the interpreter had reported that Amy did not need his services at that time. The school administrators likewise concluded that Amy did not need such an interpreter in her first-grade classroom. They reached this conclusion after consulting the school district's Committee on the Handicapped, which had received expert evidence from Amy's teacher and other persons familiar with her academic and social progress, and visited a class for the deaf.

When their request for an interpreter was denied, the Rowleys demanded and received a hearing before an independent examiner. After receiving evidence from both sides, the examiner agreed with the administrators' determination that an interpreter was not necessary because "Amy was achieving educationally, academically, and socially" without such assistance. The examiner's decision was affirmed on appeal by the New York Commissioner of Education on the basis of substantial evidence in the record. Pursuant to the Act's provision for judicial review, the Rowleys then brought an action in the United States District Court for the Southern District of New York, claiming that the administrators' denial of the sign-language interpreter constituted a denial of the "free appropriate public education" guaranteed by the Act.

The District Court found that Amy "is a remarkably well-adjusted child" who interacts and communicates well with her classmates and has "developed an extraordinary rapport" with her teachers. It also found that "she performs better than the average child in her class and is advancing easily from grade to grade," but "that she understands considerably less of what goes on in class than she could if she were not deaf" and thus "is not learning as much, or performing as well academically, as she would without her handicap." This disparity between Amy's achievement and her potential led the court to decide that she was not receiving a "free appropriate public education," which the court defined as "an opportunity to achieve [her] full potential commensurate with the opportunity provided to other children." According to the District Court, such a standard "requires that the potential of the handicapped child be measured and compared to his or her performance, and that the resulting differential or shortfall be compared to the shortfall experienced by nonhandicapped children." The District Court's definition arose from its assumption that the responsibility for "giv[ing] content to the requirement of an 'appropriate education'" had "been left entirely to the [federal] courts and the hearing officers."

A divided panel of the United States Court of Appeals for the Second Circuit affirmed. . . .

(Continued)

(Continued)

III

A

This is the first case in which this Court has been called upon to interpret any provision of the Act. "[T]he Act itself does not define 'appropriate education,'— but leaves "to the courts and the hearing officers" the responsibility of "giv[ing] content to the requirement of an 'appropriate education.'"

We are loath to conclude that Congress failed to offer any assistance in defining the meaning o f the principal substantive phrase used in the Act. It is beyond dispute that, contrary to the conclusions of the courts below, the Act does expressly define "free appropriate public education":

> The term 'free appropriate public education' means *special education* and *related services* which (A) have been provided at public expense, under public supervision and direction, and without charge, (B) meet the standards of the State educational agency, (C) include an appropriate preschool, elementary, or secondary school education in the State involved, and (D) are provided in conformity with the individualized education program required under section 1414(a)(5) [Now § 1414(d)] of this title.

"Special education" as referred to in this definition, means "specially designed instruction, at no cost to parents or guardians, to meet the unique needs of a handicapped child, including classroom instruction, instruction in physical education, home instruction, and instruction in hospitals and institutions." "Related services" are defined as "transportation, and such developmental, corrective, and other supportive services . . . as may be required to assist a handicapped child to benefit from special education."

According to the definitions contained in the Act, a "free appropriate public education" consists of educational instruction specifically designed to meet the unique needs of the handicapped child, supported by such services as are necessary to permit the child "to benefit" from the instruction. Almost as a checklist for adequacy under the Act, the definition also requires that such instruction and services be provided at public expense and under public supervision, meet the State's educational standards, approximate the grade levels used in the State's regular education, and comport with the child's IEP. Thus, if personalized instruction is being provided with sufficient supportive services to permit the child to benefit from the instruction, and the other items on the definitional checklist are satisfied, the child is receiving a "free appropriate public education" as defined by the Act. . . .

When . . . express statutory findings and priorities are read together with the Act's extensive procedural requirements and its definition of "free appropriate public education," the face of the statute evinces a congressional intent to bring previously excluded handicapped children into the public education systems of the States and to require the States to adopt *procedures* which would result in individualized consideration of and instruction for each child.

Noticeably absent from the language of the statute is any substantive standard prescribing the level of education to be accorded handicapped children. Certainly the language of the statute contains no requirement like the one imposed by the lower courts—that States maximize the potential of handicapped children "commensurate with the opportunity provided to other children."

B

(i)

. . . By passing the Act, Congress sought primarily to make public education available to handicapped children. But in seeking to provide such access to public education, Congress did not impose upon the States any greater substantive educational standard than would be necessary to make such access meaningful. . . .

Thus, the intent of the Act was more to open the door of public education to handicapped children on appropriate terms than to guarantee any particular level of education once inside. . . .

Mills and *PARC* both held that handicapped children must be given access to an adequate, publicly supported education. Neither case purports to require any particular substantive level of education. That the Act imposes no clear obligation upon recipient States beyond the requirement that children receive some form of specialized education is perhaps best demonstrated by the fact that Congress, in explaining the need for the Act, equated an "appropriate education" to the receipt of some specialized educational services.

(ii)

Respondents contend that "the goal of the Act is to provide each handicapped child with an equal educational opportunity." We think, however, that the requirement that a State provide specialized educational services to handicapped children generates no additional requirement that the services so provided be sufficient to maximize each child's potential "commensurate with the opportunity provided other children."

The educational opportunities provided by our public school systems undoubtedly differ from student to student, depending upon a myriad of factors that might affect a particular student's ability to assimilate information presented in the classroom. The requirement that States provide "equal" educational opportunities would thus seem to present an entirely unworkable standard requiring impossible measurements and comparisons. Similarly, furnishing handicapped children with only such services as are available to non-handicapped children would in all probability fall short of the statutory requirement of "free appropriate public education"; to require, on the other hand, the furnishing of every special service necessary to maximize each handicapped child's potential is, we think, further than Congress intended to go. Thus to speak in terms of "equal services" in one instance gives less than what is required by the

(Continued)

(Continued)

Act and in another instance more. The theme of the Act is "free appropriate public education," a phrase which is too complex to be captured by the word "equal" whether one is speaking of opportunities or services.

The legislative conception of the requirements of equal protection was undoubtedly informed by the two District Court decisions referred to above. But cases such as *Mills* and *PARC* held simply that handicapped children may not be excluded entirely from public education. In *Mills*, the District Court said:

> If sufficient funds are not available to finance all of the services and programs that are needed and desirable in the system then the available funds must be expended equitably in such a manner that no child is entirely excluded from a publicly supported education consistent with his needs and ability to benefit therefrom.

The *PARC* court used similar language, saying "[i]t is the commonwealth's obligation to place each mentally retarded child in a free, public program of education and training appropriate to the child's capacity. . . ." The right of access to free public education enunciated by these cases is significantly different from any notion of absolute equality of opportunity regardless of capacity. To the extent that Congress might have looked further than these cases which are mentioned in the legislative history, at the time of enactment of the Act this Court had held at least twice that the Equal Protection Clause of the Fourteenth Amendment does not require States to expend equal financial resources on the education of each child. . . .

Assuming that the Act was designed to fill the need identified in the House Report—that is, to provide a "basic floor of opportunity" consistent with equal protection—neither the Act nor its history persuasively demonstrates that Congress thought that equal protection required anything more than equal access. Therefore, Congress' desire to provide specialized educational services, even in furtherance of "equality," cannot be read as imposing any particular substantive educational standard upon the States. . . .

(iii)

It would do little good for Congress to spend millions of dollars in providing access to a public education only to have the handicapped child receive no benefit from that education. The statutory definition of "free appropriate public education" in addition to requiring that States provide each child with "specially designed instruction" expressly requires the provision of "such . . . supportive services . . . as may be required to assist a handicapped child to *benefit* from special education." We therefore conclude that the "basic floor of opportunity" provided by the Act consists of access to specialized instruction and related services which are individually designed to provide educational benefit to the handicapped child.

The determination of when handicapped children are receiving sufficient educational benefits to satisfy the requirements of the Act presents a more difficult problem. The Act requires participating States to educate a wide spectrum of handicapped children, from the marginally hearing-impaired to the profoundly retarded and palsied. It is clear that the benefits obtainable to children at one end of the spectrum will differ dramatically from those obtainable by children at the other end, with infinite variations in between. One child may have little difficulty competing successfully in an academic setting with nonhandicapped children while another child may encounter great difficulty in acquiring even the most basic of self-maintenance skills. We do not attempt today to establish any one test for determining the adequacy of educational benefits conferred upon all children covered by the Act. Because in this case we are presented with a handicapped child who is receiving substantial specialized instruction and related services, and who is performing above average in the regular classrooms of a public school system, we confine our analysis to that situation.

The Act requires participating States to educate handicapped children with nonhandicapped children whenever possible. When that "mainstreaming" preference of the Act has been met and a child is being educated in the regular classrooms of a public school system, the system itself monitors the educational progress of the child. Regular examinations are administered, grades are awarded, and yearly advancement to higher grade levels is permitted for those children who attain an adequate knowledge of the course material. The grading and advancement system thus constitutes an important factor in determining educational benefit. Children who graduate from our public school systems are considered by our society to have been "educated" at least to the grade level they have completed, and access to an "education" for handicapped children is precisely what Congress sought to provide in the Act.*

C

When the language of the Act and its legislative history are considered together, the requirements imposed by Congress become tolerably clear. Insofar as a State is required to provide a handicapped child with a "free appropriate public education," we hold that it satisfied this requirement by providing personalized instruction with sufficient support services to permit the child to benefit educationally from that instruction. Such instruction and services must be provided at public expense, must meet the State's educational standards, must approximate the grade levels used in the State's regular education, and must comport with the child's IEP. In addition, the IEP, and therefore the personalized instruction, should be formulated in accordance with the requirements of the Act and, if the child is being educated in the regular classrooms of the public education system, should be reasonably calculated to enable the child to achieve passing marks and advance from grade to grade.

(Continued)

* We do not hold today that every handicapped child who is advancing from grade to grade in a regular public school system is automatically receiving a "free appropriate public education." In this case, however, we find Amy's academic progress, when considered with the special services and professional consideration accorded by the Furnace Woods school administrators, to be dispositive.

(Continued)

The provision that a reviewing court base its decision on the "preponderance of the evidence" is by no means an invitation to the courts to substitute their own notions of sound educational policy for those of the school authorities which they review. The very importance which Congress has attached to compliance with certain procedures in the preparation of an IEP would be frustrated if a court were permitted simply to set state decisions at nought.

Therefore, a court's inquiry in suits brought under sec. 1415(3)(2) is twofold. First, has the State complied with the procedures set forth in the Act? And second, is the individualized educational program developed through the Act's procedures reasonably calculated to enable the child to receive educational benefits? If these requirements are met, the State has complied with the obligations imposed by Congress and the courts can require no more.

. . .

B

In assuring that the requirements of the Act have been met, courts must be careful to avoid imposing their view of preferable educational methods upon States. The primary responsibility for formulating the education to be accorded a handicapped child, for choosing the educational method most suitable to the child's needs, was left by the Act to state and local educational agencies in cooperation with the parents or guardian of the child. . . .

We previously have cautioned that courts lack the "specialized knowledge and experience" necessary to resolve "persistent and difficult questions of educational policy." We think that Congress shared that view when it passed the Act. As already demonstrated, Congress' intention was not that the Act displace the primacy of States in the field of education, but that States receive funds to assist them in extending their educational systems to the handicapped. Therefore, once a court determines that the requirements of the Act have been met, questions of methodology are for resolution by the States.

V

Entrusting a child's education to state and local agencies does not leave the child without protection. Congress sought to protect individual children by providing for parental involvement in the development of state plans and policies, and in the formulation of the child's individual educational program.

As this very case demonstrates, parents and guardians will not lack ardor in seeking to ensure that handicapped children receive all of the benefits to which they are entitled by the Act. [The Act does not require the provision of a sign language interpreter in this case.] . . .

Dissent Justices White, Brennan, and Marshall

The majority opinion announces a different substantive standard, that "Congress did not impose upon the States any greater substantive educational standard than would be necessary to make such access meaningful." While "meaningful" is no more enlightening than "appropriate," the Court purports to clarify itself. Because Amy was provided with *some* specialized instruction from which she obtained *some* benefit and because she passed from grade to grade, she was receiving a meaningful and therefore appropriate education.

This falls far short of what the Act intended. The Act details as specifically as possible the kind of specialized education each handicapped child must receive. It would apparently satisfy the Court's standard of "access to specialized instruction and related services which are individually designed to provide educational benefit to the handicapped child," for a deaf child such as Amy to be given a teacher with a loud voice, for she would benefit from that service. The Act requires more. It defines "special education" to mean "specifically designed instruction, at no cost to parents or guardians, to *meet the unique needs* of a handicapped child. . . ." Providing a teacher with a loud voice would not meet Amy's needs and would not satisfy the Act. The basic floor of opportunity is instead, as the courts below recognized, intended to eliminate the effects of the handicap, at least to the extent that the child will be given an equal opportunity to learn if that is reasonably possible. Amy Rowley, without a sign-language interpreter, comprehends less than half of what is said in the classroom—less than half of what normal children comprehend. This is hardly an equal opportunity to learn, even if Amy makes passing grades.

Although the IDEA does not require a "potential maximization" standard, some states have done so. This is demonstrated in *Barwacz v. Michigan Department of Education,*[4] in which the court addressed the validity of Michigan's state statute that requires educational agencies to "provide special education programs and services designed to develop the maximum potential of each handicapped person." The educational agency had argued that because Michigan's statute was enacted before the 1975 Education for All Handicapped Children Act (EAHCA) (now IDEA), the later standard as interpreted by *Rowley* was the correct standard. The court did not accept that argument and held that the potential maximization standard should apply. The court further noted, however, that the higher standard still does not require that the best possible education be provided. These standards, which go beyond what the Act requires, have been upheld as being valid.

One case applied the *Rowley* determination of appropriateness to emphasize that in the choice of education content, significant deference would be given to the school. In that case, *Rettig v. Kent City School District,*[5] the parents of a teenage boy with a severe disability requested summer classes, continuous occupational therapy, and an hour of extracurricular activity each week. The court remanded the case to the lower court on the issue of extracurricular activity, but held that as to the other requests, it was not up to the courts to "choose between competing educational theories and impose that selection upon the school system," because courts lack the expertise to do so. This degree of deference to educational decision makers is not universal. In *Beasley v. School Board,*[6] the court reviewed an individual education plan for a 15-year-old boy with a learning disability. The program was basically a continuation of a reading program that had not benefited Darren Beasley. He had remained a nonreader after almost five years in the school's program. The court noted that neither the best education nor the maximization of potential was required, but it noted the following in finding the educational program not appropriate within the IDEA:

> The evidence of the . . . 1983–84 school year . . . coupled with the evidence in the whole record, established that Darren in fact could learn to read, and consequently was not benefiting from the continued program in the Campbell County schools. [A] reading disability, and particularly one that can be overcome, warrants special efforts within the formal educational process. In that context, while he remained a nonreader, the fact that Darren was able to progress in other areas of his education by artificial support, such as oral instructions and examinations is not persuasive. . . . Darren remained a non-reader in the Campbell County school system. The 1984–85 proposed education plan was essentially a continuation of that which had not benefited Darren in the past to overcome his disability. His ability to learn to read in a proper program was demonstrated by his experience [for one year in a private program] which offered a program not available within the [public school system].

The IDEA has been amended several times since the *Rowley* decision and there have been numerous court decisions that have expanded on *Rowley*'s requirements. One of the major changes to the IDEA since the *Rowley* decision was moving past the "floor of opportunity" that *Rowley* mentions. The IDEA now addresses more than just providing students with access to public education services. It also focuses on the quality of services students receive and the outcomes they achieve as a result of the services. As noted in prior chapters, the IDEA now sets high expectations for students with disabilities, and the instruction provided to students with disabilities must be designed to ensure that the student can access and progress in the general curriculum.[7]

Courts since the *Rowley* decision have generally interpreted the appropriateness component of FAPE to require "meaningful educational benefit," which is generally measured by assessing the student's progress or lack of progress. Following *Rowley*, courts have maintained that school districts are not obligated to maximize a student's potential (as noted in *Rowley)*, but more than minimal progress is required. A student's ability is considered in determining whether the progress made is sufficient.[8]

In short, FAPE does not require schools to educate to a student's fullest potential as noted in *Rowley*, but it also does not permit services that result in minimal progress by the student. FAPE is something in between the best and the minimum and varies from student to student depending on the student's needs and abilities.

Extended School Year (ESY) Services

In a line of cases that arose around the time that *Rowley* was being decided, parents challenged state policies of providing only 180 days of school to children with disabilities because that was all that was being provided to children who are not disabled. The courts have consistently struck down such policies as being inconsistent with the requirement that education be individualized and appropriate. The following is one of the most important decisions.

ALAMO HEIGHTS INDEPENDENT SCHOOL DISTRICT V. STATE BOARD OF EDUCATION

790 F.2d 1153 (5th Cir. 1986)

Steven G. was born July 30, 1972. He lives with his mother, Beverly G., within the boundaries of the Alamo Heights Independent School District. Steven suffers from cerebral dysplasia or hyperplasia, which is an abnormal development of the brain. Steven's hands and face are deformed. He has an unusual laxity in his joints, an uncoordinated gaze, a significant lack of muscle tone, and can walk only with assistance. He has been diagnosed as severely mentally retarded, has frequent tantrums, and cannot communicate by oral expression, although he does communicate by means of pointing to pictures and symbols on a "communication board." Because of Steven's mental and physical handicaps, he is not, in education terminology, considered "educable," but rather is "trainable," that is, he can be taught to communicate with others and to take care of his physical needs. [From 1975 to 1977 he was in a year-round program, and later had other programming. In spring of 1980, summer programming was requested by Mrs. G., but none was provided. When it was denied again the following summer, Mrs. G. pursued legal challenges.]

II

The School District argues that it has a legal duty to provide summer placement only if a handicapped child will suffer "severe regression in cognitive skills gained and disciplines learned" due to an interruption of programming. . . .

Thus, the issue presented is whether this particular child, Steven G., is entitled under the Act to have structured summer programming included in his IEP.

Pursuant to the provisions of the EAHCA, the School District is required to provide Steven with a "free appropriate public education." That mandate includes "the requirement that the education to which access is provided be sufficient to confer some educational benefit upon the handicapped child." [Citing *Rowley*] "The basic substantive standard under the Act, then, is that each IEP must be formulated to provide some educational benefit to the child," in accordance with "the unique needs" of that child. The some educational-benefit standard does not mean that the requirements of the Act are satisfied so long as a handicapped child's progress, absent summer services, is not brought "to a virtual standstill." Rather, if a child will experience severe or substantial regression during the summer months in the absence of a summer program, the handicapped child may be entitled to year-round services. This issue is whether the benefits accrued to the child during the regular school year will be significantly jeopardized if he is not provided an educational program during the summer months. This is, of course, a general standard, but it must be applied to the individual by the ARD [Admission, Review and Dismissal] Committee in the same way that juries apply other general legal standards such as negligence reasonableness. . . .

(Continued)

(Continued)

In *Tatro v. Texas*, Judge Gee, writing for the court, stated that the EAHCA has "placed primary responsibility for formulating handicapped children's education in the hands of state and local school agencies in cooperation with each child's parents." In deference to this statutory scheme and the reliance it places on the expertise of local education authorities, we stated in *Tatro* that the Act creates a "presumption in favor of the education placement established by [a child's] IEP," and "the party attacking its terms should bear the burden of showing why the educational setting established by the IEP is not appropriate." . . .

The testimony concerning Steven's particular regression-recoupment tendencies was directly conflicting: The School District's employees and consultants were unanimous that they observed no significant regression, while the doctors, therapists, and former teachers who testified on behalf of Steven all agreed that Steven required a continuous structured program in order to prevent significant regression. The record thus clearly supports, although it does not compel, the district court's assessment of the facts presented—"that Steven G. would suffer at least substantial regression without continuous, structured programming."

The district court carefully phrased its conclusion and, while it did not explicitly state that the educational program offered by the School District did not meet the "some educational benefit" standard of *Rowley*, the district court showed that it was aware of that decision and its judgment is therefore tantamount to such a conclusion. Hence, we hold that the district court applied the appropriate standard to the factual determinations supported by the record. The general injunctive relief granted by the court was appropriate to ensure that Steven receives the summer programming to which he is entitled under the Act.

The *Alamo Heights* decision is one of several decisions invalidating policies of denying summer programming. The landmark case on that issue was *Battle v. Commonwealth*.[9] That case was a class action in which the policy was struck down, but the individual complaints were remanded for case-by-case determination. The fact that post-*Rowley* decisions, such as *Alamo Heights*, have reached similar results emphasizes that the standard of appropriateness will sometimes require programming beyond the basic time frame of regular educational programming. These services are called extended school year (ESY) services. The IDEA's regulations now specifically require IEP teams to consider whether a child requires ESY services as part of the IEP process.[10] ESY services must be provided to the student if the team determines that such services are necessary to provide FAPE. The services must be provided at no cost to the parents.[11]

When deciding if a student requires ESY services, many states use a "regression and recoupment" standard that looks at the level of regression a student will incur without ESY services, and how difficult it will be for the student to recoup the information after the break from school.[12] Under this approach, students likely to experience severe, substantial, or significant regression that cannot be recouped within a reasonable period of time after school starts again are generally eligible for ESY services.[13]

It may be difficult to accomplish the least restrictive environment principles during summer programs because there are not programs for peers who do not have disabilities attending. There is little litigation on whether this is required, but at least one court has determined that educational agencies are not required to "provide extended year services to nondisabled students" in these situations.[14]

Summary

One of the major underlying principles of the IDEA is that special education and related services granted to students with disabilities must be appropriate. The term *appropriate*, however, can be highly subjective and evades precise definition. The Supreme Court made an attempt to define the term in its 1982 opinion in *Board of Education v. Rowley*. In that case, the Court held that a child was being provided an appropriate special education if the child was receiving personalized instruction with sufficient supportive services to permit the child to benefit from the instruction. In addition, the educational agency must have provided the program at public expense, the program must approximate the child's age-appropriate grade level, and the IEP must be complied with. The IDEA due process procedures must also be complied with. The Court was correct in anticipating that this standard would not always be easily applied to all situations. Numerous judicial opinions since the *Rowley* decision have continued to address these issues and found that appropriateness requires "meaningful educational benefit," which does not require the school to maximize the student's potential, but does require more than minimal progress.

While the IDEA does not require that the child's potential be maximized in order for the child to be viewed as receiving an appropriate education, it is within an individual state's discretion to adopt this or any other higher standard that is consistent with the IDEA. The Supreme Court's opinion in *Rowley* also indicated that substantial deference to the educational agency would be given in determining whether the child's program is appropriate. While it would seem that a substantial number of subsequent judicial opinions have deferred to the educational agency's programmatic recommendations, it is noteworthy that this deference has not been absolute.

Of the issues that have come under question within the requirement of appropriateness, one is the application and existence of policies that make no allowance for the individual needs of the child. Policies of providing only 180 days of school per year, for example, have consistently been struck down as invalid because of this reasoning. The revised IDEA language now provides for ESY services. Similar policies, such as providing only a certain number of hours of education per day, are likely to meet similar attack with equivalent results in the courts. The fact that such a policy is struck down, however, does not mean that every child with a disability who is affected by such policies is automatically eligible for the extended-year or extended-day programming. Entitlement to such programs is to be determined on an individual basis.

Questions for Reflection

1. What standard did the lower courts in *Rowley* apply?

2. What standard did the Supreme Court apply?

3. Will the *Rowley* standard work when applied to other types of cases, that is, when a student who is severely retarded is not placed in the regular program?

4. Did the fact that Amy Rowley was bright actually work to her detriment? What would happen if a child needed the interpreter to pass from grade to grade?

5. What happens if a child needs a particular service for which funds are not available?

6. Once a school develops an individualized education program, what role is left for the courts?

7. What standard of review are the courts to apply?

8. What is the burden of proof?

9. How likely is it that the educational agency's decision will be overridden by the courts?

10. What is the concern of the dissent in *Rowley*?

11. The Court indicated that protection for the child was available by virtue of the procedural safeguards, and the fact that parents do "not lack ardor in seeking to ensure that handicapped children receive all the benefits [of the Act]." This assumes that all parents are aware of their rights and have the means to pursue them. How valid is that assumption?

12. Ashley is 5 and autistic. The evaluations done by the parents' evaluators indicate that Ashley requires a full-day program in order to benefit from an educational program. In the state where Ashley resides, public kindergarten is currently provided, but only for half a day. Must the school provide a full-day program to Ashley?

NOTES

1. 20 U.S.C. § 1412(a)(1). See also Laura Rothstein & Julia Rothstein, *Disabilities and the Law* § 2:20 (Thomson West 2006).
2. 20 U.S.C. § 1412(a)(4).
3. 20 U.S.C. § 1401(9).
4. 674 F. Supp. 1296, 1303–1306 (W.D. 1987). Other states with higher standards include New Jersey (*Geis v. Board of Education*, 774 F.2d 575 (3d Cir. 1985)) and Massachusetts (*David D. v. Dartmouth School Committee*, 775 F.2d 411 (1st Cir. 1985)).
5. 720 F.2d 463, 446 (6th Cir. 1984).
6. 367 S.E.2d 738, 742 (Va. App. 1988).

7. 34 C.F.R. § 300.39(a)&(b); for more information about the changes to the IDEA since the *Rowley* decision, see Scott F. Johnson, "Reexaming *Rowley*: A New Focus in Special Education Law," 2 *BYU Education & Law Journal* 561 (2003).

8. See, e.g., *T.R. v. Kingwood*, 205 F.3d 572 (3d Cir. 2000); *Roland M. v. Concord School Comm.*, 915 F.2d 983, 991 (1st Cir. 1990).

9. 629 F.2d 269 (3d Cir. 1980), *cert. denied*, 449 U.S. 1109 (1981).

10. 34 C.F.R. § 300.106.

11. *Id.*

12. While most ESY services are provided over the summer break, they are not limited to summer break and can be provided during other breaks from school as well. See Assistance to States for the Education of Children With Disabilities and Preschool Grants for Children With Disabilities; Final Rule 71 Fed. Reg. 46582 (August 14, 2006).

13. For more information about ESY services and regression and recoupment standards, see Candace Cortiella, *Services Beyond the School Year for Students With IEPs*, available at http://www.greatschools.net/cgi-bin/showarticle/1210?cpn=20080409ld (last accessed July 10, 2008).

14. *Travis G. v. New Hope-Solebury School Dist.*, 544 F. Supp.2d 435, 443 (E.D. Pa. 2008).

10

Related Services

Related services are part of the free appropriate public education that must be available to all children with disabilities within the state in order for the state to be eligible for funding under the Individuals with Disabilities Education Act (IDEA). The child must need the services to benefit from special education. A child who needs no special education is not eligible for related services under the IDEA. The statute defines related services as

> transportation, and such developmental, corrective, and other supportive services (including speech-language pathology and audiology services, interpreting services, psychological services, physical and occupational therapy, recreation, including therapeutic recreation, social work services, school nurse services designed to enable a child with a disability to receive a free appropriate public education as described in the individualized education program of the child, counseling services, including rehabilitation counseling, orientation and mobility services, and medical services (except that such medical services shall be for diagnostic and evaluation purposes only) as may be required to assist a child with a disability to benefit from special education, and includes the early identification and assessment of disabling conditions in children.[1]

One issue that frequently becomes a point of contention about related services is the extent to which the provision of such services can impede the goal of full inclusion. For example, certain services such as physical therapy or health-related services may be administratively easier to provide in a setting that is more restrictive. It is not always easy in some cases to balance the mandate to have appropriate programming and appropriate related services with the least restrictive environment goal. Legal guidance on this issue is found in case law interpretation rather than directly in the statute or regulation.

Another problem that arises in the related service context is the problem of public agency and other provider responsibility. Many of the related services required by the IDEA are services that were provided by other agencies before passage of the IDEA. Some counseling services provided in residential settings for children with severe emotional involvement or certain kinds of therapy may have been previously provided by state agencies such as departments of health and human services and departments of welfare. Other health-related services were provided or at least paid for by family health insurance agencies, although changes in managed care have affected access to health insurance. The IDEA makes the state education agency the primary supervisor for the provision of related services that are required for the child to benefit from special education. State educational agencies must have the general supervisory role for coordinating service delivery by other agencies,[2] but the IDEA provides no real means to mandate that other agencies provide certain services. The IDEA states that it is not to be viewed as limiting "the responsibility of [other] agencies . . . from [providing or paying] for some or all of the costs of a free appropriate public education."[3] The IDEA requires the adoption of interagency agreements including a mechanism for resolving interagency disputes.[4]

The state education agencies often lack not only the authority but also the funding to provide all the services they are now responsible for. A number of states have developed workable plans for interagency cooperation and systems for funding. Some of these plans have developed through agency-initiated agreements, others by state legislative mandate. Where good interagency cooperation does not exist, agencies sometimes compete to provide certain types of inexpensive services and yet try to refuse responsibility for expensive services, particularly residential placements.

An increasingly common practice is that of educational agencies billing third-party payees for related services provided by school personnel. This and related problems affect cost issues discussed in Chapter 14, but there are some nonfinancial implications.

The following sections address some of the related services where legal questions arise.

Transportation

Schools are required by the IDEA to provide transportation necessary to bring the child with disabilities to and from school.[5] The issue of transportation is important because of the cost involved. Transportation includes travel to and from school, between schools, and in and around school buildings.[6] Schools must also provide specialized equipment if it is needed to transport the student. For example, the school may be required to purchase special lift equipment for a bus or other special equipment such as a van to ensure that the student can get to and from school and to benefit from school once the student is there. Many states supplement the IDEA-mandated transportation requirements regulating matters such as maximum amount of time in transit and location of bus stops.

A number of legal questions are raised in providing transportation. Many of these are not directly answered by the IDEA or its regulations, nor are they answered in judicial interpretation. These issues have often been debated at the administrative hearing level. It should be noted that the Americans with Disabilities Act (ADA) specifies that its transportation requirements do not apply to public school transportation and have limited applicability to private schools.

When Must Transportation Be Provided?

Under the IDEA, if a child needs transportation in order to benefit from special education, the service must be made available. Additionally, for students who are not eligible under the IDEA, where the school provides transportation to other children, the failure to provide a special lift or other method to transport the student in a wheelchair might be viewed as denial of a reasonable accommodation and thus violating Section 504 of the Rehabilitation Act and/or the ADA. It is not clear, however, whether the reasonable accommodation requirement of Section 504 and the ADA would mandate the purchase of expensive equipment. As mentioned previously, the IDEA requires the purchase of specialized equipment such as lifts, if the child requires transportation.

What if the child lives within a certain range where transportation is normally not provided? For example, what if a school district only normally provides transportation to children outside a 4-mile radius of a school? Must the school provide transportation? The sparse case law indicates that the school should provide transportation beyond the usual area of service.[7]

What about the child in a residential placement? Must the school provide transportation for the child to visit home and for parental visits to the placement site? Case law indicates that where parental visits are essential for developing interpersonal family relationships, the transportation cost of these visits must be compensated.[8]

What Is the Extent of Transportation Service?

The requirements relating to the location of bus stops, the time in transit, and the degree of assistance required are not specifically covered by federal law. Many state and local agencies have adopted and implemented regulations and guidelines on these matters. Whether there are regulatory guidelines or not, limits can and should be specified in the individualized education plan (IEP).

Unusual instances of liability can result when appropriate safety measures relating to bus stops are not taken. In one case, the school was found liable to the driver of a car for emotional trauma when she struck and killed a 4-year-old deaf child. The bus driver had not taken proper care to ensure the child reached safety after letting the child off the bus.[9] Negligent selection of transportation personnel might also be the basis of liability, in cases where the schools are not protected by the immunity defense.[10]

One question not clearly answered by the IDEA is whether, when transportation is provided, it must be door to door, and if so what is meant by door to door. If a child is unable to get to the regular bus stop, door-to-door transport is probably required.[11] But what is meant by *door to door?*

For children living in high-rise buildings, it means that parents have the responsibility of getting the child to the curbside location and meeting the child at the end of the day. To require the driver to take a child to the door of an 11th-floor apartment is probably outside what is contemplated by the IDEA. This would require that the driver leave other children unattended, or the school would have to provide additional personnel to assist. Although the IDEA may not mandate such service, state or local regulations or the IEP may do so. The *Hurry v. Jones* decision in the next section offers two views of this issue.

Excessive time in transit can be damaging to a student's level of energy, ability to concentrate, and so forth. For that reason it is important in developing an IEP to take this into account and to designate the amount of time to be spent on the bus. The *Hendricks* decision in Chapter 11 illustrates judicial recognition of this concern.

Parent-Provided Transportation

Where the parent is providing transportation as a matter of preference and the school has made available appropriate transportation services, the school need not reimburse the parents. Because special education and related services are to be provided at no cost to the child's family, the school is required to reimburse parents for transportation costs necessitated by the school's failure to provide appropriate transportation or where the parents and school agree to parent-provided transportation in lieu of school-provided service.[12] As the following decision demonstrates, the parents' recovery may not necessarily be limited to out-of-pocket expenses.

HURRY V. JONES

734 F.2d 879 (1st Cir. 1984)

Defendants/appellants, who are school and transportation officials in Providence, appeal from a decision . . . awarding damages to George Hurry, a physically and mentally handicapped minor, and to his parents. The district court found that appellants' failure to provide George with door-to-door transportation to and from school violated both the Education for All Handicapped Children Act of 1975 (EAHCA) and the Rehabilitation Act of 1973. The court awarded $14,546.00 under the EAHCA and $5,000.00 under section 504 of the Rehabilitation Act; appellants challenge both awards.

George Hurry (George) suffers from cerebral palsy and a degree of mental retardation, and is confined to a wheelchair by spastic quadriplegia. He has attended various special education programs in the Providence area. Until January 1976 the City of Providence provided him with door-to-door bus transportation to and from school. By January of 1976, however, George had reached a weight of 160 pounds, and the bus drivers deemed it unsafe to continue to carry him up and down the steep concrete steps that led from his front door to the street. Mr. and Mrs. Hurry began to transport George to and from school in their van.

Starting in June 1976 Mr. Hurry held a position that required him to work until 5:15 P.M. each day. Because Mrs. Hurry could not lift George from the van and carry him up the steps without her husband's aid, he had to wait in the car for several hours each day until Mr. Hurry left work. He frequently missed school when the weather was too hot or too cold to permit him to wait in the van. In December of 1977, Mr. and Mrs. Hurry stopped transporting him to school; George did not attend school again until the fall of 1979.

The Hurrys discussed their transportation problem with the Providence School Department, but the parties were unable to reach a satisfactory solution. Plans to construct a permanent wheelchair ramp at the Hurrys' home failed when the Mayor's office refused to provide public funding for the project unless multiple liens on the property were discharged. The Hurrys refused the School Department's offer of home instruction for George because they believed that this instruction would not provide their son with the "least restrictive environment" available. In September of 1978 the Rhode Island Protection and Advocacy System (RIPAS) requested that the Providence School Department conduct a hearing on the Hurrys' problem. When the School Department did not respond to the request within the statutory time limit, RIPAS contacted the State Commissioner of Education on November 7, 1978, to request a hearing. This second request likewise failed to produce the statutorily required hearing, and RIPAS filed this action in the Hurrys' behalf on December 19, 1978. By October 29, 1979, the parties had agreed on an Individual Educational Program for George that provided him with transportation to and from school and obviated the need for injunctive relief.*

RIPAS withdrew from the action at this point, but the Hurrys pursued claims for damages for the period during which George attended school only if they were able to transport him and for the period during which he did not attend school at all.

The Hurrys based their claims for damages on the EAHCA, the Rehabilitation Act, [and other statutes and constitutional provisions]. The court found, and the parties do not dispute, that further pursuit of administrative remedies would have been futile, and that the action was properly before the court. [Authors' Note: The court denied recovery under some statutory and constitutional provisions that the Hurrys did not contest.] The court did award damages under the EAHCA and the Rehabilitation Act, and defendants challenge these awards on appeal.

I. Damages Under the Education for All Handicapped Children Act

The EAHCA provides that a state receiving federal assistance for education of the handicapped must assure "all handicapped children the right to a free appropriate public education." The Act further provides that parties aggrieved by decisions affecting a handicapped child's education may bring a civil action in state or federal court, and that the court hearing such an action may grant "such relief as the court determines is appropriate."

(Continued)

---

* The initial solution was for the school bus to pick George up at his home before his father left for work so that Mr. Hurry could carry him down the steps, and to transport George to another school in the afternoon where he could wait in comfort until his father left work and took him home. Ultimately, Mrs. Hurry's mother purchased an adjoining property with a sloping driveway, and the Hurrys were able to wheel George out the back door of their house and down the driveway to meet the school bus.

Appellants argue that the Hurrys had a duty to "mitigate damages" by helping to engineer an appropriate solution to the problem at an earlier date. We note that this theory is doubtful at best; but since it was never raised before the district court, we decline to address it on appeal.

(Continued)

A number of courts have interpreted the relief provision of the EAHCA as being limited to injunctive remedies, and have held that damages are not recoverable under the Act absent exceptional circumstances.

At the time the district court reached its decision, this circuit subscribed to the . . . view that reimbursement is available to parties aggrieved by violations of the EAHCA only in exceptional circumstances. We have since adopted a more expansive view of reimbursement under the EAHCA, allowing reimbursement of interim educational and related expenses even when the "exceptional circumstances" . . . are not present. Under this approach, it is clear that the district court correctly found that the Hurrys are entitled to reimbursement under the EAHCA for the interim transportation services they provided until the parties agreed on an appropriate Individual Educational Program for George. . . .

The district court made three separate damage awards to the Hurrys under the EAHCA. First, it reimbursed Mr. and Mrs. Hurry $1,150.00 for the out-of-pocket expense of driving George to school. It calculated this expense by multiplying the 92 school weeks in 1976 and 1977 during which the School Department failed to supply transportation by Mr. Hurry's $12.50 estimate of the weekly cost he incurred in transporting George himself. The parties did not contest this portion of the award, so we have no need to address it on appeal. Second, the court awarded the Hurrys $4,600.00 for their contributed services in driving George to and from school. It arrived at this figure by compensating the Hurrys at a rate of $10.00 per day for the 92 five-day school weeks during which the Hurrys transported George themselves. Third, the court awarded George $8,796.00 for the period from January 1978 until June 1979 during which he did not attend school at all. This award represented "the amount Defendants were not required to expend" on George's education, an amount the court calculated by multiplying the average per pupil cost for special education during the relevant period by the number of months George was absent. Appellants did not challenge the district court's method of computing damages; instead, they contend that the award to the Hurrys for contributed services and the award to George were improper.

The award of $4,600.00 for Mr. and Mrs. Hurry's contributed services in driving George to school requires us to determine whether the reimbursement available under the EAHCA is limited to out-of-pocket expenses, or whether it may also include compensation for the expenditure of time and effort. We see no reason why the latter type of expense should not be reimbursed, except for the possibility that, when reimbursement is given for the monetary equivalent of time and effort, excessive payments might be made. To the extent that this could occur, the distinction between "reimbursement" and "damages" would be blurred. Here, however, we are considering the district court's award of $10.00 per day for two daily round trips of ten to fifteen miles, taking several hours of the Hurrys' time. This is obviously a bare-bones figure, well within any reasonable estimate of fair reimbursement. Moreover, it cannot be argued that the service in question—transporting George to and from school—called for any special skill or training that the Hurrys lacked.

It is clear that if the Hurrys had hired a private agency to drive George to and from school, this expense would have been reimbursable under the EAHCA, just as the expense of placing George in a private school would have been reimbursable had the School Department wrongfully declined to provide him with an appropriate public education. The fact that the Hurrys performed the service themselves rather than hiring someone else to perform it should not bar them from recovering the reasonable value of their time and effort.

The $4,600.00 award to the Hurrys also requires us to consider whether they waived their right to reimbursement by engaging in "self-help" rather than seeking court approval for the action that gave rise to their claim for reimbursement. In this case, the Hurrys . . . undertook to transport the child to the school where the School Department had placed him. Under these circumstances, we do not believe that the Hurrys' self-help should bar their recovery. We affirm the award of $4,600.00. [The court denied compensation for the time George was not in school and denied recovery under the Rehabilitation Act.]

Dissent

I concur in those portions of the opinion that deny recovery, but cannot in the part ordering reimbursement for transportation. I am sorry to dissent over what, in dollars and cents, is not a large matter, but I feel I must because, with great respect, I believe the court, in declining to face a dispositive issue, is being basically unfair. Both to demonstrate the unfairness, and the consequence to defendants, I first consider the merits, viz., that in spite of a regulation calling for transportation of handicapped children from and to their street-level front door, defendants have been charged with additional burdens due to the fact that plaintiffs' front door was twelve damaged steps above the street.

The district court found,

> Bus drivers for the school department would carry George from the front door of his home down approximately twelve steps to the street level and into the bus. By January of 1976, however, George had gained weight and was so heavy (160 lbs.) that the bus drivers would no longer carry him. In addition to the child being over-weight, the concrete steps were steep and cracked in some places, making it somewhat unsafe for anyone to attempt to carry George down to the street.

According to defendants' witness's uncontradicted testimony,

> The stairs were extremely steep. The stairs were broken and uneven in places . . . [The] regulations said street level . . . [The supervisor] came back to me and said nobody will accept the liability of carrying George Hurry, with all his problems, who also has an obesity problem, for fear they might fall and there might be some legal ramification.

(Continued)

(Continued)

The underlying statute, Education for All Handicapped Children Act (EAHCA), 20 U.S.C. §§ 1413(a)(4)(B) and 1401(17), required furnishing, simply, "transportation." The Rhode Island regulation, which the court quoted, and considered, spelt this out, one with respect to transportation generally ("door to door") and one specifically with regard to assistance, manifestly defining what was meant by "door."

1.0. Responsibility—All handicapped children who need special transportation as a related service and as determined by the evaluation process and described in the I.E.P. shall be provided such service. It shall include free transportation to and from the home (door to door, if necessary) to the educational program in which he/she is enrolled. . . .

2.0. Transportation Needs of Handicapped Children.

2.1.2. A minimum of one aide assigned to each bus. Such aide, in addition to providing general care and supervision of all handicapped children on such bus, shall also provide assistance (from street level entrance of dwelling) to such children lacking the mobility to leave the home and board transportation vehicles, and shall further assist such children in debarking the vehicle and entering the school.

The district court found these regulations "clear," and that, in failing to arrange for George's reaching the street level, defendants "ignored their obvious duty." I find them clear, but just the reverse. In my opinion "street level" means exactly what it says, and the court, although recognizing, ante, that the door was above the street level, excised from the regulation, without even discussion, precisely what had caused all the difficulties.

My brethren feel that because defendants did not attack it, the district court's interpretation is the law of the case. Before reaching that question, I must first consider whether the ruling was wrong. I believe it plainly so. If anything seems clear, it is that there is a difference in kind between a street level entrance from which, if need be, a physically handicapped child may be taken in a wheelchair, or otherwise safely guided by the bus attendant, and the door twelve dangerous steps up, requiring a special attendant, or possibly two, and the risk of a substantial claim for negligence if anything goes wrong.

This decision and the dissent highlight some of the challenges for public schools in determining the limits of responsibility. The decision incorporated state law requirements, so it is not clear what would be required under the IDEA.

Disciplinary Problems

What happens when a child's behavior is such that if the child were not disabled, the child would be suspended from riding the bus? Can a special education student ever be suspended from transportation services? Case law suggests that if the behavior relates to the disability, complete withdrawal of service is not permitted. It may be that the school needs to change the mode of transportation, or provide supervision or monitoring on the bus to address the behavioral issues. Homebound instruction might be required pending resolution of disciplinary matters in some cases. There is an exception in the IDEA for short-term emergency situations where immediate threat to safety is involved. And in such emergency situations, a prompt meeting of the IEP team should address the issue and make appropriate recommendations. The issue of discipline in all contexts is discussed more fully in Chapter 16.

Psychological Services and Counseling

"Psychological services" and "counseling" are specifically included in the IDEA as related services.[13] Counseling about hearing loss, as well as speech and language disorders for both the child and the family, is within the related service mandate.[14] Providing information to parents about child development and helping them acquire skills to allow them to support the implementation of their child's IEP is also required.[15] Specific psychological services to be provided also include assessing the child and using the information to develop an appropriate learning program as well as a program of counseling if needed.[16] Individual and family counseling are also contemplated under the heading of "social work services" that would be included as related services.[17]

Because of the expense involved in providing some psychological and counseling services, a number of cases have addressed this issue. The general result in those cases is that where the service is so related to the special educational program that it is necessary if the student is to benefit from special education, the service must be provided at the school's expense.[18] This issue will be discussed in more detail in Chapter 12 on out-of-district and private school placements. In the following case, the court addresses the issue of whether the parents may be compensated for counseling services performed by a psychiatrist.

MAX M. V. ILLINOIS STATE BOARD OF EDUCATION

629 F. Supp. 1504 (N.D. Ill. 1986)

Max M. attended New Trier West, a public high school in Northfield, Illinois, from 1977 to 1981. Because of his disorganization, difficulty in writing, and anxiety, his academic performance was poor. In January of Max's freshman year, Max was referred to New Trier's Department of Special Education for evaluation. Max was examined by New Trier's consultant, Dr. Traisman, who later issued a written report recommending long-term "intensive psychotherapy" for Max. Although the parents and Dr. Traisman believed that Max should be seen by a male therapist, no male therapists were provided by New Trier for Max during his freshman year.

New Trier recommended to Max' parents that he be placed in two special education classes for the remainder of his freshman year, but the Ms rejected this recommendation as too drastic. Instead, a compromise was reached allowing Max to spend one hour a day in a resource room where a student is allowed to work individually with a teacher on a particular subject.

(Continued)

(Continued)

Shortly thereafter, New Trier again proposed that Max be enrolled in a special education math class, and this time the parents agreed. Max' first semester freshman grades in his major subject were four Ds. After a special education component was implemented during Max' second semester, Max received three Cs and one D in his major subjects.

During the summer following his freshman year, Max attended summer school at New Trier. The Ms met with representatives of New Trier that summer to discuss Max, and the Ms formally requested that their son receive psychotherapy from Frank Brull, a New Trier social worker. Also during that summer, Max saw a private psychotherapist, Dr. Burg, for four sessions.

New Trier developed an Individual Education Program (IEP) for Max to commence in September of his sophomore year. The IEP included one special education class, attendance in the resource room three days a week, and four standard courses in which Max was to be mainstreamed with the general student body. This IEP was shown to the Ms sometime in late November. Although the IEP did not so state, Max was also offered psychotherapy twice a week by New Trier social worker, Frank Brull. Max, however, failed to attend his therapy sessions with Mr. Brull on a regular basis. By the end of his sophomore year, Max' academic and social behavior had shown serious deterioration. Max received a D in the class he took during the summer between his freshman and sophomore year and received three Cs and two Fs in his first semester sophomore year. During his second semester, Max received three Ds and one F.

On May 30, 1979, New Trier recommended that Max attend the Central Campus Learning Center (CCLC), New Trier's off-campus facility designed for emotionally disturbed or behavior disordered students. In the CCLC a core teacher is assigned to each student and acts as instructor in most if not all the classes in which the student is enrolled. Students at the CCLC have no unsupervised time. Between 1979 and 1981, the maximum number of students attending CCLC at any one time was forty, and the average class size was eight.

On July 6, 1979, Max began receiving psychotherapy from Dr. Robert Rosenfeld, a psychiatrist. Aside from providing psychotherapy for Max, the Ms relied on Dr. Rosenfeld for input for Max' junior year placement. In that regard Rosenfeld first met with New Trier personnel on August 6, 1979 to discuss the proposed CCLC placement for Max' junior year. Rosenfeld informed the Ms that the CCLC placement could not be made without their knowledge and permission. Although Rosenfeld and the Ms discussed the possibility of a residential placement for Max, they all agreed not to pursue this option.

New Trier called a second meeting on August 20, 1979 to discuss Max' junior year placement. In addition to Dr. Rosenfeld, Dr. Wolter, New Trier's Director of Special Education, as well as the Ms, were in attendance. At this meeting, the CCLC placement for Max' junior year was approved by the parties. Rosenfeld felt the CCLC placement was a reasonable next step in addressing some of the problems Max had experienced in the larger setting of New Trier West. The Ms were informed by Dr. Wolter that if the CCLC placement did not work out, a due process hearing could occur.

A specific Individualized Education Plan (IEP) was prepared for Max naming Judy Knox as Max' core instructor. Knox observed that when Max first arrived at the CCLC, he seemed afraid to socialize with the other students, but as the year progressed he became much more socially interactive with his fellow classmates. At the end of his first semester at CCLC, Max received one A, two Bs, and one C. At the end of his second semester, Max received three As and one B. Max' scholastic improvement was a result of certain modifications in the regular CCLC program which enabled Max to succeed academically despite his insistence on not performing written work. Max was held accountable for work that he did not perform. The Ms received several low scholarship notices during his junior year explaining that Max was not completing his assigned work. Max' classroom behavior also showed improvement by the end of his junior year.

Aside from the educational component of Max' IEP, Max received group therapy at CCLC. Although family therapy sessions were to be provided by New Trier for the Ms, time conflicts with scheduling eventually led to a mutual agreement to discontinue the sessions. During Max' junior year, Dr. Rosenfeld was also providing private psychotherapy for Max at the Ms' expense. From July of 1979 to January of 1980, Rosenfeld saw Max twice a week. Thereafter he saw Max once a week. This reduction in sessions per week was due to the Ms' financial constraints.

Rosenfeld discussed Max' senior year placement with the Ms and a decision was reached allowing Max to continue at CCLC. Max' senior year IEP was discussed with the Ms in a conference on October 20, 1980 with New Trier. Ms. Knox noticed that Max began to socialize and interact more successfully with his classmates during his senior year. However, Max began to experience problems academically. During his first semester senior year, Max received one C, two Ds, and two Fs. Second semester senior year, Max received two Cs and three Ds. Although Ms. Knox felt that Max met the minimal expectations that she had for him in every class, she agreed that Max had many of the same problems at the end of his senior year as at the beginning of his junior year. Max' weakening academic performance was reflected to the Ms through a series of low scholarship notices. The notices universally cited Max' lack of preparation and failure to complete assigned work.

By the end of Max' senior year he had earned more than the required amount of credits to graduate and was ranked 455 out of 546 students in the senior class. On May 15, 1981, the Ms filed a request for a due process hearing. Because of financial considerations, the Ms decided to discontinue Max' psychotherapy from Dr. Rosenfeld on June 16, 1981, and concentrate their resources on the due process hearing. The Ms expended a total of $8,855 for Max' private psychiatric care while he attended New Trier and CCLC.

Max graduated on June 11, 1981. Both Max and his parents rejected the idea of continuing at CCLC during the pendency of the due process hearing. Instead, the Ms wanted a different special education program combining advanced academic work, vocational training, and therapy. No such special education program was offered by New Trier. In September of 1982, the Ms enrolled Max at Brehm Preparatory School, a residential facility for learning disabled and behavior disordered children. After several months of attendance at Brehm, Max developed acute psychiatric problems and was hospitalized at Hartgrove Hospital. Max was discharged to the Ridgeview Shelter Care Facility in Evanston, Illinois, on October 10, 1983, and received outpatient psychotherapy from Dr. Gary Phillips, a clinical psychologist. The Ms spend between $16,000 and $17,000 to place Max at Brehm and incurred approximately $3,500 in fees from Dr. Phillips.

(Continued)

(Continued)

Meanwhile, on October 13, 1981, Dr. Robert Monks conducted the due process hearing requested by the Ms. On October 16, 1981, Dr. Monks issued a decision revoking Max' graduation and ordering that services be continued and that an appropriate IEP be prepared. New Trier promptly appealed the Monks' decision and on February 12, 1982, the Illinois State Board of Education (ISBE) issued an Administrative Order reversing the hearing officer's decision. Both the hearing officer's opinion and the ISBE's Administrative Order found that Max had been denied an appropriate education with related services because New Trier failed to provide Max with the intensive psychotherapy recommended by the school district's psychologist, Dr. Thraisman. The ISBE order reversing the hearing officer's decision to revoke Max's diploma and continue services was based on an alleged pleading defect on the part of the Ms.

On October 26, 1982, the Ms filed their complaint in this Court. Although the Ms' initial complaint challenged the ISBE order on various federal and state statutory and constitutional provisions, this Court's four prior decisions limited the Ms' complaint to two basic claims under the EAHCA: (1) reimbursement from Local Defendants of the $8,855 expended by the Ms for Max' psychiatric treatment while attending New Trier; and (2) compensatory remedial educational services from all defendants to compensate Max for the alleged deprivation of EAHCA benefits while he attended New Trier and an injunction revoking Max' diploma to reestablish his eligibility under the EAHCA. [The lengthy opinion in this case covered a number of issues. Only the portion relating to the related services is included.]

Although the EAHCA is interpreted to include psychotherapy as a related service school districts must provide, limitations exist on required medical services. Specifically, services provided by a licensed physician are limited to diagnosis and evaluation. Due to the Local Defendants' failure to apprise the Ms of their rights under the EAHCA and provide Max with the psychotherapy he was identified as entitled to receive, this Court ruled that the Ms' uninformed selection of a psychiatrist would not bar their claim for reimbursement.

The EAHCA's limitation on physician provided services was held to reflect a conscious effort on the part of Congress to limit costs by requiring a school district to provide only the minimum level of health care personnel recognized as legally and professionally competent to perform an EAHCA required service. Since many of the enumerated "related services" under the EAHCA could be provided by a physician or nonphysician, this Court reasoned that Congress intended to limit the nature of the services required rather than the personnel who provided the service. In that line of reasoning this Court held that where a school district failed to provide services required under the EAHCA and failed to properly inform the deprived EAHCA recipients of their right to seek review, the school district would be liable to reimburse the deprived recipients for the cost of privately obtained required services, even if a physician provided the services. Reimbursement for these physician rendered related services were subject to certain limitations. Specifically, the school district could be held liable for no more than the cost of the service as provided by the minimum level health care provider recognized as competent to perform the related service. The liability of the school district in such a case would be computed from the amount that such qualified personnel would normally and reasonably charge for the EAHCA services obtained privately by the deprived party. Thus, if the deprived party is not fully reimbursed, then the portion of the cost the deprived party must incur is the cost of exercising the freedom to select a special care provider. . . .

Max M. III [592 F. Supp. 437 (N.D. Ill. 1984)] represented an effort to reconcile the EAHCA's requirement that each child receive an appropriate and free public education including related services with the EAHCA's limitations on expenditures for medical services. To abandon the limitation on reimbursement for physician rendered related services in *Max M. III* would require this Court to completely ignore the clear language of the statute which limits medical services to diagnosis and evaluation. *Burlington* simply cannot be read to encompass the question of physician administered related services decided in *Max M. III.* [Authors' Note: The *Burlington* case is included in Chapter 21.] Thus, the Ms' motion for reconsideration as to the reimbursement limitation imposed in *Max M. III* is denied.

Health Services

School health services and school nurse services are specifically included under the IDEA as related services.[19] They are also specifically defined in the IDEA's regulations as "health services that are designed to enable a child with a disability to receive FAPE as described in the child's IEP."[20] School nurse services must be provided by a qualified school nurse. School health services may be provided by the school nurse or by another qualified person.[21]

Some students with disabilities may require health services at school, but may not be eligible for services under the IDEA. For example, a child with asthma might need assistance in the use of a respirator or a child with allergies might require assistance with administering medication during school hours. That child might not need special education. Although such services would not be covered under the IDEA, it is likely that Section 504 of the Rehabilitation Act and/or the ADA would require that such services be provided as a reasonable accommodation in order to allow that child to participate in school. Most of the cases, however, have relied on the IDEA for a discussion of when the education agency must provide health services.

One of the early cases decided by the Supreme Court under the IDEA related to health services. The service at issue was catheterization, and the question was whether it was a medical service not required under the IDEA or whether it was a related health service.

IRVING INDEPENDENT SCHOOL DISTRICT V. TATRO

468 U.S. 883 (1984)

Chief Justice Burger delivered the opinion of the Court.

We granted certiorari to determine whether the Education of the Handicapped Act or the Rehabilitation Act of 1973 requires a school district to provide a handicapped child with clean intermittent catheterization during school hours.

I

Amber Tatro is an 8-year-old girl born with a defect known as spina bifida. As a result, she suffers from orthopedic and speech impairments and a neurogenic bladder, which prevents her from emptying her bladder voluntarily. Consequently, she must be catheterized every three or four hours to avoid injury to her kidneys. In accordance with accepted medical practice, clean intermittent catheterization (CIC), a procedure involving the insertion of a catheter into the urethra to drain the bladder, has been prescribed. The procedure is a simple one that may be performed in a few minutes by a layperson with less than an hour's training. Amber's parents, babysitter, and teenage brother are all qualified to administer CIC, and Amber soon will be able to perform this procedure herself.

In 1979 petitioner Irving Independent School District agreed to provide special education for Amber, who was then three and one-half years old. In consultation with her parents, who are respondents here, petitioner developed an individualized education program for Amber under the requirements of the Education for All Handicapped Children Act of 1975. The individualized education program provided that Amber would attend early childhood development classes and receive special services such as physical and occupational therapy. That program, however, made no provision for school personnel to administer CIC. Respondents unsuccessfully pursued administrative remedies to secure CIC services for Amber during school hours. In October 1979 respondents brought the present action in District Court against petitioner, the State Board of Education, and others. They sought an injunction ordering petition[er] to provide Amber with CIC and sought damages and attorney's fees. . . . [Lower court proceedings omitted.]

II

This case poses two separate issues. The first is whether the Education of the Handicapped Act requires petitioner to provide CIC services to Amber. The second is whether Section 504 of the Rehabilitation Act creates such an obligation. We first turn to the claim presented under the Education of the Handicapped Act.

States receiving funds under the Act are obliged to satisfy certain conditions. A primary condition is that the state implement a policy "that assures all handicapped children the right to a free appropriate public education." . . .

A "free appropriate public education" is explicitly defined as "special education and related services." "Related services" are defined as

> transportation, and such development corrective, and other *supportive services (including* speech pathology and audiology, psychological services, physical and occupational therapy, recreation and *medical* and counseling *services, except that such medical services shall be for*

diagnostic and evaluation purposes only) as may be required to assist a handicapped child to benefit from special education, and includes the early identification and assessment of handicapping conditions in children.

The issue in this case is whether CIC is a "related service" that petitioner is obliged to provide to Amber. We must answer two questions: first, whether CIC is a "supportive servic[e] . . . required to assist a handicapped child to benefit from special education"; and second, whether CIC is excluded from this definition as a "medical servic[e]" serving purposes other than diagnosis or evaluation.

A

The Court of Appeals was clearly correct in holding that the CIC is a "supportive servic[e] . . . required to assist a handicapped child to benefit from special education." It is clear on this record that, without having CIC services available during the school day, Amber cannot attend school and thereby "benefit from special education." CIC services therefore fall squarely within the definition of "supportive services."

As we have stated before, "Congress sought primarily to make public education available to handicapped children" and "to make such access meaningful." A service that enables a handicapped child to remain at school during the day is an important means of providing the child with the meaningful access to education that Congress envisioned. The Act makes specific provision for services, like transportation, for example, that do no more than enable a child to be physically present in class, and the Act specifically authorizes grants for schools to alter buildings and equipment to make them accessible to the handicapped. Services like CIC that permit a child to remain at school during the day are no less related to the effort to educate than are services that enable the child to reach, enter, or exit the school.

We hold that CIC services in this case qualify as a "supportive servic[e] . . . required to assist a handicapped child to benefit from special education."

B

We also agree with the Court of Appeals that provision of CIC is not a "medical servic[e]," which a school is required to provide only for purposes of diagnosis or evaluation. We begin with the regulations of the Department of Education, which are entitled to deference. The regulations define "related services" for handicapped children to include "school health services," which are defined in turn as "services provided by a qualified school nurse or other qualified person." "Medical services" are defined as "services provided by a licensed physician." Thus, the Secretary has determined that the services of a school nurse otherwise qualifying as a "related service" are not subject to exclusion as a "medical service," but that the services of a physician are excludable as such.

This definition of "medical services" is a reasonable interpretation of congressional intent. Although Congress devoted little discussion to the "medical services" exclusion, the Secretary could reasonably have concluded that it was designed to spare schools from an obligation to provide a service that might well prove unduly expensive and beyond the range of the competence. From this understanding of congressional purpose, the Secretary could reasonably have concluded that Congress intended to impose the obligation to provide school nursing services.

(Continued)

(Continued)

Congress plainly required schools to hire various specially trained personnel to help handicapped children, such as "trained occupational therapists, speech therapists, psychologists, social workers and other appropriately trained personnel." School nurses have long been a part of the educational system, and the Secretary could therefore reasonably conclude that school nursing services are not the sort of burden that Congress intended to exclude as a "medical service." By limiting the "medical service" exclusion to services of a physician or hospital, both far more expensive, the Secretary has given a permissible construction to the provision.

Petitioner's contrary interpretation of the "medical services" exclusion is unconvincing. In petitioner's view, CIC is a "medical service," even though it may be provided by a nurse or trained layperson; that conclusion rests on its reading of Texas law that confines CIC to uses in accordance with a physician's prescription and under a physician's ultimate supervision. Aside from conflicting with the Secretary's reasonable interpretation of congressional intent, however, such a rule would be anomalous. Nurses in petitioner's school district are authorized to dispense oral medication and administer emergency injections in accordance with a physician's prescription. This kind of service for nonhandicapped children is difficult to distinguish from the provision of CIC to the handicapped. It would be strange indeed if Congress, in attempting to extend special services to handicapped children, were unwilling to guarantee them services of a kind that are routinely provided to the nonhandicapped.

To keep in perspective the obligation to provide services that relate to both the health and educational needs of handicapped students, we note several limitations that should minimize the burden petitioner fears. First, to be entitled to related services, a child must be handicapped so as to require special education. In the absence of a handicap that requires special education, the need for what otherwise might qualify as a related service does not create an obligation under the Act.

Second, only those services necessary to aid a handicapped child to benefit from special education must be provided, regardless how easily a school nurse or layperson could furnish them. For example, if a particular medication or treatment may appropriately be administered to a handicapped child other than during the school day, a school is not required to provide nursing services to administer it.

Third, the regulations state that school nursing services must be provided only if they can be performed by a nurse or other qualified person, not if they must be performed by a physician. It bears mentioning that here not even the services of a nurse are required; as is conceded a layperson with minimal training is qualified to provide CIC.

Finally, we note that respondents are not asking petitioner to provide *equipment* that Amber needs for CIC. They seek only the *services* of a qualified person at the school.

We conclude that the provision of CIC to Amber is not subject to exclusion as a "medical service," and we affirm the Court of Appeals' holding that CIC is a "related service" under the Education of the Handicapped Act.

The *Tatro* decision left open a number of questions, some of which were addressed in the following decision.

CEDAR RAPIDS COMMUNITY SCHOOL DISTRICT V. GARRET F.

526 U.S. 66 (1999)

Justice Stevens delivered the opinion of the Court.

The Individuals with Disabilities Education Act (IDEA), was enacted, in part, "to assure that all children with disabilities have available to them . . . a free appropriate public education which emphasizes special education and related services designed to meet their unique needs." Consistent with this purpose, the IDEA authorizes federal financial assistance to States that agree to provide disabled children with special education and "related services." The question presented § 1401 in this case is whether the definition of "related services" in § 1401(a)(17) [Now § 1401(26)] requires a public school district in a participating State to provide a ventilator-dependent student with certain nursing services during school hours.

I

Respondent Garret F. is a friendly, creative, and intelligent young man. When Garret was four years old, his spinal column was severed in a motorcycle accident. Though paralyzed from the neck down, his mental capacities were unaffected. He is able to speak, to control his motorized wheelchair through use of a puff and suck straw, and to operate a computer with a device that responds to head movements. Garret is currently a student in the Cedar Rapids Community School District (District), he attends regular classes in a typical school program, and his academic performance has been a success. Garret is, however, ventilator dependent, and therefore requires a responsible individual nearby to attend to certain physical needs while he is in school.*

During Garret's early years at school his family provided for his physical care during the school day. When he was in kindergarten, his 18-year-old aunt attended him; in the next four years, his family used settlement proceeds they received after his accident, their insurance, and other resources to employ a licensed practical nurse. In 1993, Garret's mother requested the District to accept financial responsibility for the health care services that Garret requires during the school day. The District denied the request, believing that it was not legally obligated to provide continuous one-on-one nursing services.

(Continued)

* He needs assistance with urinary bladder catheterization once a day, the suctioning of his tracheotomy tube as needed, but at least once every six hours, with food and drink at lunchtime, in getting into a reclining position for five minutes of each hour, and ambu bagging occasionally as needed when the ventilator is checked for proper functioning. He also needs assistance from someone familiar with his ventilator in the event there is a malfunction or electrical problem, and someone who can perform emergency procedures in the event he experiences autonomic hyperreflexia. [Explanation of this condition omitted.]

(Continued)

[Administrative proceedings omitted. The administrative judge concluded that the IDEA required the District to bear financial responsibility for all of the services in dispute, including continuous nursing services. The district and appellate court agreed with the administrative decision. These proceedings are omitted.]

II

The District contends that § 1401(a)(17) [Now § 1401(26)] does not require it to provide Garret with "continuous one-on-one nursing services" during the school day, even though Garret cannot remain in school without such care. However, the IDEA's definition of "related services," our decision in *Irving Independent School District v. Tatro,* 468 U.S. 883 (1984), and the overall statutory scheme all support the decision of the Court of Appeals.

The text of the "related services" definition, broadly encompasses those supportive services that "may be required to assist a child with a disability to benefit from special education." As we have already noted, the District does not challenge the Court of Appeals' conclusion that the in-school services at issue are within the covered category of "supportive services." As a general matter, services that enable a disabled child to remain in school during the day provide the student with "the meaningful access to education that Congress envisioned."

This general definition of "related services" is illuminated by a parenthetical phrase listing examples of particular services that are included within the statute's coverage, § 1401(a)(17) [Now § 1401(26)]. "Medical services" are enumerated in this list, but such services are limited to those that are "for diagnostic and evaluation purposes." The statute does not contain a more specific definition of the "medical services" that are excepted from the coverage of § 1401(a)(17).

The scope of the "medical services" exclusion is not a matter of first impression in this Court. In *Tatro* we concluded that the Secretary of Education had reasonably determined that the term "medical services" referred only to services that must be performed by a physician, and not to school health services. Accordingly, we held that a specific form of health care (clean intermittent catherization) that is often, though not always, performed by a nurse is not an excluded medical service. We referenced the likely cost of the services and the competence of school staff as justifications for drawing a line between physician and other services, but our endorsement of that line was unmistakable. It is thus settled that the phrase "medical services" in § 1401(a)(17) does not embrace all forms of care that might loosely be described as "medical" in other contexts, such as a claim for an income tax deduction.

Based on certain policy letters issued by the Department of Education, it seems that the Secretary's post-*Tatro* view of the statute has not been entirely clear. We may assume that the Secretary has authority under the IDEA to adopt regulations that define the "medical services" exclusion by more explicitly taking into account the nature and extent of the requested services; and the Secretary surely has the authority to enumerate the services that are, and are not, fairly included within the scope of § 1407(a)(17). But the Secretary has done neither; and, in this Court, she advocates affirming the judgment of the Court of Appeals. We obviously have no authority to rewrite the regulations, and we see no sufficient reason to revise *Tatro,* either.

The District does not ask us to define the term so broadly. Indeed, the District does not argue that any of the items of care that Garret needs, considered individually, could be excluded from the scope of § 1401(a)(17). It could not make such an argument, considering that one of the services Garret needs (catheterization) was at issue in *Tatro,* and the others may be provided competently by a school nurse or other trained personnel. As the [Administrative Law Judge] concluded, most of the requested services are already provided by the District to other students, and the in-school care necessitated by Garret's ventilator dependency does not demand the training, knowledge, and judgment of a licensed physician. While more extensive, the in-school services Garret needs are no more "medical" than was the care sought in *Tatro.*

Instead, the District points to the combined and continuous character of the required care, and proposes a test under which the outcome in any particular case could "depend upon a series of factors, such as [1] whether the care is continuous or intermittent, [2] whether existing school health personnel can provide the service, [3] the cost of the service, and [4] the potential consequences if the service is not properly performed."

The District's multi-factor test is not supported by any recognized source of legal authority. The proposed factors can be found in neither the text of the statute nor the regulations that we upheld in *Tatro.* Moreover, the District offers no explanation why these characteristics make one service any more "medical" than another. The continuous character of certain services associated with Garret's ventilator dependency has no apparent relationship to "medical" services, much less a relationship of equivalence. Continuous services may be more costly and may require additional school personnel, but they are not thereby more "medical." Whatever its imperfections, a rule that limits the medical services exemption to physician services is unquestionably a reasonable and generally workable interpretation of the statute. Absent an elaboration of the statutory terms plainly more convincing than that which we reviewed in *Tatro,* there is no good reason to depart from settled law.

Finally, the District raises broader concerns about the financial burden that it must bear to provide the services that Garret needs to stay in school. The problem for the District in providing these services is not that its staff cannot be trained to deliver them; the problem, the District contends, is that the existing school health staff cannot meet all of their responsibilities and provide for Garret at the same time. Through its multi-factor test, the District seeks to establish a kind of undue-burden exemption primarily based on the cost of the requested services. The first two factors can be seen as examples of cost-based distinctions: intermittent care is often less expensive than continuous care, and the use of existing personnel is cheaper than hiring additional employees. The third factor—the cost of the service—would then encompass the first two. The relevance of the fourth factor is likewise related to cost because extra care may be necessary if potential consequences are especially serious.

(Continued)

(Continued)

The District may have legitimate financial concerns, but our role in this dispute is to interpret existing law. Defining "related services" in a manner that accommodates the cost concerns Congress may have had, is altogether different from using cost itself as the definition. Given that § 1401(a)(17) does not employ cost in its definition of "related services" or excluded "medical services," accepting the District's cost-based standard as the sole test for determining the scope of the provision would require us to engage in judicial lawmaking without any guidance from Congress. It would also create some tension with the purposes of the IDEA. The statute may not require public schools to maximize the potential of disabled students commensurate with the opportunities provided to other children; and the potential financial burdens imposed on participating States may be relevant to arriving at a sensible construction of the IDEA. But Congress intended "to open the door of public education" to all qualified children and "require[d] participating States to educate handicapped children with nonhandicapped children whenever possible."

This case is about whether meaningful access to the public schools will be assured, not the level of education that a school must finance once access is attained. It is undisputed that the services at issue must be provided if Garret is to remain in school. Under the statute, our precedent, and the purposes of the IDEA, the District must fund such "related services" in order to help guarantee that students like Garret are integrated into the public schools.

The judgment of the Court of Appeals is accordingly Affirmed.

[Dissenting opinion by Justices Thomas and Kennedy omitted.]

Garret F. needed intensive and expensive and constant services. This type of service can raise concerns for the school about liability for performances of such services.[22] While providing such a related service is certainly a major challenge to an educational agency from both a financial and a personnel standpoint, there are a number of other more common health services that raise challenges. These include providing services to medically fragile students who may need assistance with taking medication during the day. It can be particularly challenging where services should be performed by a school nurse, and the school is a small school without a nurse on staff. In many situations, other personnel can be trained to provide certain health services, but in some situations school union agreements or other local or state limitations may make it difficult to provide such services on a cost-effective basis. The provision of mental health services can also be challenging.

Other Related Services

A number of other potential questions arise under the issue of related services. One area of controversy involves interpreters in the classroom for children who are deaf. The *Rowley* case involved that issue. While the *Rowley* decision did not require an interpreter, it left the door open for an alternative result if the factual circumstances were different. A more recent issue under the IDEA is a school's obligation regarding cochlear implants for students with disabilities.[23] There is a substantial rift in philosophy between advocates of the *aural* method (those promoting teaching deaf children to speak and read lips) and advocates of *signing* as the primary mode of communication. This debate makes it even more difficult to resolve questions about the obligation to provide interpreters. It should also be noted that the related services provision does not require that the school purchase a hearing aid for the child; however, the school is to ensure that hearing aids are functioning properly.[24]

In addition to the related services required under the IDEA for the students themselves, Section 504 of the Rehabilitation Act and the ADA require that certain services be provided as reasonable accommodations or modifications both to the students and to others. One example was mentioned previously in the section on health services. Students needing medication for asthma or other medical problems would probably be entitled to assistance when necessary as a reasonable accommodation. There will also be occasions where the parents are disabled and require reasonable accommodations. For example, a deaf parent who attends a graduation program might be entitled to an interpreter as a reasonable accommodation under Section 504 or the ADA. While these are not technically related services in the same sense as required under the IDEA, education agencies should be aware of these additional obligations related to students and others with disabilities who are involved with the schools.

Summary

Although the IDEA regulations specifically list which related services are to be provided to children with disabilities who qualify for special education, this issue remains the subject of debate and litigation. Transportation as a related service raises questions about the actual extent of transportation service to be provided. That is, what is meant by door-to-door service? When must transportation be provided? How much time can be spent in transit? How much supervision and assistance are necessary? Can parents be reimbursed for the costs of providing transportation themselves? The issue of the extent of transportation is not well resolved by the courts. Neither is the question of when transportation must be provided. Issues of time in transit and supervision are usually addressed in state regulations. What is not clear from such requirements, however, is whether the parents may bring an action for damages if injuries occur as a result of noncompliance with state requirements. One issue that is somewhat consistently treated by the courts is reimbursement for parent-provided transportation. If the school had an obligation to provide the transportation and failed to do so, generally parents will be permitted to recover the costs they incur in carrying out the service themselves. An issue likely to be subject to future litigation is whether disciplinary measures can be taken to deny a student with a disability access to transportation. These cases are likely to follow the same reasoning that courts apply to disciplinary measures for students with disabilities generally.

As a general rule, courts will require the school to provide psychological services when these are necessary for the child to benefit from special education. Whether these services will be viewed as medical services—and therefore not within the related services definition, when they are provided by a psychiatrist—is not clearly resolved. It would seem that the issue should not be answered based on who is providing the services but rather on the nature of the service itself. Because psychological counseling can be provided by either a psychologist or a psychiatrist, it is arguable that it should be a covered related service in either case when it is necessary for the child to benefit from special education.

Like psychological counseling, health services, which are in the nature of medical services, need not be provided by the school. The only exception is medical service for diagnostic and evaluation purposes. The Supreme Court addressed this issue in 1984 in *Irving Independent School District v. Tatro.* In holding that catheterization is a required related service, the Court focused on the fact that catheterization is a school health service and not a medical service that had to be performed by a licensed physician. One factor mentioned in that case is likely to be relevant to future litigation involving health services. The Court noted that catheterization is not unduly expensive or disruptive so as to be unreasonably burdensome. More recent litigation, including the 1999 Supreme Court decision in *Cedar Rapids Community School District v. Garret F.*, has begun to clarify when some services are to be provided by the public educational agency.

As was noted at the beginning of the chapter, a child who does not need special education is not eligible for related services under the IDEA. In many cases, however, a child who has a disability as defined under the Rehabilitation Act or the ADA may need related services but not special education. While the IDEA would not provide the basis for such services, it is important to keep in mind that both Section 504 of the Rehabilitation Act and the ADA require that reasonable accommodations be provided in certain circumstances. This requirement applies not only to students but also to parents and members of the public involved with the school. Services such as minor assistance with devices needed for medical conditions such as asthma, diabetes, or allergies and interpreters for parents and others participating in certain school events might well fall under this requirement.

Questions for Reflection

1. Why should social service agencies acquiesce to the authority of the state educational agency to coordinate and require service delivery?

2. The Smith family lives at the end of a "hollow" in rural West Virginia. The lack of paved roads prevents regular school buses from getting closer than 2 miles from the Smith home. Abby Smith has a mobility impairment and cannot walk to the bus pickup point. Her IEP indicates that transportation is to be provided as a special service. Must the school purchase a special vehicle that can reach the Smith home?

3. What provision in the IDEA or its regulations would relate to ensuring that bus drivers do not shout at children who are emotionally disturbed who are on the bus?

4. Philip is an adolescent with a behavior disorder resulting from alcohol and drug problems. He rides the regular school bus each day and because he lives in a large

metropolitan area, bus transportation is essential if he is to attend school. After several incidents of misbehavior on the bus, he is told that he can no longer ride the school bus. Because his parents are unable to take Philip to school, he has effectively been excluded from school. Is there any remedy under the IDEA?

5. In *Hurry v. Jones,* a court footnote mentioned that the school argued that the parents should be required to mitigate damages. Is that position valid? Why or why not?

6. In *Hurry v. Jones,* the school did not address the regulation's validity because of its reliance on the issue of a good-faith standard, a standard that changed during the litigation. Tactically, what should the school's attorney have done?

7. Ricky has an average IQ, and he had no major problems until he reached high school and fell in with a bad crowd. His parents are both career-oriented and have had little time for Ricky in recent years. Ricky has turned to drugs and alcohol to the point where he is having serious problems in school and clearly needs drug counseling. Must the school pay for this service? Suppose Ricky's parents have an annual income of $250,000?

8. In the *Max M.* case, would the school have fared better had it insisted that Max attend the therapy sessions with Frank Brull or that family therapy take place?

9. What if Texas law required that CIC be performed only by a physician? Would the result in *Tatro* have been different?

10. Karen is a 6-year-old with a condition requiring that a tracheal tube be permanently placed in her throat. She has no mental disabilities requiring special education. Occasionally the tube becomes clogged, and a relatively simple emergency procedure is required to clear the tube. If it is not performed within a few minutes, Karen could die. The teacher in the regular classroom in which Karen is to be placed has been told of the situation and that training for the procedure will be provided to the teacher before Karen begins class. The teacher is concerned about liability should something go wrong. In addition, she feels that teachers should not be required to perform these procedures. Is the school required to admit Karen? May the teacher refuse to have Karen in the class? If so, what steps should the teacher take to protect herself from liability? What if the teacher's union agreement or contract states that teachers are not required to perform such services?

NOTES

1. 20 U.S.C. § 1401(26). See also Laura Rothstein & Julia Rothstein, *Disabilities and the Law* §§ 2.22–2.26 (Thomson West 2006).
2. 20 U.S.C. § 1412(a)(11).
3. 20 U.S.C. § 1412(a)(11)(B).
4. 20 U.S.C. § 1412(a)(12)(A)(iii).
5. 20 U.S.C. § 1401(26)(a).
6. 34 C.F.R. § 300.34(c)(16). See also *Disabilities and the Law* § 2:26.

7. *Alamo Heights Independent School District v. State Board of Education,* 790 F.2d 1153 (5th Cir. 1986).

8. *Cohn v. School Board,* 450 So.2d 1238 (Fla. 1984).

9. *Clomon v. Monroe City School Board,* 490 So.2d 691 (La. Ct. App. 1986).

10. See Chapter 18.

11. In *Kennedy v. Board of Education,* 337 S.E.2d 905 (W.Va. 1985), the school had to purchase a special vehicle to reach a child because the regular school bus could not use unpaved mountain roads.

12. *Taylor v. Board of Education,* 649 F. Supp. 1253 (N.D.N.Y. 1986).

13. 20 U.S.C. § 1401(26)(A).

14. 34 C.F.R. § 300.34(c)(1)&(c)(15).

15. 34 C.F.R. § 300.24(c)(8).

16. 34 C.F.R. § 300.24(c)(10).

17. 34 C.F.R. § 300.24(c)(14).

18. See *Disabilities and the Law* § 2:25.

19. 20 U.S.C. § 1401(26).

20. 34 C.F.R. § 300.34(c)(13).

21. *Id.*

22. See cases cited in *Disabilities and the Law* § 2:24, fn. 9.

23. 34 C.F.R. § 300.34. See also Robert A. Crouch, "Letting the Deaf Be Deaf: Reconsidering the Use of Cochlear Implants in Prelingually Deaf Children," 27 *Hastings Center Report* 14 (July 17, 1997).

24. 458 U.S. 176 (1982). See also Chapter 11. In 1993, the Supreme Court held that the cost of interpreter service could be paid for by the public schools even when the student was attending a parochial school. This is discussed more fully in Chapter 12.

11

Placement and Least Restrictive Environment

IDEA Foundations

Statute and Regulations

One of the primary principles of the Individuals with Disabilities Education Act (IDEA) is the concept of educating children with disabilities along with children who are not disabled to the maximum extent appropriate, ideally in the regular classroom. In the early years after passage of the IDEA, this was often referred to as *mainstreaming*, although the term was not found anywhere in the statutory or regulatory language under the IDEA. The term more commonly used today is *inclusion*. The term *mainstreaming* often refers to placement into selected classes, whereas *inclusion* implies the presumption of placement in the regular class, and *full inclusion* means that all special education programming would take place in the regular classroom. There are debates about these presumptions as a policy matter.[1]

The IDEA does not require full inclusion, but does have as a key underlying principle the goal of ensuring that education be provided in nonsegregated settings. The statute provides that

> to the maximum extent appropriate, children with disabilities, including children in public or private institutions or other care facilities, [should be] educated with children who are not disabled, and that special classes, separate schooling, or other removal of children with disabilities from the regular educational environment [should occur] only when the nature or severity of the disability is such that education in regular classes with the use of supplementary aids and services cannot be achieved satisfactorily.[2]

It is in the regulations, rather than the statute, however, that the concept of least restrictive environment is provided for. The regulations allow for a "continuum of alternative placements" and that "in selecting the least restrictive environment, consideration [should be] given to any potential harmful effect on the child or on the quality of services which he or she needs."[3] The goal of providing education to children with disabilities in the regular classroom does not discount the requirement to individualize a child's program and to respond to situations where the child is disruptive in the regular classroom.[4]

In the early years after the IDEA was passed, some educators mistakenly thought that the Act requires all children with disabilities to be placed in the regular classroom, and they expressed anxiety over such a mandate. It should be emphasized that the least restrictive placement must also be *appropriate*. For some children, a more restrictive placement may be necessary.

Philosophy Behind Least Restrictive Environment

The philosophy of placing students in a setting that is as "normal" as possible, where education takes place along with peers who do not have disabilities, is based on several principles. One principle is that, as a general philosophy, separation in education is inherently stigmatizing. Another concern is that once a child is placed in a separate special education setting, the self-fulfilling prophecy occurs—for example, the child will only be expected to perform at a particular level, and the expectations will generally be borne out by the child's performance. Another principle, which is discussed in the cases included in this chapter, is the value of peer interaction for children with disabilities as well as those who do not have disabilities.

It should be emphasized that, while the concept of least restrictive environment is one of the major principles of the IDEA, it is not the sole consideration. That education be individualized and appropriate are other major considerations. It is clear that the IDEA incorporates the philosophy that in some situations separation may be necessary to ensure that the education is appropriate. The IDEA, however, can be viewed as requiring a presumption of nonseparation—for example, that as much as possible the education should be provided in the regular classroom environment with necessary supplementary aids and services. The following cases demonstrate to some extent the debate that still occurs at a judicial level.[5]

RONCKER V. WALTER

700 F.2d 1058 (6th Cir. 1983)

. . . The plaintiff's son, Neill Roncker, is nine years old and is severely mentally retarded. He is classified as Trainable Mentally Retarded (TMR), a category of children with an IQ of below 50. Less severely retarded students are classified as Educable Mentally Retarded (EMR) and are generally educated in special classes within the regular public schools.

There is no dispute that Neill is severely retarded and has a mental age of two to three with regard to most functions. Neill also suffers from seizures but they are not convulsive and he takes medication to control them. No evidence indicated that Neill is dangerous to others but he does require almost constant supervision because of his inability to recognize dangerous situations.

In 1976, Neill was evaluated and recommended for the Arlitt Child Development Center. It was believed that he would benefit from contact with nonhandicapped children. In the spring of 1979, a conference was held to evaluate Neill's Individual Education Plan (IEP) as required by the Act. Present at the conference were Neill's parents, school psychologists, and a member of the Hamilton County Board of Mental Retardation. After evaluating Neill, the school district decided to place him in a county school. Since these county schools were exclusively for mentally retarded children, Neill would have received no contact with nonhandicapped children. . . .

While the dispute over placement continued, Neill began attending a class for the severely mentally retarded at Pleasant Ridge Elementary School in September 1979. Pleasant Ridge is a regular public school which serves both handicapped and nonhandicapped children. Neill's contact with nonhandicapped children at Pleasant Ridge is limited to lunch, gym and recess. Neill has remained at Pleasant Ridge during the pendency of this action. . . .

The Act does not require mainstreaming in every case but its requirement that mainstreaming be provided to the maximum extent appropriate indicated a very strong congressional preference. The proper inquiry is whether a proposed placement is appropriate under the Act. In some cases, a placement which may be considered better for academic reasons may not be appropriate because of the failure to provide for mainstreaming. The perception that a segregated institution is academically superior for a handicapped child may reflect no more than a basic disagreement with the mainstreaming concept. Such a disagreement is not, of course, any basis for not following the Act's mandate. In a case where the segregated facility is considered superior, the court should determine whether the services which make that placement superior could be feasibly provided in a non-segregated setting. If they can, the placement in the segregated school would be inappropriate under the Act. Framing the issue in this manner accords the proper respect for the strong preference in favor of mainstreaming while still realizing the possibility that some handicapped children simply must be educated in segregated facilities either because the handicapped child would not benefit from mainstreaming, because any marginal benefits received from mainstreaming are far outweighed by the benefits gained from services which could not feasibly be provided in the non-segregated setting. Cost is a proper factor to consider since excessive spending on one handicapped child deprives other handicapped children. Cost is no defense, however, if the school district has failed to use its funds to provide a proper continuum of alternative placements for handicapped children. The provision of such alternative placements benefits all handicapped children.

(Continued)

(Continued)

In the present case, the district court must determine whether Neill's educational, physical or emotional needs require some service which could not feasibly be provided in a class for handicapped children within a regular school or in the type of split program advocated by the State Board of Education. Although Neill's progress, or lack thereof, at Pleasant Ridge is a relevant factor in determining the maximum appropriate extent to which he can be mainstreamed, it is not dispositive since the district court must determine whether Neill could have been provided with additional services, such as those provided at the county schools, which would have improved his performance at Pleasant Ridge. . . .

Dissent

. . . Congress has expressed a clear preference for educating handicapped children in the regular classrooms of the public schools. Handicapped children should be removed from regular classes only when their education cannot be achieved satisfactorily with the use of supplementary aids and services. Despite this preference for "mainstreaming," however, the statute clearly contemplates that there will be some separate schools and schooling. Section 1412(5) [Now § 1412(a)(5)(A)] does not require that classes for the severely mentally retarded, such as Neill Roncker, whose only interaction with nonhandicapped children is to observe them, be located in the regular elementary school. Rather, this section is directed to the handicapped child who can spend some time in the regular classroom if given special aids or assistance.

Other than costs, the District Court in the present case has fully considered whether Neill Roncker could be educated in a self-contained handicapped classroom in a regular school. The severity of Neill's handicap is such that even with supplementary aids and services, the District Court found that Neill cannot achieve a satisfactory education or indeed any education in a regular class.

The appellant has nevertheless argued that if Neill must be educated in a 169 program, that program must be provided within the "regular school environment" even if the only benefit from such placement is to avoid the stigma of attending a special school. Because the 169 program requires children of chronological age with roughly the same developmental ability to be placed together, a classroom for each age could not be located at each regular school. However, the classrooms for one age could be at one school and those for another at a different school. The children could probably be bused to assemblies. Special gym teachers, physical and occupational therapists and special remedial teachers could go from school to school. Appellant argues that this is required unless the children could learn "zero" in such environment.

The appellant's arguments essentially represent one of two competing educational theories presented by this case. The first is that a program with all of the components of the 169 program can only be fully implemented in a separate school. This program alone, it is argued, is appropriate for severely handicapped children such as Neill Roncker who cannot benefit from any regular classroom experience. The second theory is that all handicapped children (except those who can be in the regular classroom) must be placed in special classrooms located in regular elementary schools, unless a child would get zero benefit from a classroom so situated. . . .

Section 1412(5) [Now § 1412(a)(5)(A)], far from unambiguously requiring that school districts place severely handicapped children in the regular school environment even if they cannot be satisfactorily educated in that environment, requires only that handicapped children be "mainstreamed" to the maximum extent appropriate. For those more severely retarded children, such as Neill Roncker, who are unable to be satisfactorily educated in any respect in a regular classroom, the statute does not prohibit the school district from making the judgment as to where their classrooms should be located.

The following case presents another point of view.

DANIEL R.R. V. STATE BOARD OF EDUCATION

874 F.2d 1036 (5th Cir. 1989)

Daniel R. is a six year old boy who was enrolled, at the time this case arose, in the El Paso Independent School District (EPISD). A victim of Downs Syndrome, Daniel is mentally retarded and speech impaired. By September 1987, Daniel's developmental age was between two and three years and his communication skills were slightly less than those of a two year old.

In 1985, Daniel's parents, Mr. and Mrs. R., enrolled him in EPISD's Early Childhood Program, a half-day program devoted entirely to special education. Daniel completed one academic year in the Early Childhood Program. Before the 1986–87 school year began, Mrs. R. requested a new placement that would provide association with nonhandicapped children. Mrs. R. wanted EPISD to place Daniel in Pre-kindergarten—a half-day, regular education class. Mrs. R. conferred with Joan Norton, the Pre-kindergarten instructor, proposing that Daniel attend the half-day Pre-kindergarten class in addition to the half-day Early Childhood class. As a result, EPISD's Admission, Review and Dismissal (ARD) Committee met and designated the combined regular and special education program as Daniel's placement.

This soon proved unwise and not long into the school year Mrs. Norton began to have reservations about Daniel's presence in her class. Daniel did not participate without constant, individual attention from the teacher or her aide, and failed to master any of the skills Mrs. Norton was trying to teach her students. Modifying the Pre-kindergarten curriculum and her teaching methods sufficiently to reach Daniel would have required Mrs. Norton to modify the curriculum almost beyond recognition. In November 1986, the ARD Committee met again, concluded that Pre-kindergarten was inappropriate for Daniel, and decided to change Daniel's placement. Under the new placement, Daniel would attend only the special education, Early Childhood class; would eat lunch in the school cafeteria, with nonhandicapped children three days a week if his mother was present to supervise him; and would have contact with nonhandicapped students during recess. Believing that the ARD had improperly shut the door to regular education for Daniel, Mr. and Mrs. R. exercised their right to a review of the ARD Committee's decision.

(Continued)

(Continued)

Determining Compliance with the Mainstreaming Requirement

Determining the contours of the mainstreaming requirement is a question of first impression for us. In the seminal interpretation of the EHA [Education of the Handicapped Act], the Supreme Court posited a two-part test for determining whether a school has provided a free appropriate public education: "First, has the State complied with the procedures set forth in the Act. And second, is the individualized educational program developed through the Act's procedures reasonably calculated to enable the child to receive educational benefits."

Despite the attractive ease of this two part inquiry, it is not the appropriate tool for determining whether a school district has met its mainstreaming obligations. In *Rowley*, the handicapped student was placed in a regular education class; the EHA's mainstreaming requirement was not an issue presented for the Court's consideration. Indeed, the Court carefully limited its decision to the facts before it, noting that it was not establishing a single test that would determine "the adequacy of educational benefits conferred upon all children covered by the Act."

We must agree with the Sixth and Eighth Circuits that the *Rowley* test does not advance our inquiry when the question presented is whether the Act's mainstreaming requirement has been met.

Although we have not yet developed a standard for evaluating mainstreaming questions, we decline to adopt the approach that other circuits have taken. In *Roncker*, visiting the same question which we address today, the Sixth Circuit devised its own test to determine when and to what extent a handicapped child must be mainstreamed. According to the *Roncker* court,

> [t]he proper inquiry is whether a proposed placement is appropriate under the Act. . . . In a case where the segregated facility is considered superior, the court should determine whether the services which make the placement superior could be feasibly provided in a non-segregated setting. If they can, the placement in the segregated school would be inappropriate under the Act.

We respectfully decline to follow the Sixth Circuit's analysis. Certainly, the *Roncker* test accounts for factors that are important in any mainstreaming case. We believe, however, that the test necessitates too intrusive an inquiry into the educational policy choices that Congress deliberately left to state and local school officials. Whether a particular service feasibly can be provided in a regular or special education setting is an administrative determination that state and local school officials are far better qualified and situated than we are to make. Moreover, the test makes little reference to the language of the EHA. Yet, as we shall see, we believe that the language of the Act itself provides a workable test for determining whether a state has complied with the Act's mainstreaming requirement.

Nor do we find the district court's approach to the issue the proper tool for analyzing the mainstreaming obligation. Relying primarily on whether Daniel could receive an educational benefit from regular education, the district court held that the special education class was the appropriate placement for Daniel. According to the court, "some children, even aided by supplemental aids and services in a regular education classroom, will never receive an educational benefit that approximates the level of skill and comprehension acquisition of nonhandicapped children." In these cases, regular education does not provide the child an appropriate education and the presumption in favor of mainstreaming is overcome. As no aspect of the Pre-kindergarten curriculum was within Daniel's reach, EPISD was not required to mainstream him. Given the nature and severity of Daniel's handicap at the time EPISD placed him, we agree with the district court's conclusion that EPISD was not required to mainstream Daniel. We disagree, however, with the court's analysis of the mainstreaming issue, finding it troublesome for two reasons: first, as a prerequisite to mainstreaming, the court would require handicapped children to learn at approximately the same level as their nonhandicapped classmates. Second, the court places too much emphasis on the handicapped student's ability to achieve an educational benefit.

First, requiring as a prerequisite to mainstreaming that the handicapped child be able to learn at approximately the same level as his nonhandicapped classmates fails to take into account the principles that the Supreme Court announced in *Rowley*. Our public school system tolerates a wide range of differing learning abilities; at the same time, it provides educational opportunities that do not necessarily account for all of those different capacities to learn. As the *Rowley* Court noted,"[t]he educational opportunities provided by our public school systems undoubtedly differ from student to student, depending upon a myriad of factors that might affect a particular student's ability to assimilate information presented in the classroom."

With the EHA, Congress extended the states' tolerance of educational differences to include tolerance of many handicapped children.

We recognize that some handicapped children may not be able to master as much of the regular education curriculum as their nonhandicapped classmates. This does not mean, however, that those handicapped children are not receiving any benefit from regular education. Nor does it mean that they are not receiving all of the benefit that their handicapping condition will permit. If the child's individual needs make mainstreaming appropriate, we cannot deny the child access to regular education simply because his educational achievement lags behind that of his classmates.

Second, the district court placed too much emphasis on educational benefits. Certainly, whether a child will benefit educationally from regular education is relevant and important to our analysis. Congress's primary purpose in enacting the EHA was to provide access to education for handicapped children. Implicit in Congress's purpose to provide access is a purpose to provide meaningful access, access that is sufficient to confer some educational benefit on the child. Thus, the decision whether to mainstream a child must include an inquiry into whether the student will gain any educational benefit from regular education. Our analysis cannot stop here, however, for educational benefits are not mainstreaming's only virtue. Rather, mainstreaming may have benefits in and of itself. For example, the language and behavior models available from nonhandicapped children may be essential or helpful to the handicapped child's development. In other words, although a handicapped child may not be able to absorb all of the regular education curriculum, he may benefit from nonacademic experiences in the regular education environment.

(Continued)

(Continued)

Ultimately, our task is to balance competing requirements of the EHA's dual mandate: a free appropriate public education that is provided, to the maximum extent appropriate, in the regular education classroom. As we begin our task we must keep in mind that Congress left the choice of educational policies and methods where it properly belongs—in the hands of state and local school officials. Our task is not to second-guess state and local policy decisions; rather, it is the narrow one of determining whether state and local school officials have complied with the Act. Adhering to the language of the EHA, we discern a two part test for determining compliance with the mainstreaming requirement. First, we ask whether education in the regular classroom, with the use of supplemental aids and services, can be achieved satisfactorily for a given child. See § 1412(5)(B) [Now § 1412(a)(5)(A)]. If it cannot and the school intends to provide special education or to remove the child from regular education, we ask, second, whether the school has mainstreamed the child to the maximum extent appropriate. A variety of factors will inform each state of our inquiry; the factors that we consider today do not constitute an exhaustive list of factors relevant to the mainstreaming issue. Moreover, no single factor is dispositive in all cases. Rather, our analysis is an individualized, fact-specific inquiry that requires us to examine carefully the nature and severity of the child's handicapping condition, his needs and abilities, and the schools' response to the child's needs.

In this case, several factors assist the first stage of our inquiry, whether EPISD can achieve education in the regular classroom satisfactorily. At the outset, we must examine whether the state has taken steps to accommodate the handicapped child in regular education. The Act requires states to provide supplementary aids and services and to modify the regular education program when they mainstream handicapped children.

If the state has made no effort to take such accommodating steps, our inquiry ends, for the state is in violation of the Act's express mandate to supplement and modify regular education. If the state is providing supplementary aids and services and is modifying its regular education program, we must examine whether its efforts are sufficient. The Act does not permit states to make mere token gestures to accommodate handicapped students; its requirement for modifying and supplementing regular education is broad.

Although broad, the requirement is not limitless. States need not provide every conceivable supplementary aid or service to assist the child.

Furthermore, the Act does not require regular education instructors to devote all or most of their time to one handicapped child or to modify the regular education program beyond recognition. If a regular education instructor must devote all of her time to one handicapped child, she will be acting as a special education teacher in a regular education classroom. Moreover, she will be focusing her attentions on one child to the detriment of her entire class, including, perhaps, other, equally deserving, children who also may require extra attention. Likewise, mainstreaming would be pointless if we forced instructors to modify the regular education curriculum to the extent that the handicapped child is not required to learn any of the skills normally taught in regular education. The child would be receiving special education instruction in the regular education classroom; the only advantage to such an arrangement would be that the child is sitting next to nonhandicapped students.

Next, we examine whether the child will receive an educational benefit from regular education. This inquiry necessarily will focus on the student's ability to grasp the essential elements of the regular education class. For example, if the goal of a particular program is enhancing the child's development, as opposed to teaching him specific subjects such as reading or mathematics, our inquiry must focus on the child's ability to benefit from the developmental lessons, not exclusively on his potential for learning to read. We reiterate, however, that academic achievement is not the only purpose of mainstreaming. Integrating a handicapped child into a nonhandicapped environment may be beneficial in and of itself. Thus, our inquiry must extend beyond the educational benefits that the child may receive in regular education.

We also must examine the child's overall educational experience in the mainstreamed environment, balancing the benefits of regular and special education for each individual child. For example, a child may be able to absorb only a minimal amount of the regular education program, but may benefit enormously from the language models that his nonhandicapped peers provide for him. In such a case, the benefit that the child receives from mainstreaming may tip the balance in favor of mainstreaming, even if the child cannot flourish academically. On the other hand, placing a child in regular education may be detrimental to the child. In such a case, mainstreaming would not provide an education that is attuned to the child's unique needs and would not be required under the Act. Indeed, mainstreaming a child who will suffer from the experience would violate the Act's mandate for a free appropriate public education.

Finally, we ask what effect the handicapped child's presence has on the regular classroom environment and, thus, on the education that the other students are receiving. A handicapped child's placement in regular education may prove troublesome for two reasons. First, the handicapped child may, as a result of his handicap, engage in disruptive behavior. "[W]here a handicapped child is so disruptive in a regular classroom that the education of other students is significantly impaired, the needs of the handicapped child cannot be met in that environment. Therefore regular placement would not be appropriate to his or her needs." Second, the child may require so much of the instructor's attention that the instructor will have to ignore the other students' needs in order to tend to the handicapped child. The Act and its regulations mandate that the school provide supplementary aids and services in the regular education classroom. A teaching assistant or an aide may minimize the burden on the teacher. If, however, the handicapped child requires so much of the teacher or the aide's time that the rest of the class suffers, then the balance will tip in favor of placing the child in special education.

If we determine that education in the regular classroom cannot be achieved satisfactorily, we next ask whether the child has been mainstreamed to the maximum extent appropriate. The EHA and its regulations do not contemplate an all-or-nothing educational system in which handicapped children attend either regular or special education. Rather, the Act and its regulations require schools to offer a continuum of services.

Thus, the school must take intermediate steps where appropriate, such as placing the child in regular education for some academic classes and in special education for others, mainstreaming the child for nonacademic classes only, or providing interaction with nonhandicapped children during lunch and recess. The appropriate mix will vary from child to child and,

(Continued)

(Continued)

it may be hoped, from school year to school year as the child develops. If the school officials have provided the maximum appropriate exposure to nonhandicapped students, they have fulfilled their obligation under the EHA.

EPISD's Compliance with the Mainstreaming Requirement

After a careful review of the voluminous administrative record, we must agree with the trial court that EPISD's decision to remove Daniel from regular education does not run afoul of the EHA's preference for mainstreaming. Accounting for all of the factors we have identified today, we find that EPISD cannot educate Daniel satisfactorily in the regular education classroom. Furthermore, EPISD has taken creative steps to provide Daniel as much access to nonhandicapped students as it can, while providing him an education that is tailored to his unique needs. Thus EPISD has mainstreamed Daniel to the maximum extent appropriate.

Continuum of Placements

The IDEA regulations provide for a "continuum of alternate placements" to be available.[6] Within the educational community, there has been developed a "cascade system" of placement alternatives that places the regular classroom as the least restrictive placement and the ideal goal, and hospital placement as the most restrictive placement. Between these two extremes are the following placements: regular classroom with special education consultant, regular classroom with itinerant teachers, regular classroom with use of resource room for part of the time, part-time special class, full-time special class, special day school, and residential school.

While some children may never be placed in the regular classroom for academic work, the philosophy of least restrictive environment is to place the child in a setting that is the least restrictive placement *appropriate* to the child's needs and that will not cause undue disruption to other children.

It is essential that educators and parents be conscious of the fluid nature of placements. It may be necessary for a particular child to be placed in a full-time special class for the first part of a school year, or even for an entire school year, but at least annually the placement must be reviewed and a less restrictive one considered. It may well be that the child's appropriate placement is to continue in the full-time special class for most of the school day. It is important to note that moving to a less restrictive point on the continuum is the goal of the mainstreaming mandate. Therefore, the behaviors or needs that are necessitating the segregated placement should be targeted for remediation on the IEP.

Some advocates argue for a concept known as full inclusion. This refers to the practice of educating all children in neighborhood classrooms and schools in the regular school setting. This would end labeling and educating students with disabilities in segregated special classes, but it would not end the necessary supports and services. Some of the cases in this chapter raise the issues involved in the debate about the full inclusion principle.

An examination of compliance with mainstreaming or inclusion principles shows several contexts in which the issue arises. If the child is placed in the regular classroom, to what extent should the child be placed with age-appropriate peers? To what extent should there be true interaction with peers in the regular classroom? Is it always possible to provide supportive services within the regular classroom, or is temporary removal from the regular classroom better in some cases? If the separate resource room or separate special education class is located within the regular public school facility, where must it be placed? How can appropriate interaction for separately placed children occur for at least some activities? Does the child have a right to be placed in a neighborhood school? And finally, when are completely separate facilities appropriate?

The following sections address some of these issues.

The Classroom

The Importance of Peer Interaction

The following case involves an unusual factual setting, and it demonstrates the importance of peer interaction and the problems of cost that can arise in meeting the mainstreaming mandate.

ESPINO V. BESTEIRO

520 F. Supp. 905 (S.D. Tex. 1981)

This action was brought by Raul Espino, Jr., a seven-year-old multihandicapped child who cannot adequately regulate his body temperature, by and through his parents, seeking declaratory and injunctive relief and damages for the alleged failure of Defendants to provide him with an education in the "least restrictive environment appropriate to his individual needs." It is alleged that the failure of Defendants to provide Raul with a fully air-conditioned classroom wherein he can interact fully with his peers, and their decision instead to provide him with an air-conditioned plexiglass cubicle within a regular non air-conditioned classroom, violate the Education for All Handicapped Children Act of 1975. . . .

Raul had suffered a broken spine at the age of 11 months, which had resulted in quadriplegia and damage to his nervous system preventing proper body temperature regulation. Raul needed to be in an environment where the temperature was between sixty-eight and seventy-eight degrees Fahrenheit. Raul attends school in Brownsville, Texas, and during the warmer months of the year, air-conditioned classrooms are necessary. Raul attended kindergarten in an air-conditioned classroom.

During first grade Raul was placed in a regular first grade classroom within a portable five-foot-by-five-foot plexiglass cubicle with an air-conditioning unit. Raul's grades during first grade were exceptional and he had very positive peer interaction during that time. The cost of air-conditioning the entire classroom was about $5,700 per year. The school district had $250,000

(Continued)

(Continued)

earmarked for special education. It was when Raul was to enter second grade that his parents challenged the cubicle solution and requested that his entire classroom be air-conditioned. . . .

The "mainstreaming" provisions of the EAHCA [Education for All Handicapped Children Act], as set out previously, require that a handicapped child be educated with his non-handicapped peers "to the maximum extent appropriate" and that any removal from the regular education environment occurs only when the nature of the handicap is such that education in regular classes with the use of supplementary aids "cannot be achieved satisfactorily." In the case at bar, it is undisputed that air-conditioning is a supplementary aid or "related service" which Raul Espino, Jr. needs in order to be able to attend school during the hotter months of the year. There is no evidence to suggest that a fully air-conditioned environment would be inappropriate for Raul's educational needs. There is also no evidence which suggests that [the] regular classroom at Egly Elementary cannot be satisfactorily modified to provide such an environment. In this set of circumstances it seems self-evident that the decision to provide air-conditioning for Raul in a plexiglass cubicle, and therefore at times segregate him from his non-handicapped classmates, is prima facie a violation of the mainstreaming provisions of the EAHCA.

Assuming that Raul's placement in the cubicle is not to the "maximum extent appropriate," the analysis then must focus on whether it is a reasonably appropriate accommodation in that it provides for Raul's special needs "to the maximum extent practicable" and consistent with the mainstreaming provisions of the Act. One court has suggested that the important personal needs of an individual handicapped child must be balanced against the realities of limited funding in reaching a reasonable accommodation. At least one commentator has recognized that "appropriate" cannot mean the best possible education a school can provide if given access to unlimited funds, but that the EAHCA contemplates a standard between the best education and merely opening the doors of a regular classroom to those capable of learning without special assistance. Defendants in this case have not made a serious contention that maintaining a fully air-conditioned environment for Raul is prohibited by the financial condition of the [Brownesville Independent School District] BISD. The evidence presented suggests that the cost of air-conditioning a classroom would be minimal in relation to the amount of federal funds received by BISD and BISD's total budget. Balancing the important needs of Raul Espino, Jr. for an air-conditioned environment within which he can be effectively mainstreamed and interact fully with nonhandicapped students, against the cost to BISD of providing him with such an environment, it cannot be said that the provision of an air-conditioned cubicle, with its concomitant isolative effect on Raul when it is being used, represents a reasonable accommodation resulting from the fiscal impracticability of providing air-conditioning for him to the maximum extent appropriate.

Realizing that the concept of "practicability" is not necessarily limited to monetary consideration, this court must analyze the other reasons advanced for the existence of the cubicle to determine whether it presents a reasonably appropriate accommodation. Superintendent Besteiro felt that a fully air-conditioned classroom for Raul's class might open "Pandora's box" in that parents of children in non-air-conditioned classrooms and the children's teachers would complain of unequal treatment in that one teacher and Raul's classmates would receive the benefits of air-conditioning during the hot months of the school year. Yet, Mr. Besteiro testified that he had received no official requests seeking air-conditioning for students other than Raul. A purely theoretical risk of parental or teacher complaints is probably insufficient to offset the countervailing needs of Raul Espino, Jr. for an education with his peers "to the maximum extent appropriate" and does not substantially justify segregation from his classmates in the cubicle. . . .

Dr. Schraer feels that Raul's sterling performance in the first grade proves that he is being provided with an appropriate education. While there is no question that Raul's grades establish that he is receiving an "adequate" education, this does not necessarily mean that he is receiving an "appropriate" education. One court has held that an "appropriate" education is one which lies between the extremes of a merely adequate education (i.e., one that is substantial enough to facilitate a child's progress from grade to grade) and one which enables a handicapped child to achieve his or her full potential. . . .

It is apparent that Raul misses out on a great deal of class interaction and group participation while he is confined to the cubicle. This is of particular significance in Raul's case since the [Admission, Review and Dismissal] ARD committee which decided to mainstream Raul felt that the Moody facility was "too restrictive" to meet his "intellectual and social needs." Full social interaction is an important part of today's educational curriculum and is even more vital to a child like Raul who necessarily suffers a certain degree of isolation as a result of his handicap. While it is true that Raul's scholarship is superb and he displays no psychological damage as a result of his semi-isolation in the cubicle, he derives no education benefits from it. Under the circumstances it is doubtful that Raul is being provided an opportunity for maximization of his social interaction skills commensurate with that provided to other students in his class. Raul's excellent academic performance and his ability to get along with his classmates attest to his courage and tenacity, and he should not be penalized for the fruits of his own efforts. For these reasons this Court feels that the placement of Raul in the cubicle may deprive him of a full educational opportunity and may not be in conformity with his IEP as originally espoused in the ARD committee's original report. If this indeed is the case, Raul is not being provided with an "appropriate" education under the EAHCA.

Age Appropriateness as a Mandate

The court in *Besteiro* recognized the importance of peer interaction for both intellectual and social needs. The court in *Roncker* noted that children should be placed with other children of roughly the same chronological age and developmental ability. While these two courts recognized these factors as part of an "appropriate" placement, neither the IDEA nor its implementing regulations specifically states anything about chronological age placement.[7]

Some states have recognized the importance, however, of chronological age placement and have adopted specific age span requirements for classrooms. For example, a state regulation might provide that students in a separate class for children who are mentally retarded be no more than four years apart in age. This would prevent the placement of a 13-year-old with children who are 6 or 7. State age span requirements can also relate to placements within the regular classroom.

Whether state regulations require it or not, there is support in education literature for the philosophy of age-appropriate placements. The underlying principle is that education involves not only academic development, but also social development.[8] Students need to have experience with age peers to encourage modeling of age-appropriate behavior.

Thus, while there is substantial support among educators for age-appropriate placements, and the Supreme Court in *Board of Education v. Rowley*[9] notes that an appropriate placement must "approximate the grade levels used in the State's regular education," there is little guidance at the federal statutory or regulatory level as to the parameters of age-appropriate placement requirements.

Location of Classrooms

The principle of mainstreaming and its underlying philosophy of social interaction can be used as a basis to support the importance of locating separate special education in the "mainstream" of the school facility itself. In addition, the stigmatizing effect of separate placements should be avoided by encouraging proximity of special education classrooms to regular classrooms rather than "clustering" them in separate wings or portions of the building.

Unfortunately, in some schools the separate special education classes and resource rooms are located in trailers, basements, or other locations not physically proximate to the regular education program. While neither the IDEA nor its regulations make any specific statement about where within a facility a special education program should be placed, it is certainly questionable whether the intent and spirit of the least restrictive environment mandate has been met when the physical location of special education isolates students with disabilities from students who are not disabled. Unless regular classes are located in trailers or basements on an equivalent basis, it is probable that these placements violate Section 504 of the Rehabilitation Act and the Americans with Disabilities Act (ADA).

There is little discussion of this issue in judicial decisions, but administrators should give careful thought to it when deciding where to locate special education classrooms within a public school facility. One of the few cases discussing this issue is the following. It describes the status of special education in the intermediate unit in Pennsylvania schools.

HENDRICKS V. GILHOOL

709 F. Supp. 1362 (E.D. Pa. 1989)

Non-comparable Facilities

From 1982 to the present, some CLIU [Carbon-Lehigh Intermediate Unit] classes have been located in facilities that are not comparable to those provided non-handicapped students in terms of size, sanitation, noise levels, furniture, lighting, and ventilation.

Relocation of Classes

From 1982 to the present, CLIU students—typically children in multi-district classes with more severe handicaps—have been shifted among classroom locations to make classroom space available to non-handicapped children. In some instances, these moves have been to a less central location, i.e., farther from the students' homes. As a result, some handicapped children presently ride a school bus for up to one and three quarter hours in each direction.

Restrictive and Separate Facilities

From 1982 to the present, as a result of CLIU's inability to obtain adequate classroom space in regular schools, some CLIU students have been educated in facilities that are separate from and more restrictive than the regular school environment. Such facilities have included separate schools or centers, separate wings or sections of regular schools, and mobile classrooms and trailers.

Inability to Open Classrooms

From 1982 to the present, as a result of CLIU's inability to obtain adequate space in regular schools, the CLIU has been unable to open enough special education classes to meet the needs of class members. In some instances, school districts have refused to make space available for classes of children with particular types of handicaps, e.g., students with severe or profound mental retardation or social or emotional disturbances. In several instances, the proposed classes were necessary to ensure that the children received appropriate special education programs.

CLIU is an intermediate unit serving fourteen school districts thus properly chargeable for the violations of the EHA alleged by plaintiffs, and has the power to remedy the alleged violations through the exercise of its statutory authority. For these reasons, I find that the Carbon-Lehigh Intermediate Unit and the local school districts are not necessary parties under Rule 19, and I shall not require their joinder.

(Continued)

(Continued)

Statutory Violations

1. *Non-comparable classrooms:* The defendant concedes that because of the failure of local school districts to furnish adequate classroom space for CLIU classes, handicapped children served by the intermediate unit have not had access to "comparable" facilities, i.e. "space that is comparable in quality to that provided to non-handicapped students." I do not believe that the EHA and § 504 require that the classroom space afforded CLIU students be precisely equivalent to that afforded non-handicapped students. Such a standard would impose a nearly impossible burden on school administrators charged with allocating classroom space to special education programs. However, the thirteen examples of non-comparable facilities described in the factual stipulation do not represent trivial or insignificant disparities. The CLIU classrooms noted in the stipulation are unequal to those furnished non-handicapped students in several important areas including size, sanitation, ventilation, noise level, and furnishings. Because of the significance of these disparities, I hold that the defendant has violated the plaintiffs' statutory rights by failing to ensure that plaintiffs' educational facilities are comparable to those enjoyed by non-handicapped students.

2. *Disruptive Relocation of Classes:* The inability of the CLIU to obtain adequate classroom facilities has also resulted in the relocation of several CLIU classes which have been shuffled between schools, and on some occasions to schools in other districts, in order to make classroom space available for non-handicapped students. As a result of these relocations, some handicapped students have been assigned to schools at a considerable distance from their homes, requiring them to ride a bus up to one and three quarter hours in each direction in order to attend school.

The extent of the relocation problem on a systemwide basis is not evident from the stipulated facts. Considering the size of the CLIU program, I may reasonably assume that some classroom relocations were necessitated by legitimate programmatic and logistical concerns of the CLIU and the involved school districts. However, the defendant concedes that classes have been relocated on occasion to make room for non-handicapped children. Given the disruption of the educational programs of CLIU students that is inherent in such relocations, and the inequity of forcing handicapped youngsters to travel extended distances in order to attend their relocated classes, I do not consider the accommodation of non-handicapped students to be a sufficient reason to justify these moves. Accordingly, I hold that inter-school or interdistrict CLIU classroom relocations resulting from a failure of the school districts to provide adequate space for CLIU classes constitutes a violation of the defendant's statutory duty to ensure that handicapped students do not suffer discrimination in the provision of educational facilities.

3. *Restrictive Classroom Settings:* A further result of the CLIU's inability to obtain adequate classroom space in regular schools is that CLIU students "have been educated in facilities that are separate from and more restrictive than the regular school environment," including "separate

schools or centers; separate wings or sections of regular schools; and mobile classes or trailers." Despite the statutory preference for mainstreaming, 20 U.S.C. § 1412(5) [Now § 1412(a)(5)(A)] also evidences Congress' recognition "that regular classrooms simply would not be a suitable setting for the education of many handicapped children. . . . The Act thus provides for the education of some handicapped children in separate classes or institutional settings."

Although the defendant does not press this point, I may safely assume that in the case of children with particularly severe mental, emotional, or physical handicaps, education in separate facilities, or separate sections of regular schools, may not only be warranted by logistical exigencies, but may be required for the students' appropriate education.

However, the defendant has conceded that many CLIU children "are capable of being educated in special classes located in regular schools attended by their non-handicapped peers." In the case of such children, the mainstreaming objective of the EHA is thwarted if disabled youngsters are shunted off to separate facilities, or unnecessarily segregated in isolated classrooms in regular schools, solely because the local school districts refuse to provide adequate classroom space for CLIU students. I thus hold that this practice is a violation of the defendant's duty to assure that handicapped children are educated in the "regular educational environment" to the maximum extent appropriate to the needs of the handicapped children. My holding is of course limited to those CLIU students who are capable of being educated in regular schools.

4. *Failure to Open Necessary Classes:* The most distressing admissions by defendant are those relating to the CLIU's inability, because of inadequate classroom space, to open enough special education classes to meet the needs of class members. The defendant concedes that in at least four recent instances, proposed classes which were needed to ensure the appropriate special education of handicapped children were not opened because no district would provide classroom space. I have little difficulty in holding that the failure to open classes necessary for the appropriate special education of class members runs afoul of the commonwealth's duty under the EHA and the implementing regulations of § 504 to assure that handicapped children receive "a free appropriate education." 20 U.S.C. § 1412.

The Local School

The IDEA does not create an absolute right to be placed in the neighborhood school, but it does require, in its regulations, that the student with disabilities should be placed "as close as possible to . . . home."[10] The child is to be "educated in the school which he or she would attend if nondisabled" unless the IEP provides otherwise.[11]

The local neighborhood school goal must be balanced with the requirement that education be appropriate and individualized. The regulations are unclear on what "as close as possible" means. Must support services such as therapy or a resource room be provided at every local school site? Or is it permissible to place a child in a reasonably proximate school that is not the child's neighborhood school but that provides a particular support service necessary for the child to benefit from the education program? The courts have uniformly held that the IDEA does not mandate a right to have appropriate special education provided in the neighborhood school. These cases, however, have not involved situations where school choice options (such as magnet schools, vouchers programs, inter- and intra-district transfers, and charter schools) have been available. School districts that provide school choice options may eventually be challenged by parents of students with disabilities under Section 504 and the Americans with Disabilities Act (ADA) if these programs do not provide proportionate opportunities to these students.

Regulations under Section 504 of the Rehabilitation Act do not require that every existing facility be made barrier free, and they recognize compliance if the program is accessible when viewed in its entirety.[12] It should be emphasized, however, that new construction should be accessible within current design standard specifications.[13] This could be interpreted as permitting placement of a student with a mobility impairment in a barrier-free building that is not the child's neighborhood school. There is some case authority for requiring delivery of therapy or programming in the neighborhood school, but it is not a well-settled issue. It would seem, then, that a similar analysis could be applied to other programs. It could be argued, by analogy, that a child could be placed in a school other than the neighborhood school in order to have access to certain types of therapy or other special educational programming.

The Americans with Disabilities Act (ADA)[14] requires new construction of both public and private schools to meet specific accessibility design requirements. Existing facilities must also remove barriers to the extent it is not unduly burdensome to do so. The ADA also contemplates removing barriers unless the program is accessible when viewed in its entirety for public schools. For private schools, the ADA requires the removal of barriers to the extent it is readily achievable.

The mainstreaming principle supports education with peers who are not disabled. If that can be achieved by providing the education at a school other than the neighborhood school, it would seem at least that part of the principle would be satisfied by providing education in a reasonably close regular school. It is, of course, desirable to provide the education to the child in the neighborhood school, if possible. By doing so, this provides the child the opportunity to be educated with children who are neighbors and with whom the child may have interaction outside the classroom. It also avoids the concern about having a child spend an undue amount of time being transported to and from home. But it may be unduly expensive and in some cases impossible to provide every support service and program in every local neighborhood school.

Urban areas provide greater opportunity than do rural areas for creative arrangements. For example, one school site could be made barrier free to serve several closely surrounding local school site populations. A similar plan could be applied for children needing physical therapy or speech therapy, or several local neighborhood schools could be served by having a particular type of program available at one of them. An argument could be made that such placements are for administrative convenience rather than to address the individual needs of the children. It is important in setting up consortium-type arrangements that there are not so many placements of special education students at one site that the result is a "special education school." There is no specific federal statutory guidance of what percentage of the student population should be nondisabled. Many special education advocates take the position that the percentage of students with disabilities in a school should be no more than what occurs in natural proportions in the community. The avoidance of "ghetto-izing" special education students, however, is an important consideration for school district planners.

Another relevant factor in deciding to place a child in a regular school other than the child's neighborhood school is the time the child will spend in transit. Although the school will most probably be required to provide transportation in such cases, lengthy trips should be avoided. Depending on the age and disability of the child, long bus rides can have serious detrimental effects on students. In addition, time spent in transit cannot be counted as instructional time and cannot be used to reduce the length of the school day. Where possible, it may be better to have certain services or programming provided by itinerant personnel. For the student with certain types of related service needs, such as suctioning, it is not an alternative.

While it is certainly an ideal goal that all children (particularly those in elementary school) attend the neighborhood school, there are sometimes countervailing policies. Busing children to other than the neighborhood school has been used to achieve the policy of racial desegregation. For students with disabilities, the ability to provide appropriate programming efficiently is another important social policy. But when transporting students with disabilities to distant schools for the sake of efficient delivery of special education services has a significantly adverse effect on the student or is done solely for administrative convenience, it is probable that the placement is not going to be viewed as "appropriate."

Separate Facilities

For some students, temporary placement in a residential institution or hospital is necessary in order to benefit from education. Chapter 12 addresses issues of residential placements in greater detail. It should be noted here, however, that any placement in a separate facility is viewed as restrictive, and such placements should be made only when absolutely necessary.

Recent years have brought a movement in both directions for residential placements. The IDEA and other federal and state laws provided the basis in the late 1970s and early 1980s for moving students who are mentally retarded back into the local communities and into the local schools. The movement in the other direction came from parents of students whose problems were alcohol or drug related. Because of the heavy emotional demands such students place on their families, some parents may prefer residential placement for their children. The high costs of these placements, however, often cause schools to avoid approving them.

Another population about which there is dispute over separate facilities is deaf students. A significant diversity of opinion exists over whether deaf students should be educated in special schools or centers or whether education in the regular school is desirable.

The following case illustrates one judicial response to that debate.

LACHMAN V. ILLINOIS STATE BOARD OF EDUCATION

852 F.2d 290 (7th Cir. 1988)

Benjamin Lachman is a profoundly deaf seven-year-old child who resides within the district boundaries of the east Maine, Illinois School District No. 63 ("the school district"). The school district is a member of the Maine Township Special Education Program ("MSTEP") and through MSTEP contracts with Northern Suburban Special Education District to provide services for its hearing-impaired students through a Regional Hearing Impaired Program ("RHIP"). Since the time Benjamin became eligible for participation in the RHIP pre-school program, in September, 1984, his parents and the school district have disagreed as to the manner in which his education should be facilitated. That disagreement eventually led the Lachmans to initiate his private cause of action [under] the Education for All Handicapped Children Act [EAHCA].

I

The Lachmans believe that Benjamin can best be educated at a neighborhood school near his home, in a regular classroom with the assistance of a full-time cued speech instructor.*

In contrast, the school district has consistently proposed that all or at least half of Benjamin's school day be spent in a RHIP self-contained classroom with other hearing-impaired children. Those self-contained classrooms are located in schools outside Benjamin's neighborhood. The placements advocated by the school district have all incorporated components providing that, to varying degrees, Benjamin would be integrated into classes and activities with the non-hearing-impaired children in the regular classrooms at those schools. The course of education recommended by the school district centers on the use of the total communication approach to educating hearing-impaired children, which relies primarily upon sign language as a means of communication. The school district has proposed only interim utilization of the cued speech approach, to the extent necessary to effectively transition Benjamin into the total communication-based program. . . .

At its core the complaint alleges that the IEP proposed by the RHIP and the school district, and approved by the Illinois State Board of Education, fails to provide Benjamin with a free appropriate public education as required by § 612(1) of the EAHCA.**

---

* Cued speech is a technique for aiding hearing-impaired persons to understand spoken language. It is used in conjunction with speech (lip) reading and employs eight hand shapes held in four positions close to the mouth to clarify phonetic ambiguities.

** [The IEP] proposed that Benjamin be placed at Forest View School in a self-contained total communication hearing-impaired program at the primary level. An FM auditory training unit would be provided. Benjamin would be mainstreamed with an interpreter in social studies, science, gym and art. He would receive reading and math in the self-contained classroom at an early second grade level. He would receive interpreter services. He would participate in a pilot project in the areas of speech development and introduction of new vocabulary. Cued speech would also be utilized to assist Benjamin in the transition to signed English. Forest View is an integrated K–5 school with 317 students, thirty-five of whom are hearing-impaired.

[This is an appeal from the dismissal of the parents' complaint.]

It is well established that in reviewing the outcomes reached through the §§ 1415(b) and (c) [Now § 1415(g)] administrative appeals procedure, a district court is to make an independent decision as to whether the requirements of the Act have been satisfied. That decision is to be based on a preponderance of the evidence, giving due weight to the results of those state administrative proceedings. The district court's determination that the IEP proposed for Benjamin by the school district constituted a free appropriate public education as required by the EAHCA is founded on its application of the relevant provisions of the Act to the facts attendant to Benjamin's circumstance. We review the determination of that mixed question of law and fact *de novo*. . . .

III

Examination of the district court opinion reveals that it considered the focal point of the disagreement between the Lachmans and the school district to be a question of whether Benjamin's education can best be facilitated by utilization of the cued speech technique or the total communication concept. The Lachmans dispute that inference by the district court. They perceive that the outcome-determinative question in this case is whether the challenged IEP fails to satisfy the Act's § 612(5) requirement that "to the maximum extent appropriate" Benjamin, as a handicapped child, be "educated with children who are not handicapped," and that he be removed from the regular classroom environment and placed in a special class only to the extent that "the nature or severity of [his] handicap is such that education in regular classes with the use of supplementary aids and services cannot be achieved satisfactorily." 20 U.S.C. § 1412(5)(B) [Now § 1412(a)(5)].

In *Rowley*, the Supreme Court was not directly confronted with a claim that the § 1412(5)(B) [Now § 1412(a)(5)(A)] mainstreaming goal had not been satisfied. In that opinion, the Court made only a passing reference to the "preference" for mainstreaming handicapped children reflected in § 612(5)(B) of the Act. *Rowley*, 458 U.S. at 202–03. Thus, the Lachmans claim that the district court erred because, in applying the *Rowley* test for satisfaction of the Act's general requirement that Benjamin be provided a free appropriate public education, it failed to adequately address the issues raised by the § 1412(5)(B) [Now § 1412(a)(5)(A)] preference for mainstreaming handicapped children.

The district court opinion is carefully drawn and fully addresses the components of the *Rowley* test for compliance with the general, overriding requirement of the EAHCA, imposed by § 1412(1) [Now § 1412(a)(1)], that Benjamin Lachman be provided with a free appropriate public education. However, because it believed the real point of contention between the Lachmans and the school district to be a disagreement as to which of two communication methodologies should be used to facilitate Benjamin's early primary education, the district court engaged in a prototypal *Rowley* analysis, devoting only one paragraph to the issue of mainstreaming. That paragraph concludes with the observation that under the proposed IEP "Benjamin will be completely mainstreamed in a short period of time."

(Continued)

(Continued)

Rowley makes clear that "once a court determines that the requirements of the Act have been met, questions of methodology are for resolution by the State." The mainstreaming preference articulated in § 1412(5)(B) [Now § 1412(a)(5)(A)] is one of the "requirements of the Act" referred to in the above excerpt from *Rowley.* Because the parties' disagreement as to the extent to which Benjamin is to be mainstreamed is inexorably intertwined with their disagreement as to the choice between the cued speech and total communication methodologies, we must first ascertain which of those issues, if any, predominates here.

In order to divine the true crux of the dispute that prompted the present cause of action, we must establish the nature of the mainstreaming obligation created by § 1412(5)(B) [Now § 1412(a)(5)(A)] and clarify the relationship of that statutory language to the general § 1412(1) [Now § 1412(a)(1)] requirement that handicapped children be provided with a free appropriate public education. Several post-*Rowley* decisions by the U.S. Courts of Appeals for the Sixth, Eighth and Ninth Circuits, as well as a small number of reported district court opinions, have addressed this topic. . . .

[I]t is clear that the courts considering this issue have determined that the Act's mainstreaming preference is to be given effect only when it is clear that the education of the particular handicapped child can be achieved satisfactorily in the type of mainstream environment sought by the challengers to the IEP proposed for that child. . . .

We are convinced that appellants' effort to characterize the sole, true issue in this case as whether the proposed IEP satisfies the § 1412(5)(B) [Now § 1412(a)(5)(A)] mainstreaming preference is misdirected. Undoubtedly, this case does present a valid question of whether the IEP proposed by the school district and affirmed by the Illinois State Board of Education would result in Benjamin being mainstreamed to the "maximum extent appropriate" as contemplated by § 1412(5)(B) [Now § 1412(a)(5)(A)]. However, on careful examination, it becomes apparent that a determination of whether the IEP proposed for Benjamin provides for mainstreaming to the maximum extent appropriate can be made only within the context of the methodology employed to facilitate his education.

The degree to which a challenged IEP satisfies the mainstreaming goal of the EAHCA simply cannot be evaluated in the abstract. Rather, that laudable policy objective must be weighed in tandem with the Act's principal goal of ensuring that the public schools provide handicapped children with a free appropriate education. A major part of the task of local and state officials in fashioning what they believe to be an effective program for the education of a handicapped child is the selection of the methodology or methodologies that will be employed. "The primary responsibility for formulating the education to be accorded a handicapped child, *and for choosing the education method most suitable to the child's needs*, was left by the Act to state and local education agencies in cooperation with the parents or guardians of the child."

The Lachmans' contention that their son can be fully mainstreamed rests squarely on their belief in, and preference for, the cued speech technique. They do not maintain that the fully-mainstreamed placement they seek would be possible without the use of cued speech and the utilization of a cued speech instructor working at Benjamin's side, full-time, in the classroom. Further, appellants do not claim that Benjamin could be mainstreamed in any greater extent than called for in the proposed IEP, if the total communication methodology is utilized. The reasons relied on by the school district for refusing to place Benjamin in a regular classroom full-time focus on its lack of confidence in the cued speech technique as a means of facilitating immediate, full mainstreaming in Benjamin's case. Instead, the school district believes that the total communication concept is the most appropriate way to facilitate Benjamin's early primary education and it has selected that methodology for his IEP.

On the facts of this case, it is clear that [the] § 1417(5)(B) [Now § 1412(a)(5)(A)] issue of mainstreaming is subsumed by the parties' disagreement as to methodology. In the absence of the parties' difference of opinion as to that question of educational methodology, there would be no disagreement between them as to the extent of mainstreaming that could presently be achieved for Benjamin. Given the nature of the disagreement between the parties and the concomitant thrust of the Lachmans' cause of action, we can only conclude that the district court did not err when it framed its substantive analysis in a manner closely tracking the *Rowley* opinion, without expressly addressing the § 1412(5)(B) [Now § 1412(a)(5)(A)] mainstreaming issue.

IV

We have determined that the core, dispositive issue in the controversy that underlies this cause of action is one centering on a disagreement between appellant parents and appellee school district as to the most appropriate method whereby the education of the parents' handicapped child is to be facilitated. . . .

Rowley and its progeny leave no doubt that parents, no matter how well motivated, do not have a right under the EAHCA to compel a school district to provide a specific program or employ a specific methodology in providing for the education of their handicapped child. . . .

It is clear that the IEP proposed by the school district is based upon an accepted, proven methodology for facilitating the early primary education of profoundly hearing-impaired children. Further, nothing in the record indicates that the proposed IEP does not provide that Benjamin will be educated in a regular classroom environment to the maximum extent appropriate as required by § 612(5)(B) of the Act. Given these findings, we conclude that the proposed IEP will provide Benjamin Lachman with a free appropriate public education as required by § 612(1) of the Act. Accordingly, the judgment of the district court is AFFIRMED.

It is important to note that a decision about whether to mainstream is to be based on the individual needs, abilities, and other factors for that student. Several judicial decisions have addressed factual situations involving students who are deaf and mainstreaming, and these decisions have reached a variety of results in terms of the appropriate placement.[15]

In all cases, the decision about separate facilities should be based on an individualized determination about what is appropriate *for that student.* The least restrictive environment mandate establishes a presumption that separate placement is inappropriate, and the party wanting a more restrictive placement has the burden of justifying it. To the extent that a separate facility is permitted as being temporarily necessary for the child's educational needs, it should be required that the "facility and the services and activities provided therein are comparable to the other facilities, services, and activities of the program."[16]

Other Issues

Nonacademic Programming

The IDEA is very clear that not only should the academic portion of the program be provided in the least restrictive setting possible but also that nonacademic and extracurricular services and activities be nonrestrictive. These activities include meals, recess periods, sports, and student organizations.[17] For some children, whose "academic" placement is very restrictive—that is, placement in a separate class within the regular school setting—the interaction in nonacademic programming such as a physical education class may be the only opportunity to benefit from the experience of age-peer interaction. Not only should it be stressed that mainstreaming is a requirement for such activities, but it will be important that the staff and faculty who are responsible for these activities have appropriate training in working with children with disabilities.[18]

One of the issues that arises in the context of sports and athletics is the potential risk to the child. For some activities, the concern for risk may have to be addressed by providing more supervisory personnel. There are, however, certain activities, such as contact sports, where the risk cannot be alleviated by greater supervision. According to the weight of judicial opinion, a student who is blind in one eye or who has one kidney may be legally excluded from certain contact sports. The courts have generally recognized that students under the age of majority cannot appreciate the risk in such cases, and cannot waive liability.

For students with minimal disabilities or disabilities that do not qualify the individual as a student with a disability under the IDEA, protection against discrimination will be provided only under Section 504 of the Rehabilitation Act and the ADA rather than the IDEA. These students would not have available the detailed procedural safeguards available under the IDEA. Section 504 and the ADA, however, would require that reasonable accommodation be provided to those students who were otherwise qualified for the activity. One interesting case related to this issue involved a high school student with a limb deficiency that significantly impaired her walking ability. She was prevented from participating in a trip to Spain by the school because she could not do the walking required for the trip. The court upheld the exclusion and found that because the student was not otherwise qualified, there was no violation of Section 504.[19]

The Interests of Students Who Are Not Disabled

The interest of the student with a disability in being integrated with age-appropriate peers occasionally is at odds with the interest of students who are not disabled in being able to be provided education. Where the student with a disability is so disruptive that the education of the other students is significantly impaired, removal from the regular classroom may be allowed in appropriate circumstances. The student with a disability must still be provided education, but not in the regular classroom setting. The issues that will be subject to dispute, of course, are whether the disruption is "significant" and whether support personnel or different modifications might not prevent the disruption. The 1997 amendments to the IDEA allow for placement in an alternative educational setting in appropriate circumstances, and the 2004 amendments provided additional clarification. This issue is discussed more fully in Chapter 16.

In addition, a child whose health condition poses a risk of contagion to other children may be removed without violating the IDEA, Section 504, or the ADA. The issue in such cases will be whether there actually is a risk.

It should be noted that consideration for the student who does not have a disability should not be overridden by the least restrictive environment mandate for the student with a disability. There is, however, research supporting the positive effects on children who are not disabled in many cases of integration. In cases involving disruptive students, appropriate staffing or programming often eliminates the negative effect of a child whose behavior interferes with the education of other children.

Cost as an Issue

The issue of cost is addressed more fully in Chapter 14, but it is of interest to note that at least one court has recognized cost as a relevant factor in a decision involving mainstreaming. In assessing whether a school is required to place an elementary-aged boy who was severely mentally retarded in a regular elementary school, the court in the following case considered cost. The district court analysis was accepted by the Eighth Circuit in its holding.

A.W. V. NORTHWEST R-1 SCHOOL DISTRICT

813 F.2d 158 (8th Cir. 1987)

In light of the minimal benefit A.W. would receive from placement in House Springs, the Court finds that the placement is not feasible. The specific difficulty with placement at the House Springs School is that there is no teacher who is certified to teach severely retarded children like A.W. The addition of a teacher is not an acceptable solution here since the evidence before the Court shows that the funds available are limited so that placing a teacher at House Springs for the benefit of a few students at best, and possibly only A.W., would directly reduce the educational benefits provided to other handicapped students by increasing the number of students taught by a single teacher at [State School No. 2]. The Court finds that although the plaintiff presented evidence that A.W. might benefit from exposure to nonhandicapped peers, this possible

(Continued)

(Continued)

benefit is insufficient to justify a reduction in unquestioned benefits to other handicapped children which would result from an inequitable expenditure of the finite funds available. . . .

It is consistent with the Supreme Court's conclusion in *Rowley* that the Act does not require states to provide each handicapped child with the best *possible* education at public expense, and the Court's recognition that available financial resources must be equitably distributed among all handicapped children. . . .

We decline to construe the Act in the manner A.W. urges. To do so would tie the hands of local and state educational authorities who must balance the reality of limited public funds against the exceptional needs of handicapped children. To do so would also encourage the federal courts to ignore the Supreme Court's admonition that "[t]he primary responsibility for formulating the education to be accorded a handicapped child, and for choosing the education method most suitable to the child's needs, was left by the Act to state and local educational agencies in cooperation with the parents or guardian of the child." *Rowley*, 458 U.S. at 207. We hold that the district court did not err in considering whether A.W. would benefit from placement in House Springs or in considering the cost to Northwest R-1 of such a placement.

At least one other circuit considered state finances in addressing a mainstreaming issue, and at least three other circuits have considered cost as a factor in placement decisions in general.[20]

Summary

One of the underlying principles of the IDEA is that the education of children with disabilities is to be provided to the maximum extent appropriate along with children who are not disabled. Judicial interpretation of this principle has added age appropriateness as an element of this requirement.

The goal of inclusion or the provision of education in the least restrictive environment does not require that every child be educated in the regular classroom. The statute and regulations specifically contemplate that more restrictive placements may be necessary, and that the schools should provide a continuum of alternative placements to meet these situations.

The general principle of inclusion is based on a recognition of the stigma of separate placement and the benefit of peer modeling. Courts have looked to these factors in addressing issues of inclusion within the classroom itself, the location of the classrooms within the school building, the right to attend the local school, placement in totally separate facilities, and participation in extracurricular activities. They have reached a variety of conclusions in applying these factors to such issues. In these cases, courts have also had occasion to consider the interests of the students who are not disabled and cost considerations as additional factors to weigh in determining whether a particular placement is too restrictive. It has generally been recognized as appropriate for courts to take these factors into account.

Questions for Reflection

1. Should a child who is severely mentally retarded, such as Neill Roncker, who could interact in a regular gym or music class be required to be mainstreamed into a regular school setting?

2. What are the differences between the *Roncker* decision and the *Daniel R. R.* decision?

3. The court in the *Besteiro* decision issued a temporary injunction requiring that an air-conditioned classroom be provided. It is likely from the language in the opinion that this would be the result if the plaintiffs were seeking a permanent injunction. The court did not, however, address several other issues. Should the school be required to air-condition the entire school building, so that Raul could attend music, art, and other classes?

4. *Besteiro* was decided before the *Rowley* Supreme Court decision clarifying the meaning of "appropriate." Would the fact that Raul was making straight A's change this court's decision as to whether Raul was receiving an appropriate education in the separate cubicle?

5. The 1986 amendments to the IDEA provide for incentive programs to allow programming for children with disabilities from birth to age 5. Most states do not have preschool programming available to all children within the state and, as a result, must place students with disabilities in private programs. As a practical matter, can the goal of inclusion be accomplished in the preschool setting without requiring states to establish preschool programs for children who are not disabled on a broad scale? Is the inclusion philosophy important for preschool children?

6. What obligation does the school have to protect the child with a disability who is placed in the regular classroom from undue teasing by other students?

7. If peer interaction is deemed to be essential in a particular case, how can that be accomplished if the child also needs year-round programming? In other words, how will peer interaction occur during the summer months?

8. If public school buildings are used for non-school-sponsored programs, such as Boy Scouts and Girl Scouts, is it permissible to have separate Scout troops for children who are mentally retarded? Does this violate the IDEA or is there a constitutional violation at issue?

9. If a state requires that eligibility for certain extracurricular activities be based on maintaining a particular grade point average, is there any problem with such a policy for students with disabilities? Should it make a difference if the eligibility requirements apply only to major sports rather than all extracurricular activities such as the Choral Club?

10. In 1985, the Department of Education considered, but ultimately rejected, a policy that would require that a placement in a regular program be tried before a more restrictive placement could be attempted. Would this be a good policy? Why or why not?

NOTES

1. Katie Shultz Stout, "Special Education Inclusion," posted on http://www.weac.org/resource/june96/speced.htm, updated March 15, 2007 (last accessed June 14, 2008).

2. 20 U.S.C. § 1412(a)(5)(A). See also Laura Rothstein & Julia Rothstein, *Disabilities and the Law* § 2:18 (Thomson West 2006); Patrick Howard, "The Least Restrictive Environment: How to Tell?" 33 *Journal of Law & Education* 167 (2004).

3. 34 C.F.R. §§ 114 and 300.115.

4. The issue of removal for disciplinary reasons is discussed more fully in Chapter 16.

5. See also Stacey Gordon, "Making Sense of the Inclusion Debate Under IDEA," 2006 *BYU Educ . & L. J.* 189 (2006); Mark C. Weber, "The Least Restrictive Environment Obligation as an Entitlement to Educational Services: A Commentary," 5 *U.C. Davis J. Juv. L. & Pol'y* 147 (2001).

6. 34 C.F.R. § 300.115.

7. For a discussion of this issue, see *Comment,* "Age Appropriateness as a Factor in Educational Placement Decisions," 40 *Law & Contemporary Problems* 93 (1985).

8. This principle is supported in *Brown v. Board of Education,* 347 U.S. 483 (1954).

9. 458 U.S. 176, 189 (1982).

10. 34 C.F.R. § 300.116(b)(3).

11. *Id.* § 300.115(c).

12. 34 C.F.R. § 300.104.22(a). It should be emphasized, however, that new construction should be accessible within current design standard specifications.

13. *Id.* at § 104.23.

14. 42 U.S.C. §§ 12101 *et seq.*

15. See *Disabilities and the Law* § 2:18, note 14.

16. See *Briggs v. Board of Education,* 882 F.2d 688 (2d Cir. 1989) (separate placement of hearing-impaired boy was not appropriate when it was feasible to provide integrated setting); *Visco v. School Dist.,* 684 F. Supp. 1310 (W.D. Pa. 1988) (placing two deaf children in a school for hearing-impaired children was appropriate because the mother was also deaf and unable to assist in developing aural skills); *Lachman v. Illinois State Board of Education,* 852 F.2d 290 (7th Cir. 1988) (appropriate to place child who is profoundly hearing impaired in self-contained classroom for half a day); *Barwacz v. Michigan Department of Education,* 674 F. Supp. 1296 (W.D. Mich. 1987) (student who is deaf was appropriately mainstreamed).

17. 34 C.F.R. § 300.117.

18. 20 U.S.C. § 1412(a)(14)(A); 34 C.F.R. § 300.156.

19. *Wolff v. South Colonie Cent. School Dist.,* 534 F. Supp. 758 (N.D.N.Y. 1982).

20. *Tokarcik v. Forest Hills School Dist.,* 665 F.2d 443, 458 (3d Cir. 1981) (mainstreaming did not affect state finances); *Department of Education v. Katherine D.,* 727 F.2d 809, 813–814 (9th Cir. 1983); *Age v. Bullitt County Public Schools,* 673 F.2d 141, 145 (6th Cir. 1982); *Doe v. Anrig,* 692 F.2d 800, 806–807 (1st Cir. 1982). See also Larry J. Bartlett, "The Cost of FAPE: Can LRE Make a Difference?" *ED. LAW Briefing Papers* (March 1992).

12

Private School Placements, Residential Placements, and Public School Choice Programs

This chapter addresses educational placements that are in settings other than the public school placement that would ordinarily be made for a student. Such placements include those in private schools (both placements by the public agency and those made by the parents), residential placements, and placements in a variety of school choice settings such as through vouchers, in magnet schools, and in charter schools. Private school placements in special schools and residential placements are often expensive, and in many situations there is a dispute between the school and the parents about the appropriateness of the placement and payment for it. Providing special education services to students who are placed for reasons other than obtaining special education can be challenging for the educational agency. School choice placements in magnet schools, charter schools, and other school choice placements can raise additional issues. These issues include financial responsibility, service responsibility, transportation, and permissibility of providing services to religious schools.

The 1997 and 2004 amendments to the Individuals with Disabilities Education Act (IDEA) clarified some of the unresolved and confusing questions regarding some of these issues, but because of the high stakes in some of these placements, there is a substantial amount of litigation addressing these issues.

Public Agency Placement in Private Schools

After the individualized education program (IEP) team develops the student's IEP, it must determine the appropriate placement for the student. If the public school is not able to implement the student's IEP, or is otherwise not an appropriate placement for the student, the team may decide to place the student in a private school to receive special education and related services. When the team decides to make such a placement, the public school pays the private school tuition and other costs related to the provision of special education and related services.[1] These students are entitled to the full array of services and procedural protections under the IDEA, and the public school is responsible for ensuring that the student receives a free appropriate public education (FAPE) at the private school. Such placements can include residential programs as well as day only programs.

If the parents object to the team or public agency's recommended placement, they can seek redress through the dispute resolution mechanisms and procedural safeguards described in other chapters.

Parental Placements in Private Schools

There are a number of situations where parents have chosen to place their child in a private school. Some parents have chosen to have the child attend a private school for reasons of personal preference, because the school emphasizes college preparation or because of its religious emphasis, or because the parents just think it is a better school than the public school to which the child is assigned. In other situations, the parents have placed their child in a private school because they believe that the public school was not providing their child with FAPE.

The law treats parental placements differently depending on the reason for the placement. Students who are placed in private schools when FAPE is at issue (meaning the parents allege the public school was not providing FAPE and placed their child in a private school to receive special education and related services) are in one category. Students who are placed in a private school for personal preference reasons (like those noted above) when FAPE is not at issue are in another category.

For students in the first category, the parents place their child in the private school without the agreement or assistance of the local school district and then try to recover the costs for the placement from the public school. This is called a "unilateral placement" when FAPE is at issue. The parents pay for the placement and all related expenses up front and then have the option of seeking reimbursement for these expenses from the local school district.[2]

Parents are entitled to reimbursement only if the local school district did not make FAPE available to the child in a timely manner and if the placement chosen by the parents is appropriate under the IDEA.[3] Where the local educational agency made FAPE available to the child in a public school setting, it is not responsible for the cost of education, including special education and related services, at a private school or facility.[4]

Students placed in private school because of personal preference are in a different category and do not have the same rights as students who are enrolled in public school. For example, they no longer have the right to FAPE and have limited procedural rights. The public educational agency has discretion about which services to provide these students (explained in more detail below) and is not required to provide them with an IEP. Instead, the public educational agency develops a "services plan" that details the services the school is willing to provide. The public agency that is responsible for making the services available is the public school in the school district where the child attends private school, not where the child resides.[5]

Public schools do still have child find obligations for students who are placed in private schools when FAPE is not at issue.[6] These students are to be counted in the funding formula for federal Department of Education grants to state educational agencies.[7] The 2004 IDEA amendments build on changes from the 1997 amendments and address the obligation to find and count students with disabilities in private schools. They also establish the funding formula to provide for such students and set limits on how much must be spent on special education for parent placements in private schools for personal reasons. The amendments also clarify the extent to which children in these situations have access to the procedural safeguards under the IDEA.[8] The IDEA limits do not mean that a state or local educational agency cannot choose to do more in terms of providing these services. But it sets the limits for what is required under federal mandates.

Services in Private Religious Schools

A further clarification of the permissibility of providing special education and related services to students in private schools addresses students in religious schools. The current language provides that "such services . . . may be provided . . . on the premises of private, including religious, schools, to the extent consistent with law."[9] This provision addressed the confusion arising from a series of judicial decisions addressing this issue. Significant problems arise in trying to provide special education and related services to students in parochial schools. This is because of constitutional concerns over separation of church and state. The first amendment to the United States Constitution provides that "Congress shall make no law respecting the establishment of religion, or prohibiting the free exercise thereof." This means that federal grant statutes, such as the IDEA, must not support the establishment of religion. In the area of educational services in general, the Supreme Court has held that not all public educational services provided to parochial schools will be considered to establish religion. The test to determine what support is permissible is found in the case of *Lemon v. Kurtzman.*[10] The Supreme Court permits government services that (1) have a secular purpose, (2) have a primary effect of neither advancing nor inhibiting religion, and (3) do not involve the state in excessive entanglement with religion. In the *Lemon* case, the Supreme Court held that salary supplements for teachers of nonreligious subjects in parochial schools would not be permitted.

The limitations on providing services to children in private parochial schools have eroded substantially in recent years. In 1997, the Supreme Court in *Agostini v. Felton*[11] held that public school teachers may provide special education and related services to children in private schools. The following excerpt highlights some of the challenges in addressing this issue.

ZOBREST V. CATALINA FOOTHILLS SCHOOL DISTRICT

509 U.S. 1 (1993)

Chief Justice Rehnquist delivered the opinion of the Court.

[This case addressed whether James Zobrest, who had been deaf since birth, could receive sign-language interpreter services at a Roman Catholic high school under IDEA. He had received these services in public schools before he attended high school. The case went through various administrative and judicial reviews.]

We have never said that "religious institutions are disabled by the First Amendment from participating in publicly sponsored social welfare programs." For if the Establishment Clause did bar religious groups from receiving general government benefits, then "a church could not be protected by the police and fire departments, or have its public sidewalk kept in repair." Given that a contrary rule would lead to such absurd results, we have consistently held that government programs that neutrally provide benefits to a broad class of citizens defined without reference to religion are not readily subject to an Establishment Clause challenge just because sectarian institutions may also receive an attenuated financial benefit.

[Discussion of two Supreme Court precedents and their applicability omitted.]

That same reasoning [of these Supreme Court decisions] applies with equal force here. The service at issue in this case is part of a general government program that distributes benefits neutrally to any child qualifying as handicapped under the IDEA, without regard to the "sectarian-nonsectarian, or public-nonpublic nature" of the school the child attends. By according parents freedom to select a school of their choice, the statute ensures that a government paid interpreter will be present in a sectarian school only as a result of the private decision of individual parents. In other words, because the IDEA creates no financial incentive for parents to choose a sectarian school, an interpreter's presence there cannot be attributed to state decision-making. . . . When the government offers a neutral service on the premises of a sectarian school as part of a general program that "is in no way skewed towards religion," it follows under our prior decisions that provision of that service does not offend the Establishment Clause. [U]nder the IDEA, no funds traceable to the government ever find their way into sectarian schools' coffers. The only indirect economic benefit a sectarian school might receive by dint of the IDEA is the handicapped child's tuition—and this is, of course, assuming that the school makes a profit on each student; that, without an IDEA interpreter, the child would have gone to school elsewhere; and that the school, then, would have been unable to fill that child's spot.

[R]espondent argues that this case more closely resembles *Meek v. Pittenger,* 421 U.S. 349 (1975), and *School Dist. of Grand Rapids v. Ball,* 473 U.S. 373 (1985). In *Meek,* we struck down a statute that, inter alia, provided "massive aid" to private schools—more than 75% of which were church related—through a direct loan of teaching material and equipment. The material and equipment covered by the statute included maps, charts, and tape recorders. According to respondent, if the government could not place a tape recorder in a sectarian school in *Meek,* then it surely cannot place an interpreter in Salpointe [the private high school]. The statute in *Meek* also authorized state-paid personnel to furnish "auxiliary services"—which included remedial and accelerated instruction and guidance counseling—on the premises of religious schools. We determined that this part of the statute offended the First Amendment as well. *Ball* similarly involved two public programs that provided services on private school premises; there, public employees taught classes to students in private school classrooms. We found that those programs likewise violated the Constitution, relying largely on *Meek*. According to respondent, if the government could not provide educational services on the premises of sectarian schools in *Meek* and *Ball*, then it surely cannot provide James with an interpreter on the premises of Salpointe.

Respondent's reliance on *Meek* and *Ball* is misplaced for two reasons. First, the programs in *Meek* and *Ball*—through direct grants of government aid—relieved sectarian schools of costs they otherwise would have borne in educating their students. . . . For example, the religious schools in *Meek* received teaching material and equipment from the State, relieving them of an otherwise necessary cost of performing their educational function. "Substantial aid to the educational function of such schools," we explained, "necessarily results in aid to the sectarian school enterprise as a whole," and therefore brings about "the direct and substantial advancement of religious activity." So, too, was the case in *Ball:* The programs challenged there, which provided teachers in addition to instructional equipment and material, "in effect subsidize[d] the religious functions of the parochial schools by taking over a substantial portion of their responsibility for teaching secular subjects." "This kind of direct aid," we determined, "is indistinguishable from the provision of a direct cash subsidy to the religious school." The extension of aid to petitioners, however, does not amount to "an impermissible 'direct subsidy'" of Salpointe. For Salpointe is not relieved of an expense that it otherwise would have assumed in educating its students. And, as we noted above, any attenuated financial benefit that parochial schools do ultimately receive from the IDEA is attributable to "the private choices of individual parents." Handicapped children, not sectarian schools, are the primary beneficiaries of the IDEA; to the extent sectarian schools benefit at all from the IDEA, they are only incidental beneficiaries. Thus, the function of the IDEA is hardly "'to provide desired financial support for nonpublic, sectarian institutions.'"

Second, the task of a sign-language interpreter seems to us quite different from that of a teacher or guidance counselor. Notwithstanding the Court of Appeals' intimations to the contrary, the Establishment Clause lays down no absolute bar to the placing of a public employee in a sectarian school. Such a flat rule, smacking of antiquated notions of "taint," would indeed exalt form over substance. Nothing in this record suggests that a sign-language interpreter would do more than accurately interpret whatever material is presented to the class as a whole. In fact, ethical guidelines require interpreters to "transmit everything that is said in exactly the same way it was intended." James' parents have chosen of their own free will to place him in a pervasively sectarian environment. The sign-language interpreter they have requested will neither add to nor subtract from that environment, and hence the provision of such assistance is not barred by the Establishment Clause.

The IDEA creates a neutral government program dispensing aid not to schools but to individual handicapped children. If a handicapped child chooses to enroll in a sectarian school, we hold that the Establishment Clause does not prevent the school district from furnishing him with a sign-language interpreter there in order to facilitate his education. The judgment of the Court of Appeals [barring the interpreter at public expense] is therefore *Reversed.*

The *Zobrest* decision and subsequent Supreme Court interpretations more broadly interpret what is constitutionally allowable for public agencies to provide as special educational programming. Neither these decisions, nor the IDEA itself, however, mandate that publicly provided special education services must be provided to parochial schools, and when such services are provided that they be provided at the parochial school site.

Unusual situations can occur for some religious groups. One such case involved a school district created to completely match the neighborhood boundaries of a Hasidic Jewish sect in order to provide special education to the children in that community without requiring them to attend public schools attended by nonmembers of the group. The Court in *Board of Education v. Grumet*[12] held that such a plan violates the establishment clause of the first amendment to the Constitution. The Court allowed the possibility of providing special education at the public school or a neutral site near the village's parochial school. The current version of the IDEA specifically allows providing services on the religious school site, "to the extent consistent with law."[13] This recognizes that some federal constitutional limitations may limit services as discussed in *Zobrest,* and that some states may regulate how such services are provided.

The current statutory language of the IDEA further clarifies that special education and related services (including materials and equipment) provided to children in private schools shall be "secular, neutral, and nonideological."[14]

Services in Private Placements Generally

When the parents have made a private placement for reasons of personal preference, the public agency's obligation under the IDEA is limited. The funding support that is required is an amount that is "equal to proportionate amount of Federal funds made available" through the IDEA.[15]

As noted earlier, these students no longer have an individual right to the special education and related services that the student would receive if enrolled in a public school.[16] These students also do not have the right to an IEP or to FAPE. Rather, the school district develops a services plan that describes the specific special education and related services that the school district will provide to the individual student in light of the services that the school district has determined it will make available to all privately schooled children with disabilities.[17]

The decision about what services will be provided to all students with disabilities must be done in consultation with representatives of private schools and representatives of parents with children with disabilities placed in private schools.[18] The school district where the private school is located, in consultation with these groups, decides which children will receive services, what services will be provided, how and where the services will be provided, and how the services provided will be evaluated.[19]

Special education and related services can be provided in private schools by a number of means. In a school with a small population of students with disabilities, the service might be provided by an itinerant teacher. In other situations, a public school teacher or therapist may remain at the same private school site at all times.

Services might also be provided by paying a private school employee for the costs of providing the services.

Some state constitutions prohibit public funds from being used to support private purposes. Several judicial decisions have found certain types of support to private schools to fall within the ban on supporting private purposes. It may be necessary in some states, therefore, to require that the services of a public school employee be provided outside of regular working hours. In states with stringent requirements in this regard, it may be impermissible for the state to provide equipment or physical plant renovations at the private school.

While one solution is to allow services at the public school site, this can create significant logistical and administrative problems in moving children back and forth from public site to private site. This has the additional adverse result of requiring children to spend time in transit rather than in learning.

The Americans with Disabilities Act (ADA)[20] creates obligations for private schools in their education of students with disabilities that did not exist under Section 504 of the Rehabilitation Act,[21] which applies only to programs receiving federal financial assistance. Title III of the ADA prohibits certain private programs considered to be public accommodations from discriminating on the basis of disability. Private schools fall under this mandate. The ADA not only prohibits discrimination, but also mandates reasonable accommodations and adopts the least restrictive environment principle.

The ADA requirements create the potential for private schools being required to carry more of the burden for providing and paying for special education and related services at least indirectly in the form of reasonable modifications, rather than having the public education agency being responsible for all of these costs. The ADA mandates private school responsibility for reasonable modifications (such as barrier removal or assistance in providing asthma medication) that are not considered to be special education or related services under the IDEA. The ADA does not require private schools to develop an IEP or to provide procedural safeguards similar to those under the IDEA.

It is possible that private schools that are faced with these new responsibilities under the ADA will attempt to claim undue burden. The ADA provides that programs need not provide accommodations that present an undue burden either financially or administratively. The issue of undue burden seems likely to raise a question similar to the one in which private insurance coverage or other public social service eligibility could apply to certain special education or related service programming. That question is whether the private school may require the parents first to seek payment for or provision of services through the public education agency because of the public agency's IDEA obligations. For example, a student who is deaf and attending a private school and who needs a sign language interpreter to participate in the educational program might request the private school to provide the interpreter as a reasonable accommodation under the ADA. May the private school require the student to first seek eligibility through the public school IDEA process? Additionally, there are concerns that private schools might begin to discriminate (although illegally) against students with disabilities in their admission because of concerns that such students will cost them more than they had in the past.

School Choice and Students With Disabilities

There is an increasing trend toward school choice. These options include vouchers for children attending private schools of the parents' choice and attending charter schools, which are private schools chartered by state or local governmental agencies to provide education to students. They also include attending magnet school programs within the public school system. The goals of these programs vary, but they often include the goal of providing competition for public schools.

One of the problems with school choice options is that the private schools receiving the vouchers, the charter schools, and the magnet programs may not provide access to education to students with disabilities on an equivalent basis. Such schools may have entrance requirements that have a disparate impact on students with disabilities, or there may be architectural barriers that prevent enrollment of students with certain disabilities. To the extent that such programs discriminate against students with disabilities, they would violate Section 504 of the Rehabilitation Act and the ADA. There is already some evidence that some of these programs do not provide an equivalent opportunity for students with disabilities. An additional issue is whether a public educational program that supports a system allowing children with disabilities to be disparately left in the regular neighborhood school or not having equivalent access to school choice options is a violation of the mainstreaming principle of the IDEA. These programs have not been subjected to significant legal challenges applying these theories. In light of the movement toward increasing the number of choice options, it is almost certain that such litigation will occur in the future and that policymakers will have to plan for these challenges.[22]

Charter schools are relatively new. These are schools created as a result of state charter school statutes that allow local school districts or even the state to directly "charter" a school that will receive public funding. The school is to be given substantial freedom from most state and local regulations. They are, however, not exempt from IDEA requirements. The current IDEA provisions clarify that students in public charter schools are entitled to a higher level of support than students placed in other private schools. Children placed in charter schools must be provided special education services and funding by the local agency in the same manner in which it is provided to other public school programs.[23] The procedural safeguards they are entitled to may depend on what type of charter school it is.[24]

Residential Placements

General Principles

Like private school placements, residential placements fall within the category of placements where the child receives services outside of the public school system. These services are expensive and they are viewed as restrictive. Nonetheless, there are situations in which such a placement is appropriate. Residential placements are contemplated by the IDEA regulations:

> If placement in a public or private residential program is necessary to provide special education and related services to a child with a disability, the program, including non-medical care and room and board, must be at no cost to the parents of the child.[25]

The need for residential placements arises in primarily three different situations. First is the individual with a severe or profound disability who needs highly intensive programming.[26] While some of these children can be educated in a regular day program, for others the educational programming is so integrated into the teaching of self-help skills and behavior modification programming that a residential placement may be necessary, at least for some period of time. Another group of individuals whose parents have increasingly been seeking residential placements are children (especially adolescents) who have serious emotional problems, in some cases relating to drug and alcohol dependency. Third, individuals with significant visual or hearing impairments are sometimes educated in a residential setting. There is much debate about whether the best education for these students is in a residential setting, but this issue is usually addressed on a case-by-case basis.

These situations can be contrasted with the student who is mildly or moderately mentally retarded, who before the 1970s might well have been placed in an institution or "residential placement." These individuals were generally moved out of institutions in the late 1970s and early 1980s and are very unlikely to be placed in an institution in the first place.

Residential placements are important for educational agencies to address because they can be extremely expensive, costing as much as $200,000 per year.[27] That can be a very large portion of a local school district's budget. Several questions must be addressed in looking at residential placements under the IDEA. These questions include the following: (1) Is the program the least restrictive appropriate placement? (2) Must all of the costs be borne by the school district? and (3) What if there is no appropriate accredited placement available?[28]

Some additional policy questions also might be raised. These include whether the programming, such as toilet training and other self-help skills, is really "education" that must be provided to children with profound disabilities and whether adolescents with drug-related or emotional problems resulting primarily from family situations should be provided expensive placements at public expense, particularly when the parents are able to bear the cost. While some of these questions are addressed by existing law, many are not, and they raise complex social problems for the families.

Least Restrictive Appropriate Placement

A placement in a residential program is usually viewed as very restrictive. Thus, such a placement will be given careful scrutiny in light of the IDEA's philosophy of preferring the least restrictive appropriate placement. In spite of its restrictive nature, the placement will be considered appropriate if it is necessary for the child to benefit from education. There is, however, a significant degree of difficulty in separating educational and noneducational needs in this area, and in some cases the placement may result from medical, social, or emotional problems separate from the learning process. These difficulties result from the interrelationship of various problems.

The following case is one of the earliest major decisions on residential placements. It still is frequently cited as a standard on this issue.

KRUELLE V. NEW CASTLE COUNTY SCHOOL DISTRICT

642 F.2d 687 (3d Cir. 1981)

[Paul Kruelle] is profoundly retarded and is also afflicted with cerebral palsy. At age thirteen he has the social skills of a six-month-old child and his I.Q. is well below thirty. [H]e cannot walk, dress himself, or eat unaided. He is not toilet trained. He does not speak, and his receptive communication level is extremely low. In addition to his physical problems, he has had a history of emotional problems which result in choking and self-induced vomiting when experiencing stress. . . .

[T]he district court concluded that Paul required a greater degree of consistency than many other profoundly retarded children. Specifically, it held that the present educational program [a day program] provided by the [school district] was not a free appropriate public education within the meaning of the Act. Then, in a supplemental order, the district court directed the State Education Board to provide Paul with a full-time residential program. . . .

Significantly, all parties concede that Paul needs full-time assistance from the state of Delaware beyond that available in any day school program. It is also uncontroverted that the Education Act specifically provides for residential placement in certain instances. The question, then, is whether the trial judge correctly construed the Education Act as requiring more continuous supervision for Paul than he was receiving under the [day program] in order to meet the standard of a free appropriate education.

Based on our careful review of the record, we cannot find that the district court erred in holding that the six-hour day provided by the [day] program was an inappropriate education given the terms of the Act. The trial judge's conclusion that Paul required more continuous care is supported generally by the logic of [prior case law].

The school district centers its challenge on the proposition that here the residential placement is required only for reasons of medical and domiciliary care, not for educational purposes. But . . . the concept of education is necessarily broad with respect to persons such as Paul. "Where basic self-help and social skills such as toilet training, dressing, feeding and communication are lacking, formal education begins at that point." And Congress was clearly aware of children with needs similar to those of Paul, and was quite conscious of the foundational nature of their education. The Education Act unqualifiedly provides for a free appropriate education for all handicapped children, "regardless of the severity of their handicap." . . .

Analysis must focus, then, on whether full-time placement may be considered necessary for educational purposes, or whether the residential placement is a response to medical, social or emotional problems that are segregable from the learning process. This Court is not the first to attempt to distinguish between residential placement that is a necessary predicate for learning and the provision of services that are unrelated to learning skills. One of the early cases to grapple with this issue, . . . actually collapsed the distinction by declaring the impossibility of separating emotional and educational needs in complex cases. [That] case is almost indistinguishable on the facts from the present case. It also involved the same issue: whether placement was required for emotional problems and was therefore the responsibility of the parents or social service agencies or whether full-time placement was a necessary ingredient for learning. [That] court enjoined the school board from denying a sixteen-year-old multiply-handicapped epileptic free placement in a residential academic program because it found the social, emotional, medical and educational problems to be so intertwined "that realistically it is not possible for the court to perform the Solomon-like task of separating them." However, as later cases demonstrate, the claimed inextricability of medical and educational grounds for certain services does not signal court abdication from decision-making in difficult matters. Rather, the unseverability of such needs is the very basis for holding that the services are an essential prerequisite for learning. . . .

[H]ere, consistency of programming and environment is critical to Paul's ability to learn, for the absence of a structured environment contributed to Paul's choking and vomiting which, in turn, interferes fundamentally with his ability to learn. [U]ltimately any life support system or medical aid can be construed as related to a child's ability to learn. But this would ignore the very limitations the legislation provides. The statutory language requires courts to assess the link between the supportive service or educational placement and the child's learning needs. Thus, . . . inasmuch as the statute comprehends only services "as may be required to assist a handicapped child to benefit from special education," "a life support service would not be a related service if it did not have to be provided during school hours, but instead could be performed at some other time." The relevant question in the present case is whether residential placement is part and parcel of a "specially designed instruction . . . to meet the unique needs of a handicapped child."

. . . And we cannot conclude that the district judge misapplied the statutory standard in determining that "because of his combination of physical and mental handicaps, [Paul] requires a greater degree of consistency of programming than many other profoundly retarded children" and that "it would appear that full-time care is necessary in order to allow Paul to learn." Indeed, it would be difficult to conceive of a more apt case than Paul's for which the unique needs of a child required residential placement. . . .

Of course, before ordering residential placement, a court should weigh the mainstreaming policy embodied in the Education Act which encourages placement of the child in the least restrictive environment. The district judge here, however, carefully undertook such a calculation. He noted that in the past attempts to provide in-home care and after-school instruction had been singularly unsuccessful; all had occasioned regression for Paul. Once a court concludes that residential placement is the only realistic option for learning improvement, the question of "least restrictive" environment is also resolved. "Only when alternatives exist must the court reach the issue of which is the least restrictive." If day school cannot provide an appropriate education it is, by definition, not a possible alternative.

The standard for decision making in the *Kruelle* case, the "intertwined needs" with "educational link" test, is only one approach to making decisions about residential placements. While this probably represents the current trend of majority opinion, there are other judicial approaches that have been used. One commentator has categorized and analyzed four major approaches.[29]

First is the "uneducable approach." The premise is that for certain extremely low-functioning populations educational residential placements are not required because these children are "uneducable." The *Timothy W.* case discussed in Chapter 5 is one of the major rejections of this principle.

Second is the "separate and balance" approach. This approach involves an attempt to separate a child's educational needs from other needs including those commonly referred to as medical, custodial, social, emotional, and behavioral. The next step is to determine which of the needs are most responsible for necessitating the residential placement. If it is determined that the child's educational needs are not primarily responsible for the placement, the school district is not obligated under the IDEA.[30]

One problem with this approach is that "[i]t is often . . . impossible to draw neat lines between the various needs. . . ."[31] Another problem is that the placement may address only the primary needs of the child because many residential programs have a primary emphasis.

The third approach is referred to as the "intertwined needs approach."[32] This approach initially attempts to separate the needs but recognizes that in certain cases, such as children with multiple and severe disabilities, this will not be possible. This approach, however, does not really assign responsibility to the school district for the placement.

It is the fourth approach that was used in the *Kruelle* decision, namely an "intertwined needs" approach that added an "educational link" component.[33] The test first determines that the needs are not severable, and then asks if the placement is "necessary for the child to benefit from education." This test seems to be the one adopted in a significant number of rulings. The danger of applying this approach, however, is in a restricted view of what it means to benefit from education. Some courts tend to look only at academic progress. At the other extreme is whether requiring a residential placement that mandates psychiatric services is a violation of the IDEA provision exempting educational agencies from providing medical services.[34]

The commentator's suggested approach would be that

> decision makers should acknowledge that social, behavioral, and other such difficulties, in and of themselves, warrant remedial intervention as educational needs rather than as opposed to or impacting upon educational needs.[35]

A few courts and administrative decision makers have adopted this approach.[36] Additionally, the IDEA now requires schools to address more than just academic needs. Social and emotional, developmental and functional needs must now be addressed as part of FAPE.[37]

It is important to understand that the IDEA does not require schools to provide the *best* program, but they must provide an appropriate program. Even though parents may not like the program the school is offering, as long as what the school is offering is appropriate, that is all the educational agency is required to provide. Parents may, of course, choose to place their child in an alternative program at their own cost.

A residential placement can mean a variety of settings—from the traditional "institution" to a group home or foster care. It could be argued that placement in a more "normal" setting should be made whenever appropriate because of the importance of complying with the least restrictive environment mandate. Like any special education placement, a residential placement should be reviewed at least annually. States may set higher standards for an appropriate placement, as the following decision demonstrates.

DAVID D. V. DARTMOUTH SCHOOL COMMITTEE

775 F.2d 411 (1st Cir. 1985)

The only factual matter truly at issue is whether David's special needs are severe enough to warrant a full-time, residential program or whether, instead, David is being educated to the degree legally imposed as a minimum standard by attendance at a special education day program with some supplementary services in the local school district.

David is a seventeen-year-old adolescent with Down's Syndrome, who learns and has skills at the kindergarten level. Although he has been gaining academic skills during the time he has been a student at the Dartmouth school, he has in recent years exhibited a range of seriously inappropriate behavior showing little or no self-control in unstructured or unfamiliar situations. David's parents are concerned that some of the behavior he has been exhibiting will result in his being unable to become a productive adult with a job in a sheltered workshop and denial of his access to and living within the mainstream community. Such has been predicted by special education professionals as the likely outcome, given the range, gravity and frequency of his inappropriate behavior. The parents maintain that the Dartmouth School Committee (Town) has not taught and will not be able to teach David self-control, rendering the IEP the Town proposed for him fatally deficient. The district court agreed with the parents and reversed the decision of the state educational agency. The court expressed the additional concern that David will come into conflict with the law if he persists in a lack of self-control.

The evidence presented at both the administrative hearing and at trial showed that David has repeatedly and unrelentingly engaged in sexual and aggressive behavior directed at persons and animals. He has repeatedly grabbed at students' genitals, lain on the floor of his classroom attempting to look up female students' dresses, tried to touch female staff and students' breasts, and tried to embrace complete strangers. He has repeatedly attempted to engage in sexual play with neighborhood dogs. He has entered neighbors' homes uninvited and has refused to leave. In every valuative setting, David was observed engaging in seriously inappropriate behavior of a sexual and aggressive nature.

(Continued)

(Continued)

The district court carefully reviewed the testimony of special educational professionals who had had experience with David. Except for his classroom teacher, each recounted and characterized David's behavior as extreme even when compared with that of students with similar cognitive functioning. . . .

All parties to the case agreed that social and personal skills including sex education are part of David's special education needs and that his educational program should effectively address these objectives. The conclusion of all four of the independent evaluators was the same: that David needed a comprehensive 24-hour, highly structured special education program that would address his social and behavioral needs in a consistent way by a trained staff throughout his waking hours. These experts, whom the district court credited, uniformly believed that given the frequency and intensity of his unacceptable actions, the Dartmouth IEP would not be sufficient to address David's need for continuous training. They were of the opinion that learning the self-control essential to living in the mainstream community would take from one to two years, and after that, David could and should be returned to the community. . . .

[The court then addressed the issue of whether the state could have more stringent standards than the IDEA and have these enforced through IDEA procedures.]

We do not think Congress envisioned having handicapped children's plans subject to double legal standards dependent solely upon the aggrieved party's choice of forum. Neither do we discern any intention that the federal Act preempt and reduce all state standards to the federal minimum. Rather, we think Congress contemplated, and due process requires, that a consistent body of law would be applied throughout all stages of the due process hearing system. Congress intertwined federal and state standards into one body of law, and did not leave EHA cases dependent upon whether an appeal is taken to a state or federal court.

The next question is whether a state's overall substantive standard for determining the sufficiency of a handicapped child's IEP is to be treated differently from other substantive requirements mandated by the state. The Congress explicitly defined a free appropriate public education as an education which "meets the standards of the State educational agency" and expressly authorized review of the question whether the education actually provided (or proposed) met those standards. Where a state has chosen to provide by law greater benefits to handicapped children than the federal Act requires, we believe Congress explicitly mandated that the courts—both federal and state—determine whether those state standards have been met. We need not decide at this time the extent of what constitutes "relevant" state substantive law; we hold only that a state's overall standard for evaluating the IEPs of handicapped children is incorporated by the federal Act. . . .

We now turn to the district court's decision, which we have no difficulty affirming in its entirety. The overwhelming evidence showed that a change in David's IEP was warranted. The district judge carefully reviewed the administrative findings, received additional evidence, and discussed David's needs as a unique individual, rather than as an abstract representative of the category of children with Down's syndrome. She found that while David was making progress in some of the academic areas within the Dartmouth School Committee's classroom, his inappropriate sexual behavior continued unabated and posed a serious threat to David's ability to live in the community. The importance of "maximizing [David's] potential for eventual placement in a community-based program or private employment" had already been identified by the state hearing officer as an appropriate objective of the IEP.

The district judge was especially concerned that, although David had performed relatively well in the rather cloistered and familiar environment of the school he had been attending for several years, in less familiar situations, or where relatively unsupervised, he frequently showed little or no self-control in his conduct towards other persons. The court pointed to a variety of situations where this had occurred, including David's being sent home from a camp for handicapped youths, and his rejection from other programs. The court was especially concerned because some of the special education experts who evaluated David regarded his lack of self-control and related behavior grave enough to warrant rejection of him from developmentally disabled service programs, and predicted that he would not be admitted to sheltered workshops for employment or community-based programs. As the court concluded, the evidence uniformly shows that the behavior problem in unstructured or unfamiliar situations has become less controlled over the past two years in the Dartmouth Schools rather than improved.

The district court also found that since Massachusetts law mandated a level of substantive benefits superior to that of the federal Act, the state standard would be utilized as determinative of what was an "appropriate" education for the child. The court noted that the Massachusetts Supreme Judicial Court "in a recent decision interpreted [state education law] as requiring the Department of Education to administer special education programs 'to assure the maximum possible development of a child with special needs.'" Since both the federal and state Acts require that education be provided in the least restrictive environment, the district court stated the issue as "whether Dartmouth's IEP addresses plaintiff's special educational needs so as to assure him maximum possible development in the least restrictive environment consistent with that goal." We think that the court both phrased and answered the question correctly.

Cost Issues

If residential placement is necessary for the child to benefit from education, then the school is responsible not only for paying the educational expenses but also for ensuring that the cost of room and board and transportation costs to and from the residential placement are provided at no cost to the parents. The school is not required to pay for medical expenses involved in a residential placement.[38]

Because residential placements are expensive, particularly if the placement is in an out-of-state or private facility, there is an incentive for educational agencies to develop programs and services that would alleviate the need to have residential placements. Such programs and services would include extended day programming, support service in the home, respite care, family counseling, and training for parents in behavior management and other skills. It is important to recognize that it is stressful to have a child with a severe disability and with behavioral and emotional problems in the home. For some parents, there may be a conflict of interest between the need for relief of family stress and the best interests of the child. Providing support services in the home, in some cases, would help to achieve the goal of least restrictive environment (LRE). Exhausted parents, however, may prefer relief to carrying out this goal. While these feelings are understandable, the IDEA does not address the preferences of parents but rather the interest of the child.

Because of the costly nature of these services, disputes often arise over which educational agency (local or state) is responsible for these costs. This is also an issue that is likely to lead to interagency disputes. These issues are addressed more fully in Chapter 14. The 2004 amendments to the IDEA recognize the burden that expensive placements can place on local school districts, and provide for some cost sharing.[39]

Lack of Available Placement

A problem arises in some cases when there is no appropriate placement available in the state. If necessary, the student must be sent to an out-of-state placement. The more difficult problem arises when the only appropriate placement is an unaccredited program and the state will not fund placements in unaccredited programs. One possible way around this might be for an accredited school simply to contract for a private program to provide the services under the supervision of the school, but the success of this approach would depend in part on the relevant state law provisions. As yet, no consistent judicial viewpoint exists on these issues.

Reimbursement for Unilateral Placements

In situations where a parent places a child in a private program, including a residential placement, because the parent does not believe the public agency is providing or will provide appropriate special education, disputes may arise about reimbursement for expenses. This issue is addressed in much greater detail in Chapter 21 on remedies. Briefly, however, the standard is that where the school has provided an appropriate placement, ordinarily the parents may not be reimbursed for these expenses. As noted, the complexities of applying this standard are discussed in Chapter 21.

Summary

Students placed by the public school or educational agency in a private school are entitled to the benefits of a free appropriate public education at no cost to the parents, with the full array of procedural safeguards. The fact that a child's parents have chosen to place the child in a private school does not necessarily relieve the public educational agency from an obligation to provide special education or related services. As a general rule, if the parents request such services from the public educational agency, the agency must make some services available on at least a proportional basis. The 1997 and 2004 amendments to the IDEA clarified how entitlement to special education in placements made by parents works. There remain issues about the constitutionality of providing certain services to a child in a religious school, although recent Supreme Court rulings have provided more flexibility on this issue.

Providing special education services for a child in a private placement does not mean the child is entitled to receive them at the private school site. Making special education available to children who are not physically in attendance at the public school facility can present administrative and logistical problems. Such problems are not a defense, however, to the general obligation to provide such services.

Whenever the special education and regular education are provided at different sites, there will be logistical problems. These include coordinating the services between the various educators and the time and disruption that will be spent in traveling back and forth between the regular school and the school where the special education will be provided.

A residential placement is inherently a restrictive placement. The student is separated from family and from peers who are not disabled. In extreme situations, however, placement may be necessary for the needs of the student. Residential placements necessary for the child to benefit from education must be provided at no cost to the parents. Parents are not required to pay for room and board. Parents pay for medical expenses. Where no other funding source is available, the educational agency may be financially obligated. Because of the high cost of such placements, schools are reluctant to approve them. As a result, this issue is frequently subject to resolution by the courts, which have taken a variety of approaches to determining when the residential placement is necessary. While a single judicial test has yet to be consistently applied, there is a general recognition of the fact that educational needs and other needs are often inextricably intertwined, and where such needs are not severable, the placement will be made if this is what is necessary for the child to benefit from education.

Because of the high cost of such placements, courts are likely to begin developing the application of cost as a factor in educational decision making in cases of this sort.

Questions for Reflection

1. The *Zobrest* case resulted in a finding that it is permissible to pay for an interpreter. What is the likely application to other related services or to special education programming generally?

2. If special education programming is to be given at a neutral site or public school for parochial school students, additional time in transit will frequently become a necessity. How can this be balanced if it is determined that for a child's program to be "appropriate" the child should not spend an undue amount of time in transit?

3. Will undue burden become a common defense to ADA litigation against private schools?

4. Justin (age 9) is a child who is seriously emotionally disturbed and who exhibits some autistic-type behaviors. In order for Justin to benefit from education, he needs a great deal of behavior modification, and this must be provided on a 24-hour basis to avoid daily regression. The parents, who both work in blue-collar jobs, have

been unable to control Justin's behavior, and they are concerned about the fact that their other son, Reggie, age 5, is not given a sufficient amount of attention. They would like to have Justin placed in a residential program, at a cost of $85,000 annually. Does the school have to pay for this? Should the school have to pay for this? What if the parents are not willing to carry out school-provided parent training?

5. Emily is 15. Until recently she had no apparent serious problems. Last year, however, her parents got divorced, she broke up with her boyfriend, and her grades began to suffer. Emily lives with her father, who is an engineer at a petroleum company and makes $80,000 per year. She has had episodes of running away and suicide "attempts." Her father would like to have her placed in a private residential program at a cost of $100,000 annually. What kind of facts must be developed in order for the school to be required to pay for such a placement?

6. What if the counseling needed for a child to benefit from education is provided in the residential setting by a psychiatrist? Is this a "medical expense" to be paid by the parents?

7. Educational programming for children who are not disabled could potentially be adversely affected if scarce resources have to be used for expensive residential placements. Could such a situation be the basis for a reverse discrimination lawsuit by parents of the children who are not disabled? Could cost ever be a legitimate defense?

NOTES

1. 20 U.S.C. § 1412(10)(B).
2. 34 C.F.R. § 300.148.
3. 34 C.F.R. § 300.148; 20 U.S.C. § 1412(a)(10)(C); *Florence County School District v. Carter*, 510 U.S. 7 (1993); *School Committee of Burlington v. Department of Education of Mass.*, 471 U.S. 359 (1985).
4. 34 C.F.R. § 300.148(a).
5. 20 U.S.C. § 1412(10)(A)(i).
6. 20 U.S.C. § 1412(10)(A)(ii), referencing § 1412(3).
7. 20 U.S.C. § 1411.
8. For an excellent overview of the issues raised in these situations, see Mark C. Weber, "Services for Private School Students Under the Individuals with Disabilities Education Improvement Act: Issues of Statutory Entitlement, Religious Liberty, and Procedural Regularity," 36 *Journal of Law & Education* 163 (2007).
9. 20 U.S.C. § 1412(10)(A)(i)(III).
10. 403 U.S. 602 (1971), *rehearing denied*, 404 U.S. 876 (1971).
11. 521 U.S. 203 (1997).
12. 512 U.S. 687 (1994).
13. 20 U.S.C. § 1412(10)(A)(i)(III).
14. 20 U.S.C. § 1412(10)(A)(vi)(II).
15. 20 U.S.C. § 1412(10)(A)(i)(I).
16. 34 C.F.R. § 300.137(a).

17. 34 C.F.R. § 300.37; 34 C.F.R. § 300.132(b); 34 C.F.R. § 300.137(c); 34 C.F.R. § 300.138(b).

18. 20 U.S.C. § 1412(a)(10)(A)(iii); 34 C.F.R. § 300.134(B).

19. *Id.;* 34 C.F.R. § 300.139.

20. 42 U.S.C. §§ 12101 *et seq.*

21. 29 U.S.C. § 794.

22. Laura Rothstein, "School Choice and Students With Disabilities," chapter in *School Choice and Social Controversy,* edited by Stephen Sugarman & Frank Kemerer (Brookings Institution 1999); Shanon S. Taylor, "Special Education, Private Schools, and Vouchers: Do All Students Get a Choice?" 34 *Journal of Law & Education* 1 (2005).

23. 20 U.S.C. § 1413(5). See also Joseph R. McKinney, "Charter Schools' Legal Responsibilities Toward Children With Disabilities," 126 *Education Law Reporter* 565 (1998); Jay Heubert, "Schools Without Rules? Charter Schools Federal Disability Law and the Paradoxes of Deregulation," 32 *Harv. Civ. Rts.—Civ. Lib. L. Rev.* 301 (1997).

24. 34 C.F.R. § 300.209.

25. 34 C.F.R. § 300.104.

26. See Laura Rothstein, "Educational Rights of Severely and Profoundly Handicapped Children," 61 *Neb. L. Rev.* 568 (1982).

27. In *Clevenger v. Oak Ridge School Board,* 744 F.2d 514 (6th Cir. 1984), the court held that cost considerations could not be a factor in placing a child who was seriously emotionally disturbed in an $88,000/year residential placement.

28. See Laura Rothstein & Julia Rothstein, *Disabilities and the Law* § 2:27 (Thomson West 2006).

29. Dennis Cichon, "Educability and Education: Filling the Cracks in Service Provision Responsibility Under the Education for All Handicapped Children Act of 1975," 48 *Ohio St. L. J.* 1089, 1114–1128 (1987).

30. *Id.* at 1116.

31. *Id.* at 1117.

32. *Id.* at 1119–1121.

33. *Id.* at 1121.

34. *Id.* at 1123, citing *Clevenger v. Oak Ridge School Board,* 744 F.2d 514 (6th Cir. 1984).

35. Cichon at 1123.

36. *Id.* at 1127, citing *David D. v. Dartmouth School Committee,* 615 F. Supp. 639 (D. Mass. 1984), *aff'd,* 775 F.2d 411 (4th Cir. 1985).

37. 20 U.S.C. § 1414(b)(3)(A)(ii).

38. 34 C.F.R. § 300.104.

39. 20 U.S.C. § 1413(A)(4)(iii).

13

Special Issues With Secondary Students

Most of the case law on special education has focused on elementary-age children. This is usually the age at which the initial placement decision and educational planning occurs. There are, however, several issues that have unique impact on students at the secondary school level.

The uniqueness occurs as a result of two major factors. First, students at the secondary school level have unique behavior and social problems that can affect their physical and emotional development. Students who may have had no disability prior to adolescence may develop emotional or behavior problems as a result of social pressures, lack of self-esteem, or family problems. The severity of these problems may require the student to have counseling or even residential placement in order to benefit from education. These problems may even result in incarceration as a result of criminal conduct.

The second unique factor is that the secondary school level is often the end of the line for receiving services under the Individuals with Disabilities Education Act (IDEA). Once the student graduates from high school with a regular high school diploma, the IDEA no longer requires that the individual receive special education and related services. The student may be eligible for vocational rehabilitation services or may be protected from discrimination by Section 504 of the Rehabilitation Act, the Americans with Disabilities Act (ADA), or state laws. The entitlement to a special education program and due process protections under the IDEA, however, usually ends at graduation. Thus, the impending termination of services raises two major issues. One is what event—graduation, reaching a certain age, or some other event—terminates the obligation. Another is how to ensure that public school programs provide appropriate services to facilitate transition to the world of adulthood, employment, and independence for individuals with disabilities.

The following sections focus on these issues. The issue of services for students with emotional or behavioral problems requiring counseling or residential placement has been discussed in previous chapters.[1]

Graduation Requirements

The issue of graduation requirements involves two different questions of obligation to educational agencies. The first is whether diploma requirements may be imposed on students with disabilities. The second is whether there is an obligation to a student with a disability once the diploma has been awarded.

Diploma Requirements and Minimum Competency Testing

Since about 1990, the move by education administrators toward excellence has resulted in requiring minimum competency testing in many states before a high school diploma can be awarded. These requirements have been challenged in a number of cases. The decisions in those cases establish that as a general rule these tests are permissible under the due process and equal protection clauses of the Constitution, as long as there has been adequate notice that the tests would be required, and if the tests cover material taught to the student in the curriculum. The lead case on this issue is *Debra P. v. Turlington*,[2] in which the court recognized the validity of such exams, but held that in this case there was inadequate notice of the requirements. The application of minimum competency requirements to children with disabilities has been addressed by the courts and has been held to be valid as evidenced in the following case. This issue is relevant in light of the No Child Left Behind standards requiring special education students to meet statewide assessment standards.[3]

BROOKHART V. ILLINOIS STATE BOARD OF EDUCATION

697 F.2d 179 (7th Cir. 1983)

Plaintiffs are fourteen handicapped elementary and secondary students who are challenging a Peoria School District (School District) requirement that they pass a "Minimal Competency Test" (M.C.T.) in order to receive a high school diploma.

Plaintiffs manifested a broad spectrum of handicapping conditions. One student was physically handicapped, one was multiply handicapped, and four were educably mentally handicapped. The other eight were learning disabled.

In the spring of 1978, the School District decided to require all students eligible for graduation in the spring of 1980 to pass an M.C.T. as a prerequisite to receipt of a diploma. The test is given each semester. It contains three parts—reading, language arts, and mathematics—and a student must score 70% on each part in order to receive a diploma. If a student fails any particular part, he is eligible to retake that part until he passes or becomes 21 years of age. . . .

Students who do not pass, but otherwise qualify for graduation, receive a Certificate of Program Completion at graduation time, and may continue to take the M.C.T. until age 21.

After the M.C.T. policy was adopted in 1978, the School District undertook to notify students of the additional requirement through distribution of circulars in the schools, individual mailings to some parents, and repeated announcements in the mass media. . . .

Plaintiffs claim that the M.C.T. as applied to handicapped students violates federal and state statutes, as well as the due process and equal protection clauses of the Fourteenth Amendment. We note at the outset that in analyzing these claims deference is due the School District's educational and curricular decisions. The School District's desire to ensure the value of its diploma by requiring graduating students to attain minimal skills is admirable, and the courts will interfere with educational policy decisions only when necessary to protect individual statutory or constitutional rights. . . .

[T]he EHA [Education of the Handicapped Act] does not require "specific results," but rather only mandates access to specialized and individualized educational services for handicapped children. Denial of diplomas to handicapped children who have been receiving the special education and related services required by the Act, but are unable to achieve the educational level necessary to pass the M.C.T., is not a denial of a "free appropriate public education."

Plaintiffs further contend that the imposition of the M.C.T. violates the EHA and corresponding regulation mandating that "no single procedure shall be the sole criterion for determining an appropriate educational program for a child."

Yet plaintiffs admit that graduation requirements in Peoria are threefold: earning seventeen credits, completing State requirements such as a constitution test and a consumer education course, and passing the M.C.T. In the face of this admission, passing the M.C.T. is clearly not the sole criterion for graduation.

1. Rehabilitation Act of 1973

Plaintiffs also argue that application of the M.C.T. requirement constitutes unlawful discrimination under Section 504 of the Rehabilitation Act of 1973 (RDA), providing:

> No otherwise qualified handicapped individual in the United States . . . shall, solely by reason of his handicap, be excluded from the participation in, be denied the benefits of, or be subjected to discrimination under any program or activity receiving Federal financial assistance. . . .

[The] Supreme Court [has] held that an "otherwise qualified" individual entitled to the protection of Section 504 is "one who is able to meet all of a program's requirements in spite of his handicap." . . .

The statute does not require "an educational institution to lower or to effect substantial modification of standards to accommodate a handicapped person."

Plaintiffs in this case have no grounds on which to argue that the contents of the M.C.T. are discriminatory solely because handicapped students who are incapable of attaining a level of minimal competency will fail the test. Altering the content of the M.C.T. to accommodate an individual's inability to learn the tested material because of his handicap would be a "substantial modification," as well as a "perversion" of the diploma requirement. A student who is unable to learn because of his handicap is surely not an individual who is qualified in spite of his handicap. Thus denial of a diploma because of inability to pass the M.C.T. is not discrimination under the EHA.

(Continued)

(Continued)

However, an otherwise qualified student who is unable to disclose the degree of learning he actually possesses because of the test format or environment would be the object of discrimination solely on the basis of his handicap. It is apparent, as the district court said, that "to discover a blind person's knowledge, a test must be given orally or in braille . . ." [F]ederal law requires administrative modification to minimize the effects of plaintiffs' handicaps on any future examinations. . . .

Plaintiffs' final argument is that the School District provided them inadequate notice of the M.C.T. requirement, thus depriving them of a protected liberty or property interest without due process of law. Although the issues in this case do not fit easily into a traditional procedural due process analysis, we conclude, after close consideration, that the School District failed to satisfy constitutional requirements.

The first question to be decided is whether the plaintiffs have a protected liberty or property interest at stake. Denial of a diploma clearly affects a student's reputation. It attaches a "stigma" that will have potentially disastrous effects for future employment or educational opportunities. Though the Supreme Court held that injury to reputation alone does not implicate a liberty interest, it went on to say in the same opinion that liberty interests are implicated when injury to reputation is combined with "governmental action [that] deprived the individual of a right previously held under state law." It was the removal of the right or interest "from the recognition and protection previously afforded by the State, which we found sufficient to invoke the procedural guarantees contained in the Due Process Clause of the Fourteenth Amendment.

Plaintiffs in this case have more than merely an interest in protecting their reputations and avoiding the stigma attached to failure to receive a high school diploma. They, too, had a right conferred by state law to receive a diploma if they meet the requirements imposed prior to 1978: completion of seventeen course credits and fulfillment of the State's graduation requirements. In changing the diploma requirement, the governmental action by the School District deprived the individual of a right or interest previously held under state law. Plaintiffs thus have a liberty interest sufficient to invoke the procedural protections of the due process clause.

The consequence of identifying a protected liberty interest is that governmental action cannot be used to deprive an individual of that interest without due process of law. Traditionally, a procedural due process right means "an opportunity to be heard on the factual basis underlying the loss of a liberty or property interest. . . ."

This case does not fit into the traditional procedural due process mold. Plaintiffs here do not contest the factual basis underlying the loss of a liberty interest; in fact, they admit that they did not pass the M.C.T. Rather, they demand procedures which would provide sufficient notice of the M.C.T. to enable them to prepare adequately to satisfy the new requirement.

We think that procedural due process protections are flexible enough to encompass notice of this kind. The issue arose . . . in *Debra P. v. Turlington,* where the Fifth Circuit stated its view that inadequate notice to students that they would be required to pass an exit examination before qualifying for diploma violated procedural due process. . . .

[W]e hold that plaintiffs were entitled to notice permitting reasonable preparation for the M.C.T. . . .

We must now consider whether the notice provided to plaintiffs was sufficient to satisfy constitutional requisites. The older eleven plaintiffs were informed that they were subject to the M.C.T. requirement during their junior year in high school. The State Superintendent found they therefore had approximately one and a half years to master the skills necessary to pass the M.C.T.; the district court found that all plaintiffs had notice of the M.C.T. requirement one year prior to graduation. Despite the fact that plaintiffs had between a year and a year and a half to be exposed to the material on the M.C.T., the record shows that individual petitioners lacked exposure to as much as 90% of the material tested.

Plaintiffs' educational programs were developed in accordance with 20 U.S.C. § 1414(a)(5) [Now § 1414(d)] requiring that each handicapped student receive an individualized educational program (IEP).

[T]he record reflects that the plaintiffs' programs of instruction were not developed to meet the goal of passing the M.C.T., but were instead geared to address individual educational needs. Since plaintiffs and their parents knew of the M.C.T. requirements only one to one and a half years prior to the students' anticipated graduation, the M.C.T. objectives could not have been specifically incorporated into the IEP's over a period of years. If they were incorporated at all, it could only have been during the most recent year and a half. . . .

[P]arents had only a year to a year and a half to evaluate properly their children's abilities and redirect their educational goals. We agree with the parents and the State Board that this was insufficient time to make an informed decision about inclusion or exclusion of training on M.C.T. objectives. . . .

The private interest at stake here is an interest in protecting reputation and in qualifying for future employment opportunities. The governmental interest in upgrading the value of a diploma is also significant. However, the risk of an erroneous deprivation of plaintiffs' interest in this case is overwhelming because of the near-total lack of exposure to the material tested. Requiring earlier notice and the attendant opportunity to learn the material will greatly decrease the risk of erroneous deprivation. . . .

Though we are unable on this record to define "adequate notice" in terms of a specific number of years, the School District can be assured that the requirement would be satisfied if one of the following two conditions for adequate notice is met. The School District can, first, ensure that handicapped students are sufficiently exposed to most of the material that appears on the M.C.T., or second, they can produce evidence of a reasoned and well-informed decision by the parents and teachers involved that a particular high school student will be better off concentrating on educational objectives other than preparation for the M.C.T.

We turn finally to the question of remedy. Plaintiffs argue that the only proper remedy is issuance of diplomas. . . . The School District suggests that plaintiffs should be denied diplomas, but allowed more time to participate in remedial classes and further opportunities to take the M.C.T.

Plaintiffs argue that it is impossible to put them back in the position that they would have been in had they received adequate notice while still in school. Several are employed and would

(Continued)

(Continued)

be forced to leave their jobs in order to participate in the remedial program and prepare for the M.C.T. Eleven plaintiffs have been away from school for over two years, since June of 1980, and it would be difficult, both psychologically and academically, for them to make up for lost time. They ask, essentially, why they should endure these hardships when the School District was at fault for providing inadequate notice.

We agree with the School District that, in theory, the proper remedy for a violation of this kind is to require it to provide free, remedial, special education classes to ensure exposure to the material tested on the M.C.T., and a reasonable opportunity for plaintiffs to learn that material. In this particular case, however, it is unrealistic to assume that eleven of these plaintiffs would be able to return to school without undue hardship. Consequently, the School District may not require those plaintiffs to pass the M.C.T. as a prerequisite for a diploma.

The judgment of the district court is reversed with directions to order the School District to issue high school diplomas to the eleven plaintiffs who satisfy the remaining graduation requirements.

Although competency requirements are likely to be upheld as valid, many educational agencies have implemented a practice of awarding a certificate of achievement to special education students. Such a certificate, while a good means of recognizing effort, is not a substitute for a diploma under the IDEA and does not relieve the agency of further responsibility to provide a free appropriate public education (FAPE) to that student.[4] Instead, the student remains entitled to receive FAPE until he or she is no longer a "child with a disability" under the IDEA, or reaches the maximum age of entitlement for services (either 18 or 21, depending on state law).

Schools that have competency requirements to receive a high school diploma are likely to be given deference by courts in setting those requirements as long as they are based on the educational standards that the state establishes for students to achieve. More recent policy adjustments under national education policy and laws such as No Child Left Behind have addressed the issue of ensuring that students with disabilities are required to meet these kinds of state standards.

Compensatory Relief

The *Brookhart* case involved the situation where the educational agency did not want to award the diploma because the student had not completed the minimum competency requirements. The reverse of this is not an uncommon occurrence. An educational agency interested in eliminating the continuing obligation to educate certain difficult students—such as adolescents with severe behavioral problems—may simply award the diploma and claim that once the diploma has been awarded there is no further obligation to provide education. Problems can also arise when a student actually does meet the minimum competency requirements for graduation but has not been appropriately educated up to that point.

Chapter 21 discusses this issue further, but it is important to address one aspect of it here. At what point does the obligation to provide FAPE end? Is it at the point the diploma has been awarded? What if the diploma is awarded even though minimum competency has not been met, or if the diploma has been earned but the student was not appropriately educated?

The IDEA addressed some of these questions in 2004 by noting that the student must be provided with a regular high school diploma in order for the obligation to provide FAPE to end. An alternative degree that is not fully aligned with state educational standards does not suffice to end the obligation to provide FAPE.[5]

Additionally, if the student was not appropriately educated as required by the IDEA, the student may have a claim for compensatory education, which can require the school to provide services even after graduation with a regular diploma.[6] An argument can also be made that awarding a diploma in a clearly inappropriate case (such as to a student with a behavior disorder who has not met the requirements), or providing grossly inappropriate educational programming, constitutes educational malpractice. This theory has not been widely accepted, however, and is explored further in Chapter 20. Such an award may also be a violation of procedural due process.

School Attendance Requirements

In many states, students are not required to attend school beyond a certain age, usually around 14 to 16. This raises the interesting question of whether a student who is receiving special education may elect to stop attending school. For example, a student who has reached 16 in a state where that age is the cutoff for mandatory attendance may wish to stop attending school. If that student is receiving some programming for a learning disability, for example, what is the obligation of the school to try to keep that student in school? Is there any greater obligation for that student than there is for a student who is not receiving special education? What happens if the parents do not care? Is there any greater obligation to try to persuade the parents to "force" the child to attend because the student is receiving special education? Once the student becomes 18, the parents no longer have the legal power to force the student to attend anyway.

These issues have not really been addressed by the courts, but they raise an interesting dilemma. If the student simply stops attending and the school makes no effort to try to keep the student in school, can the student later claim negligence by the school, or a failure to provide FAPE? Is there a heightened duty to special education students by virtue of the fact that educational programming may be more essential for them than for other students? While current law does not seem to resolve these questions, school administrators would do well to develop policies to address them.

Vocational Education

For many students with disabilities, preparation for the outside world of independence and employment will require some type of vocational training rather than an emphasis on academics. Many students will not be qualified to attend institutions of higher education. Thus, it is important for this group to have the advantage of public education to prepare for the transition to a world where comprehensive programming will not be available as it is under the IDEA.

In spite of the importance of vocational training for students with disabilities, vocational education teachers may often be unprepared for the presence of students with disabilities in the classroom. There has been a lack of development of special vocational programs for students with disabilities and a lack of adaptation of general vocational programs to incorporate and include special education students. For example, a secondary school that has an automobile repair training program may exclude the student with a disability by having certain qualifications for the program that cannot be met by the student with a disability. This is probably not permissible under the IDEA, Section 504 of the Rehabilitation Act, or the ADA.

One area where there is some relevant law relates to personnel training. Vocational education teachers, like all other teachers, are supposed to be adequately prepared for the presence of special education students.[7] This will mean that the teacher in a woodshop class or a home economics class, for example, will need to be aware of the characteristics of students with disabilities and to be aware of the need to provide appropriate instructions or adequate supervision. In *Collins v. School Board,*[8] the issue of liability was raised: A substitute teacher in the shop class was held to be negligent when a student with an emotional disability was sexually assaulted by another student. It is important to set up mechanisms for communicating necessary accommodations to vocational education teachers to avoid liability. A student with a learning disability may have difficulty understanding instructions on machinery in a shop class. A student with cerebral palsy may be at risk in operating an electric mixer in a cooking class. While immunity and other defenses may in some cases protect the school from liability, it is better to rely on prevention and to be sure personnel are adequately prepared.

Transition Services

In 1990, Congress responded to the concern that special education students leaving public education were not adequately prepared for higher education, employment, or independent living. In the 1990 IDEA amendments, transition services were added to the types of services to be provided to students eligible for special education. These services are defined as

> a coordinated set of activities . . . designed to be within a result-oriented process, that is focused on improving the academic and functional achievement of the child with a disability to facilitate the child's movement from school to post-school activities, including post-secondary education, vocational education, integrated employment (including supported employment), continuing and adult education, adult services, independent living, or community participation.[9]

These services are to be individualized, taking into account strengths, preferences, and interests of the child. They are to include "instruction, related services, community experiences, the development of employment and other post-school adult living objectives, and, when appropriate, acquisition of daily living skills and functional vocational education."[10] "Beginning not later than the first IEP to be in effect when the child is 16, and updated annually thereafter," the individualized education program (IEP) is to include age-appropriate postsecondary goals and the services needed to reach those goals.[11]

The IEP team must invite the student to attend IEP meetings when the team is considering and developing transition goals for the IEP. If the student does not attend, other methods must be used to ensure that the student's preferences and interests are considered.[12]

Interagency cooperation is often required for effective transition programs, because outside agencies often provide at least some of the transition services. When outside agencies or organizations are involved, they must be invited to team meetings to the extent appropriate and with the consent of the parents.[13] The IDEA requires the IEP team and the public school to ensure that the transition services noted in the IEP are provided. If outside agencies are supposed to provide services and do not, the IEP team must meet and develop alternative strategies to meet the transition goals set forth in the IEP.[14]

Postsecondary Academic Education

The IDEA has resulted in a substantial increase in the number of individuals with disabilities who are admitted to and enroll in institutions of higher education, including community colleges and four-year colleges and universities. The transition for these students can be an adjustment because they have been accustomed to the substantive and procedural protections of the IDEA. Both they and their parents may be surprised to find the difference in rights, benefits, and presumptions and burdens for students with disabilities in a postsecondary educational setting. The IDEA is a comprehensive special education statute, requiring the educational agency to identify the student, to pay for the testing, and to provide substantially greater special education services than Section 504 or the ADA require.

Upon reaching higher education, students with disabilities and their parents are often unaware that the burden shifts to the student to self-identify (and pay for the documentation). The services to be provided are only those viewed as reasonable accommodations. Both high school counselors and admissions and student service administrators in postsecondary education programs might avoid some disputes by taking a proactive approach to educating this population about these differences, and helping them to plan for them.[15]

Summary

Students in their teenage years present two major issues relating to special education. The emotional upheaval that normally goes with adolescence can trigger even greater problems for a student with disabilities. Moreover, individuals who are not disabled may become so emotionally distraught as a result of the changes in their lives during this period that they can actually develop emotional problems and be categorized as disabled. Thus, it is particularly critical that students in this age range be given appropriate special education and, to the extent possible, that this education prepare these students for the transition into the world of work, higher education, and independent living.

One issue relating to special education for teenagers is whether the educational agency can impose competency requirements for graduation. Such requirements might adversely affect students with certain disabilities. As a general rule, courts have upheld the legality of minimum competency testing for the award of a diploma as long as adequate notice has been given. A related issue, less well resolved, is whether a state is no longer obligated to provide any special education once the diploma is awarded. Courts have reached a wide range of results in addressing this question. Similarly, courts have not reached any conclusion about whether there is a remedy against an educational agency that awards a diploma to a student who has not met the minimum competency requirements generally imposed.

Students in this age-group who have disabilities are less likely to attend institutions of higher education than are their peers who are not disabled. This makes vocational education a very important program for high school students with disabilities. Unfortunately, although the need is extremely high, the training that vocational education teachers receive does not always provide them adequate preparation for teaching students with special needs. The sparse case law on these issues seems primarily to be decisions in which vocational education personnel are being sued for inappropriate supervision. This fact alone demonstrates the importance of placing a high priority on training vocational education teachers to teach students with disabilities.

In recognition of the importance of moving a student from the school setting toward higher education, employment, or independent living, the IDEA provides for transition services for students by age 16 or sooner if determined appropriate by the IEP team.

It should also be recognized that students with disabilities may be able to attend institutions of higher education. One of the express purposes or goals of the IDEA is to prepare students with disabilities for postsecondary educational opportunities. School counseling programs may not exclude such students from their college counseling and advising. In addition, these students and their parents should be counseled about the different rights and responsibilities of a student with a disability in a postsecondary setting.

Questions for Reflection

1. Is there harm done to the public by awarding a student a diploma when the student has not completed competency requirements? Is this different from a situation involving higher education? That is, is it less harmful to award a high school diploma because of inadequate notice than it would be to award a nursing certificate to a student who has not met minimal competency requirements?

2. Would it be permissible to allocate all vocational training funds for students with disabilities to separate programs? Should *all* vocational training programs integrate students with disabilities and students who are not disabled?

3. If a school district withdraws transition services for secondary students claiming lack of funding, what recourse does the special education teacher have? What recourse does the parent or student have?

4. What legal basis could be used for challenging a practice of omitting the names of special education students from lists of those who should take college prep classes in high school?

5. What steps should an IEP team take if the student requires transition services from an outside agency and the agency has a waiting list of 3 to 6 months for providing services?

6. How might schools best prepare students who will attend higher education programs for dealing with the differing legal requirements?

NOTES

1. See Chapters 10 and 12.
2. 730 F.2d 1405 (11th Cir. 1984).
3. See Chapter 3.
4. 34 C.F.R. § 300.102.
5. 34 C.F.R. § 300.102(a)(3).
6. See Chapter 21 for more information.
7. 34 C.F.R. § 300.156(a).
8. 471 So.2d 560 (Fla. Dist. Ct. App. 1985).
9. 20 U.S.C. § 1401(34).
10. *Id.*
11. 20 U.S.C. § 1414(d)(1)(A)(i)(VIII).
12. 34 C.F.R. § 300.321(b).
13. *Id.*
14. 34 C.F.R. § 300.324(c).
15. Laura Rothstein, "Millennials and Disability Law: Revisiting *Southeastern Community College v. Davis*," 34 *Journal of College & University Law* 169 (2007).

14

Cost Issues

Free Appropriate Public Education

Under the Individuals with Disabilities Education Act (IDEA), free appropriate public education means, among other things, education "provided at public expense, under public supervision and direction, and without charge."[1] States providing this service to children with disabilities in compliance with the IDEA mandates are eligible to receive supportive funding from the federal government under a funding formula based on the number of students with disabilities. Because special education on average costs about twice as much per pupil as regular education, cost issues are a major concern for state and local educational agencies. For certain types of placements, such as residential placements, the concern is even greater. While the IDEA funding provides a subsidy for special education, the federal funding does not cover all the additional costs of providing special education and related services.

Cost issues have been mentioned earlier and will be raised in subsequent chapters. This chapter reviews issues introduced earlier and also addresses some new ones.

What Expenses Are Covered Under the IDEA?

The first issue to address is which costs are covered under the IDEA; that is, which costs must be paid at public expense?

Educational Programming

The special educational programming and related services themselves are, of course, covered, but it is not always easy to identify when a particular service is part of the educational program and which supportive services are covered under the IDEA. The statutory language and the regulations specify what related services are covered within the IDEA and define special education.[2] Special education programming to be provided at no cost includes residential placements that are "necessary to provide special education and related services . . . including non-medical care and room and board."[3] The medical expenses of such a placement, however, need not be provided by the educational agency.

Another issue that occasionally arises is whether certain programs such as those teaching self-help skills are really "education" that must be paid for by the educational agency under the IDEA.[4] A similar question could arise in a context where a comatose child is being provided regular muscle therapy or being provided background music to try to bring the child out of the coma. Is that education? These issues have not been addressed to a great extent by the courts, so there is little clear resolution of them.

It should be noted that "free" does not preclude the school district's charging incidental fees to students with disabilities. For example, the school might charge all students for the cost of a field trip. The students with disabilities whose expenses might be higher because of related service costs could not be charged more, however.

Related Services

In addition to educational programming, the educational agency must pay for related services, including identification and assessment services, needed to enable the child to benefit from special education.[5] Chapter 10 discussed these issues and illustrated how expensive some related services, such as transportation, can be. The *Tatro* case[6] involving catheterization as a related service pointed out that while some services may be defined as medical services, which are not related services under the IDEA, whenever the service is a related service within the IDEA, it must be provided at no cost.

Assessment services fall within the category of related services. As the *Seals v. Loftis*[7] decision illustrated, it can become quite costly to complete all of the necessary assessments to determine the child's disability. If these assessments are necessary to determine the special education program, they must be paid for by the school, even if the parents have insurance benefits to cover them in certain instances.

Procedural Protections

One area that has not been previously discussed is the right to procedural safeguards to ensure that the IDEA has been complied with. These procedural safeguards include a right to have a hearing when there is disagreement over a child's disability, placement, program, and so on; a right to be represented at the hearing; a right to a record of the hearing; a right to appeal to the state administrative agency; and a right to seek review in court. It should be pointed out that having certain procedural rights does not always mean that these rights must be provided at no cost. The IDEA offers clarification on most of these issues. For example, the school is not required to pay for the cost of attorney representation for the parents unless the parents are prevailing parties.[8]

The state or local educational agency is obligated for the other costs of the due process hearing itself.[9] These costs include payment to the hearing officer, the cost of tape-recording or transcribing the proceedings, and the cost of sending copies of the findings of fact to the parents.[10] These are not minor costs, and as a practical matter, when local educational agencies are responsible for the cost of the administrative proceedings, they often weigh these costs when deciding whether to grant the parents' request for a service or program. Costs of conducting an administrative review at the state level are also borne by the state educational agency.[11]

Questions relating to attorneys' fees and costs for expert witnesses, production of documentary evidence, and other costs of representation are treated separately. These costs are initially paid by the parents, but some of them may be reimbursed if the parents are prevailing parties.

School Records

In preparation for a placement decision or a hearing, parents may wish to obtain copies of their child's school records. Their rights of access are discussed more fully in Chapter 19. While parents have a right to inspect and review school records, the school may charge a reasonable fee for providing copies necessary for effective review unless doing so would preclude parents from access to due process.[12] A fee for search and retrieval may not be charged to the parents.[13]

Budgetary Constraints on Educational Agencies

Technically, if a particular program or service is determined to be necessary for a child with a disability to receive an appropriate education under the IDEA, it must be provided regardless of cost.[14]

There is nothing in the statute or regulations that permits budgetary constraints to be a complete defense when a school fails to provide mandated special education and related services, but it is arguable that the *Mills* case, which was a foundation for passage of the IDEA, establishes that

> if sufficient funds are not available to finance all of the services and programs that are needed and desirable in the system, then the available funds must be expended equitably in such a manner that no child is entirely excluded from a publicly supported education consistent with his needs and ability to benefit therefrom.[15]

The IDEA, however, seems to have moved past these foundational statements by requiring that a free appropriate public education (FAPE) be made available to all students, that states maintain certain levels of funding to ensure that FAPE is available, and that states use whatever state, local, or federal sources are available to meet these requirements.[16] States must also ensure that the implementation or delivery of special education and related services to students is not delayed due to funding determinations.[17]

Additionally, even assuming the *Mills* statement is relevant to interpreting the IDEA, one can imagine the difficulty of determining how to cut back all programming. Perhaps the complexity of doing so explains why this defense is rarely raised by the educational agencies. While there is no clear guidance from current judicial interpretation of the IDEA, two major decisions indicate that cost may be a legitimate factor in determining whether certain services must be provided.

In *Irving Independent School District v. Tatro,*[18] the Supreme Court, in discussing whether catheterization must be provided as a related service, stated that it would be reasonable for the Secretary of Education to conclude that the medical services exclusion was "designed to spare schools from an obligation to provide a service that might well prove unduly expensive." Another major case in which cost was raised as an issue is *Roncker v. Walter,*[19] in which the major issue was whether it was appropriate to place children who were severely retarded in separate schools. The court held that "cost is a proper factor to consider since excessive spending on one handicapped child deprives other handicapped children." But the court cautioned against a conservative view of when a particular service would benefit only one child with a disability in its statement that

> cost is no defense . . . if the school district has failed to use its funds to provide a proper continuum of alternative placements. . . . The provision of such alternative placements benefits all handicapped children.

Case law also supports the school's selection of the less expensive placement where there is a choice between appropriate placements since either placement would provide the child with FAPE.[20]

It would seem, therefore, that the circumstances under which cost can be used as a defense are limited to those where the child will still receive FAPE with the less expensive service or placement. It should be noted that while the educational agency's fiscal status for the most part is irrelevant to deciding its obligation to provide services, the parents' right to services for the child is not dependent on family income. Parents with an annual income of a million dollars have as much right to free special education for their child as do parents on welfare.

As a policy matter, this may seem troublesome. As a practical matter, however, the transaction costs of determining a sliding scale of parental obligation based on parents' resources would be extremely burdensome. Because access to a free regular education is not based on income, it is really questionable whether special education should be so conditioned. The difference, of course, is that regular education costs about the same for each child. Special education can be vastly more expensive for certain programs.

Which Public Agency Is Responsible?

Where a determination has been made that a program or placement is appropriate to the student, the program should be provided at no cost to the parents. The issue of which public agency is responsible may still be undecided. First, there are issues as to whether the placement is one that the state educational agency should be responsible for instead of the local agency. And if it is determined that a particular program is to be a local responsibility, the question may become one of residency; that is, which local school district has responsibility for a particular child?

And there are further questions in some cases as to whether the educational agencies (local or state) are responsible at all. It may be that in some cases, social service agencies such as departments of welfare, corrections, or health have total or partial financial or programmatic responsibility. Where careful interagency agreements have not been worked out, these issues are more likely to arise. Some of these questions were answered in the 1997 IDEA amendments.

State Versus Local Agency Responsibility

While the state educational agency has the primary and ultimate responsibility for providing special education under the IDEA, states have a great deal of latitude in deciding whether to provide direct services themselves or to permit local agencies to provide direct services. In actuality, in most states it is the local agencies that have been given the primary responsibility of providing direct services for most types of placements. In some states, certain expensive placements such as residential programs and placements in schools for students who are deaf are arranged for and paid for by the state rather than the local educational agency. The 2004 amendments to the IDEA contemplate a system of state responsibility for expensive placements. The IDEA now provides for funding for high-need assistance programming to cost share and reimburse local school educational agencies that provide services to students who need "catastrophic, or extraordinary aid."[21]

The question that can arise is what happens if the local educational agency does not provide the services it is supposed to provide according to the state-established system of resource allocation. Is it the state's obligation to take care of placements when the local educational agency has failed to do so? This issue was addressed in the decision of *Doe v. Maher,* by the Ninth Circuit. The case, which addressed the issue of whether a child could be removed from the classroom for a disciplinary reason, was ultimately decided by the Supreme Court. The Supreme Court addressed the discipline and removal issues, but did not really rule directly on the issue of state responsibility, although the State Superintendent of Public Instruction sought review of that issue. The Court was evenly divided on the issue, and thus the Ninth Circuit decision holding the state responsible was affirmed.

The following excerpt is only a small portion of the Ninth Circuit's opinion. Although the issue has not been resolved by the Supreme Court, other circuit courts have reached results similar to the Ninth Circuit's disposition of the state agency responsibility issue.

DOE V. MAHER

793 F.2d 1470 (9th Cir. 1986)

The state contends that the district court erred in enjoining it to provide services directly whenever, in any individual case, it determines that a local educational agency is unable or unwilling to maintain programs of free appropriate public education for handicapped students. According to the state, section 1414(d) [Now § 1413(g)] of the EAHCA [Education for All Handicapped Children Act] requires it to provide services directly, not in individual instances of local inaction, but only when localities maintain no programs of special education whatsoever.

We think the state conceives its role under section 1414(d) [Now § 1413(g)] too narrowly. When read in its entirety, the provision imposes on the state a broader duty. Although the state stresses the language in 20 U.S.C. section 1414(d)(1) (1982) that speaks of the state's responsibility for direct action when the locality fails to maintain "programs" of free appropriate education, section 1414(d)(3) specifically requires direct action when a local education agency "has one or more handicapped children who can best be served by a regional or State center

(Continued)

(Continued)

designed to meet the needs of such children." *Id.* It would seem incontrovertible that, whenever the local agency refuses or wrongfully neglects to provide a handicapped child with a free appropriate education, that child "can best be served" on the regional or state level. . . .

Although the state has broad responsibilities under the EAHCA, those responsibilities are not absolute. The state is not obligated to intervene directly in an individual case whenever the local agency falls short of its responsibilities in some small regard. The breach must be significant (as in this case), the child's parents or guardian must give the responsible state officials adequate notice of the local agency's noncompliance, and the state must be afforded a reasonable opportunity to compel local compliance.

The 1997 amendments to the IDEA addressed this issue by providing that where a local educational agency has not met its responsibility to provide services, the state educational agency may use the funds that would have gone to the local agency to provide the services directly.[22]

Residency Issues

In addition to controversies regarding responsibility between state and local educational agencies, disputes can arise regarding which local educational agency or which state is responsible for the education of a particular child. These issues usually reach the formal dispute resolution level when placements such as residential placements or other expensive programming is involved.

The IDEA is not very helpful in clarifying these types of residency issues. Resolution is usually found by examining state education and state residency statutes. Problems arise in cases where a residential placement has been made and the parents have later moved, when the child is placed in a foster home or with a guardian or someone other than the parents, and if the child is a ward of the state. It is difficult to find any national trend in how these cases are being resolved because so much depends on individual state law.[23] The *Roncker* case and the *A.W. v. Northwest R-1 School District* case in Chapter 11 discuss the cost issue in the context of least restrictive environment under the IDEA. The following judicial opinion is an example of the type of analysis that courts are likely to consider in these cases.

CATLIN V. AMBACH

644 F. Supp. 161 (N.D.N.Y. 1986)

Plaintiff, Dunbar Elliot ("Dell") Catlin, is a 13-year-old child who was born in New York City on April 22, 1973. Shortly after Dell was born, his parents Daniel and Dundeen Catlin learned that Dell had been born with Down's Syndrome. After several consultations, the Catlins decided to place Dell in a family home with Samuel and Elizabeth Conde ("the Condes") in Edmeston, New York. Dell went to Edmeston directly from the hospital and has lived there continuously since that time. He has never resided with his natural parents and he has never even visited their home.

The Catlins pay for the cost of Dell's care in Edmeston and no part of those costs is paid by any social service agency. It is not controverted that the Catlins have always intended that Dell reside with the Condes. The center of Dell's civic, social, religious and family life is in Edmeston, New York. The Condes' is the only home Dell has ever known and the people with whom he resides are his "family." Dell refers to the Condes as "Mama" and "Dad" and has longstanding, extended family relationships with two of the Condes' natural children who reside in the area.

Dell shares a room with another child, one year younger than he, who like Dell, has lived in Edmeston since shortly after his birth. The relationship between Dell and his roommate is brotherly; they attend school together and have become virtually inseparable over the years. Both the Catlins and the Condes believe that it would be extremely harmful for Dell to leave Edmeston and the setting the Condes have provided for him.

The Condes are completely responsible for day-to-day decisions regarding Dell's care and supervision.

Selection of schools was not a factor in choosing to place Dell in Edmeston with the Condes. Since 1978, when he came of school age, Dell has attended the BOCES-Mt.Vision School in Edmeston, based upon the recommendation of the Edmeston School District Committee of the Handicapped. The placement has been reviewed each year and has been reaffirmed on each of those occasions. The Catlins never attended any of the meetings related to Dell's placement; the school district has dealt solely with the Condes on all matters related to Dell and his education.

Up to mid-1985, the Catlins resided in New York State, within the Bedford Central School District. From the time the child started attending school through 1985, the Bedford Central School District assumed financial responsibility for his tuition and paid that tuition to the Edmeston Central School District.

In the summer of 1985 the Catlins moved from their home in Bedford to the State of Massachusetts. The Bedford Central School District advised the Nantucket Public School System that "now that the family has moved to Nantucket, we are no longer responsible for tuition and the burden of Dunbar's education falls on your school district." The Bedford Central School District also informed the Edmeston Central School District that Bedford would no longer pay Dell's tuition. . . .

[The issue in this case is whether the Edmeston School District or another locality bears responsibility for Dell's education.] All parties agree that the only remaining issue is the State's determination of Dell's residence. Plaintiff's first claim hinges on an equal protection challenge to the New York residence rule as applied in the present case. [In the present case,] an intermediate scrutiny standard applies in cases where the classifications, "while not facially invidious, nonetheless give rise to recurring constitutional difficulties; in these limited circumstances we have sought the assurance that the classification reflects a reasoned judgment consistent with the ideal of equal protection by inquiring whether it may fairly be viewed as furthering a substantial state interest." Given that the Commissioner's application of the statute affects a subclass

(Continued)

(Continued)

of children by limiting their access to a state-created right, and given the importance of education for this society, the application of the New York residence statute is subject to the *intermediate standard* of furthering a substantial goal of the state.

New York Education Law places the obligation to provide schooling without payment of tuition on the school district in which the child resides. N.Y. Educ. L. section 3202(1) (McKinney 1981). The Commissioner's finding that Dell was not a resident of Edmeston School District for educational purposes was based on section 3202(4)(b) of the New York Education Law, which states:

> b. Children cared for in free family homes and children cared for in family homes at board, when such family homes shall be the actual and only residence of such children and when such children are not supported or maintained at the expense of a social services district or a state department or agency, shall be deemed residents of the school district in which such family home is located.

Although the statutory language would seem to point directly to deeming the child a resident "of the school district in which such family home [at board] is located," the Commissioner concluded that, since the Catlins had financial control over Dell, Dell's residence is that of his natural parents. The Commissioner's conclusions are specifically as follows: (1) It is undisputed that Dell is cared for in a family home at board which is licensed by the Department of Social Services, and that he is not supported by a social services district or a state department or agency. (2) The Board's decision is that the family home at board in which Dell resides is not his actual and only residence, because the child's parents continue to have parental authority and control over the child and are financially responsible for him. (3) A child's residence is presumed to be that of his parents, even if the child is not physically present in the parent's home; the presumption can be overcome by demonstrating that the parent neither exercises control over the child nor is financially responsible for the child. (4) The Catlins continue to be financially responsible for their son's support and maintenance; the responsibility delegated to the Condes can be terminated at any time. Thus, the Commissioner concluded that there was no basis upon which to conclude that the residence of the child should not be deemed to be that of his natural parents.

The State contends that the Commissioner's findings are only an application of constitutionally acceptable bona fide residence requirements. Furthermore, the State contends that "the same public interests and State interests in applying a bona fide residence test under traditional standards are present in this case."

A bona fide residence requirement, appropriately defined and uniformly applied, furthers the substantial state interest in assuring that services provided for its residents are enjoyed only by residents. A bona fide residence requirement simply requires that the person does establish residence before demanding the services that are restricted to residents.

The question before this court is, therefore, whether the New York residence requirement, as applied, does further the substantial state interests.

The interests on the child's side are fairly easy to identify. It is not controverted that Dell's reason for the claim to residence in Edmeston School District is not solely to benefit from the free school system. Dell's social, civic and actual family life centers around the home the Condes have provided. It is also uncontroverted that unless the Edmeston School District assumes the cost of Dell's education, Dell will have to move, probably to Massachusetts, for the Catlins could not bear the cost of the child's tuition in New York. Moving Dell would disrupt his world as he has always known it, with results which presumably would be very harmful to him. Or the child would have to be removed from school, remaining in Edmeston, also with serious detriment resulting for him.

The State's interests are [first] "local control over the operation of schools; local autonomy has long been thought essential both to the maintenance of community concern and support for the public schools and to the quality of the educational process." . . . This case presents no problem whatsoever with local autonomy. All decisions regarding Dell's education have been made pursuant to consultation with the Condes, and primarily, if not absolutely, according to their judgment. Another related interest, proper planning and operation of the schools, would not be affected at all by allowing Dell to remain in Edmeston at the school district expense.

Other concerns related to the planning problems that would result from substantial school population fluctuations, simply are not present in this case.

Other possible arguments, regarding the school district's interest in assuming that services provided for residents are enjoyed only by residents, could be read as an interest in limiting education to children of those who support the school system as taxpayers. This argument, and the closely related one of preservation of resources, have been clearly rejected as legitimate state interests absent a clear showing of the state's purpose.

Another argument reflects the interest school districts have in having somebody with whom "a school official may deal . . . effectively and authoritatively in matters of punishment, educational progress and medical needs." The Edmeston School District's recognition of the Condes as the persons responsible for decisions regarding Dell's education makes this a moot issue. De facto, the Condes are the persons in charge of Dell's education and the school district has never challenged their authority.

The court concludes therefore, that the State has failed to show that the New York residency statute, as applied in this case, furthers any substantial state interest. As applied in this case, the New York residence requirement offends the Equal Protection Clause of the Fourteenth Amendment. Other grounds for plaintiffs' claims need not be addressed.

Given that the Edmeston School District has continued to provide Dell with school services during this dispute, this judgment is limited to invalidating the Commissioner's determination as to residence.

While this case illuminates, at least in one jurisdiction, how to determine the residency of the child, it does not determine the responsibility of each local school district. The responsibility varies depending on whether the school district or parent makes the placement. When a local educational agency (or school) makes the placement, it is responsible for the costs of the placement, and the local educational agency (or school) making the placement is generally the one where the student resides.[24] Where the child is placed by the parents as a matter of personal preference and FAPE is not at issue, the public school district where the private school is located is responsible for providing services.[25]

Obligations of Other Social Service Agencies

Under the IDEA, the state educational agency has the primary responsibility of ensuring the provision of special education to all children with disabilities within the state. That does not preclude state lawmakers and administrators from implementing programs whereby social service agencies other than the educational agency bear at least some of the financial or programmatic responsibility for the placement of a child with a disability. One problem that can arise is the issue of what happens if the educational agency has never had the opportunity to participate in a placement decision made by another social service agency. The following case illustrates the importance of ensuring that the educational agency is involved in the process.

IN RE TODD P.

509 A.2d 140 (N.H. 1986)

In 1980, the Henniker school system found that Todd P. was educationally handicapped, and it established an individual education plan (IEP) for him. In September 1983, Todd began attending the Hillsboro-Deering Middle School, which found that he was emotionally disturbed. In January 1984, the Hillsboro-Deering School District established an IEP for Todd, finding that Todd's educational needs could be addressed within the school district. The IEP provided for psychological counselling, parent consultation, and academic monitoring.

In March 1984, Todd was adjudicated a delinquent child. . . . The court ordered that Todd be placed outside the home, and placed Todd on probation. The court subsequently found that Todd was guilty of violating its order, and ordered that he be detained at the Youth Development Center (YDC), subject to a suspension of the order upon a petition showing "either [an] alternative placement or other good cause." On March 23, 1984, the court suspended Todd's placement at the YDC on the condition that Todd be placed at the Chamberlain School. He resided at the Chamberlain School until August 1985. He is now out of the placement system. . . .

The sole issue before the court was whether the Town of Henniker or, rather, the school district was liable for the educational portion of the expenses of Todd's Chamberlain School placement. . . .

The school district appealed to this court, asserting that the district court is without authority to review the substance of an IEP developed by the school district. It argues that the district court has no jurisdiction to issue liability orders against a school district for an educational program that was not part of an IEP established by it. We agree.

The issues before us arise out of the tangled interrelationship of New Hampshire's juvenile justice system and special education laws. This interrelationship is the result of the fact that many children are both delinquent and educationally handicapped. Todd's needs, which stem from both his delinquency and his educational handicap, must be addressed through both the juvenile statutes and the special education laws. . . .

The district court has the authority to issue liability orders against the town declared the legally liable unit. This provision also grants the district court the authority to issue a liability order against a school district for educational expenses incurred. Todd's expenses at the Chamberlain School, however, were not voluntarily chosen by the school district as part of the IEP developed, and therefore were not chargeable to the school district. . . .

The school district's lack of participation in Todd's placement by the juvenile court permitted it in this case to evade its financial responsibility for Todd's special education needs. The juvenile court's disruption of special education services may be remedied by ensuring its awareness of the child's educational needs. The school district's participation in the juvenile justice process will permit the juvenile court to place a child on the basis of both the child's delinquency and his or her special education needs, and to assign liability accordingly. On its own initiative, the school district should review a child's IEP after a delinquency adjudication, or the district court may order review. If the school district refuses to review the IEP, or its decision after review is still unsatisfactory to the parents or legal guardian of the educationally handicapped child, they may take an appeal.

Hillsborough county asserts that because the special education administrative appeals process does not provide for the participation of the legally liable unit in a delinquency proceeding, exhaustion of administrative remedies is a futile requirement. Although the legally liable unit under the juvenile justice laws may not participate in the administrative appeals process, parents of a child involved in a delinquency adjudication have an incentive to appeal a school district's decision because the legally liable unit has a right of reimbursement against the parents for the expenses of the placement charged to it. The administrative process is not futile here because the State Board of Education, or the superior court or federal district court, has the power to determine that the IEP is inadequate. Without the use of this administrative process, however, no administrative record exists to guide the court in evaluating the substance of an IEP.

Once a child is placed by the juvenile court, and the school district is ordered to review the child's IEP, the school district is financially responsible for the educational portion of the placement while administrative remedies are pursued. The assumption is that the special education portion of a placement under the juvenile justice laws is the responsibility of the school district.

In this case, however, the Peterborough District Court determined liability after Todd's placement had taken place, and the school district had not been ordered to review the IEP. No administrative appeal was pending. The district court had the authority to order a review of Todd's IEP, but had no authority to issue a liability order against the school district for the educational expenses of a placement that the school district had not established as part of Todd's IEP. Todd's placement at the Chamberlain School was the result of a delinquency adjudication, and the legally liable unit is responsible for the expenses of that placement.

In response to difficulties that might arise with respect to various agencies having different responsibilities, the IDEA includes a plan for a statewide interagency coordinating council.[26] The council is to include parents; service providers; state legislators; individuals involved in personnel preparation; representation from early intervention service agencies, preschool providers, state Medicaid agencies, Head Start, child care agencies, health insurance agencies, homeless children and youth coordinators, foster care representatives, and mental health agencies; and other members as appropriate. While there is provision for meetings and duties, it is not clear how disputes are to be handled within the IDEA framework. It would seem that this provision is aspirational; it does not guarantee a system to resolve disputes. Such agreements, if effective, can be important, because for some children Medicaid and other benefits funding programs may be available to cover the cost of some related services.

Private Obligations

As was mentioned earlier in this chapter, the income of the parent is irrelevant in a determination that the education should be provided at no cost by the school. An issue that is likely to arise increasingly is the question of whether certain expenses should be borne by private insurance companies or the public educational agency. The *Seals v. Loftis* opinion excerpted in Chapter 6 should be reviewed at this point. The result in that case is probably the appropriate outcome in any case involving special education—namely that if the payment by the private insurance company will reduce the lifetime benefits or in any other way have an adverse financial impact on the family insurance benefits available to it, the parents should not be required to use their insurance benefits to cover educational expenses. These expenses include the cost of special education and related services.[27]

The less clear issue is whether the private insurance company can raise the educational agency's obligation to provide special education and related services as a defense against its own obligation to pay certain expenses in instances where the parents are willing to have their insurance benefits cover certain expenses, or where the obligation of the insurance company to pay would not affect the parents' benefits. The resolution will depend both on the terms of the insurance contract between the parents and the insurance company and on the judicial interpretation of the validity and meaning of these contract terms. In its decision in *Chester County Intermediate Unit v. Pennsylvania Blue Shield*,[28] a case decided before 1997, the court addressed whether private insurance companies could limit their obligations to cover services that are considered special education and related services under the IDEA. The court held that nothing in special education policy precluded privately negotiated contracts to provide such limitations. The case involved whether the educational agency or the private health insurance company was obligated to pay for the costs of physical therapy. The court held that based on the plain terms of the exclusions in the policy, the insurer was not liable for the costs of physical therapy. There are few other cases on this issue.

In recognition of the need for greater clarity, Congress has in 1997 and 2004 addressed at least some of those issues. The 1997 and 2004 amendments to the IDEA provide that IDEA funding is generally not to be used for services that would have been paid by another public or private source. In addition, states are not to reduce medical or other assistance or alter eligibility for social security because of any services provided under the IDEA.[29] This does not mean, however, that a private insurance company could not stipulate in an insurance contract at the outset that there would be no reimbursement for costs that an educational agency is responsible for under the IDEA.

Rehabilitation Act and the Americans with Disabilities Act

Cost can be raised as an issue for providing children with disabilities with educational services under both Section 504 of the Rehabilitation Act and the Americans with Disabilities Act (ADA).[30] Where a child might have a disability yet not meet the definition for coverage under the IDEA, the child may nevertheless be covered under Section 504, the ADA, or both. Thus the child would be entitled to reasonable accommodations or modifications for the disability. An educational agency is not required to provide an accommodation or modification that would pose an undue hardship either financially or administratively. There is little, if any, judicial interpretation of what facts would establish a case of undue financial hardship in a school setting. This is because most cases arise only under the IDEA. Perhaps the best guidance on this would be those cases involving higher education and reasonable accommodation in programs and services.

Summary

The IDEA requires that special education and related services be provided to eligible students at public expense. Some might suggest that at least certain expensive services should be paid for by parents on an ability-to-pay basis. At present, however, the IDEA does not apply this standard, and parents are not required to pay for these services regardless of their income.

The special education and related services that are to be publicly funded include not only the educational services but also the cost of procedural protections of the administrative hearing. What is not covered within the public expense mandate is the parents' cost of legal representation (attorneys' fees and costs) unless the parent is successful in the matter.

Regardless of their success at the initial administrative level, parents have a right to have a record of the hearing and a copy of the findings provided at public expense. The IDEA does not require that the school disseminate the student's records free of charge unless failure to do so would, in effect, prevent access to due process.

While courts seem to scrutinize cost defenses fairly rigorously, it would seem that cost can be used as a legitimate reason for limiting the type and level of special education programming needed by a student as long as the student still received FAPE from the services and programming that was provided. Cost cannot be a defense, however, if the result would be a total denial of FAPE to a particular student. As the number of cases that involve expensive quasi-medical and other extraordinary services increases, it is likely the courts will begin to define more clearly the circumstances under which educational agency budgetary constraints will be a defense. Although a significant number of judicial opinions have addressed cost as an issue, there is not yet a clear standard by which to evaluate such cases.

Another issue addressed by the 1997 and 2004 amendments is the availability of special education funding when other sources are available. The IDEA contemplates that other public funding sources (such as human services, health services, etc.) as well as private sources (insurance) should be used to pay for some special education and related services programming. Unfortunately, the IDEA lacks any mechanism whereby state educational agencies can exert pressure on other public agencies to play a supporting role. The law provides some incentive to coordination of services among state agencies. States receiving IDEA funding must establish a state interagency coordinating council with specific guidelines for composition and management authority.

As to the responsibility of the educational agency, it is clear that the state agency bears the primary responsibility for ensuring that services are provided, and in fact has the ultimate responsibility for directly providing the services if a local educational agency fails to do so. As to which state or local educational agency has responsibility for placements by the educational agency, this depends generally on the residency of the child. In most cases this is easily determined. But in cases where the child does not actually reside with the natural parents, where there is shared custody between divorced or separated parents, and in other situations, difficulties can arise in determining the responsible state. The IDEA does not provide any specific guidance on this issue. The resolution instead will depend on how individual states define residency in the relevant statutes and policies and how courts resolve disputes when more than one state or local jurisdiction is involved.

Because of the IDEA principle that special education is to be provided at no cost to the parents, private insurance can be required as a funding source only when it is clear that this will have no adverse economic impact (such as reduced lifetime benefit or increased premiums) on the parents. This does not prevent private insurers from precluding such coverage in the insurance contract.

In addition to the IDEA requirements related to cost, there may be some situations where a child is covered only by Section 504 of the Rehabilitation Act or the ADA. In those cases, the cost issue of whether a particular program or service must be provided would be determined under the reasonable accommodation and modification requirements of those statutes.

Questions for Reflection

1. Suppose a child had been in a residential placement for several years and the child's file contained hundreds of documents. Would it be reasonable to allow the parent an opportunity to review the file and request only specified documents?

2. What would be considered a reasonable fee for photocopying? How would that be determined?

3. Suppose a $30,000 vehicle was needed to provide transportation to a student with an orthopedic impairment who lived at the end of an unpaved mountain road. What if the local agency's entire budget was very low because of a poor local economic tax base? What if there was no chalk in the classrooms in that local school district? What if the entire state that includes the district had a low economic base? Who would set these priorities?

4. Could the *Roncker* argument, that spending benefiting only one student is a factor in using cost as a defense, be used by a school district to deny residential placement to a student because it will benefit only one individual?

5. In the *Catlin* case, could the Massachusetts school district in which the Catlins now reside be found to be obligated to pay for Dell's education? This issue was not decided in the case. If so, as a practical matter, how could they evaluate Dell and place him?

6. Keeping in mind the *Todd P.* case, as a practical matter how will schools be aware of a delinquency proceeding and know when to participate? How can juvenile court judges be apprised of the IDEA and its requirements?

7. While a child with severe impairments may have many costs paid by an educational agency until the child graduates from high school, what happens at that point when there is not the same comprehensive set of benefits available?

NOTES

1. U.S.C. § 1401(8). See also Laura Rothstein & Julia Rothstein, *Disabilities and the Law* § 2:21 (Thomson West 2006).
2. 42 U.S.C. § 1401(26). See also Chapter 10.
3. 34 C.F.R. § 300.104.
4. Laura Rothstein, "Educational Rights of Severely and Profoundly Handicapped Children," 61 *Neb. L. Rev.* 586 (1982).
5. 20 U.S.C. § 1401(26).
6. See Chapter 10.
7. See Chapter 6.
8. See Chapter 21.
9. 34 C.F.R. § 300.511(b).
10. See Chapter 21.
11. 34 C.F.R. § 300.511(b).
12. 34 C.F.R. § 99.11.
13. *Id.*
14. In *Clevenger v. Oak Ridge School Board*, 744 F.2d 514 (6th Cir. 1984), the court held that cost concerns would not be relevant where the only appropriate placement was an $88,000 residential placement.
15. *Mills v. Board of Education*, 348 F. Supp. 866, 876 (D.D.C. 1972).
16. C.F.R. § 300.100; 34 C.F.R. § 300.101; 34 C.F.R. § 300.103; 34 C.F.R. § 300.163.

17. 34 C.F.R. § 300.103.

18. 468 U.S. 882, 892 (1984). See Chapter 10 for an excerpt from the case.

19. 700 F.2d 1058, 1063 (6th Cir. 1983). See Chapter 11 for a portion of the case decision. See also *Department of Education v. Katherine D.*, 727 F.2d 809 (9th Cir. 1984).

20. *Mark C. & Ruth A. v. Grand Wood Area Educ. Agency*, 795 F.2d 52 (8th Cir. 1986) and *Springdale School District 50 v. Grace*, 693 F.2d 41 (8th Cir. 1982).

21. 20 U.S.C. § 1411(e)(3)(G).

22. 20 U.S.C. § 1413(g).

23. For citations to a number of cases addressing these issues, see *Disabilities and the Law* § 2:21, notes 37–40.

24. 20 U.S.C. § 1412(a)(10)(B).

25. As noted in Chapter 12, the rights and obligations for these students are different from those of students enrolled in public schools or placed in private schools by the public school.

26. 42 U.S.C. § 1441; 300 C.F.R. § 300.174 (for infants and toddlers).

27. "Special Education, Private Insurance and Medicaid" (March 2004), available at the Ohio Legal Rights Service Web site at http://olrs.ohio.gov/asp/olrs_SpecEd7.asp (last accessed August 10, 2008).

28. 896 F.2d 808 (3d Cir. 1990).

29. 20 U.S.C. § 1440.

30. See Chapter 18 for a more detailed discussion of Section 504 and the ADA.

15

Procedural Safeguards

An Overview

Due Process Procedures Under the IDEA

The substantive right to a free appropriate public education might well be an empty promise without the procedural safeguards mandated by the Individuals with Disabilities Education Act (IDEA).[1] The primary features of the procedural protections provided to parents under the law are the right to notice, the opportunity to participate in team meetings held to make decisions about the child, and consent. The IDEA and the implementing regulations spell out in great detail the procedural safeguards and the points at which parental involvement is guaranteed.

Notice

A key element in the procedural requirements under the IDEA is notice. Without notice of plans and proposed decisions, parental involvement would often be nonexistent. The IDEA requires written notice when the public agency or school proposes to initiate or change, or refuses to initiate or change, the identification, evaluation, or educational placement of the child, or the provision of a free appropriate public education (FAPE) to the child.[2]

The requirement of notice is based on constitutional due process principles recognized in *Mills*.[3] The IDEA expands on the general constitutional guarantee by specifying not only when notice is required but also the form of the notice and its content.

Notice must be in writing and must be in a form understandable to the general public.[4] It must be in the native language of the parents or other mode of communication if that is not feasible. In the *Rowley*[5] case, for example, the school had set up a telecommunications device for the deaf (TDD) telephone hookup not only to notify Amy Rowley's parents, who were deaf, of their procedural rights but also to allow frequent discussion of Amy's educational progress.

The regulations provide no guidance as to when it might be infeasible to provide notice in a particular language or mode of communication. It could be speculated that proposing a program for a child whose parents' native language is Hindi, but who also communicate in English, might be permitted to provide the notice in English. It is suggested that variations will probably be permitted under the infeasibility standard only where the alternative notice is reasonably designed to provide actual notice to the parents.

If parents do not communicate in written form, the educational agency must take steps to ensure that there is appropriate translation that is understood by the parents. The agency must have written evidence of what was provided.[6]

The content of the notice must include a description of options that were considered and why they were rejected; a description of the evaluation procedures and other information that was the basis for the action; a description of the available procedural safeguards; information on sources for parents to contact to understand their rights; and a description of other factors relevant to the decision.[7] This information must be in *every* notice provided relating to identification, evaluation, or placement. Notice must also include a description of the procedures, tests, or other factors used in making the proposal or refusal.[8] Notice of procedural safeguards is required only once a year except where there is an initial referral or parent request for evaluation, when due process complaints occur, during disciplinary action, and when requested by parents.[9] The content of the procedural safeguards notice must include a full explanation of all of the procedural safeguards, including time periods.[10]

Participation

Schools must provide parents with notice of the meetings that the school conducts as part of the special education process (referral, evaluation, eligibility, individualized education program [IEP], and placement meetings), so that parents can participate in these meetings as part of the team that makes decisions during the process.[11] Parents participate as full team members and must consent to some proposals before they can be implemented (see the section on consent below for more information). The school must also take steps to ensure that the parents understand what is occurring at the team meeting, including arranging for an interpreter for parents who are deaf or whose native language is other than English.[12]

Meetings do not include informal or unscheduled conversations involving school personnel. Meetings also do not include preparatory activities to develop a proposal or respond to a parent's proposal that will be discussed later at a meeting, nor conversations by school personnel about teaching methodology, lessons plans, or coordination of services.[13]

As noted in prior chapters, sometimes parents are not able, or willing, to participate in meetings for various reasons. The IDEA requires the school to make efforts to ensure parental participation at meetings. These efforts include trying to schedule the meeting at a mutually agreed upon time and place, providing notice early enough to ensure the parent can participate (in most cases 10 days notice is used as the standard), and affording parents the opportunity to participate by other means like conference calls or video conference if the parents cannot be present at the meeting location.[14]

If the school is unable to convince the parents that they should attend, the school can conduct a team meeting without the parents, but it must keep a record of its attempts to arrange a mutually agreed on time and place. Records can include things like details of telephone calls made to the parents and the results of those calls, copies of letters to the parents and responses from the parents, and visits to the parents' home or place of employment.[15]

Consent

The IDEA has a number of provisions regarding consent. As mentioned in prior chapters, parental consent is specifically required during the evaluation and reevaluation process and before the initial provisions of special education and related services.[16] Parental consent is also required in a number of other areas as well, including excusing team members from IEP meetings and when a school wants to access the parents' private insurance to help cover the costs of services. The IDEA also allows states to require consent for other services and activities in the special education process.[17]

Additionally, it is important to remember that even when consent is not specifically required, the school must provide written notice when it proposes to initiate or change, or refuses to initiate or change, the identification, evaluation, or placement of the child, or the services provided to the child to provide FAPE. The purpose of the notice requirement is to give the parents a chance to participate in the decision-making process about all of these steps. If the parent objects to the proposed change, the parent can seek an administrative due process hearing to resolve the disagreement and, when the parent does so, the proposed change often may not occur until the resolution of the hearing, unless both the parents and the school agree otherwise. This is because of the "stay-put" or pendency requirements in the law, which are discussed in more detail later in this chapter.[18]

While the terms of the stay-put or pendency requirements mention only placement, it has been interpreted to go beyond placement and require other aspects of the child's programming to remain in place as well, such as an IEP. For example, if the IEP team recommends changes to an IEP and the parent disagrees and requests a due process hearing, the stay-put provisions have been interpreted to require the services under the last agreed-upon IEP to continue to be provided until the dispute over the changes in the new IEP is resolved.[19]

Under the IDEA, informed consent means that the parent has been fully informed of all information relevant to the activity for which consent is sought and the parent understands and agrees in writing to carrying out the activity. The consent must describe the activity and list the records (if any) that will be released and to whom. The parent must also be informed that the granting of consent is voluntary on the part of the parent and may be revoked at any time. If a parent revokes consent, it is not retroactive (i.e., it does not negate an action that has occurred after the consent was given and before the consent was revoked).[20]

Enforcement

In Chapter 6, the *Quackenbush* case illustrated the possible consequences that can occur when the educational agency fails to comply with the notice requirements. That case and other cases seem to indicate that failure to comply with the notice requirement can be a procedural violation of the IDEA. The *Cerra v. Pawling School District* case in Chapter 8 provides a good example of how courts interpret some of the notice and participation requirements in the context of developing an IEP.

In the past, the remedy or consequence of a procedural violation was not always clear. If the violation was made in bad faith and had serious consequences, such as those in *Quackenbush*, there was the potential for financial liability on the part of the educational agency or perhaps some of the individuals involved in the process.[21]

As mentioned in prior chapters, the IDEA now provides that a student (or parent) is not entitled to certain remedies for procedural violations such as the failure to provide notice, unless it has impeded the right to receive FAPE, significantly impeded the parents' right to participate in the special education process, or caused a deprivation of educational benefit.[22] As a result, when enforcing the IDEA's procedural protections in court, the outcome will depend in part on the remedy sought by the plaintiff and the impact the procedural violations have on the substantive rights in the IDEA (like the right to FAPE). The following case provides an example.

GARCIA V. BOARD OF EDUCATION OF ALBUQUERQUE PUBLIC SCHOOLS

520 F.3d 1116 (10th Cir. 2008)

Jessica Garcia, on behalf of her daughter Myisha, alleges that the Albuquerque Public School District failed to formulate an individualized education program for Myisha in the Fall semester of 2003, in violation of the Individuals with Disabilities Education Act. By way of remedy, the Garcias seek certain compensatory educational services. The district court, though acknowledging the school district's procedural deficiency, held that no such services should be awarded as a matter of equity because, among other things, Myisha has dropped out of school, demonstrated an unwillingness to return to school, and could essentially receive the very services she seeks simply by re-enrolling in school. On appeal, we do not excuse the school district for neglecting its statutory duties to Myisha, but neither can we say that the district court abused its discretion in exercising its traditional equitable powers.

Turning to the district court's disposition of Myisha's claim on the merits, . . . the Garcias contend that the school district violated IDEA by failing to formulate and implement an IEP, and that this failure resulted in an effective denial of a FAPE to Myisha. The school district responds by arguing that the tardiness in formulating an IEP for Fall 2003 was merely a procedural irregularity that did not cause any substantive harm or comprise an effective denial of a FAPE. In pressing its position, the school district emphasizes that it provided Myisha with special education services even in the absence of an updated IEP and that Myisha's behavioral problems prevented her from receiving any benefit from an updated IEP even had there been one.

We approach this dispute mindful, as always, of our standard of review. Bearing this standard of review in mind, we turn to the two-step inquiry set out by the Supreme Court as our test for assessing liability: (1) Has the school district complied with the procedures set forth in IDEA? (2) Are the special education services provided to the student reasonably calculated to enable the child to receive educational benefits—or in other words, has the school district fulfilled its obligation to provide the student with a FAPE? *Rowley,* 458 U.S. at 206–07.

While "a failure to meet [either] one of these considerations may result in court ordered relief," the type of relief sought will often determine which of the two considerations is dispositive in a particular case. For example, where a school district has allegedly failed to comply with a procedural requirement of IDEA and the plaintiff seeks only an order mandating prospective compliance, then question (1) (whether the school district complied with IDEA's procedural requirements) may be the crucial inquiry, while question (2) (whether the school district provided a FAPE) may often be irrelevant because the claim seeks only to vindicate the student's *procedural,* rather than *substantive,* rights under IDEA. But where, as here, only compensatory relief is sought, the pivotal question is (2), because an award of compensatory education vindicates the student's *substantive* right to receive a FAPE and compensates for a past deprivation of educational opportunity rather than a deprivation of purely procedural rights. . . . Of course, where a procedural violation is alleged to have caused the substantive deprivation of a FAPE (the case here), question (1) still bears obvious significance.

In this appeal, the school district does not dispute that it failed to comply with IDEA's procedural requirements in Fall 2003. For that reason, and because the award of compensatory education that the Garcias seek depends primarily on question (2) of our *Rowley* analysis, we proceed directly to consider that question—namely, whether such a failure resulted in an effective denial of FAPE for Myisha. Or, more precisely, whether the procedural defect of not having a current IEP in place in Fall 2003 amounted to a substantive failure to "provid[e] personalized instruction with sufficient support services to permit the child to benefit educationally from [the school]." *Rowley,* 458 U.S. at 203.

[L]iability under IDEA is determined not by imagining the possibilities of what might have been, but rather by determining whether the preponderance of the evidence indicates that the school district's procedural failures resulted in a denial of educational benefit to the student. As the district court points out, such an inquiry implicitly seems to require determining whether the school district's actions *caused* the student to suffer an educational loss. And on the facts of this case, there is strong evidence indicating that, regardless of what actions the school district did or did not take in Fall 2003, Myisha's poor attitude and bad habits would have prevented her from receiving any educational benefit. *See, e.g.,* Hearing Officer's Decision at 39 (summarizing Myisha's patterns of behavior that contributed to her poor attendance and performance).

In addition to basing its denial of relief on its holding that the school district's procedural deficiencies did not harm Myisha and thus give rise to liability, the district court also, and alternatively, denied relief in light of various equitable considerations it identified. Because the district court's remedial decision is entitled to abuse of discretion review, and because the district

(Continued)

(Continued)

court's discretion extends to denying relief for the reasons the court stated in its disposition of Myisha's claim, we are compelled to affirm its judgment.

A

The school district asserts, and the Garcias do not deny, that, while our standard of review in assessing liability is rather searching, our review of the district court's remedial decision is limited to assessing only whether it amounts to an abuse of discretion. And, indeed, the plain language of IDEA accords district courts broad discretion in determining relief for successful IDEA claims, stating that a district court "shall grant such relief as the court determines is appropriate." 20 U.S.C. § 1415(i)(2)(C)(iii). The Supreme Court, when examining this statutory text, has echoed the point, declaring that "[t]he ordinary meaning of these words confers broad discretion on the court," *Sch. Comm. of Burlington v. Dep't of Educ. of Mass.*, 471 U.S. 359, 369 (1985), and explaining that the words of the statute "mean[ ] that equitable considerations are relevant in fashioning relief," *id.* at 374; *see also Florence County Sch. Dist. Four v. Carter,* 510 U.S. 7, 16 (1993) (recognizing that IDEA authorizes courts to "fashion[ ] discretionary equitable relief").

Where Congress affords equitable discretion to the district court, we traditionally limit ourselves to reviewing only for "abuse" of that discretion. "When Congress leaves to the federal courts the formulation of remedial details, it can hardly expect them to break with historic principles of equity in the enforcement of federally-created equitable rights." This is not to say that Congress cannot alter the federal courts' traditional equity practice by specifying a standard of review other than abuse of discretion if it so chooses; of course it may. But no such congressional intention is manifest in the text of IDEA, and the parties suggest none.

Turning first to IDEA's primary purpose of providing a FAPE to all disabled children, the district court emphasized that denying compensatory relief in this instance in no way hinders Myisha's access to a FAPE. And ample evidence supports the district court's conclusion. Myisha is, after all, *already* guaranteed the provision of a FAPE at any time she chooses to return to school, so long as she remains eligible to receive benefits under IDEA (that is, until she reaches 21).*

Relatedly, it remains unclear from the record how that provision of a FAPE would differ in any substantive (rather than formal) way from the compensatory relief Myisha seeks in this case. Neither does denying Myisha relief endanger the provision of a FAPE to other disabled children. The district court's decision does nothing to indicate that IDEA procedural failures will be tolerated or left unremedied except in limited circumstances involving students who have demonstrated a clear commitment to avoid school and disregard the educational opportunities available to them.

The district court's denial of relief also relied on IDEA's purpose of ensuring the effectiveness of efforts to educate children with disabilities. After all, the limited resources devoted to providing

* Were there any concerns that the school district would not provide her a FAPE upon her return, prospective (rather than compensatory) relief to ensure the provision of a FAPE would certainly be appropriate. But the Garcias have not raised any such concerns or sought such relief.

education benefits for disabled children are not effectively allocated where schools expend resources on students who not only fail to use the educational opportunities provided them but also affirmatively avoid attending school altogether. Along these lines, the district court emphasized that, regardless of the school district's compliance or non-compliance with IDEA's procedural safeguards, "Myisha has had no interest (with the exception of the 2004–05 school year) in obtaining an education, and . . . continues to have no interest." . . . As such, awarding compensatory relief "just in case Myisha changes her mind about getting an education at some point in the next few years is unnecessary and wasteful." . . . Ample evidence also supports the district court's conclusion on this score. Despite the school's open doors, Myisha has not regularly attended school since the Fall 2005 semester. She and her mother have affirmatively avoided the school district's attempts to cooperate in formulating new IEPs aimed at assisting Myisha in further progressing in her high school education. . . . Additionally, Myisha's significant record of disciplinary problems and truancy, while not justifying the school district's non-compliance with IDEA in Fall 2003, does tend to confirm the district court's skepticism of whether Myisha will in fact choose to benefit from the compensatory services that she might receive from the court. Myisha's superb performance during the 2004–2005 school year also demonstrates that she may well be able to make impressive academic strides simply by re-enrolling in high school, attending regularly, and avoiding the behavioral problems of her past, aided by the special education services that would be available to her should she re-enroll. Finally, as the hearing officer concluded, putting aside the lapse in updating Myisha's IEP in Fall 2003, the school district has for the most part made diligent and extensive efforts to provide Myisha with whatever special services that could help her in progressing towards graduation, while Myisha has, aside from the 2004–2005 school year, largely rejected those services.

Because the result of and reasons supporting the district court's decision accord with the relevant purposes of IDEA and are supported by the undisputed facts in the record, we cannot say that the court abused its discretion.

Affirmed.

While the *Garcia* case focuses primarily on the failure to have an IEP in place as the procedural violation at issue in the case, there were also allegations that the school improperly conducted IEP meetings without the parents. The court ultimately decided the case based on equitable grounds and found that the district court denying relief was not an abuse of discretion. Since the notice, participation, and consent requirements mentioned in this chapter fall into the procedural protections of the IDEA, like the failure to have an IEP in place, courts could also use the same approach for alleged violations of these rights.

The court in *Garcia* also noted the difference between prospective and compensatory remedies, and that played a role in the decision. As the court noted, if there were any concerns that the school district would not provide the student with FAPE upon her return, prospective (rather than compensatory) relief to ensure the provision of a

FAPE would be appropriate. Thus, in some cases, prospective relief from a court, such as ordering the school to comply with procedural protections in the IDEA going forward, may be appropriate for a procedural violation when compensatory relief (meaning an order for additional services to make up for those not provided in the past) is not.[23] More information about compensatory relief and remedies is provided in Chapter 21.

When Are Due Process Procedures Triggered?

For the IDEA to be effective, it is essential that its due process requirements be implemented at critical points. Notice is required whenever the educational agency or school proposes to initiate or change the identification, evaluation, or placement or the provision of special education or related services, or refuses to do so. The parents have the opportunity to object to the school's proposals and request a due process hearing or other means of dispute resolution at all of these points.

One critical question that can arise is whether a particular action constitutes a change in placement, thus requiring notice and the triggering of the procedural safeguards. Chapter 16 addresses disciplinary removals from a classroom and whether these constitute a change in placement. There are other situations that raise this question also. Several judicial opinions have addressed a variety of issues. As a general rule, minor changes, such as moving the class to a different room, or changing a feeding program for a child with a profound disability, or slightly increasing transportation time, are not considered to require notice.[24]

It could prove unreasonably cumbersome to require that the agency notify the parents of minor variations. In the instance of a child for whom even minor variations would be important, the IEP could reflect the fact that not even minor variations would be made without notice.

Transfer of Rights

Parental rights generally transfer to the student when the student reaches the age of majority.[25] The parent still has the right to notice along with the student. The school must notify both the parents and the student of the transfer of rights.[26] Beginning not later than one year before the student reaches the age of majority, the student's IEP must include a statement that the student has been informed of the rights that will transfer to him or her upon reaching the age of majority.[27]

One exception to the transfer of rights is when the student is deemed incompetent under state law. Additionally, the IDEA also provides that states may develop a process to appoint the parent of a child, or another appropriate individual, to represent the educational interests of the child even if the child does not reach the level of incompetency, if the child does not have the ability to provide informed consent regarding his or her educational programming.[28]

Status of Child Pending Final Decision ("Stay-Put")

The IDEA provides that while administrative and judicial proceedings are pending, the child is to remain in the present educational placement.[29] This is known as the "stay-put" provision. If the child has not been previously placed in public school, the child must be placed in the public school program pending resolution as long as the parents agree to do so.[30] The educational agency and the parents can agree to alternate placements pending resolution of the dispute.

The stay-put provision has given rise to a significant amount of litigation, primarily relating to disciplinary removals. That issue is discussed in more detail in Chapter 16. Other than disciplinary reasons, there are questions about what circumstances justify removing the student from the stay-put placement during the pendency of administrative proceedings. One situation where removal from the stay-put placement can arise is when that placement is no longer available. Examples include the school that is the stay-put placement closing or losing its certification, or the student advancing to the next grade level during the pendency of the proceedings.[31]

Summary

A key feature of the effectiveness of the IDEA in ensuring that special education will be available to those entitled to it is the procedural safeguards available under the Act. The Act and the regulations are fairly specific about the procedural requirements. These include notice to the parents at any point when a change in the identification, evaluation, or placement of the child is proposed or refused. Both the form and the content of the notice are specified, including written notice in a manner understandable to the parents to whom it is provided. Parental participation continues in the actual development of the IEP. Parents not only have a right to notice but must also give their consent before many special education actions can occur. When there is disagreement over any of these decisions, either the school or the parents may request an impartial due process hearing and the stay-put provisions may require the continuation of current agreed-upon services or placement until the dispute is resolved. If the issue cannot be resolved at that point, state administrative agency and judicial review of the decision are also available, as will be discussed in more detail in Chapter 17.

Questions for Reflection

1. What kind of notice would be required in a case where parents are illiterate?

2. Suppose a child had a record of severe anxiety on standardized tests. Would the school be required to state in the notice to parents that the test would be in a standardized form? Should it make a difference whether the school is aware of the child's aversion to such tests? See *Healy v. Ambach,* 103 A.D.2d 565, 481 N.Y.S.2d 809 (1984).

3. One remedy for procedural violations is a hearing officer or court ordering the school to comply with procedural requirements in the future. What should the remedy be if the school still continues to violate procedural requirements after the order? Should the law then provide some relief to the student even if the violations do not impede their right to FAPE, affect the parent's participation, or cause educational harm?

4. In the *Garcia* case, what role did the student and parent's actions play in the court denying relief? Would the outcome have been different if the student had stayed in school?

5. How should a state process go about determining if a student who is competent under the law is unable to provide informed consent for his or her educational programming? Does your state have such a process? If so, what does it require?

NOTES

1. 20 U.S.C. § 1415. See also Laura Rothstein & Julia Rothstein, *Disabilities and the Law* §§ 2:31–2.46 (Thomson West 2006).
2. 20 U.S.C. § 1415(b)(3).
3. For an overview of this case, see Chapter 2.
4. 34 C.F.R. § 300.503(c).
5. See Chapter 9.
6. 34 C.F.R. § 300.503(c)(2).
7. 34 C.F.R. § 300.503(b).
8. 34 C.F.R. § 300.504.
9. 34 C.F.R. § 300.504(a).
10. 34 C.F.R. § 300.504(c).
11. 34 C.F.R. § 300.322(a)(1); 34 C.F.R. § 300.322(b)(1); 34 C.F.R. § 300.501(b); 34 C.F.R. § 300.501(c).
12. 34 C.F.R. § 300.322(e).
13. 34 C.F.R. § 300.501(c).
14. 34 C.F.R. § 300.322; 34 C.F.R. § 300.328.
15. 34 C.F.R. § 300.322(d).
16. 34 C.F.R. § 300.300.
17. 34 C.F.R. § 300.300(d)(2).
18. 34 C.F.R. § 300.518.
19. See, e.g., *C.P. v. Leon County School Board*, 466 F.3d 1318 (11th Cir. 2006).
20. 34 C.F.R. § 300.9.
21. See Chapter 20.
22. 20 U.S.C. § 1415(f)(3)(E); 34 C.F.R. § 300.513(a)(2).
23. The IDEA expressly notes this as well. See 20 U.S.C. § 1415(f)(3)(E).
24. *Disabilities and the Law* § 2:43, fn. 9.
25. 34 C.F.R. § 300.520.
26. 34 C.F.R. § 300.520.
27. 34 C.F.R. § 300.320(c).
28. 34 C.F.R. § 300.520(b).
29. 34 C.F.R. § 300.518.
30. 34 C.F.R. § 300.518(b).
31. *Tilton v. Jefferson County Bd. of Education*, 705 F.2d 800 (6th Cir. 1983).

16

Discipline

Historical Context

One of the practices that Congress sought to address in enacting the Education for All Handicapped Children Act (which subsequently became the Individuals with Disabilities Education Act [IDEA]) is unilateral removal of students from their educational placements by schools and not providing the student services because of behavior that occurred as a result of the student's disability.[1] As a result, one of the guiding principles for discipline under the IDEA is that a school cannot unilaterally change a special education student's educational placement by removing the student from school for behavior that is caused by the disability. Rather, the student's programming must be changed in order to address the behavior. There are some exceptions to this principle discussed later in this chapter. Another guiding principle is that students must continue to receive a free appropriate public education (FAPE), even when they are removed from their educational placement through disciplinary procedures such as suspension or expulsion.

The first issue to be resolved with discipline is often whether there has been a change in placement at all by virtue of disciplinary removal from a classroom. A second issue results when a temporary removal is required for emergency reasons. What circumstances justify such a removal and for how long may the removal be permitted? Related to that issue is the question of what must be provided in terms of educational services during the removal. The other critical question in the context of discipline is whether the behavior that led to the disciplinary action was a result of the student's disability.

This chapter discusses all of these issues and begins with the following Supreme Court decision that addressed the issue of disciplinary removals and provided a significant degree of guidance as to these issues.

HONIG V. DOE

484 U.S. 305 (1988)

Justice Brennan delivered the opinion of the Court.

As a condition of federal financial assistance, the Education of the Handicapped Act [EHA] requires States to ensure a "free appropriate public education" for all disabled children within their jurisdictions. In aid of this goal, the Act establishes a comprehensive system of procedural safeguards designed to ensure parental participation in decisions concerning the education of their disabled children and to provide administrative and judicial review of any decisions with which those parents disagree. Among these safeguards is the so-called "stay-put" provision, which directs that a disabled child "shall remain in [his or her] then current educational placement" pending completion of any review proceedings, unless the parents and state or local educational agencies otherwise agree. 20 U.S.C. sec. 1415(e)(3) [Now § 1415(j)]. Today we must decide whether, in the face of this statutory proscription, state or local school authorities may nevertheless unilaterally exclude disabled children from the classroom for dangerous or disruptive conduct growing out of their disabilities. In addition, we are called upon to decide whether a district court may, in the exercise of its equitable powers, order a State to provide educational services directly to a disabled child when the local agency fails to do so. . . .

The EHA confers upon disabled students an enforceable substantive right to public education in participating States, and conditions federal financial assistance upon a State's compliance with the substantive and procedural goals of the Act. . . .

The primary vehicle for implementing these congressional goals is the "individualized educational program" (IEP), which the EHA mandates for each disabled child. . . .

The Act establishes various procedural safeguards that guarantee parents both an opportunity for meaningful input into all decisions affecting their child's education and the right to seek review of any decisions they think inappropriate. . . .

The "stay-put" provision at issue in this case governs the placement of a child while these often lengthy review procedures run their course. It directs that:

> During the pendency of any proceedings conducted pursuant to [sec. 1415], unless the State or local educational agency and the parents or guardian otherwise agree, the child shall remain in the then current educational placement of such child. . . . Sec. 1415(e)(3) [Now § 1415(j)].

The present dispute grows out of the efforts of certain officials of the San Francisco Unified School District (SFUSD) to expel two emotionally disturbed children from school indefinitely for violent and disruptive conduct related to their disabilities. In November 1980, respondent John Doe assaulted another student at the Louise Lombard School, a developmental center for disabled children. Doe's April 1980 IEP identified him as a socially and physically awkward 7-year-old who experienced considerable difficulty controlling his impulses and anger. Among the goals set out in his IEP was "[i]mprovement in [his] ability to relate to [his] peers [and to] cope with frustrating situations without resorting to aggressive acts." Frustrating situations, however, were an unfortunately prominent feature of Doe's school career: physical abnormalities, speech difficulties, and poor grooming habits had made him the target of teasing and ridicule as early as the first grade; his 1980 IEP reflected his continuing difficulties with peers, noting that his social skills had deteriorated and that he could tolerate only minor frustration before exploding.

On November 6, 1980, Doe responded to the taunts of a fellow student in precisely the explosive manner anticipated by his IEP: he choked the student with sufficient force to leave abrasions on the child's neck, and kicked out a school window while being escorted to the principal's office afterwards. Doe admitted his misconduct and the school subsequently suspended him for five days. [The maximum permitted in California at that time.] Thereafter, his principal referred the matter to the Student Placement Committee (SPC or Committee) with the recommendation that Doe be expelled. On the day the suspension was to end, the SPC notified Doe's mother that it was proposing to exclude her child permanently from SFUSD and was therefore extending his suspension until such time as the expulsion proceedings were completed. The Committee further advised her that she was entitled to attend the November 25 hearing at which it planned to discuss the proposed expulsion.

After unsuccessfully protesting these actions by letter, Doe brought this suit against a host of local school officials and the state superintendent of public education. Alleging that the suspension and proposed expulsion violated the EHA, he sought a temporary restraining order cancelling the SPC hearing and requiring school officials to convene an IEP meeting. . . .

Respondent Jack Smith was identified as an emotionally disturbed child by the time he entered the second grade in 1976. School records prepared that year indicated that he was unable "to control verbal or physical outburst[s] and exhibited a "[s]evere disturbance in relationships with peers and adults." Further evaluations subsequently revealed that he had been physically and emotionally abused as an infant and young child and that, despite above average intelligence, he experienced academic and social difficulties as a result of extreme hyperactivity and low self-esteem. Of particular concern was Smith's propensity for verbal hostility; one evaluator noted that the child reacted to stress by "attempt[ing] to cover his feelings of low self-worth through aggressive behavior[,] . . . primarily verbal provocations."

Based on these evaluations, SFUSD placed Smith in a learning center for emotionally disturbed children. His grandparents, however, believed that his needs would be better served in the public school setting and, in September 1979, the school district acceded to their requests and enrolled him at A.P. Giannini Middle School. His February 1980 IEP recommended placement in a Learning Disability Group, stressing the need for close supervision and highly structured environment. Like earlier evaluations, the February 1980 IEP noted that Smith was easily distracted, impulsive, and anxious; it therefore proposed a half-day schedule and suggested that the placement be undertaken on a trial basis.

At the beginning of the next school year, Smith was assigned to a full-day program; almost immediately thereafter he began misbehaving. School officials met twice with his grandparents on October 1980 to discuss returning him to a half-day program; although the grandparents

(Continued)

(Continued)

agreed to the reduction, they apparently were never apprised of their right to challenge the decision through EHA procedures. The school officials also warned them that if the child continued his disruptive behavior—which included stealing, extorting money from fellow students, and making sexual comments to female classmates—they would seek to expel him. On November 14, they made good on this threat, suspending Smith for five days after he had made further lewd comments. His principal referred the matter to the SPC, which recommended exclusion from SFUSD. As it did in John Doe's case, the Committee scheduled a hearing and extended the suspension indefinitely pending a final disposition in the matter. On November 28, Smith's counsel protested these actions on grounds essentially identical to those raised by Doe, and the SPC agreed to cancel the hearing and to return Smith to a half-day program at A.P. Giannini or to provide home tutoring. Smith's grandparents chose the latter option and the school began home instruction on December 10; on January 6, 1981, an IEP team convened to discuss alternative placements.

After learning of Doe's action, Smith sought and obtained leave to intervene in the suit. . . .

Respondent John Doe is now 24 years old and, accordingly, is no longer entitled to the protections and benefits of the EHA, which limits eligibility to disabled children between the ages of three and 21. See 20 U.S.C. sec. 1412(2)(B) [Now § 1412(a)(1)(B)]. It is clear, therefore, that whatever rights to state educational services he may yet have as a ward of the State, the Act would not govern the State's provision of those services, and thus the case is moot as to him. Respondent Jack Smith, however, is currently 20 and has not yet completed high school. Although at present he is not faced with any proposed expulsion or suspension proceedings, and indeed no longer even resides within the SFUSD, he remains a resident of California and is entitled to a "free appropriate public education" within that State. His claims under the EHA, therefore, are not moot if the conduct he originally complained of is "capable of repetition, yet evading review." Given Smith's continued eligibility for education services under the EHA, the nature of his disability, and petitioner's insistence that all local school districts retain residual authority to exclude disabled children for dangerous conduct, we have little difficulty concluding that there is a "reasonable expectation," that Smith would once again be subjected to a unilateral "change in placement" for conduct growing out of his disabilities were it not for the state-wide injunctive relief issued below.

. . .

III

The language of sec. 1415(e)(3) [Now § 1415(j)] is unequivocal. It states plainly that during the pendency of any proceedings initiated under the Act, unless the state or local educational agency and the parents or guardians of a disabled child otherwise agree, "the child *shall* remain in the then current educational placement." Faced with this clear directive, petitioner asks us to read a "dangerousness" exception into the stay-put provision on the basis of either of two essentially inconsistent assumptions: first, that Congress thought the residual authority of school officials to exclude dangerous students from the classroom too obvious for comment; or second, that Congress inadvertently failed to provide such authority and this Court must therefore remedy the oversight. Because we cannot accept either premise, we decline petitioner's invitation to re-write the statute.

Petitioner's arguments proceed, he suggests, from a simple, commonsense proposition: Congress could not have intended the stay-put provision to be read literally, for such a construction leads to the clearly unintended, and untenable, result that school districts must return violent or dangerous students to school while the often lengthy EHA proceedings run their course. We think it clear, however, that Congress very much meant to strip schools of the unilateral authority they had traditionally employed to exclude disabled students, from school. In so doing, Congress did not leave school administrators powerless to deal with dangerous students; it did, however, deny school officials their former right to "self-help," and directed that in the future the removal of disabled students could be accomplished only with the permission of the parents or, as a last resort, the courts.

As noted above, Congress passed the EHA after finding that school systems across the country had excluded one out of every eight disabled students from classes. In drafting the law, Congress was largely guided by the recent decisions in *Mills* . . . and *PARC* . . . , both of which involved the exclusion of hard-to-handle disabled students. . . .

Congress attacked such exclusionary practices in a variety of ways. It required participating States to educate all disabled children, regardless of the severity of their disabilities, 20 U.S.C. sec. 1412(2)(C) [Now § 1412(a)(3)(A)&(B)], and included within the definition of "handicapped" those children with serious emotional disturbances. Sec. 1401(1) [Now § 1401(3)(A)]. It further provided for meaningful parental participation in all aspects of a child's educational placement, and barred schools, through the stay-put provision, from changing that placement over the parent's objection until all review proceedings were completed. Recognizing that those proceedings might prove long and tedious, the Act's drafters did not intend sec. 1415(e)(3) [Now § 1415(j)] to operate inflexibly, and therefore allowed for interim placements where parents and school officials are able to agree on one. Conspicuously absent from sec. 1415(e)(3) [Now § 1415(j)], however, is any emergency exception for dangerous students. We are therefore not at liberty to engraft onto the statute an exception Congress chose not to create.

Our conclusion that sec. 1415(e)(3) [Now § 1415(j)] means what it says does not leave educators hamstrung. The Department of Education has observed that, "[w]hile the [child's] placement may not be changed [during any complaint proceeding], this does not preclude the agency from using its normal procedures for dealing with children who are endangering themselves or others." Such procedures may include the use of study carrels, timeouts, detention, or the restriction of privileges. More drastically, where a student poses an immediate threat to the safety of others, officials may temporarily suspend him or her for up to 10 school days. This authority, which respondent in no way disputes, not only ensures that school administrators can protect the safety of others by promptly removing the most dangerous of students, it also provides a "cooling down" period during which officials can initiate IEP review and seek to persuade

(Continued)

(Continued)

the child's parents to agree to an interim placement. And in those cases in which the parents of a truly dangerous child adamantly refuse to permit any change in placement, the 10-day respite gives school officials an opportunity to invoke the aid of the courts under sec. 1415(e)(2) [Now § 1415(i)(2)(c); 34 C.F.R. § 300.516, but see explanation after case as the law is different than it was when the court decided *Honig*] which empowers courts to grant any appropriate relief.

Petitioner contends, however, that the availability of judicial relief is more illusory than real, because a party seeking review under sec. 1415(e)(2) [Now § 1415(i)(2)(c)] must exhaust time-consuming administrative remedies, and because under the Court of Appeals' construction of sec. 1415(e)(3) [Now § 1415(j)], courts are as bound by the stay-put provision's "automatic injunction," as are schools. It is true that judicial review is normally not available under sec. 1415(e)(2) [Now § 1415(j)] until all administrative proceedings are completed, but as we have previously noted, parents may by-pass the administrative process where exhaustion would be futile or inadequate. . . . While many of the EHA's procedural safeguards protect the rights of parents and children, schools can and do seek redress through the administrative review process, and we have no reason to believe that Congress meant to require schools alone to exhaust in all cases, no matter how exigent the circumstances. The burden in such cases, of course, rests with the school to demonstrate the futility or inadequacy of administrative review, but nothing in sec. 1415(e)(2) [Now § 1415(i)(2)(c)] suggests that schools are completely barred from attempting to make such a showing. Nor do we think that sec. 1415(e)(3) [Now § 1415(j)] operates to limit the equitable powers of district courts such that they cannot, in appropriate cases, temporarily enjoin a dangerous disabled child from attending school. . . .

In short then, we believe that school officials are entitled to seek injunctive relief under sec. 1415(e)(3) [Now § 1415(j)] in appropriate cases. In any such action, sec. 1415(e)(3) [Now § 1415(j)] effectively creates a presumption in favor of the child's current education placement which school officials can overcome only by showing that maintaining the child in his or her current placement is substantially likely to result in injury either to himself or herself, or to others. In the present case, we are satisfied that the District Court, in enjoining the state and local defendants from indefinitely suspending respondent or otherwise unilaterally altering his then current placement, properly balanced respondent's interest in receiving a free appropriate public education in accordance with the procedures and requirements of EHA against the interest of the state and local school officials in maintaining a safe learning environment for all their students.

IV

We believe the courts below properly construed and applied sec. 1415(e)(3) [Now § 1415(j)], except insofar as the Court of Appeals held that a suspension in excess of 10 school days does not constitute a "change of placement." We therefore affirm the Court of Appeals judgment on this issue as modified herein. Because we are equally divided on the question whether a court may order a State to provide services directly to a disabled child where the local agency has failed to do so, we affirm the Court of Appeals' judgment on this issue as well [requiring the state to provide services when the local agency refuses to do so].

Legislative Revisions

As a result of the decision in this case and subsequent decisions indicating a need for clarification on the issue of disciplinary removal, Congress addressed the subject of discipline in the 1997 and 2004 IDEA amendments.[2] Among other things, Congress included provisions for dangerous students that were absent when the Court issued the *Honig* decision. Many of the requirements in the IDEA amendments codify aspects of the Court's decision in *Honig.*

For example, much of the focus in the discipline of students with disabilities is on whether or not a change in placement has occurred.[3] If the discipline action includes removal from school (such as a suspension), or sending the student to an interim alternative educational setting (discussed below), for 10 days or less, then it is not a change in placement.[4] When there is not a change in placement, a student with a disability may be treated the same as students without disabilities for discipline measures. The school does not need to go through any additional requirements and does not need to provide the student with any services for this period of time, unless it provides services to students without disabilities who are suspended for 10 days or less.[5]

If the removal from school for 10 days or less is part of a pattern that adds up to more than 10 days in the school year, then it is a change in placement.[6] To determine whether the removal is part of a pattern, the law provides a number of factors to review. These include whether the student behavior at issue is substantially similar to previous incidents of disciplinary removal, the length of each removal, the total amount of time the child is removed, and the proximity of the removals to one another.[7]

Discipline that includes removal from school for more than 10 consecutive days, or places the student in an interim alternative educational setting for more than 10 consecutive days, is a change in placement and a variety of requirements apply. These include conducting a manifestation determination, and providing the student with FAPE.[8]

The purpose of the manifestation determination is to determine if there is a relationship between the child's disability and the behavior subject to the disciplinary action. It must be conducted no later than 10 days after the date on which the decision is made to take the disciplinary action that constitutes a change in placement.[9] The manifestation determination is conducted by the individualized education program (IEP) team and other qualified personnel in a meeting that includes the parents. The team must consider all relevant information in terms of the behavior subject to disciplinary action including the student's file, the child's IEP, teacher observations, and any relevant information provided by the parents. The team must then determine

(I) if the conduct in question was caused by, or had a direct and substantial relationship to, the child's disability; or

(II) if the conduct in question was the direct result of the school's failure to implement the IEP.[10]

If the team determines that either provision listed above applies, then the behavior or conduct is a manifestation of the child's disability. The school must conduct a functional behavioral assessment and develop and implement a behavioral intervention plan to address the student's behavioral issues.[11] The school district may not impose further discipline on the student for the incident and must return the student to the placement from which the student was removed, unless the provisions regarding "special circumstances" apply (discussed below).[12] If the manifestation is due to the school not implementing the IEP, the school must take "immediate steps to remedy those deficiencies."[13]

If the team determines that the student's behavior was not a manifestation of the student's disability, then the student may be disciplined in the same manner as a student without a disability with the caveat that the student still must be provided with a free appropriate public education.[14] Therefore, while the student may technically be expelled from school, or sent to an alternative educational setting, the school district must continue to provide sufficient services to enable the student to progress in the general curriculum and to meet the goals and objectives in the student's IEP. Additionally, the school may still be required to conduct a functional behavioral assessment and develop a behavior intervention plan to address the behavior so that it does not recur in order for the student to receive FAPE.[15]

"Special Circumstances"

If the parent disagrees with the team's determination that the student's behavior is not a manifestation of the student's disability, the parent may appeal the decision and request an expedited due process hearing.[16] As mentioned previously, once a parent requests a due process hearing, the "stay-put" or pendency provisions of the law generally require the student to remain in his or her current placement until the issue is resolved. In the context of discipline, that could result in a student that the school wants to remove from school remaining in school until the conclusion of the dispute resolution process. In *Honig,* the Court noted that to address this issue, schools could go to court under the IDEA and seek an injunction or court order to remove the student from his or her current educational setting.

In addition to this process, the 2004 amendments to the IDEA provide a number of provisions that address this situation. First, school personnel can remove a student to an interim alternative educational setting for not more than 45 school days without regard to whether or not the student's behavior was a manifestation of the student's disability if the student (1) carries or possesses weapons at school, on school premises, or at school functions; or (2) knowingly possesses or uses illegal drugs or sells or solicits a controlled substance at school, on school premises, or at a school function; or (3) inflicts serious bodily harm upon another person at school, on school premises, or at a school function.[17] The student's IEP team determines the student's interim alternative educational setting and the services the student will receive in that setting.[18]

While the parents have the right to appeal the team's decision through an expedited due process hearing, the "stay-put" placement during the appeal is the interim alternative educational setting, not the current placement, unless some other agreement is reached between the parents and the school.[19] Additionally, if the student does not fit into one of the three "special circumstances" categories mentioned above, but the school feels that maintaining the student in his or her current placement is substantially likely to result in injury to the student or others, the school may request an expedited due process hearing and a hearing officer may order a change of placement to an interim alternative educational setting for not more than 45 days.[20]

Incarcerated Juveniles

Special education and adolescents who are incarcerated in detention facilities raise two issues. The first issue is whether an individual who has been receiving special education must be provided the special education in the detention facility. While there is little case law on this issue, what there is seems to indicate that it must be provided. For example, in *Green v. Johnson*,[21] the court held that incarcerated individuals under the age of 22 (the upper age limit requirement in Massachusetts) must be provided special education. In that case, the individuals involved had been receiving special education before their incarceration. A more difficult question is the obligation of the educational agency to identify incarcerated individuals as needing special education.

The second major issue involving incarcerated juveniles is whether the disability may be a factor in the behavior of the individual that resulted in the incarceration. There has been a significant amount of interest in studying the relationship of disabilities (particularly learning disabilities) to antisocial behavior that results in criminal conduct. One theory is that perhaps if appropriate educational programming were provided to some of these individuals, the misconduct would not have occurred and the student would not be incarcerated. The debate on this issue is not well resolved, and it will probably continue for some time.

The 2004 IDEA amendments address the issue of students with disabilities who are incarcerated in prisons for adults by eliminating some of the obligation to provide FAPE to them. A student aged 18 to 21 who was not identified as a child with a disability prior to incarceration, and who did not have an IEP prior to incarceration, is not entitled to FAPE if state law does not require it. The amendments also clarify that provisions of the law regarding participation in statewide assessments and transition services do not apply to students whose eligibility will end because of their age before they are released from prison.[22] Additionally, the IDEA provides that the IEP team may modify the IEP or placement of a student convicted as an adult and incarcerated in an adult prison for security or other compelling penological reasons.[23] Some of the IDEA's requirements for IEPs and the least restrictive environment requirements do not apply in this situation.[24]

Summary

The discipline provisions of the IDEA have evolved over the years but remain consistent with the original goal of protecting students with disabilities from being punished, or excluded from school, because of their disabilities. Today, much of the process revolves around whether or not the discipline action proposed by the school is a change of placement. If it is, then a variety of procedural and substantive protections apply. These include the requirement of conducting a manifestation determination and providing the student with FAPE. Functional behavioral assessments and behavior intervention plans are also often part of the process.

If the discipline is not a change of placement, then the student with a disability can be treated the same as a student without a disability for discipline purposes. The IDEA also includes "special circumstances" and other provisions to give schools more flexibility when dealing with situations involving weapons, drugs, or dangerous students.

Students with disabilities are sometimes incarcerated in juvenile detention settings. Those students who have previously been identified as disabled are required by the IDEA to be provided special education and related services even while in detention. Students not yet identified as disabled could be evaluated. A growing body of social science research indicates a relationship between learning disabilities and juvenile delinquency, making this a group that is important to reach for educational services. As a practical matter, however, the logistics of providing educational services to this transitory population are difficult. The 2004 IDEA amendments clarify that when a student with a disability is incarcerated as an adult, the rights and protections under the IDEA are more limited.

Questions for Reflection

1. As noted in this chapter, students with disabilities receive a number of protections in the discipline process. These same protections are not available to students without disabilities (unless the school knew or should have known of the student's disability and had not yet identified the student). There is an ongoing debate about whether, and to what extent, students with disabilities should be treated differently in terms of discipline. What are some of the policy justifications for doing so? What are some of the arguments for treating all students the same in the discipline process? Which are more persuasive and why?

2. One of the key discipline requirements in the IDEA is that students with disabilities must be provided with FAPE even when they are suspended or expelled from school for reasons unrelated to their disability. Why do you think Congress imposed this requirement instead of limiting the protections to discipline for actions caused or related to the student's disability?

3. Consider the following fact pattern:

> Tim is a 17-year-old student with attention deficit hyperactivity disorder (ADHD) and a learning disability. He is caught smoking cigarettes at school for the third time in the same school year. The discipline for the first infraction was 3 days in-school suspension. The discipline for the second infraction was 5 days out-of-school suspension, and the proposed discipline for this third infraction is 10 days out-of-school suspension.

Is this final discipline action a change in placement?

4. Following up on question number 3, assume the school conducts a manifestation determination meeting. Tim attends the meeting with his parents. At the meeting, Tim tells the team that smoking helps calm his nerves so he can focus in class. He also presents a note from his family physician stating that some studies have shown that

nicotine can have a temporary, calming effect on students with ADHD (though the doctor does not recommend that Tim smoke). What should the team do? Does the smoking have a direct and substantial relationship to Tim's ADHD? If so, what are the team's options? Will Tim be allowed to smoke at school when other students cannot?

5. The 1997 IDEA provisions for manifestation determinations were designed differently than the 2004 provisions. Under the 1997 law, the behavior subject to discipline was presumed to be a manifestation of the student's disability unless the team found that

   a. In relationship to the behavior subject to the disciplinary action, the child's IEP and placement were appropriate and the special education services, supplementary aides and services, and behavior intervention strategies were provided consistent with the child's IEP and placement;
   b. The child's disability did not impair the ability of the child to understand the impact and consequences of the behavior subject to disciplinary action; and
   c. The child's disability did not impair the ability of the child to control the behavior subject to disciplinary action.

If any of those three requirements were not met, then the behavior was considered a manifestation. As noted in this chapter, the 2004 IDEA amendments completely changed the standards, and now the behavior is not considered a manifestation unless the team finds the behavior was caused by the disability, had a direct and substantial relationship to the disability, or was the direct result of failing to implement the student's IEP. Which approach is better and why?

NOTES

1. Congress also sought to safeguard against disparate discipline of special education students, by including in the IDEA requirements that state educational agencies monitor discrepancies between children with and without disabilities and their suspension and expulsion patterns. See 20 U.S.C. § 1412(a)(22).

2. Perry Zirkel, "'Stay Put' Under the IDEA Discipline Provisions: What Is New?" 214 *Educ. L. Rep.* 467 (2007); Dean Hill Rivkin, "Litigating School Exclusion," 75 *Tenn. L. Rev.* 265 (2008).

3. A student who has not yet been identified under the IDEA as a student with a disability may also have protection under the IDEA with respect to disciplinary procedures if the school district had knowledge that the student is a student with a disability before the behavior that led to the discipline occurred. See 20 U.S.C. § 1415(k)(5); 34 C.F.R. § 300.534.

4. 34 C.F.R. § 300.530(b); 34 C.F.R. § 300.536.

5. 34 C.F.R. § 300.530(d)(3).

6. 34 C.F.R. § 300.530(d)(4); § 300.536.

7. 20 U.S.C. § 1415(k); 34 C.F.R. § 300.536(a)(2).

8. 34 C.F.R. § 300.536.

9. 34 C.F.R. § 300.530(e).

10. 20 U.S.C. § 1415(k)(1)(E); 34 C.F.R. § 300.530(e).

11. 20 U.S.C. § 1415(k)(1)(E)(i); 34 C.F.R. § 300.500(f).

12. 34 C.F.R. § 300.500(f)(2).

13. 34 C.F.R. § 300.500(e)(3).

14. 20 U.S.C. § 1415(k)(1); 34 C.F.R. § 300.530(c); 34 C.F.R. § 300.101(a).

15. See 20 U.S.C. § 1415(k)(1)(D); 34 C.F.R. § 300.530(d); see also 34 C.F.R. § 300.324(a)(2)(i) (requiring the IEP team to consider the use of positive behavioral supports and other strategies that address behavior when the student's behavior impedes the child's learning or that of others). See also Perry Zirkel, "Suspension and Expulsion Under Section 504: A Comparative Overview," 226 *Educ. L. Rep.* 9 (2008).

16. 34 C.F.R. § 300.532.

17. 20 U.S.C. § 1415(k)(1)(G); 34 C.F.R. § 300.530(g).

18. 20 U.S.C. § 1415(k)(2); 34 C.F.R. § 300.531.

19. 20 U.S.C. § 1415(k)(3)–(4); 34 C.F.R. § 300.532(c).

20. 20 U.S.C. § 1415(k)(3)(B); 34 C.F.R. §§ 300.532–533.

21. 513 F. Supp. 965 (D. Mass. 1981). See also Laura Rothstein & Julia Rothstein, *Disabilities and the Law* § 2:14 (Thomson West 2006).

22. 20 U.S.C. § 1414(d)(7).

23. 20 U.S.C. § 1414(d)(7)(B).

24. 34 C.F.R. § 300.324(d)(2).

17

Dispute Resolution

Due Process Procedures Under the IDEA

Chapter 15 addressed the Individuals with Disabilities Education Act (IDEA) requirements relating to parental notice, participation, and consent in the special education process. During the special education process, the parents and school members of the team may disagree on what should be done regarding the student's identification, evaluation, services, individualized education program (IEP), or placement. The IDEA provides a number of ways for the parties to resolve these disagreements. The three primary ways are (1) an administrative due process hearing, (2) mediation, or (3) filing a complaint with the state department of education. States may also develop other dispute resolution mechanisms to help parties resolve their disputes.[1]

Facilitated IEP meetings are where the state or school district provides an outside person trained in facilitating meetings to come in and be in charge of the team meeting. The purpose is to see if the parties can reach some agreement about the issues being discussed during the meeting itself.

Impartial Due Process Hearing

The IDEA provides both the school and the parent with the right to request an administrative due process hearing when there is disagreement about a proposed identification, evaluation, or placement or the provision of a free appropriate public education (FAPE) to a student (which would include IEP issues and issues regarding the special education and related services that the student should receive).[2] The IDEA provides a two-year statute of limitations to file a request for due process.[3] The two-year period begins when the parent or school knew of or should have known of the alleged action that forms the basis for the request for due process. The statute also provides for some exceptions to this two-year timeline.[4]

A due process hearing is an adversarial proceeding where the parties present evidence to a hearing officer and the hearing officer issues a decision. The request for due process must include the name and address of the student and the school the student is attending, a description of the nature of the problem including facts relating to such problem, and a proposed resolution of the problem to the extent known and available.[5] Parties receiving the request for due process who believe it does not contain enough information to let them know what the dispute is about or the requested solution have 15 days from receiving the request for due process to notify the hearing officer that they believe the request is not sufficient. The hearing officer will then decide if it is sufficient or not and inform the parties.[6]

The 2004 amendments to the IDEA include a new requirement that applies when the parents request the due process hearing. The parties must now conduct a "resolution meeting" within 15 days of the school receiving notice of the parents' request for due process.[7] The school must convene a team meeting with the parents and relevant members of the IEP team who have specific knowledge of the facts in the parents' request for due process. A person with decision-making authority from the school must also attend the meeting. At the meeting, the parents and the school discuss the request for due process and the school is provided with an opportunity to resolve the issues. If the parties do reach an agreement, a written settlement agreement explaining the agreement is drafted and signed by the parties. The parties have 3 days after the agreement is signed to review it and change the decision about the agreement.[8]

School attorneys are prohibited under the IDEA from attending the resolution meeting unless the parents are accompanied by an attorney.[9] The parents and the school can waive the resolution meeting requirement by agreement or they can agree to use mediation instead of the resolution meeting.[10]

The IDEA provides the parties in a due process hearing with certain rights, including the right to

1. Be accompanied and advised by counsel, or by individuals with special knowledge or training with respect to the problems of children with disabilities;

2. Present evidence and confront, cross-examine, and compel the attendance of witnesses;

3. Request that the hearing officer prohibit the introduction of any evidence at the hearing that has not been disclosed to that party at least 5 business days before the first day of the scheduled hearing;

4. Obtain a written or electronic verbatim record of the hearing; and

5. Obtain written findings of facts and decisions.[11]

The parents also have the right to have the child who is the subject of the hearing present, open the hearing to the public, and receive a record of the hearing and the hearing decision at no cost. Once the hearing is requested, the parents must be informed of available free or low-cost legal and other services.[12] All of the costs of the hearing, except costs of representation, are paid by the educational agency.

The hearing itself is conducted by a hearing officer appointed by the local or state educational agency. One of the essential features of the IDEA due process procedures is that the hearing officer must be *impartial*.[13] This means that the individual may not be an employee of the agency involved in educating or caring for the child or anyone having a personal or professional conflict of interest or who could not be objective.[14] In the early years after passage of the IDEA, there was confusion about whether certain individuals were impartial. In 1984, the United States Department of Education declared that state education employees could be hearing officers if they could establish impartiality. Some states allow education officials who are employed in localities other than the child's residence to act as hearing officers. Other states require that hearing officers be attorneys.

Regardless of which types of individuals act as hearing officers, the IDEA provides some specific qualifications for hearing officers in addition to impartiality. Among other things, a hearing officer must have the knowledge and the ability to understand the provisions of the IDEA and relevant state law, to conduct hearings in accordance with standard legal practice, and to render and write hearing decisions in accordance with standard legal practice.[15]

There has not been extensive litigation on the issue of hearing officers, but there have been some interesting cases. In one decision, an appellate court held that university personnel who had participated in formulating state special education policies were not impartial.[16]

The 2004 amendments to the IDEA also provide some parameters for hearing officer decisions. For example, decisions about whether a child received free appropriate public education (FAPE) must generally be based on substantive grounds (as opposed to procedural ones).[17] As noted in prior chapters, in matters involving alleged procedural violations, a hearing officer may only find that a student did not receive FAPE if the violation impeded the child's right to FAPE, significantly impeded the parent's right to participate in the decision-making process, or caused a deprivation of educational benefit.[18] A hearing officer can still order the school to comply with procedural requirements even if it does not meet any of these criteria, or deny FAPE.[19]

At the hearing itself, the process depends on the established procedures noted previously. States may also add to the procedures, or provide more specific procedures, as long as they are consistent with the IDEA's requirements. One example of this used to be state requirements regarding which party has the burden of proof at the hearing.

The IDEA does not specify which party bears the burden of proof at the administrative or the judicial level. As a result, there were different approaches taken by different states, and different court interpretations as well.

In 2005, the Supreme Court clarified the issue of burden of proof in the following case.

SCHAFFER V. WEAST

546 U.S. 49 (2005)

Justice O'Connor delivered the opinion of the Court.

The Individuals with Disabilities Education Act (IDEA) is a Spending Clause statute that seeks to ensure that "all children with disabilities have available to them a free appropriate public education," § 1400(d)(1)(A). Under IDEA, school districts must create an "individualized education program" (IEP) for each disabled child. § 1414(d). If parents believe their child's IEP is inappropriate, they may request an "impartial due process hearing." § 1415(f). The Act is silent, however, as to which party bears the burden of persuasion at such a hearing. We hold that the burden lies, as it typically does, on the party seeking relief.

I

* * *

B

This case concerns the educational services that were due, under IDEA, to petitioner Brian Schaffer. Brian suffers from learning disabilities and speech-language impairments. From prekindergarten through seventh grade he attended a private school and struggled academically. In 1997, school officials informed Brian's mother that he needed a school that could better accommodate his needs. Brian's parents contacted respondent Montgomery County Public Schools System (MCPS) seeking a placement for him for the following school year.

MCPS evaluated Brian and convened an IEP team. The committee generated an initial IEP offering Brian a place in either of two MCPS middle schools. Brian's parents were not satisfied with the arrangement, believing that Brian needed smaller classes and more intensive services. The Schaffers thus enrolled Brian in another private school, and initiated a due process hearing challenging the IEP and seeking compensation for the cost of Brian's subsequent private education.

[The administrative law decisions and lower court decisions are omitted.]

II

A

The term "burden of proof" is one of the "slipperiest member[s] of the family of legal terms." 2 J. Strong, McCormick on Evidence § 342, p 433 (5th ed. 1999) (hereinafter McCormick). Part of the confusion surrounding the term arises from the fact that historically, the concept encompassed two distinct burdens: the "burden of persuasion," *i.e.,* which party loses if the evidence is closely balanced, and the "burden of production," *i.e.,* which party bears the obligation to come forward with the evidence at different points in the proceeding. We note at the outset that this case concerns only the burden of persuasion, as the parties agree, and when we speak of burden of proof in this opinion, it is this to which we refer.

When we are determining the burden of proof under a statutory cause of action, the touchstone of our inquiry is, of course, the statute. The plain text of IDEA is silent on the allocation of the burden of persuasion. We therefore begin with the ordinary default rule that plaintiffs bear the risk of failing to prove their claims.

Thus, we have usually assumed without comment that plaintiffs bear the burden of persuasion regarding the essential aspects of their claims.

The ordinary default rule, of course, admits of exceptions. See McCormick § 337, at 412–415. For example, the burden of persuasion as to certain elements of a plaintiff's claim may be shifted to defendants, when such elements can fairly be characterized as affirmative defenses or exemptions. Under some circumstances this Court has even placed the burden of persuasion over an entire claim on the defendant. But while the normal default rule does not solve all cases, it certainly solves most of them. Decisions that place the *entire* burden of persuasion on the opposing party at the *outset* of a proceeding—as petitioners urge us to do here—are extremely rare. Absent some reason to believe that Congress intended otherwise, therefore, we will conclude that the burden of persuasion lies where it usually falls, upon the party seeking relief.

B

Petitioners contend first that a close reading of IDEA's text compels a conclusion in their favor. [Discussion of petitioner's position omitted.]

III

Finally, respondents and several States urge us to decide that States may, if they wish, override the default rule and put the burden always on the school district. Several States have laws or regulations purporting to do so, at least under some circumstances. Because no such law or regulation exists in Maryland, we need not decide this issue today. Justice Breyer contends that the allocation of the burden ought to be left *entirely* up to the States. But neither party made this argument before this Court or the courts below. We therefore decline to address it.

We hold no more than we must to resolve the case at hand: The burden of proof in an administrative hearing challenging an IEP is properly placed upon the party seeking relief. In this case, that party is Brian, as represented by his parents. But the rule applies with equal effect to school districts: If they seek to challenge an IEP, they will in turn bear the burden of persuasion before an ALJ [Administrative Law Judge]. The judgment of the United States Court of Appeals for the Fourth Circuit is, therefore, affirmed.

It is so ordered.

This decision clarified the burden of proof question. In addition to the burden of proof, another question is the credibility or weight that courts give to various parties. It has long been the case that there is substantial deference to educational agencies regarding their decisions on educational programming.

At the due process hearing itself, both sides have the right to present evidence. The law expressly allows parents to introduce independent evaluations as evidence at the hearing. Other evidence can be presented as well, with state law generally providing the parameters of what kind of evidence is admissible at the hearing.

After conducting the hearing, the hearing officer issues a decision with written findings of fact and law. The final decision by the hearing officer must be issued and a copy of the decision mailed to the parents within a certain time period. As mentioned previously, the IDEA now requires the parties to engage in a resolution session when the parents request due process. The IDEA also encourages the parties to engage in mediation (discussed later in this chapter) to resolve the dispute. As a result, the IDEA provides some time for the parties to engage in these activities. If the school is not able to resolve the issues in the due process complaint within 30 days from the time the complaint is received, the due process hearing can take place.[20]

The IDEA states that the final decision and mailing of the decision to the parents must occur no later than 45 days after the expiration of the 30-day time period mentioned above, and sooner if the parties take certain actions during the 30-day period such as waiving the resolution session or agreeing that a settlement is not possible, or if the school withdraws from the mediation process.[21]

Attorneys' fees are available to the parents' attorney if they are the "prevailing party" at the due process hearing.[22] The parents must file a separate action in federal court to recover the fees unless some agreement can be reached between the school and parents on payment for fees. There are some limitations on the payment of attorneys' fees noted in the statute. Attorneys' fees are discussed more in Chapter 21. Under a recent United States Supreme Court decision, expert fees and fees for non-attorney advocates are generally not recoverable under the federal law.[23]

The IDEA provides that schools may recover their attorneys' fees if the school is the "prevailing party" at the hearing and if there is a finding that (1) the parent's case is frivolous, unreasonable, or without foundation; or (2) if the parent or attorney continued to litigate after the litigation clearly became frivolous, unreasonable, or without foundation; or (3) the parent's case was presented for any improper purpose, such as to harass, to cause unnecessary delay, or to needlessly increase the cost of litigation.[24]

Administrative and Judicial Review of Due Process Decisions

Once the hearing decision has been reached and transmitted to the parties, either party may seek review by appealing to the state educational agency, if another agency conducted the original due process hearing, or to an intermediate agency in those states with a two-tier process. The review is based on the entire hearing record and any additional evidence necessary. Reviewing officials have the discretion to allow oral or written argument. Based on the review of this information, the reviewing official must make an independent decision and provide written findings and a decision to the parties. The state review process must be completed within 30 days after review was sought.[25] Extensions may be granted by the hearing or reviewing officer. Some states conduct the initial hearing at the state level. In those states, there is no state agency review. Any party seeking review from a state-level hearing must seek relief in court.[26]

When a matter is not resolved after a review by the state administrative agency or after a state-level hearing, either party may bring an action in state or federal court.[27] Prior to 2004, the IDEA did not specifically state a deadline to bring an action in court. As a result, most states developed their own time limitations for these actions. In 2004, the IDEA included a provision that requires the party bringing the action to do so within 90 days of the date of the hearing officer, or state-level review.[28] The IDEA also allows states that have different timelines or statutes of limitation for bringing the action, to keep those in place instead of using the IDEA's timeline.

There have been instances where parents have sought relief by going to court initially, without first seeking resolution through the administrative avenues. In those cases, the courts have fairly consistently required that administrative remedies be exhausted before seeking judicial action, at least where it would not be futile to exhaust administrative remedies.[29]

Until 2007, it was unclear whether the parents could proceed in a judicial challenge involving the IDEA without obtaining an attorney to help them do so. The reason for the uncertainty is that people generally cannot represent someone else in court, unless they are an attorney. The issue was whether the parents were representing their own interests, or their child's interests in the appeal. A number of Circuit Courts of Appeal had found that the issues revolved around the child's interest because the case involved the services the child received at school. As a result, they ruled that the parents could not proceed without an attorney as they could not represent their child in court, unless they were an attorney. One Circuit Court of Appeals ruled differently, which created a split in the circuits that the United States Supreme Court resolved in the following case.

WINKELMAN V. PARMA CITY SCHOOL DISTRICT

127 S. Ct. 1994 (2007)

Justice Kennedy delivered the opinion of the Court.

Some four years ago, Mr. and Mrs. Winkelman, parents of five children, became involved in lengthy administrative and legal proceedings. They had sought review related to concerns they had over whether their youngest child, 6-year-old Jacob, would progress well at Pleasant Valley Elementary School, which is part of the Parma City School District in Parma, Ohio.

Jacob has autism spectrum disorder and is covered by the Individuals with Disabilities Education Act (Act or IDEA). His parents worked with the school district to develop an individualized education program (IEP), as required by the Act. All concede that Jacob's parents had the statutory right to contribute to this process and, when agreement could not be reached, to participate in administrative proceedings including what the Act refers to as an "impartial due process hearing." § 1415(f)(1)(A).

The disagreement at the center of the current dispute concerns the procedures to be followed when parents and their child, dissatisfied with the outcome of the due process hearing, seek further review in a United States District Court. The question is whether parents, either on

(Continued)

(Continued)

their own behalf or as representatives of the child, may proceed in court unrepresented by counsel though they are not trained or licensed as attorneys. Resolution of this issue requires us to examine and explain the provisions of IDEA to determine if it accords to parents rights of their own that can be vindicated in court proceedings, or alternatively, whether the Act allows them, in their status as parents, to represent their child in court proceedings.

II

* * *

Our resolution of this case turns upon the significance of IDEA's interlocking statutory provisions. Petitioners' primary theory is that the Act makes parents real parties in interest to IDEA actions, not "mer[e] guardians of their children's rights." If correct, this allows Mr. and Mrs. Winkelman back into court, for there is no question that a party may represent his or her own interests in federal court without the aid of counsel. Petitioners cannot cite a specific provision in IDEA mandating in direct and explicit terms that parents have the status of real parties in interest. They instead base their argument on a comprehensive reading of IDEA. Taken as a whole, they contend, the Act leads to the necessary conclusion that parents have independent, enforceable rights. Respondent, accusing petitioners of "knit[ting] together various provisions pulled from the crevices of the statute" to support these claims.

We agree that the text of IDEA resolves the question presented. We recognize, in addition, that a proper interpretation of the Act requires a consideration of the entire statutory scheme. Turning to the current version of IDEA, which the parties agree governs this case, we begin with an overview of the relevant statutory provisions.

A

The goals of IDEA include "ensur[ing] that all children with disabilities have available to them a free appropriate public education" and "ensur[ing] that the rights of children with disabilities and parents of such children are protected." 20 U.S.C. §§ 1400(d)(1)(A)–(B). To this end, the Act includes provisions governing four areas of particular relevance to the Winkelmans' claim: procedures to be followed when developing a child's IEP; criteria governing the sufficiency of an education provided to a child; mechanisms for review that must be made available when there are objections to the IEP or to other aspects of IDEA proceedings; and the requirement in certain circumstances that States reimburse parents for various expenses. See generally §§ 1412(a)(10), 1414, 1415. Although our discussion of these four areas does not identify all the illustrative provisions, we do take particular note of certain terms that mandate or otherwise describe parental involvement.

IDEA requires school districts to develop an IEP for each child with a disability, see §§ 1412(a)(4), 1414(d), with parents playing "a significant role" in this process, *Schaffer v. Weast,* 546 U.S. 49, 53 (2005). Parents serve as members of the team that develops the IEP. § 1414(d)(1)(B). The "concerns" parents have "for enhancing the education of their child" must be considered by the team. § 1414(d)(3)(A)(ii). IDEA accords parents additional protections that apply throughout the IEP process. See, *e.g.*, § 1414(d)(4)(A) (requiring the IEP Team to revise the IEP when appropriate to address certain information provided by the parents); § 1414(e) (requiring States to "ensure that the parents of [a child with a disability] are members of any group that makes decisions on the educational placement of their child"). The statute also sets up general procedural safeguards that protect the informed involvement of parents in the development of an education for their child. See, *e.g.*, § 1415(a) (requiring States to "establish and maintain procedures . . . to ensure that children with disabilities and their parents are guaranteed procedural safeguards with respect to the provision of a free appropriate public education"); § 1415(b)(1) (mandating that States provide an opportunity for parents to examine all relevant records). See generally §§ 1414, 1415. A central purpose of the parental protections is to facilitate the provision of a "'free appropriate public education,'" § 1401(9), which must be made available to the child "in conformity with the [IEP]," § 1401(9)(D).

* * *

When a party objects to the adequacy of the education provided, the construction of the IEP, or some related matter, IDEA provides procedural recourse: It requires that a State provide "[a]n opportunity for any party to present a complaint . . . with respect to any matter relating to the identification, evaluation, or educational placement of the child, or the provision of a free appropriate public education to such child." § 1415(b)(6). By presenting a complaint a party is able to pursue a process of review that, as relevant, begins with a preliminary meeting "where the parents of the child discuss their complaint" and the local educational agency "is provided the opportunity to [reach a resolution]." § 1415(f)(1)(B)(i)(IV). If the agency "has not resolved the complaint to the satisfaction of the parents within 30 days," § 1415(f)(1)(B)(ii), the parents may request an "impartial due process hearing," § 1415(f)(1)(A), which must be conducted either by the local educational agency or by the state educational agency, *ibid.*, and where a hearing officer will resolve issues raised in the complaint, § 1415(f)(3).

* * *

If the local educational agency, rather than the state educational agency, conducts this hearing, then "any party aggrieved by the findings and decision rendered in such a hearing may appeal such findings and decision to the State educational agency." § 1415(g)(1). Once the state educational agency has reached its decision, an aggrieved party may commence suit in federal court: "Any party aggrieved by the findings and decision made [by the hearing officer] shall have the right to bring a civil action with respect to the complaint." § 1415(i)(2)(A); see also § 1415(i)(1).

IDEA, finally, provides for at least two means of cost recovery that inform our analysis. First, in certain circumstances it allows a court or hearing officer to require a state agency "to reimburse the parents [of a child with a disability] for the cost of [private school] enrollment if the court or hearing officer finds that the agency had not made a free appropriate public education available to the child." § 1412(a)(10)(C)(ii). Second, it sets forth rules governing when and to what extent a court may award attorney's fees. See § 1415(i)(3)(B). Included in this section is a provision allowing an award "to a prevailing party who is the parent of a child with a disability." § 1415(i)(3)(B)(i)(I).

(Continued)

(Continued)

B

Petitioners construe these various provisions to accord parents independent, enforceable rights under IDEA. We agree. The parents enjoy enforceable rights at the administrative stage, and it would be inconsistent with the statutory scheme to bar them from continuing to assert these rights in federal court.

The statute sets forth procedures for resolving disputes in a manner that, in the Act's express terms, contemplates parents will be the parties bringing the administrative complaints. In addition to the provisions we have cited, we refer also to § 1415(b)(8) (requiring a state educational agency to "develop a model form to assist parents in filing a complaint"); § 1415(c)(2) (addressing the response an agency must provide to a "parent's due process complaint notice"); and § 1415(i)(3)(B)(i) (referring to "the parent's complaint"). A wide range of review is available: Administrative complaints may be brought with respect to "any matter relating to . . . the provision of a free appropriate public education." § 1415(b)(6)(A). Claims raised in these complaints are then resolved at impartial due process hearings, where, again, the statute makes clear that parents will be participating as parties. See also § 1415(f)(3)(C) (indicating "[a] parent or agency shall request an impartial due process hearing" within a certain period of time); § 1415(e)(2)(A)(ii) (referring to "a parent's right to a due process hearing"). The statute then grants "[a]ny party aggrieved by the findings and decision made [by the hearing officer] . . . the right to bring a civil action with respect to the complaint." § 1415(i)(2)(A).

Nothing in these interlocking provisions excludes a parent who has exercised his or her own rights from statutory protection the moment the administrative proceedings end. Put another way, the Act does not *sub silentio* or by implication bar parents from seeking to vindicate the rights accorded to them once the time comes to file a civil action. Through its provisions for expansive review and extensive parental involvement, the statute leads to just the opposite result.

Respondent, resisting this line of analysis, asks us to read these provisions as contemplating parental involvement only to the extent parents represent their child's interests. In respondent's view IDEA accords parents nothing more than "collateral tools related to the child's underlying substantive rights—not freestanding or independently enforceable rights."

This interpretation, though, is foreclosed by provisions of the statute. IDEA defines one of its purposes as seeking "to ensure that the rights of children with disabilities and parents of such children are protected." § 1400(d)(1)(B). The word "rights" in the quoted language refers to the rights of parents as well as the rights of the child; otherwise the grammatical structure would make no sense.

Further provisions confirm this view. IDEA mandates that educational agencies establish procedures "to ensure that children with disabilities and their parents are guaranteed procedural safeguards with respect to the provision of a free appropriate public education." § 1415(a). It presumes parents have rights of their own when it defines how States might provide for the transfer of the "rights accorded to parents" by IDEA, § 1415(m)(1)(B), and it prohibits the raising of certain challenges "[n]otwithstanding any other individual right of action that a parent or student may maintain under [the relevant provisions of IDEA]," §§ 1401(10)(E), 1412(a)(14)(E). To adopt respondent's reading of the statute would require an interpretation of these statutory provisions (and others) far too strained to be correct.

* * * It is not a novel proposition to say that parents have a recognized legal interest in the education and upbringing of their child. There is no necessary bar or obstacle in the law, then, to finding an intention by Congress to grant parents a stake in the entitlements created by IDEA. Without question a parent of a child with a disability has a particular and personal interest in fulfilling "our national policy of ensuring equality of opportunity, full participation, independent living, and economic self-sufficiency for individuals with disabilities." § 1400(c)(1).

We therefore find no reason to read into the plain language of the statute an implicit rejection of the notion that Congress would accord parents independent, enforceable rights concerning the education of their children. We instead interpret the statute's references to parents' rights to mean what they say: that IDEA includes provisions conveying rights to parents as well as to children.

A variation on respondent's argument has persuaded some Courts of Appeals. The argument is that while a parent can be a "party aggrieved" for aspects of the hearing officer's findings and decision, he or she cannot be a "party aggrieved" with respect to all IDEA-based challenges. Under this view the causes of action available to a parent might relate, for example, to various procedural mandates, and reimbursement demands, see, *e.g.*, § 1412(a)(10)(C)(ii). The argument supporting this conclusion proceeds as follows: Because a "party aggrieved" is, by definition, entitled to a remedy, and parents are, under IDEA, only entitled to certain procedures and reimbursements as remedies, a parent cannot be a "party aggrieved" with regard to any claim not implicating these limited matters.

This argument is contradicted by the statutory provisions we have recited. True, there are provisions in IDEA stating parents are entitled to certain procedural protections and reimbursements; but the statute prevents us from placing too much weight on the implications to be drawn when other entitlements are accorded in less clear language. We find little support for the inference that parents are excluded by implication whenever a child is mentioned, and vice versa. * * *

Our conclusion is confirmed by noting the incongruous results that would follow were we to accept the proposition that parents' IDEA rights are limited to certain nonsubstantive matters. The statute's procedural and reimbursement-related rights are intertwined with the substantive adequacy of the education provided to a child, see, *e.g.*, § 1415(f)(3)(E), see also § 1412(a)(10)(C)(ii), and it is difficult to disentangle the provisions in order to conclude that some rights adhere to both parent and child while others do not. Were we nevertheless to recognize a distinction of this sort it would impose upon parties a confusing and onerous legal regime, one worsened by the absence of any express guidance in IDEA concerning how a court might in practice differentiate between these matters. It is, in addition, out of accord with the statute's design to interpret the Act to require that parents prove the substantive inadequacy of their child's education

(Continued)

(Continued)

as a predicate for obtaining, for example, reimbursement under § 1412(a)(10)(C)(ii), yet to prevent them from obtaining a judgment mandating that the school district provide their child with an educational program demonstrated to be an appropriate one. The adequacy of the educational program is, after all, the central issue in the litigation. The provisions of IDEA do not set forth these distinctions, and we decline to infer them.

The bifurcated regime suggested by the courts that have employed it, moreover, leaves some parents without a remedy. The statute requires, in express terms, that States provide a child with a free appropriate public education "at public expense," § 1401(9)(A), including specially designed instruction "at no cost to parents," § 1401(29). Parents may seek to enforce this mandate through the federal courts, we conclude, because among the rights they enjoy is the right to a free appropriate public education for their child. Under the countervailing view, which would make a parent's ability to enforce IDEA dependent on certain procedural and reimbursement-related rights, a parent whose disabled child has not received a free appropriate public education would have recourse in the federal courts only under two circumstances: when the parent happens to have some claim related to the procedures employed; and when he or she is able to incur, and has in fact incurred, expenses creating a right to reimbursement. Otherwise the adequacy of the child's education would not be regarded as relevant to any cause of action the parent might bring; and, as a result, only the child could vindicate the right accorded by IDEA to a free appropriate public education.

The potential for injustice in this result is apparent. What is more, we find nothing in the statute to indicate that when Congress required States to provide adequate instruction to a child "at no cost to parents," it intended that only some parents would be able to enforce that mandate. The statute instead takes pains to "ensure that the rights of children with disabilities and parents of such children are protected." § 1400(d)(1)(B). See, *e.g.*, § 1415(e)(2) (requiring that States implement procedures to ensure parents are guaranteed procedural safeguards with respect to the provision of a free appropriate public education); § 1415(e)(2)(A)(ii) (requiring that mediation procedures not be "used to deny or delay a parent's right to a due process hearing . . . or to deny any other rights afforded under this subchapter"); cf. § 1400(c)(3) (noting IDEA's success in "ensuring children with disabilities and the families of such children access to a free appropriate public education").

We conclude IDEA grants parents independent, enforceable rights. These rights, which are not limited to certain procedural and reimbursement-related matters, encompass the entitlement to a free appropriate public education for the parents' child.

Once in court, the IDEA provides that the court must receive the records of the administrative proceedings, hear additional evidence at the request of a party, and grant such relief as the court determines appropriate based on the preponderance of the evidence.[30] Litigation can be a time-consuming and expensive endeavor, and it can increase or create tensions between the parents and the educational agency. For these reasons, it is useful to consider whether alternative dispute resolution could resolve a disagreement.

Mediation

Unlike due process, mediation is a non-adversarial process where the parties voluntarily come together and try to reach an agreement regarding the dispute. The IDEA requires state educational agencies that receive IDEA funding to ensure that alternative dispute resolution procedures such as mediation are established and implemented at no cost to the complaining parties. This is a recognition of the value of mediation in resolving these disputes.[31] The IDEA states that mediation procedures must be voluntary, that they not be used to delay the parent's rights under the IDEA including the right to due process, and that the mediation be conducted by a trained, qualified, and impartial mediator.[32]

The mediator's role is to try to help the parties reach some agreement that resolves the dispute between the parties. If the parties are able to come to agreement, a written mediation agreement is drafted and signed by the parties. The agreement is then implemented by the parties.[33] If disputes arise about the implementation of the agreement, the agreement can be enforced in state or federal court.[34]

One other requirement regarding mediation is that the discussion that occurs during the process must be kept confidential.[35] This means that if the parties do not come to an agreement, statements that the parties make during the mediation cannot be used as evidence in subsequent due process hearings or other proceedings.[36]

Complaints to the State Department of Education

Parents also have the right under the IDEA to file a complaint with their state department of education with respect to any matter relating to the identification, evaluation, or placement of or provision of FAPE to the student.[37] The difference between a due process hearing and a complaint is that with a complaint, the department investigates the allegations and comes to a decision. The department decides what information it needs to obtain and can do a site visit of the school, interview relevant people, review records, and request information from the parents or the school. By contrast, in a due process hearing, the parties decide what evidence to present to the hearing officer (within the parameters set by law), who makes a decision based on that information.

After the state department of education investigates the complaint, it issues a written decision informing the parties of its findings. If the department finds that a violation of the special education laws has occurred, it can order various forms of relief, including corrective actions that require services be provided to the student, compensatory education, and monetary reimbursement to reimburse for services or evaluations that should have been provided at public expense.[38] The IDEA's regulations require the state department of education to resolve the complaint within 60 days of receipt. The deadline can be extended to 90 days in some circumstances.[39]

Dispute Resolution for Violations of Section 504, the Americans with Disabilities Act, and the Constitution

In addition to resolving complaints regarding the education of students with disabilities through the IDEA process of dispute resolution, individuals can seek redress for

Section 504, the Americans with Disabilities Act (ADA), and constitutional violations. For Section 504 and the ADA, the individual can submit a complaint to the Department of Education or seek redress directly in court. For constitutional violations, judicial redress is also available.

As was noted in Chapter 3, Section 504 of the Rehabilitation Act prohibits recipients of federal financial assistance, such as educational agencies, from discriminating against otherwise qualified individuals with disabilities. In theory, this would seem to provide a statutory basis for parents to challenge educational agency practices that discriminate against students with disabilities.

As was also noted in Chapter 3, in 1990 Congress enacted the ADA. Under the ADA, both public and private schools are prohibited from discriminating on the basis of disability and are required to provide reasonable accommodations that do not cause an undue hardship.

Similarly, the equal protection and due process clauses of the fourteenth amendment to the U.S. Constitution would seem to provide a basis for challenging public school unequal treatment of students with disabilities and denial of procedural protections to that group.[40] Section 1983 of the Civil Rights Act[41] is the statutory basis through which constitutional and federal statutory violations can be redressed. It provides that individuals deprived of rights, privileges, or immunities of the Constitution or federal laws may bring action in court. It would therefore seem that Section 1983 could be used to claim not only violations of the Constitution (such as was claimed in *PARC* and *Mills*), but also violations of Section 504 of the Rehabilitation Act, the ADA, and the IDEA.

For several years, it was unsettled whether Section 504 or Section 1983, or both, could be the basis for claiming redress in special education cases. This was an important issue because the IDEA was unclear whether damages and attorneys' fees were available. Not until a 1984 Supreme Court decision was this issue resolved to some degree. This decision resulted in a congressional amendment in 1986 to allow attorneys' fees in IDEA cases.

As was noted in the *Smith v. Robinson*[42] decision, it will be an unusual situation for Section 504 or the Constitution to provide a basis for a legal action where special education is at issue. The *Smith v. Robinson* decision clarified that the IDEA provides the exclusive avenue for relief for the vindication of constitutional claims and statutory rights under Section 504 in most instances.

Where there has been a denial of access to the procedural safeguards of the IDEA or where a child does not meet the definitional criteria of disability under the IDEA, it is possible that the IDEA will not provide relief. In those instances, reliance on Section 504 of the Rehabilitation Act, the ADA, or Section 1983 of the Civil Rights Act will be necessary. A student with HIV, who is not in need of special education, would need to resort to Section 504, the ADA, or the Constitution rather than the IDEA for relief. Where a practice or procedure is widespread or is stated or de facto policy, it will also be important to consider redress through Section 504, the ADA, or Section 1983. Although reliance on these theories will be the exception, it is still important to know the procedures for bringing such actions.

The procedures for seeking redress under Section 504, the ADA, or the Constitution are addressed in Chapter 18.

Summary

The IDEA provides parents and schools with a number of ways to resolve disputes that arise in the special education process. The law encourages the parties to resolve their disputes through non-adversarial methods such as mediation or resolution sessions that occur before an administrative due process hearing. If the parties are unable to resolve their differences through these non-adversarial methods, then either side may request an administrative due process hearing before a qualified and impartial hearing officer. The parties in an administrative due process hearing have certain rights afforded to them by the IDEA. These rights include the right to counsel, to present evidence and witnesses, and to cross-examine witnesses. After the evidence is presented, the hearing officer issues a written decision with findings of fact and law.

If the parents prevail in the administrative due process hearing, they may be entitled to have their attorneys' fees and some of their costs paid for by the school district. Conversely, the school district may be entitled to have its attorneys' fees paid for by the parents if the school district prevails and a court finds the claim of the parents who brought the due process request to be frivolous, unreasonable, or without foundation, or if it was brought for purposes of harassing or causing unnecessary delay in the process. Either party can appeal the hearing officer's decision to a state review panel, if one is available, or directly to state or federal court if one is not available.

Questions for Reflection

1. Most special education disputes are now resolved through mediation, resolution sessions, or some other non-adversarial process. Why is that so? What are some of the advantages of resolving the dispute in a non-adversarial proceeding instead of an administrative due process hearing or complaint?

2. In the *Schaffer* case, the United States Supreme Court resolved some issues regarding who has the burden of proof at an administrative due process hearing. As noted in this chapter, the Court found that the party requesting the hearing bears the burden. What impact does this ruling have on the special education process and requests for hearings? For school officials, what advantages are there to having the parents request due process and bear the burden of proof at the hearing? From the parents' perspective, what are the advantages of waiting for the school to request due process?

3. Before the *Schaffer* decision, some courts had ruled that the school district always had the burden of proof in a due process hearing since the school had the obligation to provide FAPE and school officials had more expertise and knowledge than parents regarding special education requirements and providing FAPE. What benefits to the student, if any, would this approach have over the approach set forth in *Schaffer?*

4. In *Winkelman,* the Supreme Court found that parents could proceed in an IDEA appeal in court without an attorney. Before the decision, the vast majority of the courts of appeals that considered the issue found that parents could not do so. Why did the Supreme Court decide otherwise? Does the Court's analysis make sense?

5. The dispute resolution options under the IDEA include the right for parents to file a complaint with the state department of education or a due process complaint. In what circumstances might a parent want to pursue one of these options over the other?

NOTES

1. Two common methods developed by states are neutral case evaluations and facilitated team meetings. Neutral case evaluation is a non-adversarial method of resolving disputes that the parties undertake voluntarily. It is a process where the parties obtain an opinion from a hearing officer about the strengths and weaknesses of their case. The parties meet with a hearing officer and are allowed to present limited evidence and make arguments to the hearing officer about their case. The hearing officer then makes a recommendation on how he or she would likely rule on the case given the evidence and argument she or she heard. If the parties agree with the hearing officer's assessment and recommendation, the parties enter into a written binding agreement signed by each party. If they do not agree, the parties are not bound by the hearing officer's statements and may continue through the dispute resolution process by going to mediation or to a due process hearing. The hearing officer in the neutral case evaluation does not have any further involvement in the case.
2. 20 U.S.C. § 1415(f); 34 C.F.R. § 300.507.
3. 20 U.S.C. § 1415(f)(3)(C); 34 C.F.R. § 300.507; § 300.511(e).
4. 20 U.S.C. § 1415(f)(3)(D); 34 C.F.R. § 300.511(f).
5. 20 U.S.C. § 1415(b)(7)(A); 34 C.F.R. § 300.507.
6. 20 U.S.C. § 1415(c)(2)(A),(C).
7. 20 U.S.C. § 1415(f)(1)(B); 34 C.F.R. § 300.510.
8. 34 C.F.R. § 300.510.
9. 20 U.S.C. § 1415(f)(1)(B).
10. *Id.*
11. 34 C.F.R. § 300.512.
12. 34 C.F.R. § 300.507.
13. 20 U.S.C. § 1415(f)(1)(A).
14. 20 U.S.C. § 1415(f)(3)(A)(i).
15. 34 C.F.R. § 300.511(c).
16. *Mayson v. Teague,* 749 F.2d 652 (11th Cir. 1984). See also Laura Rothstein & Julia Rothstein, *Disabilities and the Law* § 2:35 (Thomson West 2006).
17. 34 C.F.R. § 300.513.
18. 20 U.S.C. § 1415(f)(3)(E); 34 C.F.R. § 300.513(a)(2).
19. *Id.*
20. 34 C.F.R. § 300.510.
21. 34 C.F.R. § 300.510(c).
22. 20 U.S.C. § 1415(i)(3).
23. *Arlington Cent. Sch. Dist. Bd. of Educ. v. Murphy,* 548 U.S. 291 (2006).
24. 20 U.S.C. § 1415(i)(3).
25. 34 C.F.R. § 300.515.
26. 34 C.F.R. § 300.516.
27. 20 U.S.C. § 1414(i); 34 C.F.R. § 300.516.

28. 34 C.F.R. § 300.516(b).
29. See *Disabilities and the Law* § 2:40.
30. 20 U.S.C. § 1415(i)(2)(C).
31. 20 U.S.C. § 1415(e).
32. *Id.*
33. 34 C.F.R. § 300.506(b).
34. 20 U.S.C. § 1415(e)(2)(F)(iii); 34 C.F.R. § 300.506(b).
35. 34 C.F.R. § 300.506(b).
36. *Id.*
37. 20 U.S.C. § 1415(b)(6).
38. 34 C.F.R. § 300.151.
39. 34 C.F.R. § 300.152(b).
40. See Chapter 5.
41. 42 U.S.C. § 1983.
42. 468 U.S. 992 (1984).

18

Americans with Disabilities Act and Section 504 of the Rehabilitation Act

Most students with disabilities who request services related to their disabilities will receive the assurance of access to special education and related services through the Individuals with Disabilities Education Act (IDEA). As previously noted in Chapter 5, where the IDEA provides redress, it will be the exclusive avenue for doing so. The vast majority of students with disabilities will pursue remedies through the IDEA.

There are, however, still some situations where the IDEA does not provide redress, but Section 504 or the Americans with Disabilities Act (ADA) applies and provides certain protections. One example is where a student has been discriminated against based on the disability and seeks monetary damages as a remedy. Another example is when a student does not require special education and related services, but has an impairment that is considered to be a disability under the Americans with Disabilities Act and Section 504 of the Rehabilitation Act. In such a situation, the student is protected against impermissible discrimination under Section 504 and the ADA and may be entitled to certain services and accommodations under these laws as well.

Because these and other situations may arise, it is important to know how the ADA and Section 504 apply in education of students until they graduate from high school. It is also important to know the avenues for redressing discrimination claims in situations where the IDEA does not apply. These may include litigation in court, complaint to the federal Department of Education, and use of a Section 504 process within the school policy. These actions raise a number of issues. Educational agencies should consider the implications of Section 504 and the ADA in developing individualized plans for students similar to the individualized education program (IEP) plans under the IDEA.

Litigation Under Section 504 and the Americans with Disabilities Act

A student may decide to go directly to court bringing an action under Section 504, the ADA, and/or the Constitution.[1] Constitutional claims will be the exception after *Smith v. Robinson*.[2] Constitutional violations are filed directly in court, without a resort to any administrative agency. There is no immunity from a constitutional claim. The difficulty, however, is in proving that the violation is one that cannot be remedied under the IDEA.

Who Is Covered

The first element of a Section 504 or an ADA case is determining whether the individual meets the definition of being disabled within the statute and whether it is a situation that is not remedied by the IDEA. An example would be a student with a mobility impairment who cannot gain access to some areas of a school building (such as the auditorium stage or seating areas in the sports stadium) or a student who is not allowed on the basketball team because he is HIV positive. A student with severe arthritis who needs book lockers on two floors of a high school building as a reasonable accommodation illustrates another situation.

The following decision is an example of a case of discrimination not addressed by the IDEA. The case involved a 6-year-old boy with hemophilia who had gotten HIV through a blood transfusion. When the school board decided to exclude him pursuant to its policy on children with chronic communicable diseases (adopted to respond to his situation), it became necessary to resolve whether his mother was required to pursue IDEA remedies in challenging the exclusion. The excerpt illuminates the distinction between coverage under the IDEA and Section 504.

DOE V. BELLEVILLE PUBLIC SCHOOL DISTRICT

672 F. Supp. 342 (S.D. Ill. 1987)

The plaintiff . . . contends that he is not "handicapped as that term is statutorily defined in EAHCA [Education for All Handicapped Children Act], and thus is not afforded a remedy by that Act. Consequently, plaintiff argues that he is not required to exhaust his administrative remedies because his claim does not arise under EAHCA, but rather under the Rehabilitation Act.

Because defendants' argument relies on the applicability of EAHCA to the plaintiff, the court must determine if plaintiff's diagnosis of AIDS brings him within the statutory definition of a handicapped individual. EAHCA defines "handicapped children" as children who are:

> mentally retarded, hard of hearing, deaf, speech or language impaired, visually handicapped, seriously emotionally disturbed, orthopedically impaired, or *other health impaired children*, or children with specific learning disabilities, *who by reason thereof require special education and related services*.

[Emphasis added] 20 U.S.C. § 1401(a)(1) [Now § 1401(3)].

In this case the parties agree that the only category into which Johnny fits is that of "other health impaired children." That phrase is defined as children who have:

> limited strength, vitality or alertness due to chronic or acute health problems such as heart condition, tuberculosis, rheumatic fever, nephritis, asthma, sickle-cell anemia, *hemophilia*, epilepsy, lead poisoning, leukemia, or diabetes, *which adversely affect a child's educational performance.*

[Emphasis added] 34 C.F.R. § 300.5(b)(7).

In applying these definitions to the plaintiff, the Court concludes that three tests must be met before the provisions of EAHCA can be made to apply in this case: 1) there must be limited strength, vitality, or alertness due to chronic or acute health problems, 2) which adversely affects a child's educational performance, and 3) which requires special education and related services. Here, the record reveals virtually no evidence that plaintiff suffers from limited strength, vitality, or alertness. Furthermore, given such evidence as is in the record of Johnny's limited strength, there is virtually no evidence that this limitation has adversely affected his educational performance.

The Court also finds it noteworthy that, while the defendants assert that Johnny's hemophilia brings him within the statutory definition of "other health impaired children," the health impairment they are apparently concerned with is Johnny's AIDS virus. AIDS is not listed as an example of an acute or chronic health problem in the statute. Furthermore, the United States Department of Education, directly addressing the applicability of EAHCA to AIDS victims, has opined that a child with AIDS might be considered "handicapped" under EAHCA, depending upon his or her condition. More significantly, the Department's opinion concludes that a child with AIDS is not considered to be "handicapped," as the term is defined in the EAHCA, unless he or she needs special education. With respect to the availability of special education programs for children with AIDS, the opinion states:

> Children with AIDS could be eligible for special education programs under the category of other health impaired: if they have chronic or acute health problems which adversely affect their educational performance.

Based on the Department of Education's opinions and the tenor of the statutory language, the Court concludes that EAHCA would apply to AIDS victims only if their physical condition is such that it adversely affects their educational performance; i.e., their ability to learn and to do the required classroom work. There is no such showing at the present time, and it seems clear that the only reason for the Board's determination that Johnny needs "special education" is the fact that he has a contagious disease—AIDS. In the Court's opinion, given the facts of this case as they now exist, the provisions of EAHCA would not apply to the plaintiff at this time.

The decision in this case denied the defendant's motion to dismiss the claim for failure to exhaust administrative remedies because the claim was proper under the Rehabilitation Act, and exhaustion is not required under that Act. While the excerpt indicates that the student is not covered under the IDEA, it does not decide whether he was covered under the Rehabilitation Act.

One final type of case where the IDEA would not be applicable, but where discrimination might occur involves accommodations and access for parents of students with disabilities. This might include a sign language interpreter for a parent who is deaf or attendance at events by a parent with a mobility impairment. It could even apply in a situation where a child is not admitted to a preschool program because the parent is known to be HIV positive.

Section 504 of the Rehabilitation Act of 1973 provides that "no otherwise qualified individual with a disability . . . shall solely by reason of her or his disability, be excluded from the participation in, be denied the benefits of, or be subjected to discrimination under any program or activity receiving Federal financial assistance."[3] The ADA, which defines a protected individual in similar terms, prohibits such discrimination by both public and private schools.[4] While the ADA is in many ways quite similar to Section 504, in some ways it requires special attention in the context of education of students with disabilities. First, the ADA, like Section 504, provides coverage for those with impairments, or who are regarded as, or who have records of substantial impairments. Unlike Section 504, the ADA also applies to individuals with associational status. For example, under the ADA a school could not prohibit the attendance of a child whose parent had tuberculosis.

The Supreme Court in a 1987 decision addressed whether individuals with contagious diseases are disabled under Section 504. The following provides the definitional language and the application of that language in an employment setting involving a schoolteacher. This decision provides guidance in other settings as well.

SCHOOL BOARD OF NASSAU COUNTY V. ARLINE

480 U.S. 273 (1987)

In determining whether a particular individual is handicapped as defined by the Act, the regulations promulgated by the Department of Health and Human Services are of significant assistance. As we have previously recognized, these regulations were drafted with the oversight and approval of Congress.

The regulations are particularly significant here because they define two critical terms used in the statutory definition of handicapped individual. "Physical impairment" is defined as follows:

> [A]ny physiological disorder or condition, cosmetic disfigurement, or anatomical loss affecting one or more of the following body systems: neurological; musculoskeletal; special sense organs; respiratory, including speech organs; cardiovascular; reproductive, digestive, genito-urinary; hemic and lymphatic; skin; and endocrine. 45 C.F.R. § 84.3(j)(2)(i) (1985).

In addition, the regulations define "major life activities" as:

> . . . functions such as caring for one's self, performing manual tasks, walking, seeing, hearing, speaking, breathing, learning, and working. § 84.3(j)(2)(ii).

Within this statutory and regulatory framework, then, we must consider whether Arline can be considered a handicapped individual. According to the testimony of Dr. McEuen, Arline suffered tuberculosis "in an acute form in such a degree that it affected her respiratory system," and was hospitalized for this condition. . . . Thus, Arline's hospitalization for tuberculosis in 1957 suffices to establish that she has a "record of . . . impairment" within the meaning of 29 U.S.C. § 700(7)(B)(ii), and is therefore a handicapped individual.

Petitioners concede that a contagious disease may constitute a handicapping condition to the extent that it leaves a person with "diminished physical or mental capabilities," and concede that Arline's hospitalization for tuberculosis in 1957 demonstrates that she has a record of a physical impairment. Petitioners maintain, however, Arline's record of impairment is irrelevant in this case, since the School Board dismissed Arline not because of her diminished physical capabilities, but because of the threat that her relapses of tuberculosis posed to the health of others.

We do not agree with petitioners that, in defining a handicapped individual under § 504, the contagious effects of a disease can be meaningfully distinguished from the disease's physical effects on a claimant in a case such as this. Arline's contagiousness and her physical impairment each resulted from the same underlying condition, tuberculosis. It would be unfair to allow an employer to seize upon the distinction between the effects of a disease on others and the effects of a disease on a patient and use that distinction to justify discriminatory treatment.

Nothing in the legislative history of § 504 suggests that Congress intended such a result. That history demonstrates that Congress was as concerned about the effect of an impairment on others as it was about its effect on the individual. Congress extended coverage, in 29 U.S.C. § 706(7)(B)(iii), to those individuals who are simply "regarded as having" a physical or mental impairment. The Senate Report provides as an example of a person who would be covered under this subsection "a person with some kind of visible physical impairment which in fact does not substantially limit that person's functioning." Such an impairment might not diminish a person's physical or mental capabilities, but could nevertheless substantially limit that person's ability to work as a result of the negative reactions of others to the impairment.

Allowing discrimination based on the contagious effects of a physical impairment would be inconsistent with the basic purpose of § 504, which is to ensure that handicapped individuals are not denied jobs or other benefits because of the prejudiced attitudes or the ignorance of others. By amending the definition of "handicapped individual" to include not only those who are actually physically impaired, but also those who are regarded as impaired and who, as a result, are substantially limited in a major life activity, Congress acknowledged that society's accumulated myths and fears about disability and disease are as handicapping as are the physical limitations that flow from actual impairment. Few aspects of a handicap give rise to the same level of public fear and misapprehension as contagiousness. Even those who suffer or have

(Continued)

(Continued)

recovered from such noninfectious diseases as epilepsy or cancer have faced discrimination based on the irrational fear that they might be contagious. The Act is carefully structured to replace such reflexive reactions to actual or perceived handicaps with actions based on reasoned and medically sound judgments: the definition of "handicapped individual" is broad, but only those individuals who are both handicapped *and* otherwise qualified are eligible for relief. The fact that *some* persons who have contagious diseases may pose a serious health threat to others under certain circumstances does not justify excluding from the coverage of the Act *all* persons with actual or perceived contagious diseases. Such exclusion would mean that those accused of being contagious would never have the opportunity to have their condition evaluated in light of medical evidence and a determination made as to whether they were "otherwise qualified." Rather, they would be vulnerable to discrimination on the basis of mythology—precisely the type of injury Congress sought to prevent. We conclude that the fact a person with a record of a physical impairment that is also a contagious disease does not suffice to remove that person from coverage under § 504.***

We hold that a person suffering from the contagious disease of tuberculosis can be a handicapped person within the meaning of § 504 of the Rehabilitation Act of 1973, and that respondent Arline is such a person. We remand the case to the District Court to determine whether Arline is otherwise qualified for her position.

In its decision, the Supreme Court specifically stated in a footnote that it was not deciding whether someone with AIDS was protected under the Rehabilitation Act. Congress amended the Rehabilitation Act in 1987 to protect individuals with infectious diseases. The amendment is as follows:

> For the purposes of sections 503 and 504, as such sections related to employment, such term does not include an individual who has a currently contagious disease or infection and who, by reason of such disease or infection, would constitute a direct threat to the health or safety of other individuals or who, by reason of the currently contagious disease or infection, is unable to perform the duties of the job.[5]

While this amendment would seem to apply only to employment, most commentators would find it also applicable to other areas, such as education. In 1998, the Supreme Court hinted that individuals who are HIV positive, but asymptomatic, might be automatically covered as disabled under the ADA and Section 504. In *Bragdon v. Abbott*,[6] the Court held that a woman who was HIV positive, but asymptomatic, was substantially limited in her major life activity of reproduction. The Court declined to clarify whether others who were not of reproductive age would also be covered, but many scholars believe that this is an appropriate interpretation of the statutory definition.

In 2008, Congress amended the definition of disability for both the ADA and the Rehabilitation Act. The amended definition responded to a narrow interpretation of coverage from 1999 and 2002 Supreme Court decisions, which were focused on employment. Although these decisions involved employment, the interpretation had been expanded to other areas, although there were few cases involving students with disabilities in schools.[7]

The definition covers individuals who are substantially limited in one or more major life activities, those who have a record of such an impairment, and those who are regarded as having such an impairment. The Supreme Court had considered mitigating measures, such as medication, in determining substantial limitation. The Court had also applied a narrow interpretation of what constitutes a major life activity. The amendments clarified that the statute was to read broadly.

Of significance to education is that it adds the following to the list of major life activities: reading, concentrating, thinking, and communicating. This would provide broad coverage to individuals with a number of learning and related disabilities. Major life activities also include operation of major bodily functions, including functions of the immune system, digestive, bowel, bladder, neurological, brain, respiratory, circulatory, and endocrine functions. This will affect a number of students with health conditions who do not necessarily require special education or related services.

Otherwise Qualified

A determination that an individual fits the definition is only the first step toward challenging a discriminatory practice. The definition specifies that the individual must be "otherwise qualified." The first Supreme Court case to address any issue under Section 504 dealt with this requirement. In *Southeastern Community College v. Davis,*[8] the Court found that a nursing student with a hearing impairment was not otherwise qualified to participate in the nurse-training program because she could not meet the program's requirements *"in spite of"* her disability. Programs subject to Section 504 or the ADA are not obligated to make substantial modifications or fundamental alterations to the program to accommodate the disability. They are, however, required to make reasonable accommodations where these do not pose an undue hardship on the program. The Supreme Court in *Arline,* while finding tuberculosis to be a disability, remanded the case for a determination as to whether the plaintiff was otherwise qualified. The Court indicated that issues such as the duration and severity of the condition and the probability that the disease would be transmitted required a factual determination before the decision could be made that she was or was not "otherwise qualified." The Court noted: "A person who poses a significant risk of communicating an infectious disease to others in the workplace will not be otherwise qualified . . . if reasonable accommodation will not eliminate that risk."[9]

The Court further stated that a determination of that risk should be based on "reasonable medical judgments given the state of medical knowledge, about . . . the nature . . . duration . . . and severity of the risk . . . and . . . the probabilities the disease will be transmitted and will cause varying degrees of harm."[10] Two years after the Supreme Court decision, the district court found Gene Arline not to be a risk and to be otherwise qualified.

Applying this standard, the presumption should be that as a general rule a child with HIV is otherwise qualified because the weight of medical knowledge is that HIV is not transmitted by casual contact. This presumption may be rebutted in specific cases, such as where because of a child's behavior (biting) or manifestation of symptoms (open sores, oozing lesions that cannot be covered, etc.) there is a risk of communicating the disease. Also, if the child with HIV is at a point where the immune system is so depressed that exposure to ordinary childhood infections, such as flu and chicken pox, would pose a serious danger to that individual child, it may be that the child is not otherwise qualified to attend regular school. And in either case, where the child is at risk or poses a risk, the child would generally be viewed as at least "otherwise qualified" for homebound instruction, unless the child is simply too ill to do schoolwork. In response to the concern about children with infectious diseases in schools, the Centers for Disease Control (CDC) developed and published Guidelines in August 1985. The Guidelines apply to children who are HIV positive as well as those with HIV or clinical AIDS.

The Guidelines are premised on current medical evidence that indicates that "casual person-to-person contact as would occur among schoolchildren appears to pose no risk." The lack of information about younger children and children with neurological impairments lacking control of body secretions is noted as a caveat to this premise. This group is perhaps in need of different treatment in terms of both the risk of transmission of HIV to other children and the risk to the child with HIV.

The CDC recommendations provide the following:[11]

- Case-by-case decision making regarding participation
- Decision making by a team (including child's physician, public health personnel, child's parent or guardian, and personnel involved in proposed educational program, such as the classroom teacher)
- Presumption of inclusion for most children
- A more restricted environment for preschool and neurologically impaired children until further study of transmission in these settings is done
- Precautions in handling child's bodily fluids
- Routine procedures for handling bodily fluids of all children
- Continuing monitoring of the child's hygienic practices and appropriate responses to any changes
- Children in risk groups (such as those born to mothers with AIDS) might be considered for being tested for AIDS in order to avoid giving vaccinations that might be dangerous and to monitor behavior and exposure to infections
- No mandatory screening as a condition of enrollment
- Educational personnel should respect right to privacy and maintain confidentiality as much as possible
- Provide education to parents, children, and educators about AIDS and how it is transmitted

While most states and local educational agencies have adopted procedures for dealing with children who have infectious diseases, there is a need for a more comprehensive federal policy. Such a policy should address the following issues:[12]

- The need to amend the definition of individual with a disability to specifically include children with HIV under the IDEA or at least to ensure that those who are HIV positive are clearly protected under Section 504 and the ADA against discrimination

- The need for an expedited decision-making process for children with HIV because of the potential impact of the condition on the child
- The importance of having impartial parties make decisions about inclusion of children with HIV rather than school board members and other local administrators who may be influenced by political pressure
- The importance of ensuring that confidential issues are addressed more specifically in the IDEA regarding children with HIV and other infectious diseases
- Ensuring that the individualized placement program provides for ongoing monitoring of changing conditions of the child
- Personnel development to include mandatory training about HIV and its transmission and appropriate safety and hygiene practices

Reasonable Accommodation

As mentioned in Chapter 4, there are particular difficulties regarding several populations of individuals and whether they are covered under the IDEA. These include medically fragile children (whose needs may be medical as well as educational), children with attention deficit disorder (ADD) or attention deficit hyperactivity disorder (ADHD), children with health impairments (such as asthma or cancer), children with contagious diseases such as HIV or tuberculosis, those who are socially maladjusted but not emotionally disturbed, and those who are addicted to drugs or alcohol.[13] Students with diabetes raise a number of complex issues that could include whether they are disabled within Section 504 or the ADA and what kinds of accommodations might be required.[14]

As noted previously, although the child may not be entitled to special education and related services under the IDEA, the ADA and Section 504 of the Rehabilitation Act may protect the child from discrimination. The reasonable accommodation requirement under both the ADA and Section 504 may mandate that services and special programming be provided. For example, the school may be required to allow a child with asthma to carry and use an inhaler as an exception to a rule prohibiting self-administered medication. And while the school may not be required to pay for the costs of drug rehabilitation for a student addicted to drugs, it may be required to adjust attendance requirements to allow a student to attend drug therapy sessions.

There have been a number of other instances in which courts have applied Section 504 to cases involving students with disabilities. For example, in *Wolff v. South Colonie Central School District*,[15] a girl who wanted to participate in a school-sponsored trip to Spain was denied participation because her limb deficiency would make it too difficult for her to keep up with many of the activities involved in the trip. The case was decided under Section 504, and it was held that the exclusion was permissible because she was not "otherwise qualified."

Architectural Barrier Issues

Both Section 504 of the Rehabilitation Act and the ADA provide a mandate for more accessible facilities and programming. This mandate refers to a number of requirements, such as ramps and accessible restrooms. Section 504 applies to all educational agencies receiving federal financial assistance. Title II of the ADA applies to public schools and Title III to private schools.[16] Both public and private schools must ensure that new construction meets specific barrier-free design requirements. In addition, private schools are required to remove existing barriers to the extent it is readily achievable to do so. Public schools are required to conduct a self-evaluation of their programs and to ensure that the program when viewed in its entirety is accessible. This might mean that having a barrier-free school within the school district would satisfy the requirement from a student's perspective. But this may not be sufficient from the perspective of others protected by the ADA. For example, a parent with a mobility impairment attending an event such as a graduation ceremony would be protected by the ADA. For that reason, a school may be required to remove barriers in all schools to provide the required access to the public, even though the school might not be required to provide the same level of access for students in the school system in that area.

This issue does not fall directly under the topic of special education. It is important to recognize, however, that because ADA mandates apply to public events and access by parents, the barrier-free design requirements may result in all schools becoming more accessible. Therefore, a student in a wheelchair who does not require special education and related services would be more likely to be able to attend the neighborhood school because its barriers would have been removed as a result of the broader ADA mandate.

Enforcement and Remedies for Seeking Individual Redress

The disadvantage of Section 504, ADA, and Section 1983 of the Civil Rights Act actions is that they do not have the built-in administrative deadlines of the IDEA due process hearing and administrative review. Once the claim reaches court, however, there is no time advantage to an IDEA claim over the other sources of relief. The importance of these mechanisms for redress is that Section 504 and the ADA provide avenues for relief for students falling outside the protection of the IDEA, and Section 1983 provides a mechanism for ensuring that the procedural safeguards are followed.

Enforcement of the ADA under Title II (applicable to public schools) is through the procedures of Section 504 and includes the same remedies and rights. Title III (applicable to private schools) enforcement involves both private enforcement through the remedies and procedures of the Civil Rights Act of 1964 and Attorney General enforcement. Remedies available under Title III include injunctive relief, monetary damages (but only if the Attorney General intervenes), attorneys' fees, and costs.

Section 504 Plans in Schools

Although school personnel may be familiar with requirements for developing individualized programs under the IDEA, they may be less familiar with the benefit of developing a similar plan for students covered by Section 504.[17] There are a number of features that should be included in such a plan, which are suggested by a model developed by Stan Shaw, codirector of the Center on Postsecondary Education and Disability, University of Connecticut. The model, which was adapted from a number of models, includes the following elements:

• Reason for referral

• Eligibility determination (summaries of performance data, staff information, parent/student information); specification of the impairment; major life activity and the degree to which it is affected

• 504 Accommodation Plan (includes basis for determining eligibility; goals of the plan; specific services, accommodations, modifications, or assistive technology to be provided and when, where, and who will provide these services)

Complaints to the Department of Education

A student's parents may want to seek redress through complaint to the United States Department of Education, which has jurisdiction over programs that receive federal financial assistance. All public schools currently receive federal financial assistance through the IDEA grant programs. Many private schools receive federal financial assistance through subsidized lunch programs and other grant programs. Complaints under Section 504 can be filed with the United States Department of Education within 180 days of the violation. The complaint should be sent to the Office for Civil Rights of the Department of Education in the region where the school district is located. The complaint need not be on any particular form in order for investigation to proceed, but it must contain the following:

- The name, address, and telephone number of the complaining party
- The basis for the complaint, such as disability discrimination
- Who has been affected by the discrimination—individuals or groups of individuals
- The name and address of the discriminating agency if known
- The approximate date of the discriminatory conduct
- A brief description of what happened
- The signature of the complaining party[18]

An administrative investigation follows. Because administrative action in such cases is generally futile to resolution of the individual situation, the majority of courts permit individuals to bring actions directly in court. While Section 504 complaints are not a viable avenue for remedying many types of practices that may affect only one individual—because the IDEA often preempts Section 504 and because Section 504 is often too cumbersome for special education–type cases—it is important to recognize Section 504 as a tool for remedying systemic practices and policies.

For example, a practice of always conducting special education classes in separate, segregated facilities could be attacked through a complaint to the Office for Civil Rights. An investigation could lead to an order for the school to stop the practice, and this would then affect all special education students in the school. An individual complaint using IDEA due process procedures will often resolve the situation for only one student. For that reason, it is important that both advocacy groups and parents concerned about overall policy and practice recognize the value of the administrative complaint procedure under Section 504. Not only may such groups bring direct actions; they are not required to exhaust administrative remedies (including filing a complaint with the Department of Education), either, when it would be futile.

School choice programs, such as magnet schools, vouchers, and charter schools that are implemented by public educational agencies, also have the potential for challenge under Section 504 and the ADA if such programs do not provide equivalent access to students with disabilities.[19]

Summary

Students with disabilities concerned about services and programs within the educational context will be primarily covered under the requirements of the Individuals with Disabilities Education Act. In fact, if the IDEA resolves an issue, these students must use that as their exclusive avenue for redress.

Nonetheless, there are instances where either the student is not disabled within the definition of the IDEA or the IDEA does not address the concern that the student has. In such cases, it may be appropriate to seek relief under Section 504 of the Rehabilitation Act or the ADA. In these cases the student will need to meet the definition of being disabled within the statute and being otherwise qualified to carry out the requirements of the program (including not posing a direct threat). Section 504 and the ADA both prevent discrimination on the basis of disability, and they both require reasonable accommodations. Each situation is fact specific in determining what constitutes a reasonable accommodation.

There are a number of situations where the IDEA might not apply, but where Section 504 or the ADA would. One of the major ones involves students with health impairments, including having HIV. Because of the potential for coverage, educational agencies should develop individualized plans for these students, similar to IEPs under the IDEA.

In addition to redress in the courts, parents may bring complaints to the Department of Education, which has the ability to do an investigation to determine whether there has been impermissible discrimination.

Questions for Reflection

1. With reference to children with HIV, if the school requested an opinion from a private physician as to the risk of a child with HIV to other children in the classroom, and that physician determined there would be reasonable risk (although opinions of other physicians in the area were otherwise), should the court defer to the medical judgment of private physicians on which the school has relied in excluding the child?

2. The concern about privacy for a child with HIV and the need for school employees to know that a child has HIV so that appropriate precautions can be taken are both legitimate concerns. How can these concerns be reconciled?

3. Should the IDEA be amended to address issues relating to children with HIV and other contagious diseases? If so, how? Or should this be left to the state or local educational agency? Do the ADA amendments address this concern?

4. What reasons would there be for a parent to litigate under Section 504 or the ADA instead of complaining to the Department of Education.

NOTES

1. See Laura Rothstein & Julia Rothstein, *Disabilities and the Law* §§ 2:53–2:56 (Thomson West 2006); Perry Zirkel, "Suspension and Expulsion Under Section 504: A Comparative Overview," 226 *Ed. L. Rep.* 9 (2008).

2. See Chapter 3.

3. 29 U.S.C. § 794.

4. 42 U.S.C. § 12102(2).

5. 29 U.S.C. § 706(8)(D). See also *Disabilities and the Law* § 2:9.

6. 524 U.S. 624 (1998).

7. The ADA Amendments Act of 2008, Pub. L. No. 110-325 (2008), effective January 1, 2009.

8. 442 U.S. 397, 407, 413 (1979).

9. 480 U.S. at note 16.

10. 480 U.S. at 273 quoting Brief for the American Medical Association.

11. See *Guidelines for Effective School Health Education to Prevent the Spread of AIDS*, Centers for Disease Control, available at http://www.cdc.gov/mmwr/preview/mmwrhtml/00001751.htm (last accessed August 6, 2008).

12. For a detailed discussion of these issues, see Laura Rothstein, "Children With AIDS: A Need for a Clear Policy and Procedure for Public Education, 12 *Nova L. Rev.* 1259 (1988).

13. See Laura Rothstein, "Substance Abuse and Testing: Just Say 'Maybe,'" *EDLAW Briefing Paper* (June 1991).

14. Christopher W. Goddard, "Children With Diabetes: Are State Statutes Needed to Protect Students' Rights?" 34 *Journal of Law & Education* 497 (2005); Perry Z. Zirkel, "Counterpoint Intro: Students With Diabetes: Life and Law Are Not Sweet," 35 *Journal of Law & Education* 497 (2006); James F. McKethan & David H. Phillips, "State Statutes to Protect Children With Diabetes: Noble Intentions but the Wrong Approach," 35 *Journal of Law & Education* 501 (2006).

15. 34 F. Supp. 758 (N.D.N.Y. 1982).

16. 42 U.S.C. §§ 12132 & 12182.

17. Stan F. Shaw & Joseph W. Madaus, "Preparing School Personnel to Implement Section 504," 43 *Intervention in School and Clinic* 226, 226–230 (March 2008).

18. See 45 C.F.R. § 807. The U.S. Department of Education is located at 400 Maryland Avenue, S.W., Washington, DC 20202. Online complaints can be submitted to OCR@ed.gov. The Web site at http://www.ed.gov/about/offices/list/ocr/complaintintro.html provides detailed information about the process and the online complaint form.

19. See Chapter 12 for a discussion of this issue and its impact on special education.

19

Education Records

What Constitutes an Education Record?

Under the Family Educational Rights and Privacy Act (FERPA),[1] educational records are records that directly relate to the student, and are maintained by an educational agency or institution, or by a party acting for the agency or institution.[2] Records include any information about the student recorded in any way, including, but not limited to handwriting, print, computer media, video- or audiotape, film, microfilm, and microfiche.[3]

FERPA also defines certain records that are not education records. These include records by educational personnel that are kept in the sole possession of the maker, and are not accessible or revealed to any other person; records of a law enforcement unit of an educational agency; records relating to an individual who is employed by an educational agency or institution; and records on a student who is 18 years of age or older, or is attending an institution of postsecondary education, that are made or maintained by a physician, psychiatrist, psychologist, or other recognized professional or paraprofessional and maintained or used only in connection with the treatment of the student. Records that only contain information about an individual after he or she is no longer a student at that educational agency or institution are also not education records.[4]

With the passage of the Health Insurance Portability and Accountability Act of 1996 (HIPAA),[5] questions arose about whether certain records might be subject to the privacy protections of that legislation. The overlap between FERPA and HIPAA is the subject of great confusion, and a full discussion of that issue is beyond the scope of this text. Care should be taken, however, to ensure that privacy is protected and balanced with the legitimate need to know.[6]

In addition to the federal laws related to student records, many states have public health laws or state record laws that may provide additional protections. Administrators in each state should familiarize themselves with these laws as well. The primary focus of this chapter, however, is on FERPA and the records.

One common practice that was subjected to a FERPA claim was peer grading of student work. A group of parents challenged the practice contending it violated FERPA to allow students to review work of other students. The practice complained of involved students exchanging papers with each other and scoring them pursuant to teacher instructions, and returning work to the student preparing it. In some instances students reported their own grades and in others the student could call out the grade or reveal it privately to the teacher. The concern was for the embarrassment of the student. In determining that the customary practice did not result in the creation of an educational record as defined in FERPA, the Supreme Court rejected the challenge in its decision in *Owasso Independent School District No. 1-001 v. Falvo.*[7] The Court's analysis raised concerns about the burden that abandoning this common practice would place on schools. Although the case did not involve special education student issues, it raises the potential for stigma and other negative treatment for students with disabilities whose poorer performance might be highlighted by such a practice.

Access and Accuracy

FERPA limits and restricts the manner in which educational agencies and institutions may disclose educational records with respect to students and requires consent to release records with a few exceptions. FERPA applies to schools that receive federal funds.[8] The statute also provides parents and students with certain rights regarding their abilities to inspect and review and request amendments to education records.

FERPA ensures parental and student access to education records through statutory provisions and regulations that provide that a parent or eligible student must be given the opportunity to inspect and review the student's education records.[9] An educational agency or institution must respond to a request for access to records within a reasonable period of time, but within 45 days after it has received the request.[10] The educational agency must also respond to reasonable requests for explanations and interpretations of the educational records.[11] Copies of the educational records must be made for the parent or student if failing to do so would effectively prevent the parent or student from exercising the right to inspect and review the student's educational records.[12] FERPA also prohibits educational agencies, such as schools and state education agencies, from destroying any education records when there is an outstanding request to inspect and review records.[13]

Educational agencies may not disclose personally identifiable information from education records without parental (or student at the age of majority) consent. Disclosure includes oral, written, or electronic means. Personally identifiable information includes the student's or parents' name or address, any personal identifiers (like social security numbers or student numbers), and personal characteristics or other information that would make the student's identity easily traceable.[14]

There are some exceptions to the consent requirements. These exceptions include disclosure to other school officials, including teachers, within the school that have legitimate educational interests in reviewing the records.[15] There are a number of other exceptions listed in the law itself.[16]

Remedying FERPA Violations

As the court noted in *Owasso,* the issue of whether a parent (or student) could bring a claim in court to enforce FERPA was an open question at the time. The Supreme Court's decision in *Gonzaga v. Doe*[17] resolved the issue. It was a higher education case, but its reasoning applies to K–12 education programs as well. The Court held that FERPA does not create personal enforcement rights.

Pursuant to the ruling in *Gonzaga,* the sole recourse for parents regarding potential FERPA violations is to file a complaint with the Family Policy Compliance Office (FPCO) of the United States Department of Education. FPCO investigates complaints, and if it finds a violation has occurred, it can order compliance with the law. If the school does not comply with the FPCO order, the agency can withhold further federal funds, issue a complaint to compel compliance through a cease and desist order, or terminate eligibility for further federal funds.

It should be noted that the *Gonzaga* decision did not address possible rights under state tort and contract theories. Although immunity often prevents recovery under these theories in many states, educational agencies should be aware of the potential liability under these theories, even if there is not a private action under FERPA. In addition to legal liability, highly publicized cases such as this can create concerns about the integrity of the educational institution that is not careful about maintaining privacy and confidentiality.

Notice Requirements

FERPA also requires educational agencies and institutions to annually notify parents of students currently in attendance, or eligible students currently in attendance, of their rights under the Act. Eligible students are students who have reached 18 years of age and are attending an institution of postsecondary education. The annual notice must inform parents or eligible students that they have the right to

1. Inspect and review the student's education records;
2. Amend the student's education records if the parent or student believes part of the record to be inaccurate, misleading, or otherwise in violation of the student's privacy rights;
3. Consent to disclosures of personally identifiable information contained in the student's education record; and
4. File a complaint with the Department of Education concerning alleged failures by the educational agency or institution to comply with FERPA.

The notice must also include

1. The procedure for exercising the right to inspect and review education records; and
2. The procedure for requesting amendments to the records; in addition,
3. If the educational agency or institution has a policy of disclosing education records to other school officials, including teachers within the agency or institution who have a legitimate educational interest, the notice must specify the criteria for determining who constitutes a school official and what constitutes a legitimate educational interest.[18]

An educational agency or institution may provide annual notice by any means that are reasonably likely to inform the parents or eligible students of their rights.[19]

Educational Records in IDEA Procedures

FERPA[20] must be read in addition to the student record requirements under the Individuals with Disabilities Education Act (IDEA). Basically, these statutes allow parents the right to ensure that educational records are correct and to resolve disputes over them through administrative hearing procedures.[21] Because stigma may attach to inaccurate information or benefits may be denied if educational records do not reflect a student's disability status correctly, accuracy becomes an important issue. In a 1984 federal circuit court opinion, the court found that an appropriate remedy was to expunge records falsely attributing mental retardation to a student.[22] Also, because of concern about entitlement to benefits in the future, parents may want to ensure that the agency policy on handling old records does not result in important information being destroyed.

Again, because of the stigma that may attach to the information in records, it can be important to know who has access to them. FERPA, the IDEA, and state confidentiality laws are fairly restrictive about allowing access only to those who have privileged reason.[23]

Adherence to proper policies has become even more important to protect children with HIV. A teacher who has no real need to know, but who has access to a record indicating that a child has HIV, can destroy the privacy of the family if the teacher is indiscreet about telling others. The fact that there may be a legal remedy for the parents is of little comfort in such cases. It is far better to implement the protective procedures in the first place.

It can often become critical for parents to have access—to evaluate whether the student's school records are accurate, and in some instances to use as evidence at a due process hearing. There is no question that parents may inspect and review all educational records under the IDEA.[24]

The issue of medical records becomes a bit more complex. Medical records that have been used as part of the basis for making an educational placement must be included as part of the records to which parents have access. The right of access to medical records other than those used in placement decisions is covered under state law and HIPAA, which is discussed briefly at the beginning of this chapter. The next question that arises is whether the parents must pay for copies of educational records as a general rule. The answer is that reasonable charges may be assessed. Given that it may well be deemed reasonable to charge 50 cents to $1.00 for one page in some school districts, the parent of a child with a severe disability who has hundreds of pages of school records can end up paying hundreds of dollars just to get the records. The IDEA does provide that if the cost would in effect prevent the parents from obtaining access to records, the charge must be waived. In addition, the Handicapped Children's Protection Act of 1986[25] may allow for reimbursement for the cost of copying records if these are seen as related costs in an action where the parents prevail.

Summary

In enforcing any procedural right, issues of student records often come into play. The IDEA, FERPA, HIPAA, and state law must all be referenced to determine issues of accuracy, access, cost, and destruction of school records. This is not an issue receiving a great deal of discussion in the courts in the context of special education cases.

The remedies for violating one or more of these statutes often do not address the individual harm. Nonetheless, the potential loss of federal financial assistance may provide an incentive or deterrent to the educational agency in its handling of student records.

Questions for Reflection

1. In *Owasso*, the Court found that the practice of peer grading of papers did not violate FERPA, at least when it was done in the manner at issue in the case. Are there circumstances where peer grading may violate FERPA? What about allowing students without disabilities to assist students with disabilities in school? Consider the following example:

> The elementary school has a "Writing Buddies" program where fifth grade students help third and fourth grade students with learning disabilities. The fifth grade students model how to write a certain passage from a topic question and then help the third and fourth grade students complete the same task by working with them directly as the student writes out the passage in response to the topic question. The fifth grade student then reviews the student's written work and gives the third or fourth grade student some feedback on how to improve it and assigns it a number grade from 1 to 10. The written work then becomes part of the student's writing portfolio that is part of the student's overall writing grade.

Would any part of this activity violate FERPA?

2. In *Gonzaga*, the effect of the Court's decision was to take away a relatively large monetary judgment from the student. Without the ability to bring claims in court under FERPA, the remaining enforcement and remedies are through the FPCO complaint process. Are those sufficient to ensure compliance with FERPA?

3. As noted in this chapter, FERPA prohibits schools, and state education agencies, from destroying education records when there is an outstanding request to inspect and review the records. What should the remedy be if the school or state education agency violates this provision?

NOTES

1. 20 U.S.C. § 1232(g).
2. 34 C.F.R. § 99.3.
3. *Id.*
4. *Id.*
5. 29 U.S.C. §§ 1181–1191c; 42 U.S.C. §§ 300gg–300gg-2.
6. See Dixie Snow Huefner & Lynn M. Daggett, "FERPA Update: Balancing Access to and Privacy of Student Records," 152 *Educ. L. Rep.* 469 (2001).
7. 534 U.S. 426 (2002).
8. 20 U.S.C. § 1232(g).
9. 34 C.F.R. § 99.10.
10. *Id.*
11. *Id.*
12. *Id.*
13. *Id.*
14. 34 C.F.R. § 99.3.
15. 34 C.F.R. § 99.31.
16. *Id.*
17. 536 U.S. 273 (2002).
18. 34 C.F.R. § 99.7.
19. *Id.*
20. 20 U.S.C. § 1232(g).
21. 20 U.S.C. § 1415(b)(1); 34 C.F.R. § 300.619.
22. See *Carter v. Orleans Parish Public Schools,* 725 F.2d 261 (5th Cir. 1984).
23. For a discussion of all aspects of student records, see Susan P. Stuart, "Lex-Praxis of Educational Informational Privacy for Public School Children," 84 *Neb. L. Rev.* 1158 (2006).
24. 20 U.S.C. § 1415(b)(1); 34 C.F.R. § 300.501; see also Laura Rothstein & Julia Rothstein, *Disabilities and the Law* §§ 2:30 & 2:42 (Thomson West 2006).
25. See Chapter 21.

20

Special Education Malpractice

Special Education Misconduct

Since the advent of a national program of special education for students with disabilities in 1975, there has been an influx of students with a variety of disabilities into the mainstream of public schools. The presence of children with disabilities raises the potential for misconduct to occur when educational personnel are not adequately trained or prepared for children with special needs.

As a policy matter, schools and school personnel should be held accountable for at least gross misconduct; but, historically, courts have rejected "educational malpractice" as a theory of liability. A few courts, however, have looked more favorably on these cases.[1]

The best means to avoid liability is for educational policymakers and administrators to ensure that educators and other school personnel are adequately prepared for the demands of mainstreaming students with disabilities. In this chapter, special education misconduct refers to actions that could potentially be remedied through common law tort suits, Individuals with Disabilities Education Act (IDEA) claims for remedies with financial obligations, and "constitutional torts" under Section 1983 of the Civil Rights Act. The application of these theories is discussed later in this chapter.

The term *education malpractice* is often used in a context of common law tort. In the late 1970s and early 1980s, there was a flurry of litigation in the regular education context using this theory.[2] These claims often stemmed from parental dissatisfaction with a child being passed from grade to grade while failing to learn basic skills such as reading and math. The parents would then bring a malpractice action claiming that the failure was a result of the school's breach of its duty to educate. These claims were overwhelmingly rejected by the courts, primarily because of the judicial attitude that there was neither a clear duty nor proof of causation.

Unfortunately, the blanket rejection of these claims was carried over to a large extent to claims involving special education. Courts often adopted the general reasoning of the regular education "why Johnny can't read" cases without examining significant differences in the duty and other elements between regular and special education malpractice claims. This chapter discusses various types of misconduct, some of which have been referred to by courts and others as malpractice.

Injuries and Remedies

To ensure that appropriate education is provided according to the IDEA mandates, extensive practices and procedures are built into the law. Although many years have passed since the IDEA became law, some educational personnel have not been adequately trained for this mandate, and some administrators do not comply with the clear administrative requirements. The mandate that children with disabilities attend public schools and participate in the regular classroom to the maximum extent appropriate creates the potential for numerous injuries.

Actual physical injury could result from inadequate supervision of the child with either a physical or a mental disability in the regular classroom, in the playground setting, or in situations such as woodworking class. Physical injury could also result where the in-class discipline is inappropriate or where the bus driver or other educational employee who was negligently hired assaults a child.

Psychological or emotional damage could result when the teacher either ridicules or permits other children to ridicule a child with a disability or even when a teacher simply fails to give any attention to the child. Emotional damage can also result if a child spends too much time on the bus because of the injury to concentration and stress on the child, or where inappropriate disciplinary measures damage the child's self-esteem.

Finally, damage to the child's educational development and even to the child's potential to earn a living can result from a variety of failures in the educational system—failure to provide a timely evaluation, program development, or implementation (as mandated by IDEA requirements); improper suspension or expulsion of a child with a disability; failure to appropriately identify, evaluate, or place a child with a disability; or the total failure to implement an appropriate program as agreed upon.

The question is what remedies are appropriate to compensate for these injuries? In some cases, injunctive relief will be sufficient—that is, simply requiring the school to stop doing what it is doing or to start doing something else. In others, where the parents have unilaterally placed their child in an appropriate program while they dispute the school's recommended placement, a reimbursement of their expenses will adequately redress or remedy the situation.

But what if there are hospital bills for physical injuries or bills from psychiatrists or psychologists for counseling to remedy emotional damage? What if the parents cannot afford to make a unilateral placement in an expensive residential program pending a five-year litigation process, and the child remains in a grossly inappropriate program in the meantime? The damage in such cases can only be remedied by providing compensatory education or money damages for remedial education or money damages for lost potential earnings.

Barriers to Tort Type Damage Awards

There are four main reasons (other than finding no fault) that courts have not traditionally awarded money damages in special education tort type misconduct cases. These are public policy, finding that a duty does not exist, determining the IDEA does not provide a private action for these types of cases, and immunity.

Public Policy

The first reason is public policy. As a matter of policy, some courts deem it inappropriate to require educational agencies (which are supported by the taxpayer) to provide compensation for misconduct—even in some cases where the misconduct has resulted in serious damage.[3] Some courts have applied this public policy reasoning but have recognized that at least in cases where there has been bad faith or serious harm to the child, compensation could be required of the school.

The other policy reason that courts have been reluctant to permit recovery for injuries caused as a result of misconduct toward children with disabilities in the educational process is a general public policy reason. Courts are generally deferential to educational institutions in their decision making, and they do not want to get into the business of second-guessing educational practices.[4] While that makes sense for many educational decisions—such as whether a particular teacher should be given tenure or whether a particular textbook or curriculum is appropriate—it does not always make sense with respect to special education decisions.

No Duty Exists

The elements of common law tort actions are (1) a duty to adhere to a particular standard of conduct or to exercise reasonable care, (2) a breach of the duty or a violation of a standard, (3) a causal connection between the breach and the injury, and (4) resulting injury.[5] Courts have not traditionally awarded monetary damages because they have often found that the duty element of negligence is not present. The early cases denying recovery on negligence theories, because of findings that there are not clear standards of practice or a clear duty, should not be relied on as the basis for not applying a malpractice theory. Most early special education malpractice decisions involved factual settings where the conduct in question arose before there were clearly established standards of practice relating to students with disabilities as a result of the IDEA. Because standards of practice have been clarified as a result of the IDEA, in many instances it should no longer be valid to claim that the "duty" element of a malpractice case has not been met.

Private Actions Under the Individuals with Disabilities Education Act

There is no question that if the parents dispute the school's decision to evaluate, the school's assessment of a child's status, the proposed placement, or a proposed change in placement, the parents have a right under the IDEA to seek redress through an impartial hearing, review by the state agency, and ultimately review in the courts. This is discussed in other chapters.

What is less clear is whether the parents may go directly to court for an IDEA violation. What if the issue is a claim that the due process rights of the IDEA have not been complied with or that the program has never been implemented as agreed upon, or that the school has failed to reevaluate in the time frame required under the IDEA? Can the parents bring an action in court without going through administrative procedures? More important, what are the remedies available to them in these situations?

While the Supreme Court has not specifically ruled on the issue in a special education context, some courts have ruled that parents need not exhaust administrative remedies before claiming relief for IDEA violations, where it would be futile to do so.[6] Cases involving denial of access to administrative hearing procedures would be an example of a situation where resort to administrative remedies would be futile.

Where the courts have been less consistent is in the issue of remedies. While declaratory and injunctive relief are clearly available under the IDEA, the availability of other remedies is more problematic. Availability of reimbursement as a remedy was only clearly established in 1985 when the Supreme Court decided the case of *Burlington School Committee v. Department of Education.*[7]

Burlington answers the question about the availability of reimbursement as a remedy under the IDEA, and this decision would resolve situations where the parents have the financial resources to pay for residential placements or other expenses pending resolution of a dispute. The decision does not resolve, however, what remedy is available to the parents who cannot afford to make the unilateral placement, but who ultimately prevail in a dispute when the school's placement turns out to be inappropriate. In those cases, can the parents recover damages to cover costs of remedial tutoring or lost potential earnings? Can the school be required to provide compensatory education to make up for the time lost during the dispute? On these issues there is a difference of opinion among courts.

Some courts hold that damages are *never* available as a remedy.[8] Others hold that damages may be available, but do not specify under what circumstances.[9] In other jurisdictions, damages are available only in situations where there is a danger to the child's physical health or where the school has acted in bad faith.[10]

As for compensatory relief, the availability of such relief may depend on whether it is viewed as equivalent to damages. The reasoning in the *Burlington* decision holding that reimbursement is not the same as damages, because "reimbursement merely requires [payment of] expenses that . . . should have [been] paid all along," would lend itself to a similar result when looking at compensatory education. If the school wrongfully denied an educational program, providing compensatory education is simply paying for services it was required to provide all along. At least one circuit court, however, has ruled that compensatory education is equivalent to damages.[11]

Immunity

While immunity is no longer a defense to actions under the IDEA or Section 504 of the Rehabilitation Act and is probably not a defense under the Americans with Disabilities Act (ADA), it is still possible to raise the defense of tort immunity. Where the theory of the case is a tort theory (such as common law negligence or other malpractice type claim), rather than reliance on a private action under one of the federal statutes, in most states there will be immunity from such actions unless the state has statutorily waived immunity. Such waivers are common for cases involving school bus accidents but often do not apply to cases such as failure to supervise on the playground and other types of actions that might give rise to a claim of misconduct toward a student with a disability.

Trends in Awarding Damages and Compensatory Education in Misconduct Cases

Supervision and Related Conduct

In many situations, a child with a disability is in greater need of supervision than is a child of the same age who is not disabled. It is important for administrators to recognize that heightened duty and to ensure that all personnel are appropriately trained to meet their obligations.

There have been several decisions in which supervision of children with disabilities has been at issue. These cases have mixed results. Several cases involving children with disabilities have resulted in findings of liability or have left open the possibility of liability. In *Collins v. School Board,*[12] a directed verdict in favor of the school was reversed and the case was remanded for findings in a suit claiming that the substitute teacher in a shop class had been negligent in supervising the class, when a student with an emotional disability was sexually assaulted by another student. In *Hopkins v. Spring Independent School District,*[13] the court found that the state would not be immune from liability for leaving unsupervised a child with cerebral palsy who subsequently suffered head injuries as a result of being pushed into a stack of chairs. Liability by the school board was found in *Clomon v. Monroe City School Board,*[14] when a 4-year-old child who was deaf was struck and killed after alighting from the school bus because the bus driver did not make sure she reached safety. The claim in that case was brought by the driver who killed the child, claiming severe emotional trauma. The court held in *DeFalco v. Deer Lake School District*[15] that the teacher, school nurse, and principal might all be liable under Section 1983 of the Civil Rights Act for failing to provide medication to a student with hypoglycemia in a timely manner. In *Barbin v. State,*[16] an award of $185,000 was upheld, when a seventh grader who was deaf was improperly supervised in woodworking class and the injury that resulted permanently impaired the child's finger-spelling skills. Perhaps the most dramatic instance of liability is the $400,000 damage award in *Rodriguez v. Board of Education,*[17] where a child who was labeled trainably mentally retarded suffered severe head injuries after being negligently supervised during play period.

There have been a number of cases, however, in which no liability has been found. The reasons have included findings that there was no negligence. The primary reason, however, is the application of the immunity defense. The court in *Braun v. Board of Education*[18] found that there had not been negligence when a student manager with epilepsy suffered a seizure while standing on a ladder to make scoreboard alterations. Immunity was a defense in *Hicks v. Walker County School District,*[19] where a child with a disability was assaulted on the bus by two other children with disabilities but the bus driver was not willful, malicious, or acting in bad faith. In another bus driver case, a mixed result was reached. *Doe A. v. Special School District*[20] involved a bus driver who had beaten and sexually abused students with disabilities on the bus. The claim was brought under Section 1983 of the Civil Rights Act, and the court found the action permissible as against the bus driver but not against the school district or school administrators.

In at least some of the cases, the injury may have resulted not only from a failure to supervise but also from a failure on the part of the school to adequately prepare personnel for the heightened awareness necessary to supervise students with disabilities. Because of the tendency of some courts to apply the immunity defense when raised against school districts and administrators, it would seem that in many cases only the individual supervisor will be held liable. In cases involving particularly egregious misconduct, this policy seems to be wrong. In *Lopez v. Houston Independent School District*,[21] the court found that although a school bus driver may have been liable for negligence in not stopping lengthy fights on the bus, the bus driver's supervisors had not been callously indifferent and therefore were immune. It would seem that if this standard were to be applied in a case where a child had been seriously injured and sustained extensive medical expenses, an injustice might be done because the bus driver may well not have the resources to compensate the parents for those expenses.

One possible avenue for seeking redress might be through a direct action under the IDEA. If the individualized education program (IEP) states that the child is to have an assistant on the bus, or that the bus should be provided with a supervisor in addition to the driver, a violation of this requirement might give rise to direct action in court. Because the right to bring such actions is not clearly settled, and the availability of damages under the IDEA is even less well settled, there seems to be a gap in coverage at least for some instances of negligence in supervision in states with strong immunity policies.

Infliction of Emotional Distress

Like negligent supervision, a claim of infliction of emotional distress is probably going to be brought under a tort theory, or in extreme cases, under Section 1983 of the Civil Rights Act. It will not be the type of injury where a claim under the IDEA will ordinarily be appropriate. There is not a great deal of case law on this issue, but it would seem that cases alleging infliction of emotional distress will face the same obstacle of immunity in many jurisdictions. Unless the infliction of emotional distress reaches the level of a constitutional claim under Section 1983, there may well be problems of immunity.

The *Clomon* case, mentioned previously, involved a claim of emotional trauma by a passing driver against the school for the driver's negligently supervising a child getting off the bus. While in that case liability was found, immunity is probably going to be a defense in some jurisdictions. *Doe A. v. Special School District* is such a case. In that case, immunity prevented claims against the school district and school administrators although there was evidence of negligent supervision of a bus driver who beat and sexually abused children with disabilities over a long period of time.

Violations of IDEA Requirements

Since *Smith v. Robinson*,[22] a few rulings have indicated that if there is a denial of access to due process procedures and other substantive rights available under the IDEA, rather than a dispute over the appropriateness of the educational program, a claim can be made directly either under the IDEA or under Section 1983 of the Civil Rights Act. What is essential in those cases is a claim that there was a total denial or at least a substantial denial of access to the IDEA rights and procedures. It is unclear, however, whether damages are available in such cases. If damage claims are limited to instances where there is bad faith or a serious physical injury, many injuries will not be redressed. For example, the child whose parents cannot afford unilateral placement but who ultimately prevail in proving that the school's placement was inappropriate may have spent several years in an inappropriate placement. Such a wrongful placement could result in a serious detriment to the child's educational development, although it would not necessarily result in serious physical harm or even have been caused by bad faith. It is questionable whether "policy reasons" should prevent recovery of damages in such cases. The weight of authority is that damages have not been recovered in these cases.

Inappropriate Disciplinary Action

Inappropriate discipline can be of two kinds. First, using corporal punishment or another disciplinary measure that is inappropriate in a particular circumstance can result in emotional damage to a sensitive child, particularly one who is already emotionally disturbed or one who has a behavior problem. Second, improper classroom discipline can also result in physical injury to the child. The theories for remediation of these injuries in most instances follow the theories for improper supervision or infliction of emotional distress. In other words, courts may either be inclined to find that there was no duty in a particular case, or that immunity is a defense even if there was improper conduct.

For example, in *Cole v. Greenfield-Central Community Schools,*[23] the court found that it was permissible to paddle and tape shut the mouth of a child who was hyperactive and emotionally disturbed, where this was used as a last resort with an extremely disruptive child. In that case, state law permitted paddling or corporal punishment in certain situations and the student taped his own mouth and could remove the tape at any time. While the result may be correct in this case given the unique facts and specific laws involved, there is a question whether a court would find liability should it turn out that the disciplinary measures in this case were extreme and inappropriate and caused serious emotional damage to the child. In *Jefferson v. Ysleta Independent School District,* the court ruled that tying an 8-year-old to a chair and denying her access to the bathroom was improper discipline.[24] Whether or not using restraints, aversives, or corporal punishment on a student violates the IDEA, Section 504, the Constitution, or state law depends very much on the circumstances of the case.

The second type of inappropriate discipline involves disciplinary removal of a student. This could include suspension (temporary removal) or expulsion (permanent removal). As Chapter 15 demonstrated, there is now some degree of clarity about the circumstances under which either type of disciplinary measure may be imposed legally within the requirements of the IDEA.

The wrongful removal of a student can have serious detrimental effects on that student, particularly when it is a long-term removal. These effects can include damage to the academic progress of the student as well as negative psychological effects due to embarrassment and other factors.

Misconduct in Identification, Evaluation, Placement, and Programming

This is the type of issue that is most frequently considered to fall within the area of what is called *educational malpractice*. And it is in this area that the courts have traditionally been particularly reluctant to intervene. The case most frequently cited for the proposition that there is no viable cause of action for special education malpractice involves an issue of inappropriate identification and placement. In *Hoffman v. Board of Education,*[25] the New York Court of Appeals found that although Daniel Hoffman had been misidentified as mentally retarded and had wrongfully been placed in a class of children who were mentally retarded when he was not retarded, because of judicial deference to educational decision makers, the lower court award of $750,000 in damages was dismissed. In that same vein, a later decision in New York rejected a special education malpractice case for misidentification in *Torres v. Little Flower Children's Services,*[26] although a court in that state had only one year earlier upheld a $1.5 million damage award involving a physician who had improperly relied on an IQ test in recommending a child's placement in an institution.[27]

Since the IDEA was passed, courts have generally rejected special education malpractice involving misconduct in identification, placement, and programming. But in recent years, there seems to be occasional willingness to bring such cases, and at least some courts are beginning to find liability for misconduct in identification, placement, and programming types of issues. Not surprisingly, a New York ruling in *DeRosa v. City of New York*[28] held that there is no cause of action based on an educational malpractice theory for alleged negligent placement of a child who was deaf in a class for students who were mentally retarded. And in Pennsylvania, a similar result was reached in a case involving the improper placement of a student with a learning disability in a class of students who were mentally retarded.[29]

Interestingly, a court in New York has recognized educational malpractice as a basis for recovery, when a school district with knowledge that a student had psychological problems that could worsen if left untreated did not notify the student's mother.[30] Another court in New York, this time a federal court using the IDEA as the theoretical basis for the case, found that the City of New York was not in compliance with the IDEA for failing to evaluate and place children in a timely manner.[31]

While not proof of judicial attitude, a case in Connecticut was settled for $2,000 in damages plus $2,500 in attorneys' fees when the school failed to implement (through administrative errors) a program that had been agreed upon for a student with a disability.[32] This payment of damages is particularly significant because the parents had incurred no out-of-pocket expenses and the child had not suffered egregiously, and the situation was remedied. The payment was deemed to be one that would prompt more diligence by the school.

Probably the most well-known early case involving a claim of misconduct in identification and placement is the case of Karen Morse.[33] Although she had been diagnosed as being learning disabled, she was not provided with appropriate educational programming for two or three years. Although the school agreed to provide compensatory education for one year, she had to seek judicial intervention to obtain further relief. In early 1987, the New Hampshire Department of Education ordered the school to pay for an additional year of education, which amounted to $17,000 to reimburse additional remedial education after she had graduated from high school. Litigation may increase regarding appropriate methodology for certain situations, such as for children who are learning disabled or deaf. In cases where the appropriate methodology is far from settled, it is likely that courts will defer to reasonable judgment of the educational agency, as they did in *Rowley.*

General Trends

There are still too few cases to draw any sweeping conclusions about the future of cases involving special education misconduct. There does seem to be, however, at least some judicial willingness to consider such cases. And there is certainly an increased tendency for parents to litigate in cases where they believe the school has acted inappropriately.

Some of the courts have addressed school misconduct under IDEA or Section 1983 theories, and these cases have not been brought using malpractice theories. Other cases, however, have resulted in findings of liability and damage awards, where the case theory has been in terms of common law malpractice or at least tort language rather than statutory language.

A judicial willingness to recognize a duty toward children with disabilities in public schools and not to give total deference to educational decision makers and away from a general reluctance to order damages against public schools as a policy matter seems to at least occur occasionally. For example, in *Ortega v. Bibb County School District,*[34] the court indicated that there might be liability if the parents could prove intentional discrimination when a child died from asphyxiation at a pre-kindergarten facility. It may be that where an injury has resulted from serious misconduct, the courts will order the injury to be remedied. Perhaps courts will not order compensation for pain and suffering, lost potential earnings, or punitive damages, but they will at least remediate out-of-pocket expenses already incurred or provide for the cost of compensatory education.

Schools should take seriously the IDEA requirement that educational agencies implement a comprehensive system of personnel development. The specter of accountability is an important incentive to schools to ensure that their personnel are adequately trained and their procedures and practices are appropriate for the challenges and obligations imposed on the public school system by the mainstreaming mandate of the IDEA. State certification requirements, local hiring practices, and colleges of education should take account of this issue in ensuring that the regular classroom teacher, not just the special educator, is trained to recognize disabilities, to practice behavior management, and to meet legal requirements.

The following two judicial decision excerpts illustrate some of the difficulties involving special education malpractice theories. The first case involves two students who are deaf and is quite unusual in its result. The dissenting opinion raises some of the concerns about finding liability in this set of circumstances. The case is also unusual in its reliance on state nondiscrimination law as the basis for liability rather than relying on special education statutes directly. The *Greider* case demonstrates the more likely outcome in terms of using the tort theory in the context of a special education student.

BOARD OF EDUCATION V. HUMAN RIGHTS COMMISSION

385 S.E.2d 637 (W.Va. 1989)

In November, 1977, Paul Devericks, Sr. enrolled his five children in the public schools of Lewis County. Two of his children, Paul, Jr. and Barbara, were hearing-impaired. They were enrolled at Weston Central Elementary School. Paul, Jr., age 12 at the time, is profoundly deaf, and communicates only by "home-made" gestures without syntax. Barbara, age 10 at the time, is able to communicate orally. There were no other hearing-impaired children in the Lewis County school system, and it did not have an adequate program for deaf and hearing-impaired children. Paul, Jr. and Barbara were taught in a separate class for two hours a day by a speech therapist, until they could be enrolled in the Romney School for the Deaf and Blind. When they were not being privately taught by the speech therapist, they were placed in a regular classroom.

During the summer of 1978, Paul, Jr. was committed to Weston State Hospital. Paul, Jr. and Barbara enrolled in the Romney School for the Deaf and Blind in August, 1978. In September, 1978, Paul, Jr. was expelled from Romney due to behavioral problems.

The Devericks family moved to Upshur County in April, 1979, where Paul, Jr. became embroiled with legal authorities. Paul, Jr. was referred by the circuit court, utilizing juvenile jurisdiction, to the Brown School, an institution in Austin, Texas, that was capable of dealing with handicapped children who have behavioral problems. Barbara was placed in another school in Texas. Paul, Jr. was withdrawn from the Brown School because his father objected to the method of treatment utilized for him.

The Devericks returned to Lewis County in March, 1981, and the two children were again enrolled in Lewis County schools. At this point, Paul, Jr. was 16 years old and Barbara was 14 years old. It was apparent to school personnel that the two children had problems other than only their hearing impairments. In addition to Paul, Jr.'s behavioral problems, both Paul, Jr. and Barbara were at a first or second grade level in academic terms. Moreover, neither child could use or understand the "American sign," which is the standard sign language of the deaf that is generally accepted in the United States. As a result of this, their communication abilities were severely limited.

Although counseling and language therapy were provided for the two children for a half-day, two to three days per week, it became apparent that the Lewis County schools did not have the resources to provide an appropriate education for the Devericks children. The Board determined that a deaf educator was not the children's primary need. Rather, it determined that they needed placement in an institution to compensate for their deficiencies in sign language as well as development. Consequently, the Board sought to place Paul, Jr. and Barbara in such an institutional setting for the 1981–82 school year. Their father, however, refused to give permission to such a placement.

In November, 1981, Paul Devericks, Sr. filed a complaint with the West Virginia Human Rights Commission, against the Board, alleging discrimination on the basis of handicap, and asserting that his children had been deprived of an appropriate education.

Pending a decision for permanent placement, Paul, Jr. and Barbara were placed in the "Alternative Learning Center," which was a program for students who are not successful in a traditional classroom environment. This program included individual tutoring, but it also "mainstreamed" the children with other students for group activities, such as physical education.

Paul, Jr. began having behavioral problems in the Alternative Learning Center. On one occasion, he threw a chair at another student and broke a window. He was removed from the Alternative Learning Center due to safety concerns for other children. A teacher was provided to educate Paul, Jr. at home. Attendance problems arose with both Paul, Jr. and Barbara, eventually becoming a total cessation of attending school. However, no formal withdrawal from school was made. From April, 1982, to September, 1985, no educational services were provided for the Devericks children by the Board.

In the fall of 1985, as part of a negotiated agreement, Paul, Jr. and Barbara were enrolled again in the Lewis County schools. An "individual educational plan" was developed for the two children, including the services of a deaf educator. Both children were making progress at the time of the hearing before the Commission.

The Commission adopted the hearing examiner's recommended decision that the Board violated the West Virginia Human Rights Act. The Commission determined that by failing to provide the Devericks children with an appropriate education as determined by procedures which adequately considered the least restrictive environment, the Board engaged in discrimination.

The hearing examiner concluded that no monetary damages should be awarded in this case. The Commission, however, ordered that Paul, Sr., Paul, Jr., and Barbara Devericks were entitled to incidental damages in the amount of $5,000 each, and ordered that the children be provided an appropriate compensatory education until they reach the age of 24. The compensatory education is to be provided pursuant to individual education plans prepared each year, which insure placement in accordance with least restrictive environment provisions of state and federal regulations.

The Board filed a petition for an administrative appeal in the Circuit Court of Lewis County. The circuit court reversed and vacated the Commission's order.

The basic issue in this case is whether the educational program offered the Devericks children by the Board discriminated against them on the basis of their handicap.

The Board offered an educational plan which included placing the Devericks children in an institutional setting outside of Lewis County. Their father, however, objected to this, and expressed his desire to keep the children at home and trained in Lewis County.

Our review of the record in this case reveals that the Commission's decision merely ordered the Board to follow its duty as prescribed by *W.Va. Code,* 18–20–1 [1983].

(Continued)

(Continued)

In accordance with the following provisions, county boards of education throughout the State shall establish and maintain for all exceptional children between five and twenty-three years of age special educational programs, including, but not limited to, special schools, classes, regular classroom programs, home-teaching or visiting teacher services for any type or classification as the state board of education shall approve. Provisions shall be made for educating exceptional children (including the handicapped and the gifted) who differ from the average or normal in physical, mental or emotional characteristics, or in communicative or intellectual deviation characteristics, or in both communicative and intellectual deviation characteristics, to the extent that they cannot be educated safely or profitably in the regular classes of the public schools or to the extent that they need special educational provisions within the regular classroom in order to educate them in accordance with their capacities, limitations and needs. In addition, county boards of education may establish and maintain other educational services for exceptional children as the state superintendent of schools may approve.

This statute imposes upon the Board a duty to establish and maintain an educational program that provides handicap[ped] children with an appropriate education. The Commission utilized this statutory provision as well as the Federal Education of the Handicapped Act (EHA) to determine whether the education offered to the Devericks children satisfied the requirements pertaining to the education of handicapped students.

The Federal EHA is codified in 20 U.S.C. §§ 1400 to 1461 [Now §§ 1400–1487], as amended. It promotes the education of handicapped children in a "least restrictive environment."

The Commission concluded that the EHA is relevant to this case. Although the EHA expressly applies to children between the ages of three and twenty-one, the implementing state regulations to *W.Va. Code,* 18–20–1 [1983] follow the EHA in every respect applicable to this case. *W.Va. Code,* 18–20–1 [1983] provides for the education of the handicapped up to the age of twenty-four.

It is the Board's contention that a residential placement would be the better alternative for the Devericks children. The United States Supreme Court has held that, for purposes of the EHA, a "free appropriate public education" is achieved "by providing personalized instruction with sufficient support services to permit the child to benefit educationally from that instruction." *Board of Education v. Rowley,* 458 U.S. 176 (1982). Based upon that ruling of the United States Supreme Court, we believe the Commission properly extended the logic of *Rowley* to the applicable state statute and regulations.

Although the implementing regulations for *W.Va. Code,* 18–20–1 [1983] and federal law permit out-of-state and residential placements, they also require that the "least restrictive environment" plan be pursued to the maximum extent appropriate. The Commission concluded that the Board failed to consider the "least restrictive environment" placement provisions for the Devericks children, by offering to send them out of Lewis County to receive appropriate educational training and offering counseling and language therapy for a half-day, two to three days per week.

Furthermore, the Commission concluded that the procedural rights of the Devericks were not adequately protected, and that although Paul Devericks, Sr. may not have been cooperative, his lack of cooperation dealt with the Board's plan to send his children to schools outside of Lewis County. Thus, the Commission concluded that the Board did not provide an appropriate education for the Devericks children pursuant to its duty to do so under *W.Va. Code,* 18–20–1 [1983].

Hearing-impaired children, between five and twenty-three years of age, are handicapped for purposes of *W.Va. Code,* 18–20–1, as amended. Therefore, when a county board of education fails to provide an appropriate education for a hearing-impaired child between five and twenty-three years of age, such failure constitutes unlawful discrimination based upon handicap and is violative of *W.Va. Code,* 5–11–9(f), as amended.

Accordingly, Barbara Devericks is now entitled to an appropriate education until she reaches the age of twenty-four years [under state law], which insure[s] placement in accordance with least restrictive environment provisions and in accordance with an individualized education program. The circuit court merely focused on the Board's efforts during the spring of 1981, when it provided the Devericks children with counseling and language therapy for a half-day, two to three days per week, while attempting to place them in programs outside of Lewis County. Consequently, the circuit court concluded that the Board made good faith efforts to provide the Devericks children with an appropriate education. This focus was too narrow.

We now address the question of incidental damages. The Commission ordered that Paul, Sr., Paul, Jr., and Barbara Devericks were entitled to incidental damages in the amount of $5,000 each. Testimony presented at the Commission's hearing indicated that the Devericks children suffered emotional distress as a result of their frustrated attempts to obtain an education. There was also testimony presented that Paul Devericks, Sr. suffered emotional and physical pain as a result of his children's plight. The hearing examiner found that Paul Devericks, Sr. did not prove that he had been discriminated against in violation of the West Virginia Human Rights Act and concluded that no monetary damages would compensate the Devericks children for the loss of an education. The Commission adopted the examiner's findings and conclusions except the examiner's conclusion that monetary damages were not appropriate. The Commission awarded the incidental damages to which we have alluded. However, the Commission also adopted the examiner's finding that Paul Devericks, Sr. was not discriminated against in violation of the West Virginia Human Rights Act.

Our review of the record in this case indicates that Paul Devericks, Sr. was not a victim of discrimination who is entitled to incidental damages. Rather, his procedural rights were not adequately protected by the actions of the Board. Therefore, the $5,000 incidental damages awarded to Paul Devericks, Sr. was not proper, and the circuit court did not err by reversing the Commission's order in this regard. See *W.Va. Code,* 5–11–10 [1971, 1987], empowering the Commission to issue remedial orders against persons found to have "engaged in . . . any unlawful discriminatory practice[.]" Because the Board did not violate the Act with respect to Paul Devericks, Sr., it is inappropriate to order a remedy for him.

(Continued)

(Continued)

With respect to Paul, Jr., and Barbara Devericks, an award of incidental damages is appropriate. However, the $5,000 award is excessive. In *Bishop Coal Co. v. Salyers,* 380 S.E.2d 238 (W.Va. 1989), we held that the West Virginia Human Rights Commission is authorized to award up to $2,500 in monetary damages for anything other than lost wages.

Accordingly, Paul, Jr. and Barbara Devericks are each entitled to $2,500, based upon the evidence presented at the Commission's hearing that they suffered emotional distress as a result of the board's violation of the West Virginia Human Rights Act.

Neely, Justice, dissenting:

This decision sets a terrible precedent. It values the irresponsible demands of parents above the clear interest of their handicapped children. It requires exorbitant expenditures by local school boards in rural counties in what will ultimately amount to utterly futile efforts to offer an approximation of the education available at good, specialized schools for handicapped children. Under a majority's view, local school boards must divert money from conducting their usual classes—a task they do well—to setting up special local schools for a few handicapped children—a task they *cannot* do well.

The Romney School for the Deaf and Blind is an excellent school, with long experience in meeting the special needs of its students, and a long record of service to the deaf and blind children of this State. Romney School could not handle the children who are the subject of this proceeding because of their severe emotional handicaps. But this Court expects Lewis County to do so. By what logic? Commanding Lewis County to educate these children does not make it possible for Lewis County to do so. If the world could be made a better place simply by entering an order, the Russians would have achieved utopia long ago!

The majority has enshrined an unhealthy fetish for local schooling of handicapped children. In so doing it allows an accident of geography to trump the only legitimate end of these anti-discrimination statutes: the best education for handicapped children.

The majority misconstrues the federal statute's preference for the "least restrictive environment." When a handicap is severe enough that education "cannot be achieved satisfactorily" through regular classes, then it is appropriate to remove handicapped children from regular classes.

The cases break down into two basic patterns. First, the school system may seek to do slipshod in-house training, over the parents' insistence that the system pay to send the child to a specialized boarding school. The Courts tend to support the parents.

The other pattern occurs frequently. As in the case before us, the school system prefers to pay the bill to send a child to boarding school, instead of setting up an expensive inefficient in-house program for a few children. The courts often support the school system.

The bottom line of the decisions is that the best interest of the child carries the day.

Certainly there is a loss when children must be removed from regular classes and their home environment. But once that point is passed, the school board must not tarry in finding the best possible education *for the child.* It should not favor its own school system for the sake of either convenience or economy, when the local schools cannot do the job.

Having a handicapped child is a grievous misfortune for parents, but it is an even greater misfortune for the child. A child who is handicapped must be taught at an early age to compensate to the maximum possible extent. Learning to read Braille, learning Standard American Sign, learning to speak without the benefit of hearing, and learning other compensatory skills at an early age is the difference between a potentially successful life and a mere vegetable existence. Parents, however, must also bear a responsibility for their children; if parents are entirely reluctant to be separated from their children so that they can be educated in good schools, it is appropriate for the state to expect the parents to move to where such good schools are located. Ours is a world of finite resources—a consideration of which courts as well as legislatures and executives should be constantly mindful.

Where a school system is located in a large population center it may be possible to provide *high quality* compensatory education at the local level. But today's decision merely requires rural school boards to go through *the motions* of providing good education; without necessary economies of scale, it is not *possible* to duplicate in Lewis County the facilities of the Romney School or a good out-of-state school.

Because I refuse to believe that the statutes require a result so opposed to the best interests of handicapped children themselves, I must respectfully dissent.

The next case was also brought under state law and demonstrates the significant harm that can result in cases where educators are not adequately prepared. It does not, however, necessarily demonstrate the approach that other courts would take.

GREIDER V. SHAWNEE MISSION UNIFIED SCHOOL DISTRICT

710 F. Supp. 296 (D. Kan. 1989)

In the fall of 1985, plaintiff Alexander Greider ("Greider") was an eighth grader at Trail Ridge Junior High. He was enrolled in an industrial arts class taught by defendant, Mark Isenberg ("Isenberg") and was injured in that class while using a table saw. Greider had been classified by the defendant school district as a behaviorally disturbed child and therefore "handicapped" under the Education for All Handicapped Children Act of 1975 ("EHA").

One of the special education teachers at Trail Ridge Junior High determined that Greider should be enrolled in Isenberg's woodworking class. The special education instructor claims she notified Isenberg that Greider was a special education student, and further advised him of Greider's particular problems and needs. However, Isenberg does not recall receiving any such notice.

While in Isenberg's woodworking class, Greider severely injured his hand on a table saw. He now brings suit . . . contending the school district and Isenberg were negligent in several

(Continued)

(Continued)

regards. He contends that defendants failed to take reasonable steps to protect his safety. According to Greider, those failures included placing him in the class despite his behavioral disturbance, failing to properly notify Isenberg of his enrollment in the class and of his particular problems and needs, failing to properly instruct plaintiff on safety procedures while taking into consideration his behavioral disturbance, and failing to provide proper guards and warnings on the table saw. Further, Greider contends defendants were negligent in failing to properly supervise Greider's activities in the woodworking class.

In their motion for summary judgment, defendants argue that all actions of which plaintiff complains were discretionary in nature and that they are therefore entitled to immunity under the Kansas Tort Claims Act [KTCA].

The KTCA is applicable to school districts and their employees. *See* K.S.A. 75–6102(b), (c), (d). K.S.A. 75–6104 provides:

> A governmental entity or an employee acting within the scope of the employee's employment shall not be liable for damages resulting from . . . (e) any claim based upon the exercise or performance or the failure to exercise or perform a discretionary function or duty on the part of a governmental entity or employee, whether or not the discretion is abused and regardless of the level of discretion involved.

The Kansas Supreme Court most recently discussed the discretionary function exception to the KTCA in the case *Dougan v. Rossville Drainage Dist.*, 243 Kan. 315, 757 P.2d 272 (1988). The supreme court in that case stated the general doctrine that under the KTCA, "liability is the rule and immunity is the exception." No workable definition of "discretionary" is provided by the statute or the case law. However, the court's discussion of a line of Kansas cases dealing with the discretionary exception provides some guidance in this case.

Thus, in the present case, the school board is entitled to immunity only if its actions were not governed by any "readily ascertainable standard," or no legal duty to act in a certain manner existed. The burden is on the defendants to establish their entitlement to the exception. The Kansas Supreme Court has never addressed the question of whether public schools and teachers owe a duty to properly supervise students and to take reasonable steps to protect students' safety. However, it is likely that the court would recognize such a duty if the question were presented to it.

The court finds that the defendants here were under a legal duty to properly supervise Greider in the woodworking class and to take reasonable steps to protect his safety. Reasonable steps would at least include properly instructing him on safety procedures and providing proper guards and warning signs on the table saw on which he was injured. Such matters were not "discretionary" and the defendants are not entitled to immunity.

Defendants do contend that they are entitled to immunity concerning their decision to place Greider in the woodworking class and to notify defendant Isenberg of his presence there and his special needs and problems. 34 C.F.R. § 300, App. C(17)(c) requires that the child's "regular" teachers should be informed of the child's IEP. Since the district was under a legal duty to notify

Isenberg, the district would not be entitled to immunity if it failed in this duty. Finally, the court finds that in assigning Greider to the woodworking class, the school district had a duty to take into consideration Greider's safety. This of course would include determining whether Greider could safely operate the power tools in the class, despite his behavioral disorder. This is a minimal duty it would owe to any student, whether handicapped or not. Thus, the discretionary function exception does not apply in this instance, and defendants are not entitled to immunity under the KTCA. Accordingly, defendants' motion for summary judgment will be denied and plaintiff's motion for summary judgment on the issue of the applicability of the KTCA will be granted.

Defendants seek to exclude from trial any reference to plaintiff's handicapped status or the formulation or implementation of Greider's IEP. While the court acknowledges that this is not an action under the EHA, the jury must be allowed to consider all relevant factors the defendants should have properly considered to protect Greider's safety. A student's behavioral disorder could be relevant to this determination.

As was noted previously, these cases provide examples of approaches taken in some jurisdictions, but they do not illustrate how all jurisdictions would handle these issues.

Summary

The presence of students with disabilities in the public education system creates the potential for a number of types of misconduct, particularly where educational personnel have not been adequately prepared or trained to meet the needs of this population of students. Whether educational personnel or educational agencies should be held accountable for injuries that occur as a result of such misconduct is a difficult and complex issue.

As a general rule, courts have been disinclined to hold educators liable for money damages for violations of the IDEA. This judicial deference has in some situations prevented parents from recovering monetary damages of any type against educational personnel and agencies for claims involving infliction of emotional distress, violations of IDEA requirements, or misconduct in identification, evaluation, placement, and programming. Students may be able to recover damages under state law tort claims for injuries directly caused by school personnel (such as physical injuries that occurred during a restraint), but the results will depend on state law requirements including state immunity doctrines. In addition to the general tendency of courts not to hold educators liable for monetary damages, there are a number of other obstacles to such actions, particularly where damage awards are sought as a remedy. These obstacles include failure to find that the elements of negligence are present, rulings that there is no private action for damages under the IDEA, and the application of immunity doctrines in these cases.

In general, it is not likely that parents will be able to recover damages for misconduct toward their children with disabilities under the IDEA. There is some judicial law, however, that has recognized that educators should be held accountable for their misconduct, particularly when the conduct has been in bad faith or is especially egregious.

Questions for Reflection

1. In which of the following instances would the IDEA address the problem, and in which would a tort action of some type be more appropriate? In examining these situations, which individual within the school system should be held accountable and why?

    a. Kim is 6 and has a learning disability that prevents her from processing verbal instructions. She is a first grader, placed in the regular classroom for most of the day. She and her classmates have been told not to play near the swings. Kim walks in front of a swing during recess on the first day, is knocked down, and breaks her arm.

    b. Zack is autistic, and his parents want to have him placed in a full-day, rather than a half-day, kindergarten program. When the IEP meeting fails to result in agreement, his parents request a due process hearing, the request being made on June 30. The school does not hold the hearing until September, and does not render a decision until November.

    c. Mark (age 10) has a behavior disorder requiring psychological counseling. He is in the regular classroom for most of the day, but frequently runs out of the classroom. The teacher deals with this by tying Mark into his seat. His parents find out about this after it has gone on for six months.

    d. Diane is a third grader with Down's syndrome. She is educably mentally retarded and has been placed in the regular classroom for most of the day during kindergarten, first grade, and second grade. She has made excellent progress in learning academic skills such as counting and reading. Diane's IEP indicates that she is to continue learning these skills in the regular classroom. Mrs. Green, the third-grade teacher, is 57 and attends the IEP conference. Although Mrs. Green says nothing at the conference, she is philosophically opposed to mainstreaming children who are mentally retarded. She thinks the experience and demands are too frustrating and that the best thing for them is to "just love them" so they'll be happy. Once Diane arrives in the classroom, Mrs. Green places her at a table and gives her coloring and simple puzzles to do for most of the time each day. At the end of the year, Diane's progress review indicates that she has lost most of the skills she had gained before beginning third grade. What if the principal becomes aware of Mrs. Green's conduct?

2. How can educational institutions best avoid liability by ensuring that their personnel are adequately trained?

3. What can regular education teachers who are concerned that they have not been adequately prepared for children with disabilities in the classroom do to protect themselves from liability?

4. Would it be good policy to allow parents to collect tort damages against school systems, whose resources are already stretched, when the result will be that all other children will be "penalized" by educational dollars going to pay damage awards?

5. How do administrators respond when cost is a significant factor in providing a mandated service or program?

NOTES

1. For an in-depth analysis of this issue, see Laura Rothstein, "Accountability for Professional Misconduct in Providing Education to Handicapped Children," 14 *J. L. & Educ.* 349 (1985); Laura Rothstein, "Special Education Malpractice," 43 *Educ. L. Rep.* 1249 (1988). See also Laura Rothstein & Julia Rothstein, *Disabilities and the Law* § 2:57 (Thomson West 2006).

2. See generally Kathleen Conn, "The Evolution of K–12 Educational Malpractice Claims: Will the 'Reading First' Scandals Influence Statutory Causes of Action Under NCLB and IDEIA?" 221 *Educ. Law Rep.* 21 (2007); John Elson, "A Common Law Remedy for the Educational Harms Caused by Incompetent or Careless Teaching," 73 *Nw. U. L. Rev.* 641 (1978).

3. See, e.g., *Torres v. Little Flower Children's Services,* 61 N.Y.2d 119, 474 N.E.2d 223, 485 N.Y.S.2d 15 (1984), *cert. denied,* 106 S. Ct. 181 (1985) (misclassification of child).

4. *Hoffman v. Board of Education,* 49 N.Y.2d 121, 400 N.E. 2d 317, 424 N.Y.S.2d 376 (1975).

5. See W. Page Keeton, *Prosser and Keeton on Torts* (5th ed.) § 30 (West 1984).

6. See Chapter 15.

7. 471 U.S. 359 (1985). See Chapter 21.

8. *Miener v. Missouri,* 673 F.2d 969 (8th Cir.), *cert. denied,* 459 U.S. 909 (1982).

9. *Manecke v. School Board,* 762 F.2d 912 (11th Cir. 1985). See also *Disabilities and the Law* § 2:48 for a breakdown of circuit court opinions on this issue.

10. *Anderson v. Thompson,* 658 F.2d 1205 (7th Cir. 1981). The Supreme Court in *Smith v. Robinson,* 468 U.S. 992 (1984), noted the various lower court opinions on damages, but did not indicate whether any of those standards were correct.

11. *Alexopulos v. San Francisco Unified School District,* 817 F.2d 551 (9th Cir. 1987). See also *Disabilities and the Law* § 2:50.

12. 471 So.2d 560 (Fla. App. 4th 1986).

13. 706 S.W.2d 325 (1986), *aff'd,* 722 S.W.2d 471 (Tex. 1987).

14. 490 So.2d 691 (La. App. 1986).

15. 663 F. Supp. 1108 (W.D. Pa. 1986).

16. 506 So.2d 888 (La. App. 1987).

17. 104 A.D.2d 978, 480 N.Y.S.2d 901 (N.Y. 1984).

18. 151 Ill. App. 3d 787, 502 N.E.2d 1076 (1986).

19. 172 Ga. App. 428, 323 S.E.2d 231 (1984).

20. 637 F. Supp. 1138 (E.D. Mo. 1986).

21. 817 F.2d 315 (5th Cir. 1987).

22. See Chapter 3 for an excerpt.

23. 657 F. Supp. 56 (S.D. Ind. 1986).

24. 817 F.2d 303 (5th Cir. 1987). See also *Juneau v. Louisiana Board of Elementary & Secondary Education,* 506 So.2d 756 (La. 1987), where the court held a school nurse could be dismissed for unauthorized use of aversive stimuli on students with disabilities. See also Scott F. Johnson, *Preventing Physical Restraints in Schools* (Education Law Resource Center 2006).

25. 49 N.Y.2d 121, 400 N.E.2d 317, 424 N.Y.S.2d 376 (1979).

26. 64 N.Y.2d 119, 47 N.E.2d 223, 485 N.Y.S.2d 15 (1984), *cert. denied,* 474 U.S. 864 (1985).

27. *Snow v. State,* 98 A.D.2d 442, 469 N.Y.S.2d 959 (1983) (physician improperly relied on IQ test).

28. 517 N.Y.S.2d 754 (App. Div. 1987).

29. *Agostine v. School District of Philadelphia,* 527 A.2d 193 (Pa. Commwlth. 1987).

30. *Savino v. Board of Education,* 123 A.D.2d 315, 506 N.Y.S.2d 210 (1986).

31. *P. v. Ambach,* C.A. No. 79 C 270 (E.D.N.Y. 1986).

32. *P. v. New Haven Board of Education,* C.A. No. N84-64 (D. Conn., filed Feb. 6, 1984).

33. Reported by the news media, see http://query.nytimes.com/gst/fullpage.html?sec=health&res=9A0DE6DC1638F934A15753C1A960948260 and http://query.nytimes.com/gst/fullpage.html?res=9B0DEED8143DF936A25750C0A961948260 (last accessed August 11, 2008).

34. 431 F. Supp. 2d 1296 (M.D. Ga. 2006).

21

Remedies

As noted in earlier chapters, very detailed procedures protect the interests of students entitled to services under the Individuals with Disabilities Education Act (IDEA). While there are a number of deadlines set for complying with the procedures, the process can be a long one, particularly if the final administrative decision is appealed to court. The dilemma for parents in such cases is where to place the child pending the decision. Unlike employment cases, where compensation (in the form of back wages, reinstatement, and the like) can be provided for a wrongful employment decision, the development of a child cannot be put on hold and compensated for adequately at a later time. This is particularly true for younger children.

Damages

While monetary damages are available for actions under Section 504 of the Rehabilitation Act, the Americans with Disabilities Act (ADA), and Section 1983 of the Civil Rights Act in some circumstances, most actions involving students and special education will be brought under the IDEA. The courts have been inconsistent in their recognition of the availability of damages under the IDEA. As a policy matter, courts have often been reluctant to award damages under the IDEA, as the previous chapter noted. Some courts have recognized the availability of damages as a remedy under the IDEA, but no court has yet awarded damages directly under the IDEA.[1] Of those courts that have recognized the potential for damages, some have limited damages to exceptional circumstances such as danger to the child, bad faith, or failure to comply with clear requirements under the IDEA. Other courts do not allow damages under the IDEA at all, nor under Section 1983 for claims that could be brought under the IDEA.

Claims for relief other than monetary damages are more common under the IDEA and they often include requests that a hearing officer or court order the school to do something, or not do something regarding a student. This could include an order that the school evaluate the student, or find the student eligible for services, or find that the individualized education program (IEP) or placement that the school offered or provided the student does not provide free appropriate public education (FAPE). One common remedy when the school does not provide the student with FAPE is called compensatory education, where a court or hearing officer orders the school to provide additional services to make up for not providing appropriate programming in the past. Another common claim under the IDEA for not providing FAPE is tuition reimbursement at a private special education school.

Tuition Reimbursement

As noted in prior chapters, the "stay-put" or pendency provisions of the IDEA generally require the child to remain in the current placement pending a final decision in the dispute resolution process. This can be problematic when the parents are concerned that the current placement is inappropriate or may even create a serious risk for the child. As a result, some parents attempt a "unilateral placement," which is where the parents place the child in a private special education school on their own, pay for it on their own, and then request reimbursement from the school district for the tuition and related expenses. This remedy is now a specific part of the law, whereas in earlier versions of the IDEA it was not; and it was not until *Burlington School Committee v. Department of Education* was decided by the Supreme Court that it was determined whether parents could be reimbursed for these "self-help" placements. The *Burlington* case answered the major question about reimbursement but left a number of questions unanswered.

BURLINGTON SCHOOL COMMITTEE V. DEPARTMENT OF EDUCATION

471 U.S. 359 (1985)

Justice Rehnquist delivered the opinion of the Court.

The Education of the Handicapped Act requires participating state and local educational agencies "to assure that handicapped children and their parents or guardians are guaranteed procedural safeguards with respect to the provision of free appropriate public education" to such handicapped children. These procedures include the right of the parents to participate in the development of an "individualized education program" (IEP) for the child and to challenge in administrative and court proceedings a proposed IEP with which they disagree. Where as in the present case review of a contested IEP takes years to run its course—years critical to the child's development—important practical questions arise concerning interim placement of the child and financial responsibility for that placement. This case requires us to address some of those questions.

Michael Panico, the son of respondent Robert Panico, was a first grader in the public school system of petitioner Town of Burlington, Massachusetts, when he began experiencing serious difficulties in school. It later became evident that he had "specific learning disabilities" and thus was "handicapped" within the meaning of the Act. This entitled him to receive at public expense specially designed instruction to meet his unique needs, as well as related transportation. The negotiations and other proceedings between the Town and the Panicos, thus far spanning more than 8 years, are too involved to relate in full detail; the following are the parts relevant to the issues on which we granted certiorari.

In the spring of 1979, Michael attended the third grade of the Memorial School, a public school in Burlington, Mass., under an IEP calling for individual tutoring by a reading specialist for one hour a day and individual and group counseling. Michael's continued poor performance and the fact that Memorial School encompassed only grades K through 3 led to much discussion between his parents and Town school officials about his difficulties and his future schooling. Apparently the course of these discussions did not run smoothly; the upshot was that the Panicos and the Town agreed that Michael was generally of above average to superior intelligence, but had special educational needs calling for a placement in a school other than Memorial. They disagreed over the source and exact nature of Michael's learning difficulties, the Town believing the source to be emotional and the parents believing it to be neurological.

In late June, the Town presented the Panicos with a proposed IEP for Michael for the 1979–1980 academic year. It called for placing Michael in a highly structured class of six children with special academic and social needs, located at another Town public school, the Pine Glen School. On July 3, Michael's father rejected the proposed IEP and sought review by respondent Massachusetts Department of Education's Bureau of Special Education Appeals [BSEA]. A hearing was initially scheduled for August 8, but was apparently postponed in favor of a mediation session on August 17. The mediation efforts proved unsuccessful.

Meanwhile the Panicos received the results of the latest expert evaluation of Michael by specialists at Massachusetts General Hospital, who opined that Michael's "emotional difficulties are secondary to a rather severe learning disorder characterized by perceptual difficulties" and recommended "a highly specialized setting for children with learning handicaps . . . such as the Carroll School," a state approved private school for special education located in Lincoln. Believing that the Town's proposed placement of Michael at the Pine Glen School was inappropriate in light of Michael's needs, Mr. Panico enrolled Michael in the Carroll School in mid-August at his own expense, and Michael started there in September.

The BSEA held several hearings during the fall of 1979, and in January 1980 the hearing officer decided that the Town's proposed placement at the Pine Glen School was inappropriate and that the Carroll School was "the least restrictive adequate program within the record" for Michael's educational needs. The hearing officer ordered the Town to pay for Michael's tuition and transportation to the Carroll School for the 1979–1980 school year, including reimbursing the Panicos for their expenditures on these items for the school year to date.

The Town sought judicial review of the State's administrative decision in the United States District Court for the District of Massachusetts naming Mr. Panico and the State Department of Education as defendants. In November 1980, the District Court granted summary judgment against the Town. The Court of Appeals vacated the judgment.

In the meantime, the Town had refused to comply with the BSEA order, the District Court had denied a stay of that order, and the Panicos and the State had moved for preliminary injunctive

(Continued)

(Continued)

relief. The State also had threatened outside of the judicial proceedings to freeze all of the Town's special education assistance unless it complied with the BSEA order. Apparently in response to this threat, the Town agreed in February 1981 to pay for Michael's Carroll School placement and related transportation for the 1980–1981 term, none of which had yet been paid, and to continue paying for these expenses until the case was decided. But the Town persisted in refusing to reimburse Mr. Panico for the expenses of the 1979–1980 school year. When the Court of Appeals disposed of the state claim, it also held that under this status quo none of the parties could show irreparable injury and thus none was entitled to a preliminary injunction. The court reasoned that the Town had not shown that Mr. Panico would not be able to repay the tuition and related costs borne by the Town if he ultimately lost on the merits, and Mr. Panico had not shown that he would be irreparably harmed if not reimbursed immediately for past payments which might ultimately be determined to be the Town's responsibility.

On remand, the District Court entered an extensive pretrial order on the Town's federal claim. In denying the Town summary judgment, it ruled that 20 U.S.C. sec. 1415(e)(3) [Now § 1415(j)] did not bar reimbursement despite the Town's insistence that the Panicos violated that provision by changing Michael's placement to the Carroll School during the pendency of the administrative proceedings. The court reasoned that sec. 1415(e)(3) concerned the physical placement of the child and not the right to tuition reimbursement or to procedural review of a contested IEP. The court also dealt with the problem that no IEP had been developed for the 1980–1981 or 1981–1982 school years. It held that its power under sec. 1414(e)(2) [Now § 1415(i)(2)(B)] to grant "appropriate" relief upon reviewing the contested IEP for the 1979–1980 school year included the power to grant relief for subsequent school years despite the lack of IEPs for those years. In this connection, however, the court interpreted the statute to place the burden of proof on the Town to upset the BSEA decision that the IEP was inappropriate for 1979–1980 and on the Panicos and the State to show that the relief for subsequent terms was appropriate.

After a 4-day trial, the District Court in August 1982 overturned the BSEA decision, holding that the appropriate 1979–1980 placement of Michael was the one proposed by the Town in the IEP and that the parents had failed to show that this placement would not also have been appropriate for subsequent years. Accordingly, the court concluded that the Town was "not responsible for the cost of Michael's education at the Carroll School for the academic years 1979–80 through 1981–82."

In contesting the Town's proposed form of judgment embodying the court's conclusion, Mr. Panico argued that, despite finally losing on the merits of the IEP in August 1982, he would be reimbursed for his expenditures in 1979–1980, that the Town should finish paying for the recently completed 1981–1982 term, and that he should not be required to reimburse the Town for its payments to date, apparently because the school terms in question fell within the pendency of the administrative and judicial review contemplated by sec. 1415(e)(2) [Now § 1415(i)]. The case was transferred to another District Judge and consolidated with two other cases to resolve similar issues concerning the reimbursement for expenditures during the pendency of review proceedings. [Lower court proceedings omitted.] We granted certiorari, only to consider the following two issues: whether the potential relief available under sec. 1415(e)(2) includes reimbursement to parents for private school tuition and related expenses, and whether sec. 1415(e)(3) [Now § 1415(j)] bars such reimbursement to parents who reject a proposed IEP and place a child in a private school without the consent of local school authorities.

The *modus operandi* of the [Education for All Handicapped Children Act] is the "individualized educational program." The IEP is in brief a comprehensive statement of the educational needs of a handicapped child and the specially designed instruction and related services to be employed to meet those needs. The IEP is to be developed jointly by a school official qualified in special education, the child's teacher, the parents or guardian, and, where appropriate, the child. In several places, the Act emphasizes the participation of the parents in developing the child's educational program and assessing its effectiveness.

Apparently recognizing that this cooperative approach would not always produce a consensus between the school officials and the parents, and that in any disputes the school officials would have a natural advantage, Congress incorporated an elaborate set of what it labeled "procedural safeguards" to insure the full participation of the parents and proper resolution of substantive disagreements. . . .

The Act also provides for judicial review in state or federal court to "[a]ny party aggrieved by the findings and decision" made after the due process hearing. The Act confers on the reviewing court the following authority:

> [T]he court shall receive the records of the administrative proceedings, shall hear additional evidence at the request of a party, and, basing its decision on the preponderance of the evidence, shall grant such relief as the court determines is appropriate. Sec. 1415(e)(2) [Now § 1415(i)(2)(B)].

The first question on which we granted certiorari requires us to decide whether this grant of authority includes the power to order school authorities to reimburse parents for their expenditures on private special education for a child if the court ultimately determines that such placement, rather than a proposed IEP, is proper under the Act.

We conclude that the Act authorizes such reimbursement. The statute directs the court to "grant such relief as [it] determines is appropriate." The ordinary meaning of these words confers broad discretion on the court. The type of relief is not further specified, except that it must be "appropriate." Absent other reference, the only possible interpretation is that the relief is to be "appropriate" in the light of the purpose of the Act. As already noted, this is principally to provide handicapped children with "a free appropriate public education which emphasizes special education and related services designed to meet their unique needs." The Act contemplates that such education will be provided where possible in regular public schools, with the child participating as much as possible in the same activities as nonhandicapped children, but the Act also provides for placement in private schools at public expense where this is not possible. In a case where a court determines that a private placement desired by the parents was proper under the Act and that an IEP calling for placement in a public school was inappropriate, it

(Continued)

(Continued)

seems clear beyond cavil that "appropriate" relief would include a prospective injunction directing the school officials to develop and implement at public expense an IEP placing the child in a private school.

If the administrative and judicial review under the Act could be completed in a matter of weeks, rather than years, it would be difficult to imagine a case in which such prospective injunctive relief would not be sufficient. As this case so vividly demonstrates, however, the review process is ponderous. A final judicial decision on the merits of an IEP will in most instances come a year or more after the school term covered by that IEP has passed. In the meantime, the parents who disagree with the proposed IEP are faced with a choice: go along with the IEP to the detriment of their child if it turns out to be inappropriate or pay for what they consider to be the appropriate placement. If they choose the latter course, which conscientious parents who have adequate means and who are reasonably confident of their assessment normally would, it would be empty victory to have a court tell them several years later that they were right but that these expenditures could not in a proper case be reimbursed by the school officials. If that were the case the child's right to a *free* appropriate public education, the parents' right to participate fully in developing a proper *IEP*, and all of the procedural safeguards would be less than complete. Because Congress undoubtedly did not intend this result, we are confident that by empowering the court to grant "appropriate" relief Congress meant to include retroactive reimbursement to parents as an available remedy in a proper case.

In this Court, the Town repeatedly characterizes reimbursement as "damages" but that simply is not the case. Reimbursement merely requires the Town to belatedly pay expenses that it should have paid all along and would have borne in the first instance had it developed a proper IEP. Such a post-hoc determination of financial responsibility was contemplated in the legislative history. . . .

Regardless of the availability of reimbursement as a form of relief in a proper case, the Town maintains that the Panicos have waived any right they otherwise might have to reimbursement because they violated sec. 1415(e)(3) [Now § 1415(j)], which provides:

> During the pendency of any proceedings conducted pursuant to [sec. 1415], unless the State or local educational agency and the parents or guardian otherwise agree, the child shall remain in the then current educational placement of such child. . . .

We need not resolve the academic question of what Michael's "then current placement" was in the summer of 1979, when both the Town and the parents had agreed that a new school was in order. For the purposes of our decision, we assume that the Pine Glen School, proposed in the IEP, was Michael's current placement and, therefore, that the Panicos did "change" his placement after they had rejected the IEP and had set the administrative review in motion. In so doing, the Panicos contravened the conditional command of sec. 1415(e)(3) [Now § 1415(j)] that "the child shall remain in the then current educational placement."

As an initial matter, we note that the section calls for agreement by *either the State or the local educational agency.* The BSEA's decision in favor of the Panicos and the Carroll School placement would seem to constitute agreement by the State to the change of placement. The decision was issued in January 1980, so from then on the Panicos were no longer in violation of sec. 1415(e)(3) [Now § 1415(j)]. This conclusion, however, does not entirely resolve the instant dispute because the Panicos are also seeking reimbursement for Michael's expenses during the fall of 1979, prior to the State's concurrence in the Carroll School placement.

We do not agree with the Town that a parental violation of sec. 1414(e)(3) [Now § 1415(j)] constitutes a waiver of reimbursement. The provision says nothing about financial responsibility, waiver, or parental right to reimbursement at the conclusion of judicial proceedings. Moreover, if the provision is interpreted to cut off parental rights to reimbursement, the principal purpose of the Act will in many cases be defeated in the same way as if reimbursement were never available. As in this case, parents will often notice a child's learning difficulties while the child is in a regular public school program. If the school officials disagree with the need for special education or the adequacy of the public school's program to meet the child's needs, it is unlikely they will agree to an interim private school placement, while the review process runs its course. Thus, under the Town's reading of sec. 1415(e)(3) the parents are forced to leave the child in what may turn out to be an inappropriate educational placement or to obtain the appropriate placement only by sacrificing any claim for reimbursement. The Act was intended to give handicapped children both an appropriate education and a free one; it should not be interpreted to defeat one or the other of those objectives.

The legislative history supports this interpretation, favoring a proper interim placement pending the resolution of disagreements over the IEP. . . .

We think at least one purpose of sec. 1415(e)(3) was to prevent school officials from removing a child from the regular public school classroom over the parents' objection pending completion of the review proceedings. As we observed in *Rowley,* the impetus for the Act came from two federal court decisions, which arose from the efforts of parents of handicapped children to prevent the exclusion or expulsion of their children to private institutions or warehousing them in special classes. We also note that sec. 1415(e)(3) [Now § 1415(j)] is located in a section detailing procedural safeguards which are largely for the benefit of the parents and the child.

This is not to say that sec. 1415(e)(3) [Now § 1415(j)] has no effect on parents. While we doubt that this provision would authorize a court to order parents to leave their child in a particular placement, we think it operates in such a way that parents who unilaterally change their child's placement during the pendency of review proceedings, without the consent of state or local school officials, do so at their own financial risk. If the courts ultimately determine that the IEP proposed by the school officials was appropriate, the parents would be barred from obtaining reimbursement for any interim period in which their child's placement violated sec. 1415(e)(3) [Now § 1415(j)]. This conclusion is supported by the agency's interpretation of the Act's application to private placements by the parents:

(a) If a handicapped child has available a free appropriate public education and the parents choose to place the child in a private school or facility, the public agency is not required by this part to pay for the child's education at the private school or facility. . . .

(b) Disagreements between a parent and a public agency regarding the availability of a program appropriate for the child, and the question of financial responsibility, are subject to the due process procedures under [sec. 1415].

In cases decided subsequent to the *Burlington* decision, courts have reached a number of conclusions in a variety of factual settings in which the parents sought reimbursement.[2] In one case, the court held that the school need not reimburse transportation expenses when the parents had chosen to place the student in a private school setting.[3] A different decision resulted in a reimbursement for transportation and babysitting when the school refused to provide the services.[4] In one interesting decision, it was held that because the parents did not take advantage of ample opportunities to participate in the IEP, they could not be reimbursed for a unilateral placement.[5] And several courts have found that reimbursement for out-of-state placements is not required when the school has not been able to adequately assess the child.[6]

The conclusion that can be drawn from these cases is that while unilateral placement carries some risk, the pre-*Burlington* position taken by some courts—that a unilateral placement by a parent violates the "stay-put" requirement and is not subject to reimbursement—is no longer the case. The *Burlington* decision reaches a reasonable balance between the interests of the child and the concerns of the educational agency. Where the school has not provided an appropriate placement, parents may be reimbursed. As the problems at the end of the chapter illustrate, however, there are still some unanswered questions and some policy inequities.

One of those unanswered questions was whether parents could be reimbursed for placement in schools that had not been approved by the state educational agency. In *Florence County School District Four v. Carter,*[7] the United States Supreme Court held that they could, noting,

> This case presents the narrow question whether Shannon's parents are barred from reimbursement because the private school in which Shannon enrolled did not meet the § 1401(a)(18) [Now § 1401(9)] definition of a "free appropriate public education." We hold that they are not, because § 1401(a)(18)'s [Now § 1401(9)] requirements cannot be read as applying to parental placements.

Section 1401(a)(18)(A) [Now § 1401(8)(A)] requires that the education be "provided at public expense, under public supervision and direction." Similarly, § 1401(a)(18)(D) [Now § 1401(8)(D)] requires schools to provide an IEP, which must be designed by a "representative of the local educational agency," and must be "established," "revised," and "reviewed" by the agency. These requirements do not make sense in the context of a parental placement. In this case, as in all *Burlington* reimbursement cases, the parents' rejection of the school district's proposed IEP is the very reason for the parents' decision to put their child in a private school. In such cases, where the private placement has necessarily been made over the school district's objection, the private school education will not be under "public supervision and direction." Accordingly, to read the § 1401(a)(18) requirements as applying to parental placements would effectively eliminate the right of unilateral withdrawal recognized in *Burlington.* Moreover, the IDEA was intended to ensure that children with disabilities receive an education that is both appropriate and free. To read the provision of § 1401(a)(18) to bar reimbursement in the circumstances of this case would defeat this statutory purpose.

In 1997 and 2004, Congress amended the IDEA to include a number of provisions that address some of the issues left unresolved in *Burlington* and *Carter.* The statute now specifically recognizes reimbursement as a remedy when the school district did not make FAPE available to the child in a timely manner and the placement chosen by the parents is appropriate under the IDEA.[8] The amendments also provide some limitations on reimbursement if the parents do not meet certain requirements. For example, even the school's obligation to reimburse parents for the costs incurred in their placement may be reduced, or even denied, in cases where parents have not indicated at either the most recent IEP/placement meeting prior to the removal of the child, or at least 10 business days prior to removing the child from the public school, that they intend to place the child in a private placement. Parents are not entitled to reimbursement where they acted unreasonably in making the child unavailable for evaluation by the public school.[9]

One issue that has evolved under the reimbursement provisions of the IDEA is whether the student must first receive special education services from the public school before the parents can be eligible for reimbursement. The following is the district court opinion in a case involving this reimbursement issue. The opinion below was ultimately struck down by the Second Circuit Court of Appeals.[10] In 2007, the Supreme Court affirmed the circuit court's opinion, but did so by an equally divided court (Justice Kennedy did not participate), which means the decision is not binding outside of the Second Circuit.[11]

The facts in the case are important, and only the district court opinion provides the context for the decision. The following provides those facts. It is important to keep in mind that this court's decision was ultimately overruled.

BOARD OF EDUCATION V. TOM F.

2005 U.S. Dist. LEXIS 49 (S.D.N.Y. 2005)

OPINION BY: HON. GEORGE B. DANIELS

I. Background

Defendant's son, Gilbert F. ("student") has attended the Stephen Gaynor School ("Gaynor"), a private school, since kindergarten. On June 23, 1999, the Board of Education's Committee on Special Education ("CSE") conducted an annual review to determine the student's appropriate educational placement for the 1999–2000 school year. Seven people attended the CSE meeting, including an educational evaluator who signed the Individualized Education Program (IEP) as the special education teacher. The student's actual special education teacher from Gaynor was unavailable because she was in the hospital.

Following a review of several evaluations conducted by the CSE in preparation for the student's annual report, the CSE recommended that the student continue to be classified as learning disabled and that he be placed in a Modified Instructional Services-I ("MIS-I") program with a teacher ratio of 15:1. The CSE further recommended that the student receive speech/language therapy in a group twice per week and counseling in a group once per week.

(Continued)

(Continued)

The student's Final Notice of Recommendation was sent to Defendant on July 29, 1999, which placed the student at P.S. 871, a public school.

Nonetheless, Defendant continued the student's placement at Gaynor for the 1999–2000 school year and requested an impartial hearing to seek reimbursement for the cost of the student's tuition. On April 6, 2000, the Impartial Hearing Officer ("IHO") ordered the Board to reimburse Defendant for the cost of the student's tuition at Gaynor. The plaintiff, in turn, appealed to the State Education Department SRO, who affirmed the IHO's award of tuition reimbursement on grounds that the CSE was not validly constituted and, thus, resulted in an inappropriate placement.

Plaintiff now seeks to reverse the March 30, 2001 decision of the SRO [State Review Officer] granting Defendant tuition reimbursement on grounds that: (1) the IDEA precludes an award of tuition reimbursement in instances where a student has not previously received special education services from a public agency; and (2) in any event, the CSE was properly constituted.

II. Discussion

A. Standard of Review

"Federal courts assess IDEA petitions based on the 'preponderance of the evidence developed at the administrative proceedings and any further evidence presented by the parties.'" However, this assessment is not an "invitation to the courts to substitute their own notions of sound educational policy for those of the school authorities which they review." When reviewing whether a proposed IEP is appropriate, the district court must give "due weight" to the findings of a state administrative proceeding.

"[The Second Circuit] has acknowledged that '*Rowley* requires that federal courts defer to the final decision of state authorities.'" "Deference is owed to state and local agencies having expertise in the formulation of educational programs for the handicapped."

Nonetheless, as Defendant acknowledges here, the Second Circuit has differentiated between those matters where the court has been called upon to judge whether a child has been offered a free and appropriate education, and matters of statutory interpretation. The line of cases that calls for deference to administrative proceedings addresses only the former situation. In contrast, where the issue facing the court is one of statutory interpretation, the district court may review the matter de novo. Under the latter circumstances, "state administrative officials [are] in no better position than the district court to make conclusions."

Here, as in *Muller,* it is not the underlying facts that are in dispute, but rather the legal conclusions to be drawn from those facts. As a result, the concern that motivated the court in *Rowley,* of courts substituting their own notions of sound educational policy for those of school authorities, is not present. As the issues here are ones of statutory interpretation, the SRO's determinations are to be reviewed de novo.

B. Defendant's Eligibility for Tuition Reimbursement

The Board of Education argues that Defendant is barred from tuition reimbursement under the IDEA because his child did not previously receive special education under the authority of a public agency. Defendant argues that despite the plain language of the statute to the contrary, he should be permitted to receive tuition reimbursement because to hold otherwise would defeat the purpose of the IDEA.

In *School Committee of Burlington v. Department of Education,* the Supreme Court set forth the circumstances under which a parent who unilaterally enrolled a child in a private school could receive tuition reimbursement. The Court did not limit the remedy to parents of children who previously received special education in a public school. However, *Burlington* predated the amendments to the IDEA made in 1997.

The 1997 amendments to the IDEA provide, in pertinent part:

> If the parents of a child with a disability, who previously received special education and related services under the authority of a public agency, enroll the child in a private elementary or secondary school, without the consent of or referral by the public agency, a court or hearing officer may require the agency to reimburse the parents for the cost of that enrollment if the court or hearing officer finds that the agency had not made a free appropriate public education available to the child in a timely manner prior to that enrollment. [20 U.S.C. § 1412(a)(10)(C). This language is reiterated in the applicable federal regulation. 34 C.F.R. § 300.403(c).]

Interpretation of this provision is an issue of first-impression in this circuit. The clear implication of the plain language, however, is that where a child has *not* previously received special education from a public agency, there is no authority to reimburse the tuition expenses arising from a parent's unilateral placement of the child in private school.

The Court of Appeals for the First Circuit reached this conclusion in *Greenland School District v. Amy N.* 358 F.3d 150, 158–160 (2004). There, the parents of a child who had never received special education services in public school sought tuition reimbursement after having unilaterally removed the child from public school and placed her in private school. As in the instant case, the hearing officer ordered the school district to reimburse the child's tuition. However, in affirming the district court's reversal of the hearing officer's holding, the Court of Appeals concluded that the amended provision limits tuition reimbursement to children "who have previously received 'special education and related services' while in the public school system (or perhaps those who at least timely requested such services while the child is in public school)."

As neither threshold is satisfied here, the SRO's holding awarding tuition reimbursement to Defendant was erroneous.

Defendant advocates departure from the plain language of the statute on grounds that adhering to its literal interpretation would defeat the statute's very purpose. This contention is

(Continued)

(Continued)

without merit. "Only the most extraordinary showing of a contrary intention from the legislative history would justify interpretive departure from a statute's plain language." Here, however, evidence of congressional intent from the legislative history is *consistent* with the plain meaning of the text. The relevant House Report from the Committee on Education and the Workforce states:

> Section 612 [20 U.S.C. § 1412] also specifies that parents may be reimbursed for the cost of a private educational placement under certain conditions (i.e., when a due process hearing officer or judge determines that a public agency had not made a free appropriate public education available to the child, in a timely manner, prior to the parents enrolling the child in that placement without the public agency's consent). Previously, the child must have received special education and related services under the authority of a public agency.

As Plaintiff suggests, the provision ensures that a parent's rejection of a public school placement is not based on mere speculation as to whether the recommended public school placement would have been inappropriate. Therefore, it cannot be said that adherence to the plain language would defeat the purpose of the IDEA to provide every child with a disability a free and appropriate public education. See 20 U.S.C. § 1400(d)(1)(A).

Finally, Defendant relies on an opinion given by the Office of Special Education Programs ("OSEP") in response to the question of whether the 1997 Amendments to the IDEA preclude private school tuition reimbursement for children who had not previously received special education from a public agency. OSEP concluded that it did "not appear that [this] question . . . [was] answered by § 612(a)(10)(C) of IDEA '97."

"Deference to an OSEP policy letter may be appropriate where statutory language is ambiguous." However, "if the intent of Congress is clear," a court reviewing an agency's construction of a statute that it administers "must give effect to the unambiguously expressed intent of Congress." Here, where there is no ambiguity in the statutory language, deference to the OSEP letter would be inappropriate. Therefore, this Court reaches the same conclusion as to the meaning of 20 U.S.C. § 1412 (a)(10)(C) that the First Circuit reached in *Amy N.*

As the IDEA bars tuition reimbursement in the instant case, it is not necessary for the Court to address the issue of whether the educational evaluator properly served as the child's special education teacher such that the CSE was validly constituted.

III. Conclusion

For the reasons set forth above, Plaintiff's motion for summary judgment reversing the SRO's grant of tuition reimbursement to Defendant is granted, and Defendant's motion is denied. The Clerk is directed to close this case.

As the *Tom F.* district court decision notes, a First Circuit Court of Appeals decision ruled that a student had to previously receive services at the public school to be eligible for tuition reimbursement. As noted previously, the district court opinion in *Tom F.* was overturned by the Second Circuit Court of Appeals, which found that a student did not have to previously receive special education services in order to be eligible for reimbursement as a remedy under the statute.[12] This created a split among courts on the issue and the *Tom F.* case then went to the Supreme Court to try to resolve the different interpretations of the IDEA.

The Supreme Court affirmed the Second Circuit's decision without opinion in a tie vote (4 to 4), which means it left the *Tom F.* Court of Appeals decision in place in the Second Circuit. It did not, however, resolve the issue or provide any binding precedent outside of the Second Circuit (which includes the states of New York, Vermont, and Connecticut). Thus, the issue is still unresolved among the courts.

Compensatory Education

Where a student has been improperly educated in the past, one of the means of redressing the situation can be by providing compensatory education.[13] This remedy under the IDEA has been a topic of debate in a number of judicial decisions, with inconsistent results. The following is an example of a situation in which compensatory education would be ordered.

JEFFERSON COUNTY BOARD OF EDUCATION V. BREEN

853 F.2d 853 (11th Cir. 1988)

In November 1974, at age seven, Alice Breen sustained a closed head injury in an automobile accident near Mobile, Alabama. She emerged from the resulting coma with a multitude of physical and emotional problems such as impaired memory, attention, perception, and judgment. Since the accident she has engaged in impulsive behavior, self-mutilation, and suicide attempts.

Alice was placed in various public and private schools with marginal success. By the fall of 1979 she began experiencing severe psychiatric problems and had become violent. In September and December 1982 Alice was admitted to the Psychiatric Unit of University Hospital in Birmingham; the December admission was prompted by suicide attempts. From January until August 1983, Alice was under the care of Dr. Otto Eisenhardt at Hillcrest Hospital.

Alice was next treated at the Engel Day Treatment Center in Birmingham, Alabama. Apparently dissatisfied with the program at Engel, Mrs. Breen (Alice's mother) withdrew Alice in November 1983. In December 1983 and January 1984 Mrs. Breen contacted the Jefferson County Board of Education regarding an appropriate placement for Alice. The Board recommended that Alice be enrolled at Berry High School in Jefferson County and be provided a self-contained classroom with regular classes part-time.

(Continued)

(Continued)

Alice's stay at Berry was short-lived, however. She spent from April 9 to April 20, 1983 at Hillcrest Hospital recovering from a suicide attempt. She returned to Berry on April 27 but six days later overdosed on an over-the-counter drug and was admitted to Children's Hospital in Birmingham under the care of Dr. Thomas Vaughan. Alice was discharged on July 9, but readmitted two weeks later. Dr. Vaughan recommended that Alice be placed at the Ranch [Treatment Center in Austin, Texas] and on September 17, 1984 she was admitted there.

Over the next fifteen months Alice received therapeutic, educational, and related services seven days per week, twenty-four hours per day. Mrs. Breen's insurance paid for all but $9,715.26 of the costs.

Shortly after Alice enrolled in the Ranch Mrs. Breen met with the Jefferson County School Board to discuss an appropriate placement for Alice. Mrs. Breen rejected the Board's proposal that Alice be enrolled at Gilmore Bell High School because it did not provide services twenty-four hours per day, seven days per week.

At Mrs. Breen's request a hearing was held to determine whether the Jefferson County Board of Education was obligated to pay for Alice's care at the Ranch or whether by providing instate care the Board could satisfy its duty under the Act to provide an "appropriate education." The hearing officer upheld Mrs. Breen's decision to place Alice at the Ranch, concluding that a residential program was required. The hearing officer's decision was affirmed by a state administrative review officer. The review officer found that "[p]rior efforts to educate Alice in day programs were not successful." Further, "the entire group of services provided at the Ranch Treatment Center is of the type needed for Alice to be educated. The unseverability of Alice's needs met by such services is the reason for concluding that such services are an essential prerequisite for Alice's learning."

In late 1985, while the administrative proceedings were pending, Alice checked out of the Ranch and returned home. Her condition rapidly deteriorated and hospitalization was once again necessary. Alice spent most of the summer of 1986 in Brookwood Hospital and upon discharge became violent toward her mother. Over the next year Alice was frequently in and out of the psychiatric unit of University Hospital in Birmingham.

On September 8, 1986 the Board filed this lawsuit in the United States District Court for the Northern District of Alabama. The Board acknowledged that Alice required residential services, but argued that she should be placed at Bryce Hospital, a state mental hospital in Tuscaloosa, Alabama.

The district court disagreed and ordered the Board to pay Alice's $9,715.26 outstanding balance at the Ranch, to immediately place her at the Ranch, and to provide her with two years of compensatory education beyond her twenty-first birthday.

The district court placed great weight on the opinion of the Director of Neuropsychology at Bryce Hospital, Dr. Goff, who believed that Bryce did not have the facilities to adequately address Alice's problems. Dr. Goff reasoned that Alice's problems require a comprehensive treatment program combining behavioral intervention and cognitive remediation with an educational program.

The district court also considered the opinions of Dr. Julia Hannay, Professor and Director of Clinical Neuropsychology Training at the University of Houston and one of the founders of the Alabama Head Injury Foundation, and Dr. Tom Boll, Professor of psychology and the Director of the Comprehensive Head Injury Center at the University of Alabama in Birmingham. The common thread running through both opinions is that Bryce does not have the residential facilities needed to treat head injured patients such as Alice. Dr. Hannay believed that Bryce could provide a safe environment for Alice, but it could not treat her problems. Dr. Boll states that there were no facilities in the entire State of Alabama capable of providing Alice with the care she needs.

We have little difficulty deciding that the district court correctly ordered the Board to reimburse the Breens for their out-of-pocket expenses. Because the Ranch was ultimately determined to be the appropriate placement for Alice, "[r]eimbursement merely required the [Board] to belatedly pay expenses that it should have paid all along. . . ." [Citing *Burlington.*] Further, we agree with the district court that the equities weigh heavily in favor of full reimbursement.

The second issue is closely related to the first in that the district court ordered the two additional years in response to the Board's failure to provide an appropriate education prior to the court's order. Compensatory education, like retroactive reimbursement, is necessary to preserve a handicapped child's right to a free education. Without it, the child's right would depend upon his or her parent's ability to fund the education during the years of administrative proceedings and federal court litigation. Also, providing a compensatory education should serve as a deterrent against states unnecessarily prolonging litigation in order to decrease their potential liability. We believe that the district court correctly ordered the Board to provide Alice with two years' compensatory education.

One of the issues that is debated is whether compensatory education is in essence "damages" from which a state agency might be held to be immune in a particular jurisdiction. While this reasoning was adopted by the Ninth Circuit, it can be criticized in light of the *Burlington* case, in which the Court found that reimbursement should not be characterized as "damages" because these are expenses that should have been paid all along had a proper IEP been developed. This reasoning is applied in the *Breen* case, and most courts to consider the issue have not followed the Ninth Circuit's approach. Certainly compensatory education should be seen in the same light—these are expenses that are being borne to compensate for expenses that should have been paid in the first place. Whether this reasoning will ultimately be adopted by the Supreme Court remains to be seen. In those jurisdictions that do recognize damages as a possible remedy, bad faith can be a factor in making an award.

Attorneys' Fees

Are They Allowed?

The 1975 IDEA was silent as to whether attorneys' fees and costs incurred in the administrative due process and judicial proceedings of special education cases could be recovered by parents. Early cases did not really address whether there is an implied right to attorneys' fees and costs, because most cases were brought using a combination of Section 504 and Section 1983 claims. These statutes clearly provide that attorneys' fees may be recovered.[14] The same is true for actions under the Americans with Disabilities Act.[15]

Until *Smith v. Robinson,*[16] however, it was unclear whether one could use Section 504, Section 1983, and the IDEA in combination to obtain relief in special education cases. Ever since that 1984 decision, it is clear that unless the IDEA does not provide appropriate relief, Section 504 and Section 1983 (and now probably the Americans with Disabilities Act) are unavailable as avenues of redress. It thus became important to determine whether the IDEA provides for payment of attorneys' fees.

The Handicapped Children's Protection Act (HCPA) of 1986[17] was passed by Congress as an amendment to the IDEA. It provides for the award of reasonable attorneys' fees and costs to parents who are prevailing parties. What follows are the specific provisions of that amendment and the 1997 changes that have been incorporated.

20 U.S.C. § 1415(i)(3)

(B) Award of attorney's fees.

(i) In general. In any action or proceeding brought under this section, the court, in its discretion, may award reasonable attorneys' fees as part of the costs—

(I) to a prevailing party who is the parent of a child with a disability;

(II) to a prevailing party who is a State educational agency or local educational agency against the attorney of a parent who files a complaint or subsequent cause of action that is frivolous, unreasonable, or without foundation, or against the attorney of a parent who continued to litigate after the litigation clearly became frivolous, unreasonable, or without foundation; or

(III) to a prevailing State educational agency or local educational agency against the attorney of a parent, or against the parent, if the parent's complaint or subsequent cause of action was presented for any improper purpose, such as to harass, to cause unnecessary delay, or to needlessly increase the cost of litigation.

(C) Determination of amount of attorneys' fees. Fees awarded under this paragraph shall be based on rates prevailing in the community in which the action or proceeding arose for the kind and quality of services furnished. No bonus or multiplier may be used in calculating the fees awarded under this subsection.

(D) Prohibition of attorneys' fees and related costs for certain services.

(i) In general. Attorneys' fees may not be awarded and related costs may not be reimbursed in any action or proceeding under this section for services performed subsequent to the time of a written offer of settlement to a parent if—

(I) the offer is made within the time prescribed by *Rule 68 of the Federal Rules of Civil Procedure* or, in the case of an administrative proceeding, at any time more than ten days before the proceeding begins;

(II) the offer is not accepted within 10 days; and

(III) the court or administrative officer finds that the relief finally obtained by the parents or guardian is not more favorable to the parents than the offer of settlement.

(ii) IEP team meetings. Attorneys' fees may not be awarded relating to any meeting of the IEP Team unless such meeting is convened as a result of an administrative proceeding or judicial action, or, at the discretion of the State, for a mediation described in subsection (e).

(iii) Opportunity to resolve complaints. A meeting conducted pursuant to subsection (f)(1)(B)(i) shall not be considered—

(I) a meeting convened as a result of an administrative hearing or judicial action; or

(II) an administrative hearing or judicial action for purposes of this paragraph.

(E) Exception to prohibition on attorneys' fees and related costs. Notwithstanding subparagraph (D), an award of attorneys' fees and related costs may be made to a parent who is the prevailing party and who was substantially justified in rejecting the settlement offer.

(F) Reduction in the amount of attorneys' fees. Except as provided in subparagraph (G), whenever the court finds that—

(i) the parent during the course of the action or proceeding, unreasonably protracted the final resolution of the controversy;

(ii) the amount of the attorneys' fees otherwise authorized to be awarded unreasonably exceeds the hourly rate prevailing in the community for similar services by attorneys of reasonably comparable skill, reputation, and experience;

(iii) the time spent and legal services furnished were excessive considering the nature of the action or proceeding, the court shall reduce, accordingly, the amount of attorneys' fees awarded under this subsection; or

(iv) the attorney representing the parent did not provide to the school district the appropriate information in the due process complaint in accordance with subsection (b)(7)(A), the court shall reduce, accordingly, the amount of the attorneys' fees awarded under this section.

(G) Exception to reduction in amount of attorneys' fees. The provisions of subparagraph (F) shall not apply in any action or proceeding if the court finds that the State or local educational agency unreasonably protracted the final resolution of the action or proceeding or there was a violation of this section.

The 1986 amendments were criticized by some as stirring up litigation and forcing schools into actions because of the threat of litigation. The more recent amendments responded to those concerns and attempt to balance the interest of all parties.

What Is a Prevailing Party?

While the HCPA amendment clarifies that attorneys' fees are available, there still remain unanswered questions. When a party obtains all the relief sought, it is simple to demonstrate that the party prevailed. In the *Rollison v. Biggs* decision, excerpted below, the court applied a standard that prevailing parties are only those who succeed on a significant issue that achieved some of the benefit sought. Several circuit courts have addressed these issues. They have reached a variety of conclusions based on different factual settings. For example, in *Wheeler v. Towanda Area School District,*[18] the court held that because the parents did not prevail on any legal claims nor were they able to prove a causal connection between the litigation and the hiring of a new interpreter for their deaf child, they were not prevailing parties, and thus not entitled to attorneys' fees. Other cases have limited the attorneys' fees where the relief was limited or allowed all fees where the parents received a significant amount of the relief that they sought.[19]

In 2001, the United States Supreme Court decided a case that changed the landscape of attorneys' fees recovery and how courts determined prevailing party status. The case, *Buckhannon Board & Care Home Inc. v. West Virginia Dept. of Health and Human Services,*[20] determined that in order to be a "prevailing party" eligible to recover attorneys' fees, a party must obtain a judgment on the merits, a consent decree, or some similar form of judicially sanctioned relief. The decision rejected the "catalyst theory" for attorneys' fees, which had allowed parties to collect attorneys' fees short of obtaining a judgment in their favor if they could show a causal connection between their efforts and obtaining the result that the party sought in litigation through some other means (such as a settlement agreement). While the *Buckhannon* decision did not involve the IDEA, courts have applied *Buckhannon* to IDEA claims.[21]

Recovery in Administrative Actions

One of the issues stimulating much debate in the courtroom is whether attorneys' fees are available for administrative proceedings. On one hand the amendment provides that fees are to be awarded by a court, implying that they are available only for judicial proceedings. On the other hand, the amendment states that they are available for "any action or *proceeding,*" arguably including administrative proceedings in the coverage.

The strong weight of judicial opinion seems to be in favor of awarding fees in administrative proceedings.[22] Attorneys' fees are specifically disallowed for most IEP meetings under the IDEA and are generally not to be allowed for mediation proceedings that occur before a complaint is filed.[23]

What Expenses Are Recoverable?

Types of Expenses

The 1986 amendment and its current version provide for the award of "*reasonable* attorneys' fees" and related costs. The obvious question concerns what expenses are deemed reasonable. The statute itself provides some further guidance by noting that fees are to be based on rates prevailing in the community where the action arose for the type of services offered. Furthermore, the court making the award has the discretion to reduce the amount of fees if the request is excessive, in either the hourly rate or the time spent. One additional point made clear by the statute, however, is that no multiplier or bonus can be used in making these awards. This means that a court does not have the discretion to award double attorneys' fees or another type of bonus as a punitive measure.

One issue that has been addressed by at least one federal circuit court is whether lay advocates may be awarded attorneys' fees. A 1988 Third Circuit decision held that lay advocates could be denied attorneys' fees.[24]

This does not mean that lay advocates could not be advisers in IDEA matters, but that payment to such individuals does not fall within the attorneys' fees provision. It is unclear how likely this issue is to be raised in the courts. One problem that could occur should courts find lay advocates entitled to attorneys' fees is the difficulty in determining what would be a reasonable rate for such individuals.

Expenses After Settlement Offer

Congress intended that the potential for protracted litigation should not be an incentive to unnecessary attorneys' fees and costs. That recognition is manifested in the settlement portion of the amendment providing that once a reasonable settlement offer is made, attorneys' fees for services performed after the offer will not be available.

The post-settlement ban on fees applies only where the offer is a timely offer and the relief obtained by the parents is less favorable than the settlement offer. There is an exception to this limitation, however. If the rejection of the settlement was substantially justified, the parents may at the court's discretion recover post-settlement costs and fees. Factors indicating substantial justification for rejecting the offer might be claims involving novel or unusual circumstances not well resolved by the courts, unreasonable settlement offers, and offers made in situations where the parents had reason to suspect bad faith in implementation. The amendment attempts to strike a balance between the need to provide these costs to ensure access to due process and the need to avoid unnecessarily protracted controversies and litigation costs.

Expert Fees

Until 2006 it was unclear whether expert witness fees were recoverable costs under the IDEA. In *Arlington Central School District v. Murphy*,[25] the United States Supreme Court held that they were not. The Court stated that

> . . .the terms of the IDEA overwhelmingly support the conclusion that prevailing parents may not recover the costs of experts or consultants. Certainly the terms of the IDEA fail to provide the clear notice that would be needed to attach such a condition to a State's receipt of IDEA funds.

Attorneys' Fees Under Section 504 and the Americans with Disabilities Act

It has previously been noted that there will be few special education related cases brought under Section 504 or the ADA. For those few cases, however, it is important to know that successful plaintiffs can recover attorneys' fees and costs under both Section 504 and the ADA. There has not been much litigation on this issue under either of these statutes to date.[26]

Other Remedies

While it may be of little help to the student involved, termination of federal funds is a remedy that can be ordered in cases where an education agency has denied special education or discriminated on the basis of disability. The IDEA lists termination of IDEA-allocated federal funds specifically for this purpose. Such an action would also be a response to a violation of Section 504 of the Rehabilitation Act.[27]

Of more value to the individual student is the remedy of injunctive relief.[28] This would mean, for example, that the school would be enjoined from using a single criterion for special education placement or from constructing an inaccessible building. It might also include enjoining lengthy bus rides for special education students, or ordering certain services be provided to the student. Injunctive relief is clearly contemplated under the IDEA, Section 504, and the ADA.[29]

Summary

While termination of federal funds and injunctive relief are clearly available as remedies in appropriate cases involving special education, most courts have found that monetary damages are not available under the IDEA. The IDEA does provide for tuition reimbursement if the school does not provide the student with FAPE and the parent's chosen special education placement is appropriate under the law.

The Court in *Burlington School Committee v. Department of Education* in 1985 held that reimbursement could be ordered as a remedy in appropriate cases. These cases are where the parents have made an appropriate placement on their own and the school has failed to provide an appropriate placement. If the parents cannot afford to fund a placement pending dispute resolution and the parents ultimately prevail in demonstrating that the school's placement is inappropriate, the school can be required to provide compensatory education to make up for the lost time that occurred during the inappropriate placement.

Before 1984, it was unclear whether parents could recover attorneys' fees and other legal costs incurred in attaining appropriate special education and related services for their children. The IDEA was silent on the question, and while attorneys' fees and costs are permitted in Section 504, the ADA, and constitutional actions, it was unsettled whether either of these types of actions could be the basis for resolving special education disputes.

The 1984 *Smith v. Robinson* Supreme Court decision declared that, except in cases where the IDEA does not provide substantive protection, Section 504 and constitutional actions could not be used to redress special education disputes. The Court also held that the IDEA does not permit the recovery of attorneys' fees and costs. Because of the importance of true parental participation in carrying out the goals of the IDEA and the recognition that reasonable access to legal recourse requires that attorneys' fees and costs be available to successful parents, Congress amended the IDEA in 1986 to allow attorneys' fees and costs to be recovered in appropriate situations.

The attorneys' fees provisions offer an incentive for both parties to seek prompt resolution and a disincentive to needlessly protracting a dispute. While not receiving enormous amounts of attention in the courts, there are some developments relating to what types of expenses are recovered and whether such fees are available to lay advocates. These decisions have yet to provide any demonstrable patterns.

Recent amendments and judicial clarification illuminate what makes someone a prevailing party for purposes of attorneys' fees and the types of expenses that are recoverable (including expert fees).

Questions for Reflection

1. Megan is 16. A private psychiatrist has diagnosed her as emotionally disturbed. When Megan enters high school, the school recommends that she be placed in an in-school placement that the parents believe to be inappropriate. They think Megan needs a highly intensive program that integrates educational programming and counseling. Because of their concern about Megan's education and the time it will take to resolve the dispute over the placement, they put Megan into a private residential program (School A) where she receives programming year round. The program costs $80,000 per year, which the parents pay. Two years after the parents' unilateral placement, the final judicial decision finds that the school's recommended placement is not appropriate, and that the program in which Megan has been placed by her parents is appropriate. During the judicial proceedings, the school presented evidence that although it was not the program recommended by the school, there was another appropriate residential program (School B) available at the time of Megan's initial placement in School A. The cost of the program at School B is $30,000 per year.

   a. If the court were to find that School B is an appropriate placement, and that there was space in the program for Megan, how much, if anything, should the school be required to reimburse the parents?

   b. Suppose both School A and School B were appropriate placements and that School B had been offered at the time the parents placed Megan in School A. Should the school have to reimburse the parents at least $30,000 for each year, since it would have had to pay that anyway?

   c. Suppose that instead of refusing to pay the $80,000, the school agrees to pay the yearly costs pending resolution of the case, but contests its obligation to do so. Are the parents required to reimburse the school if it is later determined that the school's program was appropriate?

   d. If it is determined that a student has been provided an inappropriate program for two years, should any compensatory education order be limited to two years? What if the inappropriate programming occurred in primary grades or in preschool, where lost time is difficult to compensate because of the importance of that developmental stage?

2. As noted in the *Tom F.* case and discussion afterward, courts are split on whether a student must first receive special education services from the public school before the parent may place the student in a special education school and request

tuition reimbursement from the public school. Should a student be required to first attend public school and receive special education before being eligible to recover tuition reimbursement from a private special education school? Why or why not? How should the courts resolve this issue?

3. Is there any requirement that a parent select the least expensive attorney available? What if an attorney is selected from another city, but attorneys in the home city are available? Can travel expenses be justified in such a case?

4. Is there any basis for permitting a higher than usual hourly rate for an attorney who is an expert in special education law?

NOTES

1. Laura Rothstein & Julia Rothstein, *Disabilities and the Law* § 2:48 (Thomson West 2006).
2. See *Disabilities and the Law* § 2:49.
3. *Work v. McKenzie*, 661 F. Supp. 225 (D.D.C. 1987).
4. *Taylor v. Board of Education*, 649 F. Supp. 1253 (N.D.N.Y. 1986).
5. *Scituate School Committee v. Robert B.*, 620 F. Supp. 1224 (D.R.I. 1985).
6. *Evans v. District No. 17*, 841 F.2d 824 (8th Cir. 1988); *Lenoff v. Farmington Public Schools*, 680 F. Supp. 921 (E.D. Mich. 1988).
7. 510 U.S. 7 (1993).
8. 20 U.S.C. § 1412(a)(10)(C); 34 C.F.R. § 300.148.
9. 20 U.S.C. § 1412(a)(10)(C); 34 C.F.R. § 300.148(d).
10. 459 F.3d 356 (2d Cir. 2006).
11. 128 S. Ct. 1 (2007).
12. 459 F.3d 356 (2d Cir. 2006).
13. See *Disabilities and the Law* § 2:50.
14. 29 U.S.C. § 794(d); 42 U.S.C. § 1988. See also *Disabilities and the Law* § 2.51.
15. 42 U.S.C. § 12205.
16. 468 U.S. 992 (1984). See Chapter 3 for the case opinion.
17. 20 U.S.C. § 1415(i)(3).
18. 950 F.2d 128 (3d Cir. 1991).
19. For a list of cases on these issues, see *Disabilities and the Law* § 2:51.
20. 532 U.S. 598 (2001).
21. *John T. v. Del Co. Intermediate Unit*, 318 F.3d 545 (3d Cir. 2003); *J.C. v. Regional Sch. Dist. 10*, 278 F.3d 119 (2d Cir. 2002).
22. See, e.g., *Brown v. Griggsville Comm. Unit Sch. Dist. No. 4*, 12 F.3d 681, 683–684 (7th Cir. 1993).
23. 20 U.S.C. § 1415(i)(4).
24. *Arons v. New Jersey State Board of Education*, 842 F.2d 58 (3d Cir. 1988).
25. 548 U.S. 291 (2006).
26. 29 U.S.C. § 794(d); 42 U.S.C. § 12205.
27. 20 U.S.C. § 1416. See also *Disabilities and the Law* § 2:45.
28. 29 U.S.C. § 794a. See also *Disabilities and the Law* § 2:47.
29. See *Disabilities and the Law* §§ 1:08, 1:14, 2:47, 3:27.

22

The Status and Future of Special Education Law

Numerous commentators have found the Individuals with Disabilities Education Act (IDEA) to be positive and constructive legislation. They believe that it has already achieved its goals to a substantial degree—that most children with disabilities in this country are now receiving an appropriate education, without unreasonable disruption or consequences to the rest of regular education. Many believe that the teaching methodologies and the accountability resulting from the IDEA and No Child Left Behind (NCLB) have benefited *all* of education and that children who are not disabled benefit from the presence of children with disabilities in the mainstream of public education. Others are concerned that the implementation of NCLB creates tensions with some of the goals of the IDEA.

Some believe that the IDEA has brought unnecessary bureaucracy, paperwork, and costs to public education. Recent amendments have attempted to respond to those concerns. Some find that while the IDEA is a positive step for children with certain disabilities—such as mental retardation—it is unduly burdensome to educational agencies when children who are severely medically and psychologically involved are seeking services. These critics suggest that the appropriate avenues for such services are health, social service, and welfare agencies rather than educational agencies. Perhaps a more appropriate reaction is not that the educational agency is the wrong agency, but that there is an enormous financial burden when educating children with severe medical and psychological needs, and that the public funding for such programs needs to be rechanneled through the educational agencies. In addition, educational agencies need to be empowered at the state level to obtain support services from other agencies.

Litigation in the first 10 years after passage of the IDEA focused on major policy questions: What is appropriate? What constitutes medical services and what does not? What types of remedies are available under the IDEA? How does the IDEA interrelate with Section 504 of the Rehabilitation Act, and Section 1983 of the Civil Rights Act? Are policies permissible if they limit the amount of service available? How can testing be used to identify, evaluate, and place children?

During the early 1980s, attempts to deregulate the IDEA were unsuccessful, and the major legislation that passed during that period only added to the substance of the IDEA—by providing for additional programming for preschool children and infants and for attorneys' fees for parents who prevailed against the educational agencies.

In 1990, two major statutory changes affected special education law. The first of these was passage of the Americans with Disabilities Act (ADA). This Act mandates nondiscrimination on the basis of disability for both public and private schools. While this legislation did not add a great deal to the requirements already in place in Section 504 of the Rehabilitation Act, it has heightened awareness of disability rights. The ADA mandates related to architectural barriers (including some barrier removal in existing facilities) and its reasonable modifications requirements probably have the greatest impact.

The second major change has a more direct effect on special education. The Education for All Handicapped Children Act was amended and its name was changed to the Individuals with Disabilities Education Act. While the basic substantive, procedural, and remedial provisions of the IDEA remain, the 1990 amendments introduced several significant changes. These included providing for transition services, making available assistive technology devices and services, eliminating state agency immunity from actions brought under the IDEA, and adding autism and traumatic brain injury to the list of disabilities specifically covered.

In 1997, Congress again amended the IDEA. While not changing the existing substantive requirements significantly, the amendments clarify some of the issues that had previously been unresolved. These changes address whether disciplinary measures can be applied to students with disabilities and to what extent. They also limit the obligation of public educational agencies to provide special education services when parents have elected to place their children in private schools and when the public agency had made appropriate special education available in the public school setting.

The 1997 amendments also expressly address the quality of services provided to students with disabilities by including provisions regarding the expectations and outcomes for students with disabilities. The amendments to the IDEA in 1997 required high expectations for students with disabilities along with access to the "general curriculum."

The 2004 amendments continued with high expectations and outcomes for students with disabilities and included a number of express connections between the IDEA and the requirements in No Child Left Behind. These connections include the quality of services provided to students with disabilities, more express provisions regarding students with disabilities taking statewide assessment tests, and the qualifications for school personnel and others who provide services to students with disabilities.

The future of special education law depends to some extent on the future of our public education system generally. In the past 30 years or so, educational policy has been reshaped in response to societal changes. Schools now provide sex and drug education, more early childhood programming, after-school care, and meals. Schools are being held increasingly accountable for the performance of their students as compared with other students nationally. Schools are expected to address children's physical fitness deficiencies and to provide services for medically fragile children and those with contagious and infectious diseases. Schools are faced with challenges regarding violence in schools. Resources for education generally have been grossly inadequate to respond to all of these demands.

These demands and inadequate resources are likely to be significant factors in how special education policy is addressed by Congress, the regulatory agencies, and the courts. The trend toward school choice options, including charter schools and school voucher programs, will have a major effect on students with disabilities. Preliminary indications are that these opportunities will not be proportionately available to students with disabilities. As a result, such programs must either ensure nondiscriminatory opportunities or they will be subject to challenge under Section 504 or the ADA. Policy planners need to take this into account in developing school choice programs.

Cost issues are likely to recur. When can limited resources be used as a defense? Will damages or compensatory education be recoverable under the IDEA? Will administrators or state or local agencies become accountable for financial awards? Will improvements in secondary and vocational education occur? How will schools be required to handle custodial and medical-type placements? How will interagency agreements and funding allocations be worked out? What types of extended services will be required? How are the preschool and infant programs working? Have the refinements in disciplinary removals of children with disabilities been effective? How will children with HIV and other contagious diseases be educated? To what extent will the mainstreaming requirement be implemented? Will the burden fall on the educational agency any time a placement outside the regular school is involved? Has the availability of attorneys' fees been a positive step—has it improved the quality of representation? Has it stirred up unnecessary controversies? Or has it encouraged schools to provide appropriate programming in the first place? Is mediation improving dispute resolution?

Whether the IDEA is a good program or not, it seems that for a variety of reasons it is here to stay. Special education probably requires more attention to legal issues than any other aspect of the educational program in schools today. For that reason, teachers, education administrators, and policymakers would do well to be informed of the basic requirements of the law and to take advantage of opportunities to update their information on a regular basis. Although the IDEA may be frustrating and demanding for some on both sides because of its ambiguities and numerous requirements, it is important policy that recognizes the ability and potential of all students and the value of providing services at this developmental stage.

Questions for Reflection

1. Which of the issues noted above would best be resolved through litigation? Which through legislation? Which through regulation? Which through education? Which through communication?

2. What is the likely direction that the intersection of the IDEA and NCLB will take?

3. What changes should be made to the IDEA? To NCLB?

Appendix A*

Education and the American Legal System

In this appendix we look first at the role of state governments in education. Then we present the organization of U.S. court systems and indicate the way they relate to educational controversies.

Education and State Governments

Unlike most countries, the United States has no national system of education. In fact, the national Constitution is silent on the matter; however, under its tenth amendment, education is considered to be among the powers reserved to the states. Courts have accepted this interpretation of the Constitution, and the Supreme Court has repeatedly stated that federal courts may interfere with the actions of state and local school officials only when such actions somehow threaten a personal liberty or property right protected by the Constitution or violate federal law.

All 50 states provide in their constitutions for public education. With America's historic commitment to decentralized government and local control, states have delegated much power and responsibility over schooling to local governments. Such delegation is a choice made by the people of a state, who could, like the state of Hawaii, choose to have one statewide school district. In spite of the existence of local school districts, legally schools remain a responsibility of the state government; school officials, teachers, and staff are agents of the state when performing their official duties. This is a significant principle, because the Constitution protects individuals only against actions taken by the government.

The first ten amendments to the Constitution (more commonly, the Bill of Rights) prohibit certain actions on the part of the federal government. The fourteenth amendment

---

* Appendix adapted from Louis Fischer, David Schimmel, and Cynthia Kelly, *Teachers and the Law*, published by Allyn & Bacon, Boston, MA.

applies to actions by the states. Because all actions of school officials and school boards are "state actions," the fourteenth amendment prohibits certain arbitrary and discriminatory practices. What makes this all the more important is the historic development whereby all the guarantees of the first amendment, and many other provisions of the Bill of Rights, have been incorporated into the "liberty clause" of the fourteenth and thus made applicable to all the states. Although there is a complex and controversial legal history to this incorporation, for our purposes it will suffice to understand that all protections of the first amendment, and most protections of the other Bill of Rights provisions, apply to the actions of public school officials just as do those of the fourteenth amendment.

Thus, although states have the primary power and responsibility for public schools, their power must at all times be exercised consistently with the rights guaranteed in the national Constitution.

The Federal Court System

The U.S. Supreme Court is the only court specifically created by the Constitution (art. III, sec. 2); all other federal courts were established by Congress. Below the Supreme Court are 13 federal courts of appeal (see Figure A.1), and within each "circuit" or geographical area (except for one centralized federal court of appeals dealing with copyright and other specialized matters) are trial courts, called district courts. There are nearly 100 district courts, at least one in each state, though their exact number may change from time to time. School-related cases involving federal issues may be brought to trial in a district court; from this court an appeal may be taken to a court of appeals and eventually to the Supreme Court (see Figure A.2).

The Constitution specifies what cases the Supreme Court will consider (art. III, sec. 2, cl. 1). For all other federal courts, Congress determines which cases will be tried where, the route appeals will take, and the relationship of courts to the many administrative agencies of government. In general, federal courts take only two kinds of cases: (1) those that present substantial questions under federal laws and the Constitution, and (2) those involving different states or citizens of different states. Many cases present questions involving both federal and state laws and may initially be tried in either federal or state courts. If such a case is brought to trial in a federal court, however, the court must decide questions of state law according to the laws of the affected state. Conversely, if the case was initially filed in a state court, that court must follow the federal law governing that area.

Although decisions of the Supreme Court are applicable to the entire nation, the decisions of circuit courts are binding only within their territories; thus different rules may apply in different regions of the country until the Supreme Court decides the issue.

The State Court System

Most school-related cases are litigated in state courts. Because these courts are created by state constitutions and legislatures, however, they vary considerably in titles, procedures, and jurisdiction. A general pattern among the states is a three-tiered system, excluding lower courts of special jurisdiction such as traffic courts and small claims courts (see Figure A.3).

Figure A.1 The 13 federal judicial circuits

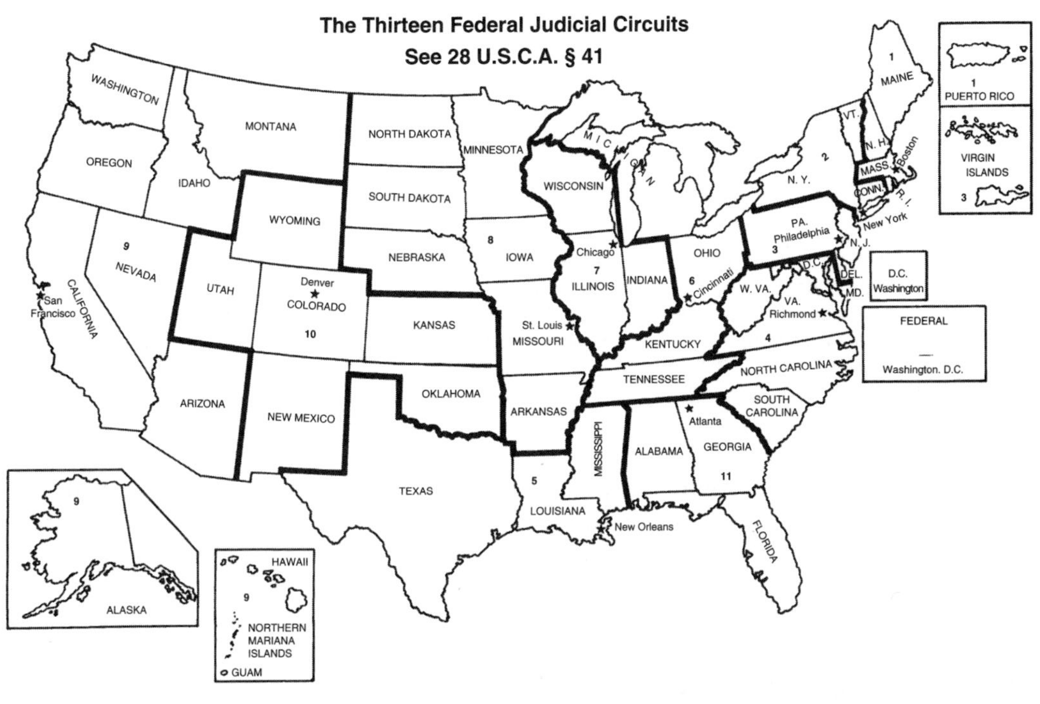

Source: Courtesy of West Group, St. Paul, Minnesota, from *The Federal Reporter*. Reprinted with permission of Thomson Reuters.

Figure A.2 The federal court system

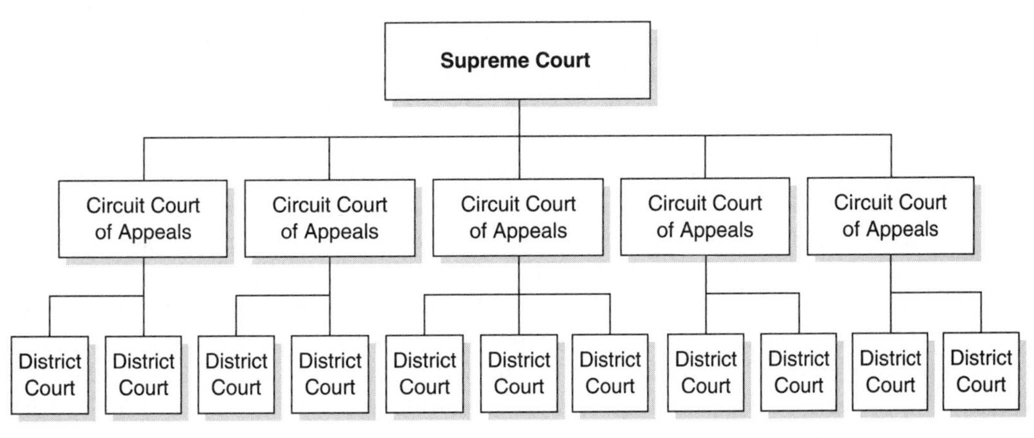

Figure A.3 A typical state court system

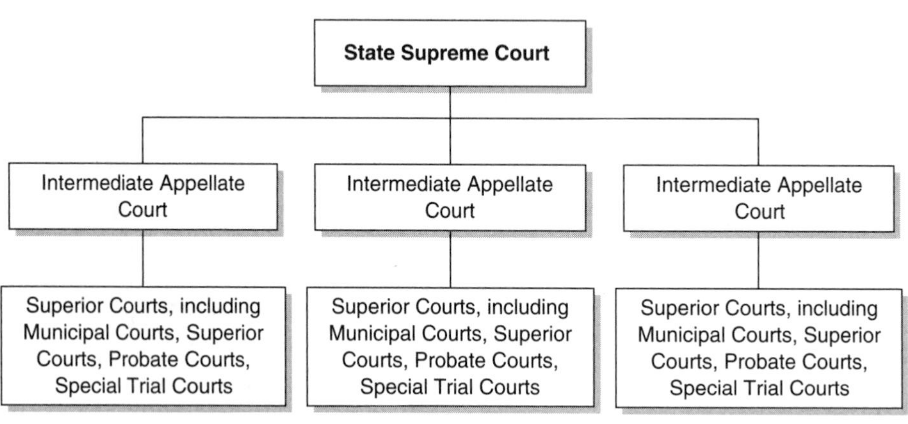

At the foundation of the state court system, we find the trial courts, often organized along county lines. From these, appeals go to intermediate appeals courts and finally to the highest court of the state, variously named in different states. For example, the highest state court is named the Supreme Judicial Court in Massachusetts, the Supreme Court of Errors in Connecticut, and the Supreme Court in California.

The Functions of Trial and Appeals Courts

A school-related controversy that cannot be resolved without a lawsuit first goes to a trial court. Here the facts are established and the relevant legal principles applied to the facts. If the case is appealed, the appellate court will not retry the case; it will usually accept the facts as established by the trial court unless it is very clear that evidence to support such facts was inadequate. The main concern of appeals courts is whether correct legal principles were applied to the facts determined by the court below it.

For example, a school may have expelled Student X for persistent acts of violence and classroom disruption. Student X could seek review of such action in a state trial court of general jurisdiction. If it were alleged that the student had been deprived of a constitutional right to due process, the case could be brought to a federal district court instead. (The student could still proceed in state court, however, because state courts have the power to decide issues of federal constitutional law.) Whichever trial court the student chose would hear evidence from both sides in order to determine what actually happened. Once the facts were established, the judge would apply the law to the facts and arrive at a decision. Even if the judge were a state judge, all laws applicable to the case, both federal and state, would be considered, because Article VI of the U.S. Constitution provides that the "Constitution, and the Laws of the United States . . . shall be the supreme Law of the Land; and the Judges in every State shall be bound thereby." If the case were appealed, the appeals court would consider whether or not the principles of law were properly applied by the trial court.

The highest state court will be the final authority on legal questions related to the law of that state unless there is federal law on the same matter. The U.S. Supreme Court is the final authority on matters arising out of the Constitution, treaties, federal laws, or conflicts among state laws. In matters that involve only state laws, the state courts have the authoritative voice.

Administrative Bodies

It is generally recognized today that the courts are overburdened and their calendars overcrowded. It is all too true that "justice delayed is justice denied," yet in many cities it takes over a year for a criminal case to come to trial and several years for a civil suit to be tried. This situation would be worse if we did not have administrative agencies acting in quasi-judicial capacities. Without a doubt, the largest and most detailed body of law, administrative rules and regulations, is created by agencies that regulate public affairs. Administrative law functions at both federal and state levels, and the lives of educators are heavily influenced by it.

How to Find Reports of Court Cases

Every county has a courthouse that contains a law library. Every law school has such a library, and most universities and colleges have legal collections. In each of these places a librarian can help one to find cases of interest. The following constitutes a brief introduction to legal research.

Appellate courts almost always publish their decisions. The decisions of the highest appellate court, the U.S. Supreme Court, can be found in the *United States Reports.* For example, the citation *Brown v. Board of Education of Topeka, Kansas,* 349 U.S. 294 (1955), indicates that the case, decided in 1955, is reported in volume 349 of the *United States Reports* at page 294. Since Supreme Court cases are reported in several publications, the same case may be followed by the notations 75 S. Ct. 753, 99 L. Ed. 1083. This means that the same case also appears in volume 75 of the *Supreme Court Reporter* at page 753 and in volume 99 of the *Lawyers Edition* at page 1083. The most recent cases decided by the Supreme Court appear in a loose-leaf volume called *United States Law Week,* cited, for example, as *Irving Independent School District v. Tatro,* 52 U.S.L.W. 5151 (July 5, 1984).

Recent cases decided by the U.S. Courts of Appeals are reported in West's *Federal Reporter, Second Series* (F.2d). For example, *Clark v. Whiting,* 607 F.2d 634 (4th Cir. 1979) would be found in volume 607 of the *Federal Reporter, Second Series* at page 634. The case was decided by the Fourth Circuit Court of Appeals in 1979. When a series becomes too long and thus the volume numbers too large, a second series is begun and cited, for example, "F.2d" rather than "F."

Decisions of the U.S. District Courts are reported in the *Federal Supplement* (F. Supp.), also published by West Publishing Company, and are cited in a manner similar to other federal court cases. For example, *Valencia v. Blue Hen Conference,* 476 F. Supp. 809 (D. Del. 1979), indicates that this case was decided by a district court in Delaware in 1979 and is reported in volume 476 of the *Federal Supplement* at page 809.

The National Reporter System of West Publishing Company, in addition to reporting the federal cases noted above, also reports cases from state courts. Most reported state appellate court decisions appear in the following volumes: *Atlantic Reporter* (A.), *North Eastern Reporter* (N.E.), *North Western Reporter* (N.W.), *Pacific Reporter* (P.), *South Eastern Reporter* (S.E.), *South Western Reporter* (S.W.), and *Southern Reporter* (So.). Cases from New York, including some trial court decisions, are available in West's *New York Supplement* (N.Y.S.); cases from California are contained in the *California Reporter* (Cal. Rptr.). Many of these same cases also appear in the respective regional reporters—the *North Eastern Reporter* and the *Pacific Reporter.*

Authors' Note: Research can now be done using the Internet and a variety of computer-searchable programs.

Appendix B

Frequently Used Acronyms and Terms

ADA Americans with Disabilities Act

ADD (attention deficit disorder) a type of learning disability that may be covered by the IDEA depending on the causative factor

ADHD (attention deficit hyperactivity disorder) a condition that may affect learning, but which is not a designated condition entitling a student to special education and related services

AIDS (acquired immune deficiency syndrome) this text refers to both AIDS and HIV infection; a viral infection that adversely affects the immune system

architectural barrier an environmental condition that adversely affects the use of the physical space by an individual with a disability

assistive technology device equipment used to increase, maintain, or improve the capabilities of individuals with disabilities as defined under the IDEA

BD (behavior disorder) often refers to a student whose behavior makes functioning in society or school difficult

case law law developed by the courts through issuing judicial opinions

catheterization removal of blood or urine from the body by insertion of a narrow tube; may be required as a related service as defined in the *Tatro* case

certiorari a discretionary writ giving a superior court the jurisdiction to review the decision of a lower court

common law law developed primarily by the courts; developed over time by usage and custom

competency achievement of a specified level of performance

consent permission of the parents (or their representatives) allowing the school to evaluate, assess, place, or make another individualized decision about a child who is or who is thought to be disabled

disability depending on the applicable legislation, it may refer to the lack of physical or mental ability such that special education is required (as in the IDEA) or an impairment that substantially affects one or more major life activities, a record of such as an impairment, or being regarded as having such an impairment (as in Section 504 of the Rehabilitation Act or the Americans with Disabilities Act)

EAHCA or EHA Education for All Handicapped Children Act or Education for the Handicapped Act (since 1990 known as the Individuals with Disabilities Education Act); also referred to as Pub. L. No. 94-142; statute requiring states receiving funding under the statute to provide special education and related services pursuant to a set of educational principles and including a specific program of procedural safeguards

ED (emotionally disturbed) often refers to a student with a behavior disorder that results in the inability to control emotions

FAPE (free appropriate public education) special education and related services provided at public expense under public supervision and direction that meets the state educational standards and conforms with the IDEA mandates

FERPA Family Educational Rights and Privacy Act (also commonly known as the Buckley Amendment); a federal statute relating to confidentiality and access involving student educational records

full inclusion the practice of educating all children in neighborhood classrooms and schools in the regular classroom for all educational programming; it implies an end to labeling and providing special education in separate classes; it is not a requirement of IDEA, but it is an ideal goal

handicap under some statutes, refers to individuals who have substantial impairments affecting major life activities, who have records of such impairments, or who are regarded as having such impairments; the preferred term in more recent legislation is disability

HCPA Handicapped Children's Protection Act of 1986; an amendment to the EAHCA (now IDEA) providing for reimbursement of attorneys' fees and costs to parents who are successful in cases against educational agencies

HIPAA Health Insurance Portability and Accountability Act; passed in 1996; provides for confidentiality of medical records, which may interrelate with FERPA

HIV (human immunodeficiency virus) a virus that affects the white blood cells and leads to a decline in the body's immune system

IDEA Individuals with Disabilities Education Act; the statute passed in 1975 as the EAHCA (see above), amended and renamed in 1990, providing for special education and related services

IDEIA Individuals with Disabilities Education Improvement Act; refers to the 2004 amendment that "renamed IDEIA," although the statute is still generally referred to as IDEA

IEP (individualized education program) the plan for students who qualify for special education and related services; developed by a team that includes parents and educational personnel

injunction an order issued by a court requiring a party to do or to refrain from doing something

IQ (intelligence quotient) an artificial number that is used to indicate mental development level

LD (learning disabled) refers to an individual who has a disorder in the psychological processes in language that affects the ability to listen, think, speak, read, write, spell, or do math

LRE (least restrictive environment) sometimes known as mainstreaming, the concept of placing children with disabilities in an environment that exposes them to children without disabilities to the maximum extent appropriate

mainstreaming a term referring to placement in the regular classroom of children with disabilities as much as possible

MR (mental retardation) significantly subaverage general intellectual functioning, existing concurrently with deficits in adaptive behavior and manifested during the developmental period, that adversely affects a child's educational performance

NCLB No Child Left Behind; federal legislation passed in 2002 that mandates highly qualified teachers, accountability, and other standards; special educational programming is expected to meet these standards

notice information provided to parents regarding proposed action to be taken toward their child and information about their legal rights under the IDEA

precedent judicial decisions applicable to the same jurisdiction that set the principles to apply to similar cases in that jurisdiction

Pub. L. No. 94-142 the original public law number for the Education for All Handicapped Children Act (now known as IDEA); passed in 1975

reasonable accommodation or modification an adaptation of a facility or program for a person with a disability that can be accomplished without undue administrative or financial burden; may include barrier removal or adjustment to policies and practices; required by Section 504 of the Rehabilitation Act and the Americans with Disabilities Act for covered programs

regular education initiative refers to a philosophy of providing all or most special education in the regular classroom

related services services provided to ensure special education is appropriate for students with disabilities

resource room a room within the school where specific special educational programming is provided in conjunction with the child's regular classroom programming

RTI (response to intervention) a policy encouraged, but not required, for special education where students identified as needing assistance are provided additional educational programming and evaluated before they are identified and labeled as qualifying for special education and related services

Section 504 the portion of the Rehabilitation Act of 1973 that provides that recipients of federal financial assistance may not discriminate on the basis of disability

special education misconduct a broad term including a variety of types of misconduct by educators or employees of education agencies, including improper supervision, infliction of emotional distress, improper discipline, or improper evaluation or placement of a child with a disability

stare decisis legal precedent, binding holdings from previous similar cases

sweep-screening group assessments of children for a specific problem, such as vision or hearing

tort law the law of private or civil wrongs arising from a violation of a duty other than a contract duty

transition services a coordinated set of activities, including instruction, community experiences, and development of employment opportunities to promote movement from school to the workplace, higher education, or other setting; required by the IDEA as appropriate

undue burden able to be accomplished without significant difficulty or expense in light of the nature and cost of the action, overall financial resources available, number of persons affected, and type of operation involved; a standard applied under the ADA to define what is a reasonable modification

zero reject under the IDEA, the philosophy that all children with disabilities can benefit from education

Index

About the Authors

Laura Rothstein is a Professor of Law and Distinguished University Scholar at the Louis D. Brandeis School of Law at the University of Louisville, where she served as Dean from 2000 to 2005. She received her B.A. in political science from the University of Kansas and her J.D. from Georgetown University Law Center. She began her career in legal education in 1976 and served on four other law school faculties before her appointment at the Brandeis School of Law. She began work on special education issues in 1979, while a visiting faculty member at the University of Pittsburgh, where she also served as an attorney in the Developmental Disabilities Law Project clinical program.

Professor Rothstein has written 12 books and dozens of book chapters, articles, and other works on disability discrimination, covering issues ranging from special education and employment to public accommodations and access to health care. Her work focuses on disability issues in schools and in higher education.

The first edition of *Special Education Law*, published in 1990, was one of the first books on the topic. Professor Rothstein's parents were public school teachers, and they reviewed the first edition of the book, ensuring that the text was accessible to both lawyers and those without formal legal training. Other publications focusing on special education issues have included work on school choice and students with disabilities, genetic testing in schools, students with HIV and other contagious and infectious diseases, and special education malpractice. She is a frequent presenter at national and regional conferences of legal and education professionals and academics.

Scott F. Johnson is a Professor of Law at Concord Law School of Kaplan University and a Special Education Hearings Officer with the New Hampshire Department of Education. He received his B.A. in political science from the University of North Carolina at Charlotte and his J.D. from Franklin Pierce Law Center. He is the author of numerous articles and books in various areas of education law, and he frequently develops professional development programs for educators and presents at national conferences. Prior to teaching, Professor Johnson practiced law and was involved in a number of precedent-setting education law cases.

SAGE

PINE
FORGE

CORWIN

CQ PRESS